CHINA
THE STEALTH EMPIRE

CHINA
THE STEALTH EMPIRE

EDWARD BURMAN

The History Press

First published 2008

The History Press Ltd
The Mill, Brimscombe Port
Stroud, Gloucestershire, GL5 2QG
www.thehistorypress.co.uk

British Library Cataloguing in Publication Data.
A catalogue record for this book is available from the British Library.

ISBN 978 0 7509 4683 4

Typesetting and origination by The History Press Ltd.
Printed in Great Britain

Contents

Appendices

A Brief Word of Explanation

This book is based on the personal experience of living and working in China for five years, travelling extensively in the many large cities and also in remote areas, and reading about China in several languages. It seeks to avoid the common obsession amongst journalists and political commentators with Taiwan, Tibet and Xinjiang, simply because they do not loom large in the minds of ordinary Chinese people. For most of them live in the broad swathe of coastal plain that stretches from Beijing to Shenzhen, where, for better or for worse, other things matter (not to mention the millions of rural Chinese who live at one remove further, sometimes even unaware that Mao has died). It also seeks to avoid clichés about the numbers of cranes and building sites, forced eviction and demolition of old buildings, and of the exploitation of young women in textile factories, because that too is not how most Chinese see it. They need the new buildings, justly crave decent sanitary conditions after decades of deprivation, and are content, as is usually the case, that their extended family's overall situation is improving. Above all, it seeks to avoid the fashions inherent in praise and criticism of China: before 2002, for example, the emphasis in Western reporting was on human rights and political dissidents; from 2003 to 2006 it was on stunning economic growth; since the beginning of 2007 it is all about the environment. Meanwhile, Chinese life goes on. The focus here is on China *going out*, as the country seeks to assume the economic and political global roles and responsibilties that its newly recovered status entails.

It has always been dangerous to write about China. A few years ago, Philip Stephens noted in the *Financial Times* that all a writer needs is a 'rush of statistics, an occasional nod to history, a Confucian aphorism or two' to write about the country's re-emergence as a global power.[1] Indeed, there are dozens of books about China that adopt this formula and, as Robert Skidelsky noticed, many of them have 'the same touristic flavor: a trip down the Huangpu River in Shanghai reveals the garish skyscrapers and low nightlife of the new moneyed metropolis.'[2] A century ago, Jay Denby was far harsher in his admonitions: 'I find that it is only after years of patient study of the native character that the student fully realizes that he knows nothing whatever about his subject, and never will. It is only the more intelligent who are able to reach this advanced stage; the remainder write books ...'[3] A counter-example to such pessimism is provided by Paul Claudel, who as a diplomat spent fifteen years in China at the turn of the twentieth century. His book of prose poems *Connaissance de L'Est* (1900) begins with evocative poems about Chinese scenes and legends, for example 'Rêves', and ends in poems that have little connection with China, such as 'Dissolution', when the China experience has simply become an integral and nearly invisible part of his life – which indeed 'dissolves' into the sea. This seems to me a better model.

There's a fair bit of history in the first half of the book. For I firmly believe that it is necessary to go deeper than most business and travel books, and broader than works by sinologists with whom the general reader and general author can never compete on their chosen terrain. History permeates the Chinese mind in a curious way, since it is led by the language into thinking of the past as something in front of it, while in European languages the past is thought of as being behind us. Moreover, in its tenseless verbs, their language itself renders past and present as indivisible. Thus, even when an individual has little historical knowledge, the past, and especially past 'injustices', inform his or her being. If nothing else, going a little deeper might protect a neophyte from the attractions of what one author calls the 'manipulative political pageantry'[4] which comes from China's propagandistic use of its past, a subject we will deal with later. The best defence is to acquire a better knowledge of the historical processes behind this change *from their point of view.*[5]

Thus Part I of this book seeks to explain what China is, and how it came to be the way it is, both in its strengths and in its rejection of imperial expansion in the past. Part II analyses the way in which China has come to possess a global empire of sorts almost in spite of itself. Finally, Part III looks at the ways in which these pasts will inform the future as China reclaims her ancient role on the world stage after a century of false starts.

Names are given in the standard contemporary form of romanisation known as Pinyin, but older names are given in their earlier Wade-Giles version in brackets at the first occurrence to avoid ambiguity.

Introduction: Meanings of Empire

Most Western definitions of empire run something like this, from the *Concise Oxford Dictionary*: 'an extensive group of states ruled over by a single monarch or ruling authority'. The monarch might be Queen Victoria or King Charles V of Spain, and the ruling authority might be Augustus or Suleiman the Magnificent, but the meaning is clear to us. As is the nature of the associated empires. For those we are familiar with have usually taken one of two main forms: land-based empires, which extend across a contiguous territory, such as the Russian Empire; and sea-borne empires, where naval strength is of paramount strategic importance, such as the British Empire. The problem is that we are so conditioned by this approach, and have recognised and used this sense of the word 'empire' since schooldays, that this is what most of us have in mind when we read the phrase 'Chinese Empire'. But the Chinese themselves understand the concept of empire – if indeed they have one at all – in a very different way, usually in the negative sense of a Western imperial power that encroached upon their country's sovereignty in the nineteenth century. So before going on to examine the 'Chinese Empire', whether past, present or future, it will be useful to clarify our starting point by asking the apparently innocuous question, what is China? For interpretations of the past and predictions about the future will be different if we consider it to be a Western-style empire, a nation-state, a party-state, a civilisation, a cultural construct, a self-perpetuating bureaucratic organisation, a 'civilization pretending to be a state',[6] or what has been described more elaborately as a 'state defined by a culture claiming to exemplify the correct universal ethical system'[7] and a 'civilization-state with a variety of autonomous regions or even a loosely structured Chinese federation of different political entities.'[8] Given their historical and contemporary importance, the absence of agreement about the exact nature of China and the Chinese Empire is on the face of things very odd. Certainly the latter doesn't sound much like the empires we are used to; moreover, to the best of my knowledge, the 'Chinese Empire' is rarely defined or described as a 'group of states'.

Imperial expansionism in the nineteenth century – the pressures of Russia in the north and west,[9] Japan in the northeast, Britain, France and Germany in the east and southeast – showed up the weaknesses of the last Chinese dynasty's particular form of imperialism. It has been argued that China's recent past can be read as a 'palimpsest of imperialisms',[10] but it might also be said that China itself was never an empire in the European sense, certainly before the eighteenth-century conquests of the Qing, which we shall examine later. But that depends on how we define empire.

Since the English word 'empire' itself derives from the Latin *imperium*, perhaps the best example of the Western concept is that of the Roman Empire, although there were of course earlier empires based on Mesopotamia, Persia and Greece. Most of them came into being as the result of a militarily strong state conquering other states with force, and then incorporating them into a larger political union with varying degrees of control. The Roman Empire is the exemplar of people moving out from a limited territorial base to occupy new land, and then recreating their own world in a foreign setting as the British were later to do in India, with forum, basilicas, temples, baths and the other physical accoutrements of citizenship. The mind-set was outgoing from the beginning. The Roman orator Cicero, quoting a king who had been banished from Troy by his father, asserted that 'wherever I am happy is my country' (*patria est ubicumque est bene*);[11] Seneca the Younger, born in Cordoba and thus a scion of empire, echoed these sentiments in a moving letter to his mother about adapting to exile in Corsica: 'wherever the Roman conquers, he inhabits' (*ubicumque vicit Romanus, habitat*).[12]

Of course things were not quite that simple. In a paper on the economics of empire building, two researchers found three distinctive types of imperial strategy, which I believe will be useful here.[13] Using their terminology, in the early stage of Roman history, from the fifth to the beginning of the third century BC, the strategy employed was one of *attempted conquest*, which entailed attacking neighbouring 'barbarian' countries (in this case, Etruria and the Latin League). This was always a risky strategy, since conquest can fail for many reasons, but it was also relatively cheap since it required a small number of legions devoted to a specific task over a short period of time. Then, in the third and second centuries BC, the Romans employed a strategy of *coerced annexation* (for example, that of the Greek states) or intimidation by a display of superior military force. This required them to deploy legions of such overwhelming strength that the target would decide to capitulate rather than seek to defend themselves in a series of extenuating battles (whose effects the Greeks knew from memories of the Peloponnesian Wars). It was a long-term and expensive strategy. Finally, as the Empire expanded far from its origins into Germany, Britain, Asia Minor and Judaea, the Romans adopted a more sophisticated strategy, which can be described as *uncoerced annexation*. This implies that the benefits of annexation were appealing enough to induce the barbarians to agree to the submission of their country to Rome, which from the Roman point of view saved enormous military expense and the problem of maintaining supply lines. It also enabled the creation of various new forms of relationships ranging from direct rule to alliance with Rome under local Roman leadership. The states that the central power gained in this way could be looked upon as 'client states'.

The British Empire, to take a more recent example, annexed countries that had been unknown or scarcely inhabited before its navy arrived, and at the same time conquered a country like India for reasons of commercial or political expediency. Over the centuries, it gradually shifted in emphasis from *coerced annexation* to *uncoerced annexation*, and transformed itself from an empire held together by military power to the less aggressive form of Commonwealth. Another form of *uncoerced annexation* derived from a strong religious impulse in late nineteenth-century imperalism, the will to convert and 'improve' the native population. New imperial powers such as the United States sent missionaries throughout the world (including China, after the Treat of Wanghia in 1844) and sought to convert the rulers they met, from the Congo to Tonga, so much so that European states 'often promoted religion as their badge of identity even when they spoke of liberalism and science.'[14]

Missionary zeal was linked to contemporary notions of progress and the individual, as may be seen in the closing words of an otherwise perceptive book about China written by Arthur H. Smith, a Doctor of Divinity and graduate of Andover Theological Seminary, after twenty-two years working as a missionary in the northern village of Panjiazhuang in Hebei Province.[15] The only way that China could achieve the 'righteousness' essential for its future, he concluded, was for the Chinese to discover the Christian god and develop a new concept of man both as an individual soul and as a member of his family and society: 'The manifold needs of China we find, then, to be a single imperative need. It will be met permanently, completely, only by Christian civilization.'[16] The most striking aspect of the journals of Sir Robert Hart (1835–1911), the celebrated Inspector General of the Imperial Maritime Custom Service in China for nearly fifty years, is his fierce devotion to the Wesleyan beliefs and virtues of his childhood and education, especially in his difficult early years in Ningbo and Guangzhou (Canton).[17] Sundays were given almost entirely to religious speculations. Such firm beliefs helped to create a negative image of imperialism, entailing features unacceptable to the Chinese then and most people today such as a notion of cultural superiority, racial superiority or the idea that the imperial power is in some way spreading the benefits of a superior civilisation to the less fortunate. For the Chinese this was an insult, and for Westerners today with the benefit of hindsight and better knowledge of Chinese culture at best ironic.

These examples will suffice to show that we have a *tradition* of empire in various forms which could lead, in the words of a critic of imperialism such as Lenin, to 'annexationist, predatory, plunderous war', or war for 'the division of the world, for the partition and repartition of colonies, "spheres of influence" and finance capital.'[18] But for the Chinese, none of this means much, except in the negative sense of having suffered it. They simply don't *think* this way.

Even when there was effectively a period of large-scale colonisation under the Western Han at the turn of the first century BC, when China 'emerged for the first time as an imperialist power on the Asian continent',[19] the Chinese refuse to describe it as 'colonisation'. Despite the fact that by an astute combination of *attempted conquest* and *coerced annexation*, the area of Han influence was extended far to the West and added over quarter of a million square miles to their territory, providing the model for planned colonisation by Han peoples in the Western regions still in use today. Moreover, although the world's largest contiguous land empire in history was that created on the *attempted conquest* model by the Mongols under Genghis Khan and his grandson Qubilai Khan, the modern Chinese does not consider the domains of Genghis Khan to be part of *his* empire as, say, he or she considers Taiwan to be (fortunately, we might add). Indeed, Qubilai practised a form of what we might almost call 'reverse *uncoerced annexation*'. For, as we will see below in more detail, he changed the official name of the Mongol dynasty to Yuan and not only decreed that the capital should be renamed Ta-Tu, the 'Great Capital', but that its plan should be drawn up on the basis of the capital city outlined in an ancient Chinese classic of government. Yet for all this acceptance and integration of their civilisational values, modern Chinese do not consider the realms dominated by Genghis Khan as part of their cultural heritage, as they do those of the Tang in the west or the Song in the south. I have heard the Yuan period described by a Chinese intellectual as 'a historical accident' – something remote from essential Chineseness. The great Arab traveller Ibn Battuta wrote in the mid-fourteenth century, during the reign of the last Mongol Emperor Toghon Temur (Shundi, 1333–68), that on leaving Hangzhou he left 'the last of the provinces of China [proper], and entered the land of Cathay [Khitá].'[20] Clearly, he, and his local informants, are referring here to 'China Proper' as the land of the Southern Song dynasty, which maintained its capital in Hangzhou until it was taken by Qubilai in 1279. The territory of the Yuan, and their world, were *beyond* China even then.

The tradition outlined above leads *us* to describe the 'Chinese Empire' as if it were a kind of Roman Empire transported a few thousand miles east. For example, Hugh Murray's popular *Encyclopedia of Geography*,[21] published in Philadelphia in 1839, described it in these terms:

> The Chinese empire, stretching from 18° to 56° of north latitude, and from 70° to 140° of east longitude, covers an area of about 5,350,000 square miles, or one-tenth of the whole land-surface of the earth. The population of this vast region, according to the most probable modern computation, is about 183,000,000, as follows:
>
> China Proper : 148,897,000
> Corea: 8,463,000
> Thibet and Boutan: 6,800,000

Mandshuria, Mongolia, Zungaria, Chinese Turkestan &c: 9,000,000
Colonies: 10,000,000

Of this vast expanse of territory, the China Proper of our maps, Mandshuria, and the eastern part of Little Bucharia, form the political China of the imperial administration.

The other regions are merely tributaries or protected states.[22]

The status of Manchuria is ambiguous here (outside China Proper, but within 'political China of the imperial administration'), and the presence of Korea even more so, but the layout and the use of terms like 'colonies' and 'protected states' make it sound very much like a European empire or at least an oriental equivalent of the British Empire of the time.[23]

Indeed, for a while the People's Republic of China seemed to think so too. For in a moment of nationalist pride following the creation of the Republic, an intriguing map was published in 1952 in a *Brief History of Modern China*, which was used as a school textbook for at least a decade. The map, which shows 'the Chinese territories taken by the Imperialists in the Old Democratic Revolutionary Era (1840–1912)', lists among the 'lost' territories that purportedly once belonged to China such places as Nepal, Bhutan, Assam, Burma, the Andaman Islands, Malaya, Singapore, Thailand, Korea, Annam (French Indochina), the Ryukyu Islands and the 'Great North-East' of Russia beyond the Amur River.[24] The purpose behind the publishing of this list remained ambiguous, but at least implicitly there is a claim of direct imperial control in the non-Communist past. The idea behind this map was to take the 'empire' at its greatest ever extent, however short-lived, and however slim the claim to effective control through tribute or other forms of relationship, and then claim that such a land-mass (together with a few strategically important islands) had always constituted China. This is the only time at which China attempted to portray itself as a Western-style empire.

The Concept of Decline and Fall

From these examples, and in general from a Western perspective, it seems evident that there is a direct connection between an empire's economic rise and fall and its growth and decline as an important military power. The notion of decline and fall is intrinsic to our concept of empire, and provides us with a ready-made vocabulary of words like 'waning', 'twilight' and 'eclipse', which signal immediate reference to authors of classical cyclical theories of history such as Edward Gibbon, Oswald Spengler and Arnold Toynbee.[25]

Gibbon (1737–94), whose *Decline and Fall of the Roman Empire* remains in print 200 years after publication, argued that over thirteen centuries a series of revolutions 'gradually undermined, and at length destroyed, the solid fabric of human greatness',[26] which was Rome at the end of the first century after Christ. This long process of decline went through three main periods, first a gentle decline that ended with the conquest of the Empire by the Goths, second the period of Lombard invasion of Italy and the loss of the eastern provinces to Islam, and third a longer period that leads to the time of a 'degenerate race of princes, who continued to assume the titles of Caesar and Augustus, after their dominions were contracted to the limits of a single city.'[27] It is easy to understand how this model can be prejudicially applied to the 'decline' of the Qing and the 'Last Emperor', the boy Puyi. Just as the Romans became indolent and pleasure-loving, so effeminate and unmilitary that they left the business of defending the empire to others, the last Qing emperors are said to have succumbed to similar temptations and through their weakness and apathy to have allowed their lands to be occupied by foreign powers. Thus Qianlong (reigned 1735–1799), a hard-working and constantly campaigning emperor who ruled over what was then the most successful economy on earth, can be described as enjoying 'a corrupt life of self-indulgence as usual'[28] in the face of substantial evidence to the contrary.

As we shall see, things are not really that simple, and today a historian could not get away with phrases like 'sheer conservatism of the Confucian bureaucracy'.[29] This is partly because the current Chinese leadership is acutely aware of its own history and the lessons to be learned from that of other countries. A few years ago, Zbigniew Brzezinski, formerly National Security Advisor to President Jimmy Carter, provided a rare glimpse into their thinking when he remarked that 'not long ago' the Politburo had invited two distinguished, Western-trained professors to a special meeting. According to Brzezinski, these unnamed professors were asked to 'analyse nine major powers since the fifteenth century to see why they rose and fell'.[30] This was a clear indication not only of the Chinese leadership's understanding of the importance of history but also why we should look deeper into history to understand their country.

At the same time, however, in their view, from 221 BC, when the first generally accepted version of a single Chinese polity came into being with the Qin dynasty, to at least the beginning of the twentieth century, some form of empire-like polity remained a constant presence in terms of political and economic power. Athough there were fluctuations in this constancy, so that the last ruler of each dynasty tended to be portrayed by his successors as a self-indulgent and licentious tyrant in order to justify his overthrow, such cycles did not go beyond a break in dynasty. There were also, in late Qing times, theories such as that of the 'three ages' of Gong Zizhen (1792–1841), which began with an age of orderly rule, followed by an age of disorder and finally an age of decay.[31] But, as we shall see, the Mandate of Heaven, which preserved 'empire' as an immanent entity transcending the temporal ruler, remained constant.

The Chinese in their own view

Behind the problem of defining the empire, there is also the difficulty of defining what it means to be *Chinese* and what exactly *China* is. This is not as simple as it might seem, for in ancient China there was no racial or blood definition. It was possible to *become* Chinese, as many Turkic peoples, Mongols and Manchus did: one definition of a 'Chinese' was a person who could read Chinese characters, who lived in a city administered by officials appointed by the emperor, and had his name registered in the emperor's census register. Since on this view 'biological extraction had nothing to do with his identity,'[32] the so-called 'barbarous' populations, known as *yi*, were simply people who did not speak Chinese and did not act like Chinese. But if they were prepared to adopt the customs and language, it was possible for them to be integrated into society and become to all intents and purposes Chinese (a schematic rendering of the relationship between the Chinese in all their manifestations and Outsiders is set out in Figures 1 and 2 (see Appendix 2); it will be clear that while it is possible from the inner core of China in Figure 1 to move outwards, the Outsider in Figure 2 will never be able to reach the centre).

This in fact occurred with entire dynasties such as the Tang (618–907), who were of partly Turkic origin, and the Qing (1644–1911), who were of Manchu – and ultimately Mongolian – origin. The first case is especially interesting, since the Tang are considered by many Chinese today to be the quintessentially Chinese dynasty, which is odd, since such markers of Chinese culture as silk and porcelain have little to do with the Tang, or indeed the north. Although Chinese history books write of the northerners as 'sinicised', it is also possible to argue that on the contrary the Chinese aristocracy was 'Turkicised'. One scholarly description of life in Tang times sounds as if it were written of another country:

> many members of the Tang court displayed many Central Asian and steppe influences: riding horses, speaking Turkic in preference to Chinese, and playing polo (even women). Tang elites also indulged in a passion for Kuchean music, for Soghdian whirling dance and for exotic western goods brought by Soghdian merchants. One Tang prince chose to live in a yurt, and would offer guests chunks of roast mutton carved off with his own dagger. Tang music was played on the lutes, viols and percussion instruments of Central Asia and India; Tang poets sang of infatuation with western dancing girls.[33]

It is for this reason that the Tang were considered cosmopolitan and so influenced Chinese culture, and also explains in part their success in pushing the western frontiers of China as far as Bokhara, Samarkand and even Iran.

In fact the very word used to mean 'Chinese' has changed with the centuries, and with changing self-perception. Before Han times, the Chinese referred to themselves as *rén* or *min*, which can both be translated as 'people', as well as *baixing*, meaning 'those belonging to the hundred surnames'; during Han times, they often referred to themselves proudly as *wanmin*, 'the myriad of people'. Then for many centuries the Chinese found themselves subservient to an invading culture, and their language became for many purposes a second-class language, or at the best *primus inter pares*; officials under the Mongol rulers spoke Mongolian and Persian, while under the Qing dynasty they used Manchu, Chinese and Mongolian. To distinguish themselves racially from the Manchus, the indigenous Chinese began to use the expression *hanrén*, 'the people of Han'. Yet this term merely stressed their ethnicity with reference to the second earliest dynasty, and had no link with a specific territory as there is in words like 'Welsh', or with a blood race like 'Caucasian'. Today, they refer to themselves by the name of their country: *zhōngguó* (China) + *rén* (person or people) = *zhōngguórén*. But, as we will see, until a century ago *zhōngguó* was not even the name of a country or nation.

For it was not until notions of the modern nation-state in Europe reached China in the mid-nineteenth century that a real awareness of being Chinese developed. This feeling arose in contraposition to the invading imperial powers: concepts that had never troubled the Chinese in their isolated certainty such as racism and nationalism drove them to similar constructs of their own. Being Chinese came to mean being substantially different to these other people, or in other words a 'non-Westerner', which was new for them since they had always considered themselves as being at the centre of the universe – with no pressing need to contrast themselves with others. Now the foreigner was no longer simply a *yi*, an unfortunate by birth without the benefits of club membership who could nonetheless apply, but a *waiguórén*, an 'outside the country person' who was irremediably distanced by birth and race and had no chance of joining the club.

In effect, it was their mutual distaste for Western imperial encroachment that unified Manchu and Han. For until the mid-nineteenth century, 'China Proper' was as much a Manchu colonial territory as Qingdao was a German concession. It has recently been emphasised how there were strong resemblances between Qing and Western conquests: 'Even more important, [the Qing's] successful rule over Chinese society was heavily dependent upon native collaboration, in return for which, as in India and other more "typical" colonial situations, the collaborators were given substantial political power.'[34] It was very successful, as was the revival of 'traditional Chinese' costume in the past decade or so. Nowadays, a young man or woman will often refer to such 'Chinese' costumes as the *qipao* (the long, short-sleeved dress with thigh-length slit) without being aware that it is actually a Manchu costume. Such confusion is something that would have been impossible just over a century ago.

There is also another level of difficulty, for Chinese culture is far from unified. Questions of ethnicity, local identity, minority languages and cultural background all create problems and ambiguity in the idea of being Chinese. A single example will suffice to illustrate the various 'origins', each one nesting in another like Russian dolls:

> A native of Taishan, for instance, is simultaneously a belonger to Siyi (the so-called 'four districts' of which Taishan is one), and a man of Guangdong, the province which encompasses Siyi. He is also a denizen of the Siyi speech area, which is encapsulated within Yue, the language known in English as Cantonese.[35]

To the average Westerner, of course, he is simply Chinese. But his language, his loyalties when he emigrates (as many of the people from Taishan did and do), and the food he eats, differ fundamentally from those of a 'denizen' of any other province of China. The first identity is that of family, followed by that of the home village (in the case of extended clans this is often the same thing) or hometown. The defining information on a Chinese tombstone is the person's place of origin, which indicates his or her ultimate identity.

Nation and Empire of Mind

Thus for the Chinese the concept of 'empire' has very different connotations. Indeed the language distinguishes between *dì guó*, meaning 'empire' but with negative connotations of 'strong' and 'bad' and used of the British Empire in the past or the American Empire more recently, and *dà zhōng huá quān*, or 'extended nation', which is what we perceive as the Chinese Empire. Although in Chinese the name of the country is now the abbreviated form *Zhōngguó*, until 1949 it was referred to as *zhōng huá mín guó*, which contains the idea of extended nation. This usage still survives in the words used to express the concept of a Chinese person, *huá rén*.

There is also an ideological problem of a historical Chinese empire or empires, since one of the central tenets of the Chinese myth of itself is that the country has always been more or less as it is now. Thus it was initially a series of smaller disparate states and principalities that were 'united' by the first emperor, with later 'unifications' of larger provinces. The paradox is that 'China' in the past was never considered as a territorial state, and therefore could not conquer its neighbour to create an empire.[36] In a vague way, the empire was already formed in itself. Moreover, to accept the notion of conquest would be to deny the myth of peaceful unification. It is typical of the many ambiguities of Chinese history, which are so complex and so much overlain by centuries of myth-making by various factions and parties for multifarious motives, that any truth – in the Western, empirical sense – is difficult to discern. What, for example, would a visitor from Mars make of this paragraph in a Chinese book of business history, about the events of June 1989:

> After suffering through a summer of intense heat and tremendous anxiety, oppression, and violent resistance, most Chinese seemed immobilized, sunk in a deep fog. Over twenty Western countries united in refusing to invite Chinese leaders to their countries. They obstructed the investments of businessmen who wanted to come to China. Foreign-invested projects that had already started work were either cancelled or delayed. Even the World Bank stopped making loans to China.[37]

Had this all happened because of the heat, our Martian might ask, and why were Western governments being so nasty? Chinese history is full of such ambiguities and deliberate conceptual fog. In this case, it is easy to penetrate the fog because the events are well-known to us; in other cases further in the past it is difficult to discern the truth, for instance as we read the dynastic history of the Han.

The idea of nation did not exist in the Chinese language at all, and had to be imported from Japanese *minzoku* as *minzu*, in 1899, with the related construct of *minzu zhuyi*, or nationalism, appearing two years later.[38] In an interesting article on sport in the late nineteenth century, Andrew Morris translated *minzu* as 'nation-race', arguing that it is a complicated term heavily laced with both national and racial meanings, and possesses an 'etymological vagueness' somewhere between 'ideas of a modern citizenry and a primeval race of descendants of the Yellow Emperor, in between Western scientific ideas of race and a Chinese community covering the realm "All Under Heaven".'[39] It was only with the revolution of 1911 that the *minzu* became part of Chinese political discourse. But the conditions that were necessary for the creation of a nation, for building what Renan called 'a large-scale solidarity', were amply present. For he wrote of the nation in 1882 as a 'soul, a spiritual principle', which was constituted by two key elements: '... a rich legacy of memories; the other is present-day consent, the desire to live together, the will to perpetuate the value of the heritage that one has received in an undivided form.'[40] Perhaps no empire or country possessed these elements in greater degree than China around 1900.

A name was needed for the new entity. The two characters that form the name *Zhōngguó* (... where the first one can be seen to represent 'middle') are usually translated as Middle Kingdom, although it would be more accurate to say Central State. The Chinese historian Xu Guoqi has performed the unenviable task of counting the occurrence of the expression *zhōngguó* in the histories of the twenty-five major dynasties and discovered that it occurs 2,259 times; it apparently occurs in the Confucian 'Thirteen Classics' no less than 613 times.[41] It is therefore a very ancient and respectable *word*. But it was always used in the past in a geographical or cultural sense, never as the name of the country. One Chinese historian explains that in the Warring States period the expression refers to 'the cultural area of the central plain' and not to any middle state or kingdom.[42]

China had been a *civilisation*, but had no name.

As the Jesuit priest Matteo Ricci (1552–1610), who spent nearly thirty years in China and died in Beijing, explains in his remarkable journal, whose wealth of detail about China opened up a new world to Europeans when it was published in 1615:

> It is a custom of immemorial age in this country, that as often as the right to govern passes from one family to another, the country itself must be given a new name by the sovereign whose rule is about to begin. This the new ruler does by imposing some appropriate name according to his own good pleasure.[43]

He explains that during his time in Beijing the country was known as 'Ta-Min', or 'great brilliance'. At the turn of the twentieth century matters were even more complicated. The Chinese often called their own country *Shi ba sheng*, the 'Eighteen Provinces'. But they also used many other expressions, such as the literary terms *Zhōnghua*, the 'Central Cultural Flowering'; *Shenzhou*, 'the Spiritual region'; *Zhōngtu*, 'the Central Land'; *Jiuzhou*, 'the Nine Regions'; and *Hwa-kwo*, the 'Flowery Kingdom'. The country was also often referred to by the name of the current dynasty, so that for the Ming it was *Da Ming Guo* (Ricci's 'Ta-Min'), 'the Great Ming State', and for the Qing dynasty it was *Da Qing Guo*, or 'the Great Qing State'. The name *China* and its variants is only used in other languages, and is thought to derive from Sanskrit *cīna* used in India from about the first century BC to refer to the already extinct Qin dynasty, and by extension to the entire country.

One reason there was no word for China as a nation is therefore that until the beginning of the twentieth century there *was* no nation, no strong sense of belonging to what we might term a '*han* nation'. In 1898, Huang Zunxian (1848–1905), a poet and reformer from Guangdong whose works were admired by the last emperor, made the extraordinary observation (for us, in its banality) that 'research indicates that the diverse countries in the world all boast of their own state names, such as England or France, the only exception being the Central States.'[44] Huang had seen diplomatic service in Tokyo, in London (as counsellor to the Legation in 1890) and also in Singapore,[45] and therefore had personal knowledge of international practice. The use of *Zhōngguó* was designed to remediate this situation. Yet there were objections even to this name when it was initially proposed; Huang himself suggested *Hua Xia*.

Another significant change, marking the transition from the old empire to a modern nation, came with the formal adoption of the solar calendar on 21 December

1911, so that for the first time China measured its years together with the rest of the world instead of according to the years of the current emperor's reign.[46] The modern Chinese nation-state made a tentative beginning with a new name, a republican president and a new calendar – with, for the Chinese, such striking innovations as Sundays and a seven-day week. The queues, or pigtails, which had created problems since Ming officials were forced to wear them in sign of submission to their Manchu conquerors, could now be cut off, often publicly or in large groups as a sign of agreement with the new order. Ironically, many resisted because after so many centuries of indoctrination they believed it was a 'Chinese' custom, and some even committed suicide in shame at something so manifestly 'foreign' as cutting their hair short.[47] In Guangdong, 200,000 queues were cut off in a single day, while in some places soldiers forcibly cut off queues at road-blocks.[48] The other, this time native Chinese, custom to be abolished was foot-binding. At the same time, high-level officials and diplomats began to use Western-style clothing, the ties and bowler hats that we see in old photographs, after the introduction of government rules on formal dress. Out of the conflict between traditional Chinese dress and modern Western dress came the compromise adopted by Sun Yat-sen, which we know wrongly today as the 'Mao suit', still worn by some elderly men. On 12 February of the New Year, the Qing dynasty came to an end with a formal declaration of abdication, although this first Republic was short-lived since the President, Yuan Shikai, soon succumbed to the weight of his new nation's past and reinvented himself as Emperor with the name Hongxian.

As for a truly national identity, that came with the 4 May protest in 1919 against the provisions of the Treaty of Versailles, which stipulated that the German colonies in China – which the Chinese had hoped to recover – were to be transferred to Japan. The 'May Fourth Movement', which was born on that day, was the great catalyst of twentieth-century Chinese revolution and nationalism, spawning both the Communist Party in 1921 and a 1924 coalition between Communists and the Nationalist Party, which adopted the 'Three People's Principles' of nationalism, democracy, and the people's livelihood (the student protests that culminated in the event which the Chinese refer to as 'June 4th' in 1989 actually began on 4 May).

The Burden of History

History weighs heavily in China, as Mao understood when he attempted to eliminate its trappings. The word itself, *shi* or *lishi*, in Chinese has a different meaning. In ancient China, *shi* referred first to an official responsible for holding records of events, so the practice of history primarily meant preserving records of the past. In its most reductive form this entailed little more than compiling the detailed genealogies of the emperors and their families in standard format and in formal language, what has been described as 'the accumulation of administrative experience'.[49] This could be a useful resource for an official who could discover how a problem such as a natural disaster had been resolved in the past. But imperial censorship and interference lessened the usefulness even here. In one outstanding case, the eighteenth-century emperor Qianlong played a very active role in the writing of history. His approval of the Ming *History*, which had taken ninety years to complete, was by no means a formality, since he believed that the purpose of history was to make judgement on the rights and wrongs of the past and to lay blame or praise on its actors when appropriate. He personally issued instructions for the compilation of historical works, edited the results and even made changes to already finished works. He himself compiled a work called the 'Edited Views of the Comprehensive Mirrors of the Successive Ages with Imperial Critiques', which included thousands of his personal interpretations and opinions. He made an anthology of his own contributions, with the 'explicit intention that his works serve as guides to reading and studying the long history of China.'[50] Such official compilations were intended to create an impression of legitimacy and continuity of rule since the first recorded events in the ninth century BC. Today this leads to confused perceptions and beliefs about the past, that the territory of the PRC is no different from that of 2,000 years ago, for example. As one contemporary historian has written, 'the Chinese refer to the Han (206 BC–220 AD) and Tang dynasties as if their greatness still provides practicable standards for contemporary Chinese culture and politics.'[51]

In fact it was only a century ago that Chinese historians began to conceive of a linear history in Western terms, and define the modern 'nation' in terms of its past. But even then traditional scholars did not see the need to adopt modern or Western ways. There were two main defences: a retreat into Confucian conservatism, and a form of Luddism; or, to express it in another way, an opposition between the perfection of classical theory as honed over the centuries and the pragmatic needs of the incipient nation. An intelligent and perceptive man like the high court official Liu Xi Hun (Liu Hsi Hun), who in 1876 travelled with the first Chinese embassy to London, embraced both extremes. In the Journal he kept of his experiences in Europe, he observed on the one hand that 'we Chinese base our culture on the pursuit of righteousness rather than the pursuit of profit, preferring to suit the taste of the people rather than to disturb them,' but then a few pages later complained that if railways were introduced to China 'the people who bare their thighs and forearms, who hold to the whip and the cord, who row the boats, who pull the carriages, to carry people or cargo, would all lose their jobs.'[52]

This dichotomy or paradox influenced many fine scholars. It was essential to remember, in the words of the political theorist and reformer Kang Youwei (K'ang Yu-Wei, 1858–1927), China's past greatness with 'principles, institutions, and culture', which were the 'most elevated in the world'. But also the fact that due to unenlightened customs and 'a dearth of men of ability, she is passively taking aggression and insult.'[53]

The challenge of resolving the paradox was taken up by one of the most renowned scholars, Zhang Zhidong (Chang Chih-Tung, 1837–1900), a man whose life and career by themselves demolish the prejudice against a decadent official hierarchy incapable of understanding the modern world. Zhang was famed for his phenomenal memory and knowledge of the Confucian classics, and was also known in traditional scholarly fashion for his total honesty and frugal lifestyle. But already in 1863, placed third in the imperial palace exams, having previously been first in the provincial level exams in his home province of Chili, he was criticised for paying too much attention to current affairs rather than classical learning. Then, during the 1880s he wrote memorials on a Sino-Russian dispute over the Ili Valley in north-western Xinjiang, which the Russians had seized in 1871, and against French influence in Vietnam. As a leading scholar and politician, and promoter of printing and the dissemination of books, he was governor of Guangdong for many years and extremely pragmatic in following his duties – creating an arsenal for manufacturing shells, establishing a school for training naval officers, and purchasing new warships. He also brought German military instructors to train a modern military force. Later, as Governor of Wuchang, he sponsored a project for a railway from Peking to Hankow,[54] and from his action in founding an important iron and steel works evidently understood very well the importance of industrial development.[55] Zhang was a vigorous supporter of the reform movement of the late 1890s, and in his book *Exhortation to Study* (1898) he coined the slogan 'Chinese learning for the fundamental principles (*ti*), Western learning for practical applications (*yong*).' This meant that scholars should '… glance over the philosophical works and belles-lettres and exquisite writings. And then they can select and make use of that Western knowledge which can make up our shortcoming.'[56] Zhang's book was an immense success, and the emperor himself ordered its distribution to all officials and students.[57] The slogan is still used today, and informs more recent slogans like 'socialism with Chinese characteristics', since the latter refer to the historical values of Chinese culture. As we will see later, it also informs President Hu Jintao's theory of a 'harmonious society' for the future China.

These ideas were reflected a few years later in the historiographical revolution (*shijie geming*) launched by Liang Qichao (1873–1929),[58] who was sponsored by Zhang. Frustrated by his failure at political reform, Liang embarked upon cultural reform instead and made intensive study of Western works on history. In 1902, while in exile in Japan, he launched an attack on traditional historiography in his *Xin shixue* (*New History*). For Liang, the major flaw in the traditional historical practice, he called it that of the old historians (*jiu shijia*), was its failure to foster the national awareness necessary for a strong, modern nation. Following the ideas of progressive thinkers in nineteenth-century Europe, he argued that history must show human progress and its causes, rather than just be an 'essentially primitive synthesis'[59] of the activities of the imperial family. For the first time in China, history was not perceived as a way simply to preserve and present the past, and provide dynastic legitimacy, but as an attempt to exploit historical knowledge in order to define a new future. He knew the problem was that China had no concept of itself as a nation, and that this demanded a new way of looking at Chinese history.

In his book *A Systematic Discussion of Chinese History* (*Zhongguoshi xulun*), published in 1901, Liang sought to resolve the problem. He divided Chinese history into three phases on the Western model corresponding to the ancient, medieval and modern: a first phase that was the 'China of China … when [the Chinese] were victorious over the barbarian races',[60] which lasted until the 'unification' in 221 BC; a second phase which was that of China in Asia, which lasted until 1796 and encompassed the expansion of ancient China into the Greater China of the nineteenth century; and a third phase, the modern, in which China would enter the world in competition with the Western powers. He also provided an interesting gloss on how it was possible to be patriotic without having a country: 'We Chinese do not lack patriotic character. As for those who do not know to love their country, it is because they do not know what a country is. China has been unified since ancient times … it was called the Earthly Realm and was not called a country.'[61]

Four years later, Wang Jingwei (1883–1944), a complex revolutionary figure who later rose to prominence as a polemicist for Sun Yat-sen but died as Governor of a Japanese-sponsored puppet government in Nanjing, produced one of the fundamental documents of Chinese nationalism, a short essay entitled 'Citizens of a Nation' (*Minzudi Guomin*). Here the young idealist defined a nation in terms of common blood, language, territory, religion and history, but in particular he argued that the strongest nation-state is one which consists of people of a single race. Hence the new importance of the word *hanrén*, 'han people' and the reduction of ethnic minorities to little more than folklore and dances in traditional costumes, as they are often portrayed today, especially on television. Wang observed that, unlike China, the powerful countries of Europe were not ruled by people of a different race. In terms that prefigure the definitions of empire used above, he creates an interesting typology of historical situations in the formation of new nations: first, races of equal strength merge to form a new nation; second, a majority conquering race absorbs the conquered minority; third, a minority conquering race assimilates a majority race; and, fourth, a conquering minority is assimilated by a conquered majority.[62] It is clear from this schema that since early times China had belonged to the second type, beginning from unification under the First Emperor in 221 BC, but that from 1644 the assimilation of the Manchus fell into the fourth type. But the most interesting point is that this essay placed history, race and the concept of nation in a single doctrine, which enabled China to emerge from its past as a *minzu* known as *Zhōngguó*, as the nation is called today.

But to imagine a *nation* required a huge creative effort as well as historical studies. A *National Products Movement* which mandated the use of Chinese materials in clothing was coterminous with the Republic and culminated in the Chinese National Products Exhibition of 1928 in Shanghai, attended by over 5 million visitors; there was even a shop on Nanjing Road in Shanghai that sold exclusively Chinese products. There was also a flourishing of 'national medicine', a 'national language', a national flag and anthem, the national opera and even a 'national father' in Sun Yat-sen and talk of 'national blood'.[63] One celebrated business success story of the period was that of Wu Yunchu, who managed to copy and produce the notorious MSG that the Chinese use so much, which had previously been imported from Japan, and founded the Tianchu Weijing Factory, or 'The Heart of Flavour from Heaven's Kitchen factory', in the early 1920s. Wu continues to be called a 'patriotic businessman' and was lauded by Zhou Enlai after the foundation of the PRC. In 1933–4, he even bought aircraft for the Nationalist Government, and had one bomber with the company's name painted on the fuselage.[64] His company was the predecessor of the State-Owned Enterprises designated 'national champions' by the present government.

Sometimes in literature it was easier to cast off the shackles of tradition. In his book *One World Philosophy* (*Datong shu*, 1902), Kang Youwei presents himself as alone in the world and seeking his true self in the midst of the society that is disintegrating around him. Rather like Descartes in discarding his previous knowledge, Kang slakes off his literary persona and begins his life again as a naked body: 'I myself am a body,' he writes, 'another body suffers; it has no connection with me, and yet I sympathize very minutely.'[65] In his fantasy, he reaches out to the galaxies and heavens before coming back to consider himself as a 'gentleman from a family with a tradition of literary studies for thirteen generations'[66] in a country with a millennial history of civilisation. In this way he discovers a new life-force that enables him to achieve an ethical awakening. Starting from new premises, Kang is then able to connect again with Chinese tradition, and seek a new way forward. In a similar vein, Liang Qichao, before asking the fundamental question 'What is a nation?', once imagined the nation, here in almost Kafkaesque fashion, as a huge first-person pronoun. For him, there was a 'small me', *xiaowo*, and a collective 'big me', *dawo*, so that both an individual and the society as a whole was a kind of 'me', which however would have a longer duration.[67] In both cases, the author begins from a fresh, new 'me', unhindered by historical baggage, and imagined a nation composed of such individuals.

Another literary approach to the problem was that of the greatest Chinese author of the time, Lu Xun (1880–1934), who asked another fundamental question: what does it mean to be Chinese? His narrative strategy, in the story 'Death of a Madman' (1918), was to write a brief, one-page introduction in classical Chinese (representing the old order) and then to allow the purported diary entries to be written in the colloquial language of the present day. The diary begins (the entire first section):

Moonlight's really nice tonight. Haven't seen it in over thirty years. Seeing it today, I feel like a new man. I know that I've been completely out of things for the last three decades or more. But I've still got to be *very* careful. Otherwise, how do you explain those dirty looks the Zhao family's dog gave me?

I've got good reasons for my fears.[68]

Here, Lu Xun brilliantly captures the fears of the time and removes the past from the narrator's consciousness. As a madman – now, fortunately, healed – the diarist is given literary license to write whatever he wishes (a device similar to the distancing effect achieved by Montesquieu in his *Persian Letters*). He becomes convinced that everyone wants to eat him, that his own Younger Sister was eaten by his Elder Brother, and that this has been going on for thousands of years. In the end he imagines that he himself has eaten other people, and realises that as 'someone with four thousand years' experience of cannibalism behind me, how hard it is to look real human beings in the eye!'[69] But, in the hope of creating a new identity and sloughing off the past, the story finishes on a note of optimism that there might be some children around who have not yet eaten human flesh. This was Lu Xun's censor-proof way of emphasising the importance of creating a new, honest Chinese identity from scratch.

Thus each writer and each citizen constructed his own private image of the nation, a 'big me'. Indeed, given the importance of the recently conquered provinces at the end of the nineteenth century, one eminent scholar has written of a 'federated nation', which in an extreme form could simply be a federation of 'big me's. The corollary of such a definition is that if there was no Nation there could of course not be, in the Western imperial sense, an Empire. In fact China was always, as we shall see, and is today in a sense, predominantly an *Empire of Mind*.

PART I

Empires of Conquest and Empires of Mind

Within the six directions, the domain of the August Emperor,
West to the flowing sands, south all the way to Beihu,
East to the eastern sea, north beyond Daxia,
Wherever human tracks may reach, there are none who are not his subjects.

(Sima Qian, *Records of the Grand Historian, c.* 100 BC)

Empire as Permanent Tribute

For two millennia the Chinese people have cultivated the myth of a single, geographically constant, centralised empire governed within the equally potent construct of Confucian ideology. They lived, as one author has expressed it, 'in a dream of their country being the eternal center of world civilization, the only place where everything was in harmony.'[70] All other people were barbarians, who could be dealt with in two ways: they could be 'benevolently transformed' and incorporated into the myth as Chinese, as happened with the ethnic minorities; or they could be expelled and kept out, as occsionally happened with foreign traders and missionaries. What we might describe as the 'Middle Kingdom syndrome' functioned as a logic gate. China was either open or closed, and could not be both at once. Another consequence was that the Middle Kingdom could not seek equal status, or enter into bilateral relations with other states, because in its own view there were no equals in the entire universe.

The 'syndrome' still functions today and impacts on foreign visitors. Whereas Westerners might think of themselves as travelling to China out of curiosity, to make money from a business deal, or as a backpacker performing a rite of passage, the average Chinese sees the visit as a form of tribute paid to the superiority of Chinese culture and to the country's rediscovered place in the world. Each photograph of a historical monument taken by us is a badge of merit for them. In a sense, the visit is *due*. Moreover, the perception of the motivation and justification of the visit depends, as in the case of Janus, which side of the coin each partner in the relationship happens to be looking at. While Jesuit priests worked in the imperial court in the hope of converting the Chinese to Christianity, the emperors employed them because to have educated foreigners in their court circle was a tangible sign of their universal power and the cosmopolitan nature of their court. The Emperor Kangxi wrote very explicitly that Christianity, or 'the teaching of the West', was not for him: 'It is contrary to orthodoxy and it is only because these apostles have a thorough knowledge of the mathematical sciences that the State employs them. Take care not to forget that.'[71] The same was true of the nineteenth-century Treaty Ports: while foreign powers saw the treaties as a charter of trading privileges that they had won for themselves, from the Chinese point of view they were a means of limiting foreign presence in China to a few well-controlled areas – as had been done with the Portuguese in Macao as long ago as 1557. Indeed, in that case, it was also useful to have a foreign power controlling what was difficult to control from an imperial capital, which was to all intents and purposes as far away as Lisbon. All is never as it seems.

China as the Centre of the World to which Tribute is Paid

The mainland territory, which came to be known as *Zhōngguó* to the Chinese and modern China to Westerners, is heavily conditioned by physical geography. The eastern border is fixed by the long coastline of the China Sea, from frozen Siberia to tropical Vietnam; the southern border is defined by the forests and swamps associated with the Mekong delta system; the south-western border is defined by the presence of massive mountain chains; the extreme west by the arid expanse of the Gobi and Taklamakan Deserts. The only 'flexible' part of this physical geography is in the north, which is why so many dynasties built walls to block marauding tribes from the steppes. These tribes always presented the greatest threat. In the case of the Mongol and Manchu invasions it led to conquest, which Chinese sophistry manages to read in reverse as the assimilation of barbarians to their culture.

This vastness was one of the reasons the Chinese failed to be curious about the world outside, which they assumed reasonably enough was part of *their* world. In origin this was a self-contained fluvial empire, with the two great rivers, Chang Jiang (Yangtze) and Huang He (Yellow River), facilitating both trade and territorial control. For rivers encourage movement and conquest, while mountains restrict them. Indeed, in one of those connections between the visual element of characters and their meaning which make Chinese such a fascinating language, the Chinese word for political order, *zhi*, is linked to the concept of dominating the river systems. The character for *zhi*, 治, is composed of the two elements 水 (*shui*, water) and 台 (*tai*, mound or wall); placed together, they can be seen as representing a dam or dyke controlling the water to the left.[72] In other words, political power was a consequence of possessing the skill to dominate rivers. Indeed, the entire Chinese civilisation is believed to have begun with legends of the ancient Yellow Emperor, whose main contribution was to bring the eponymous river under human control.

Looking inwards, they ignored us as much as we ignored them. As Matteo Ricci put it: 'The extent of their kingdom is so vast, its borders so distant, and their utter lack of knowledge of a transmaritime world is so complete that the Chinese imagine the whole world as included in their kingdom.'[73] A much later long-term resident, the diplomat and sinologist Herbert Allen Giles (1845–1935), observed that 'just as every inhabitant of the eighteen provinces believes China to be the centre of civilisation and power, so does he infer that his language and customs are the only ones worthy of attention from native and barbarian alike.'[74] Such was the disdain for the barbarian peoples who lived outside this magic circle that in ancient times the word *ti* (狄) for 'northern barbarian' was written with a character including on the left the radical for 'dog'(犭), so that policies could be literally described as being a matter of 'stick and bone', while *man* (蛮), meaning 'southern barbarian', used in the lower part the radical for 'worm' (虫). These subliminal messages in the script were used to reinforce Chineseness and depict all other peoples as subhuman. China only agreed not to use a more modern character meaning 'barbarian' as synonymous with 'foreigner' after the Treaty of Tianjin of 1858 specified 'that the character 'I' 夷 [barbarian], shall not be applied to the Government or subjects of Her Britannic Majesty.'[75] It took cannon power to force such a change.

While *Zhōngguó* is often translated as 'Middle Kingdom', there are other possible translations that are more precise: 'Central Kingdom', or, better still, 'Central State'. This myth of centrality informs the normative Chinese world view, a central state of such self-evident moral and material superiority that its values should be carried outwards to the rest of the world since its validity was universal. But then, each civilisation known to man has seen itself as being at the centre of the world, and writes its own history in this perspective. Before accusing the Chinese of hubris we should remember that the Mediterranean is known in several languages, such as German and Hebrew, as 'the Middle Sea',[76] and the Roman usage of 'our sea' (*mare nostrum*) bears the same force in being literally at the centre of the empire. Yet the unification of feudal China was dramatically different from the 'unification' imposed on the Mediterranean by the Romans. As we have already noticed, the Romans unified by military force but acknowledged the cultures of the conquered peoples when they recognised something of value; thus Greek remained the dominant language of the eastern part of the empire. In a nice example of multicultural practices, the geographer Strabo (*c.* 63 BC–24 AD), a Roman citizen with a Latin nickname meaning 'squinter' (*strabico* means 'cross-eyed' in modern Italian), was born in the town of Amasya in what is now northern Turkey (then the province of Pontius and Bithynia) and wrote his works in Greek. The first Qin emperor, conversely, imposed a standardised script, weights and measures, and customs on the territories he unified. The most remarkable thing about his achievements is of course the continuity that brought much of their substance down to modern times. By comparison, the legacy of Rome was long-lasting, especially in law, but weaker and less direct.

Yet in terms of political geography there has always been and still is a degree of ambiguity concerning the definition of China. Officially, the present state consists of twenty-three provinces (Anhui, Fujian, Gansu, Guangdong, Guizhou, Hainan, Hebei, Heilongjiang, Henan, Hubei, Hunan, Jiangsu, Jiangxi, Jilin, Liaoning, Qinghai, Shaanxi, Shandong, Shanxi, Sichuan, Yunnan and Zhejiang), five auton-omous regions (Guangxi, Nei Mongol [Inner Mongolia], Ningxia, Xinjiang and

Xizang [Tibet]), and four metropolitan areas (Beijing, Chongqing, Shanghai and Tianjin). But things are not that simple. A quick count of the provinces above will actually reveal twenty-two, since the twenty-third province is given as Taiwan. A standard, popular reference work such as the *Atlas of the People's Republic of China*, first published by the China Cartographic Publishing House in 1989, provides maps of 'Taiwan Province', described as 'the second smallest province of China' with no explanation of its political status. But whatever the real status of that ambiguous island, it is not at present considered by anyone else in the world to be a province of the People's Republic of China. Then there are the two 'special administrative regions' of Hong Kong and Macau. These three 'places', the only circumlocution which can avoid the diplomatic issues, slip in and out of China according to who is counting. A Taiwanese travels to China with a special kind of visa called 'Pass for Taiwanese Residents Travelling to the Mainland', popularly known as a *taibaozheng* or 'Compatriot Pass' – which, unusually for what is in effect a visa, makes no mention of nationality. In spite of its supposed provincial status, there are no direct scheduled flights or ferries to Taiwan, although it lies just 120 miles off the mainland province of Fujian. Citizens of mainland China still need a special document to travel to Hong Kong and Macau. 'Inward investment' from Hong Kong and Taiwan, itself an odd phrase since the two places are deemed to be part of China, is counted as Foreign Direct Investment (and notably falsifies the statistics), while Taiwanese and Hong Kong residents on the mainland must use on their cars the special black number plates reserved for foreign residents (except in Shenzhen, where dual Hong Kong/ Shenzhen plates exist). At the same time, however, Taiwan pop music is accepted by mainland youth as an integral part of their musical culture: after all, the singers do sing in Chinese and speak a language close to *Putonghua* in their interviews. The real absurdity of this ambiguity is evident at international sports events, when three 'Chinese' teams compete against each other: PRC, 'Hong Kong, China' [sic], and, in a bizarre circumlocution designed to avoid the other T-word, 'Chinese Taipei'. It is hardly surprising that in relaxed conversation many Chinese speak sometimes as if these 'places' were part of their country and sometimes as if they were not, or that schoolchildren are confused. To coin a phrase: several countries, lots of systems.

Then again, it is natural that definitions mutate in the course of history, and according to the power and conquests of successive dynasties. Let us take as example the term *hsi-yü*, or 'western regions', which has been used since the times of the Han dynasty (206 BC–220 AD). At first, this term referred to territory west of the Yumen Pass on the Silk Road near the western border of Gansu. Then gradually it came to include land west of the Pamir, such as Samarkand, Russian Turkestan and part of India, and later still Persia, Asia Minor and all of India. During the Yuan dynasty (1271–1368), the same term was used to refer to the area from the lands of the Weiwuer (Uyghurs) in modern Xinjiang through the Mongol khanates as far as Eastern Europe.[77] It is a perfect example of the flexibility of definitions in

Chinese historical geography. A mountainous and desert region of such extent that knew Mazdaism, Buddhism, Nestorian Christianity and Islam before the process of sinicisation cannot by definition be a simple territory. The ambiguity persists today: Xi'an, known today as the city of the Terracotta Warriors, is spoken of as being in the 'West' (the name itself means 'western peace'), although a glance at a map shows that it is very much east of the centre of China and only one and a half hours southwest of Beijing by plane (Urumqi, in the real west, is a four-hour flight due west).

But there is another remarkable feature of Chinese history that supports their view of themselves as unique. The vicissitudes of conquest, of new powers, religions and ideologies that have touched most other countries of the world to a greater or a lesser degree have had little impact on China. We might mention the long-term effects of the Roman Empire and Holy Roman Empire, the voyages of discovery and papal dominion of an expanding Christian world, or the threat of the Ottoman Empire. Even educated Chinese today know little of these things, just as in Europe little was known of China before late medieval travellers and merchants returned from the East. Chinese knowledge of the 'West' in ancient times mainly concerned the Parthians and Persians, with communications being opened up between China and the pre-Islamic Arab world by a roving ambassador called Zhang Qian who made a ten-year journey to the West in the second century BC. On subsequent journeys, however, envoys travelled as far west as Syria and on one occasion to the court of Augustus in Rome. Much later, at the end of the thirteenth century, an Uyghur monk called Sauma visited Naples, Rome and Genoa before meeting King Philippe le Bel in Paris and King Edward I of England in Gascony.[78] But after the Mongol empire such overland journeys came to a virtual halt, and travel to the West only began again in the second half of the nineteenth century, by sea rather than overland, when diplomatic representatives and students began to sail to Europe and the USA. Today, few Chinese, even university students, have much knowledge of basic European geography, such as the location of countries or cities of major historical importance for Western culture like Florence, a city that is crucial to modern culture but as unknown to the average Chinese as Hangzhou is to the average Westerner. 'Abroad' often means the USA.

Many reasons can be given for this historical and cultural insularity, but we will focus on one: the idea of *tianxia*, 'that which exists under heaven', as shaped during the intellectual revolution of the third century BC.

The Mandate of Heaven

Emperors often feel a need to demonstrate the legitimacy of their rule. The first Roman Emperor, Augustus, recruited Virgil to extol his virtues and recount that he was descended from the Trojan hero Aeneas, who in turn claimed descent from Venus. Thus, too, the kings of the state of Zhou during the first millennium BC needed more than brute force to placate the opposition of the nobility, and achieve something akin to uncoerced annexation of their immediate neighbours. In doing so they devised a system of divinely attributed authority, which sustained the Chinese Empire down to the early twentieth century, the *tian ming* or 'Mandate of Heaven'.

According to early Chinese writings, *tiān*, Heaven, first created mankind and then appointed a king, on the basis of personal virtue, to rule over its creation. This doctrine originated at the time of the transition of power from the Shang dynasty to the Zhou dynasty, around 1000 BC. The Zhou, which survived in a slowly fragmenting form until the rise of the unifying 'first emperor' 800 years later, needed to legitimise their new power in order to convince Shang nobles and officials to accept them as genuine rulers. This was done by arguing that the right to govern was based on a heavenly mandate: *tiān* demanded worthy behaviour from the king who had been appointed, and also had the right to remove an unworthy ruler. This relationship between heaven and man is visually manifest in the word for king, or ruler: *wáng*. Three simple steps provide an insight into Chinese culture: first, the character for *wáng* consists of three horizontal lines representing heaven, man and earth, connected by a single vertical stroke to signify the person who forms the link downwards from heaven to earth: 王; secondly, the character for jade, *yù*, is the same as that for king with a single dot added to differentiate it from *wáng*: 玉, which also explains the significance of jade in the Chinese mind; thirdly, the simplified character for country, *guó* (as in Zhōngguó), consists of a box meaning boundary or land, with the character for jade – representing the king or ruler – inside the box: 国. Thus the political theory of kingship is encapsulated in the written script, and is integral to language and culture as in no other civilisation. The centrality and the link to Heaven inform the name of the country: 中国. It could therefore be clumsily, but appropriately, translated as 'the central civilisational area which is ruled by a king mandated by Heaven'. The realm of this king was *tiānxia*, the 'All-Under-Heaven', or in other words the Universe.

Given this powerful, quasi-divine sense of legitimacy of power, it is not surprising that emperors looked upon surrounding or distant peoples with disdain. Such a view is made explicit by the first Ming Emperor, Hongwu, in a letter written to the people of northern China:

> Ever since the earliest emperors ruled all-under-Heaven, China has controlled the barbarians from within while the barbarians have respectfully looked to China from without. The barbarians have never been known to rule the empire from within China. Since the Sung was overthrown and the Yuan came as northern barbarians to rule over China, all peoples within and without have offered

submission without exception. This was hardly [the result of] human effort, but really the gift of heaven.[79]

Interestingly, *tiānxia* is used here to mean 'empire', rationally, since for Hongwu all the world *was* now his empire, although the more usual word for empire was *tiān-fu*.

We can now understand why the renewal of the mandate was one of the key tasks of the emperor's year, and why the temples which guaranteed the mandate provided the coordinates of the imperial capital of the Ming and Qing. The primary locus, the Temple of Heaven, in effect a park located in the south of Beijing housing various buildings for the annual ceremonies, was complemented by the Temple of Earth in the north, a Temple of the Sun in the east, and a Temple of the Moon in the west. Each year, on the eve of the winter solstice, the emperor left the Forbidden City to make the short journey to the Temple of Heaven in a procession of officials and imperial family members. He passed through what was known in Ming times as the 'Following Heaven Gate' (Chengtiānmén, later renamed Tiānānmén, the 'Gate of Heaven'), and was carried in an elaborate sedan chair along Tiānjie ('Heavenly Street'), which was in 1958 subsumed into the infamous square. He had already fasted for two days before this, and on arrival in the grounds of the Temple of Heaven entered the Abstinence Palace to complete the process with a final day of fasting. The next morning, at dawn, he continued the procession eastwards to a pavilion where he could change into ceremonial robes before the final short distance to an altar raised off the ground in the southern part of the park. There, accompanied by music, he 'burned incense, made supplications, made offerings of jade and silk, and bowed three times, and watched the offerings burn as a way of seeing off the deities.'[80] The whole structure of the Temple of Heaven was designed to enhance the symbolism of the ceremony: the circular altar was raised above the earth, and represented heaven while the square-shaped buildings below represented earth. The 'Hall for Prayer for a Prosperous Year' at the northern end of the complex was also circular and raised above the surrounding ground. When this ceremony was completed, and the emperor had literally stepped up to the sun to receive the mandate, he returned to the Forbidden City with his powers renewed for a year. Heaven, 天, had provided order and life, the 'mandate', 命.

In 1421, Shah Ruhk (Shahruh Mirza, 1377–1447), the son of Tamerlane who as ruler of Persia and Transoxiana controlled the central part of the Silk Road, sent an embassy from his capital at Herat including his own son Shadi Khwaja. One of the envoys, Hafiz-i Abru, wrote up a diary that provides an eye-witness account of the return of Yongle after the ritual which took place on 13 February that year:

Elephants richly caparisoned, were led out in procession, and bore on their backs a circular gilded litter. Then came standards of black, red, yellow, green and russet colours, emblazoned with the figures of sun, moon, stars, mountains, rivers and other Chinese devices both in the rear and in the van. These were followed by lancers carrying swords, halberds, spears, staves, javelins, maces, scimitars, battle-axes, long-tufted fly-whisks and Chinese fans and umbrellas, and then five more ornamented sedan chairs completely gilded carried by men on their shoulders. There were many musical bands of which it is impossible to give an idea, and there marched about five thousand men before and behind the Emperor keeping perfect steps together without daring to fall out of the marching line. No one had the courage to make any noise so that it seemed that there was not a breathing soul there but the sound of Chinese musical bands that intonated prayers for the Emperor.[81]

This impressive procession passed through what is today Tiānānmén Square, and entered the Forbidden City, after which 'everybody returned to his quarters.' Imperial power was reconsecrated and extended in time.

Hence the symbolic importance of the block-like mausoleum that was built to house the embalmed corpse of Mao Zedong (Mao Tse Tung) and placed at exactly 90° across the due north-south route that the Emperor took to renew his mandate, in order to break the sequence: tiān, Heaven > tiāntán, the Altar of Heaven > Tiānānmén Guǎngchǎn, the Gate of Heaven Square (the 2008 Olympic 'Birdcage' was built by the Communist but deeply superstitious Chinese on exactly the same axis a few miles further north, to benefit from imperial feng shui). The mausoleum straddles the sequence in the midst of the massive square, a highly charged emotional space, and literally breaks the flow of the mandate: once again, the Chinese language is explicit in the two characters that stand for revolution, 革命, *ge ming*, where the first character actually means 'take away', 'change' or 'break', and the second character means 'mandate' and also 'order'. In other words: Heaven, 天, provides the mandate, 命 (天命); revolution 'breaks', 革, the order established by the mandate 命 (革命).

For Beijing represented imperial order. The city was laid out from the beginning as a political statement, with the Inner City, the Imperial City and the so-called Forbidden City expressing a system of power. The diplomat Sir George Staunton remarked on this when he visited Beijing with Lord Macartney at the end of the eighteenth century: 'Pekin,' he wrote in his *Account* of the journey, 'is merely the seat of the government of the empire. It is not a port. It is not a place of inland trade, nor manufacture … It forms no rendezvous for pleasure and dissipation.'[82] In other words, it is not a 'natural' capital but was designed to impress both imperial subjects and foreign tributary missions. This absence of a natural identity probably explains why the city has had so many names in its history, once being merely contrasted as *bei-*, or northern capital, to *nan-*, or southern capital, *Beijing* as opposed to *Nan*jing. In Ming times, it was usually known as Jingshi ('our national capital'), but also Ducheng ('Walled Capital'), Dumen ('Gated Capital'), Huangdu ('Imperial Capital'), Dijing ('The Imperial Capital'), and even Chang'an, the ancient name of Xi'an when it was the capital of China. Apart from the better known modern name Beiping (used from 1928 to 1949), as many as seventy different names are known to have been used for the city. In fact, in the past 600 years the use of Beijing to describe the present city was 'rare'.[83]

The Tribute System

Thus in the ancient Chinese world-view, the 'Son of Heaven', *tiānzi*, was superior to all other rulers and stood at the heart of the *tiānxia*, literally 'that which exists under heaven'. If that was the case, an emperor could argue, then some form of recognition was required from other, implicitly minor, states in the *tiānxia*. There were two ceremonial ways of performing this obeisance: first, by presenting tribute to the emperor on a regular basis; second, by performing the ritual *kowtow* in the presence of the emperor. This was the essence of the tribute system, which probably had its roots in ancient customs of exchanging gifts to seal alliances.

In later times the imperial authorities issued lists of required tribute, as can be seen in the case of tribute from Korea during the Qing period. It was on the face of it a complex and costly business, for tributary states sent three or four missions a year of around thirty people plus ten times as many retainers (secretaries, ushers and heralds) throughout the Ming and Qing periods, bearing hundreds of sacks of gifts and supplies. For the Korean missions, this process entailed a journey of forty to sixty days in each direction plus a stay of up to two months in the Chinese capital; missions from some of the more distant tributaries lasted years, and often meant long waits for the right season or winds to depart once the payment of tribute had been completed. During the early Qing period, required goods for each Korean mission fell into twenty-two categories, headed by gold and silver but including thousands of pieces of cotton and silk goods, rolls of paper, knives, tea, pepper and an impressive number of animal skins: 100 leopard skins, 400 otter skins, 100 deer skins and 300 black squirrel skins in a single year. There were also elaborate lists of personal gifts for the emperor, empress and heir apparent, who reciprocated with gifts to members of the embassy, including interpreters, guards and retainers. Some idea of the immense financial burden may be gleaned from the fact that for the King of Korea the cost of receiving a single Qing mission amounted to one sixth of the entire annual budget of his government. Yet these ritualistic exchanges bought peace and relative independence: '… so long as Korea sent tribute, received imperials patents concerning matters of adoption, marriage, and the like in the royal family and remained peaceful both at home and toward China, the Ch'ing did not interfere in Korea's internal affairs.'[84]

The system was expensive for the Chinese hosts as well. Hafiz-i Abru informs us that the living conditions for imperial guests in Beijing during the early Ming were luxurious, with satin and brocade pillows, brocade slippers, sofas and beds with equally rich covers all provided free of charge. Members of the embassy were divided into groups of ten, each of which received every day:

> a sheep, a goose and two fowls, while each person was given two standard *mans* of flour, a big bowl of rice, two large loaves stuffed with sweets, a pot of honey, garlics, onions, vinegar, salts and such variety of vegetables as are to be had in China, as well as two jugs of beer, a plate of desserts together with several active and alert servants.[85]

On departure, each member of the embassy was given gifts according to his rank: Shadi Khwaja received 'ten bags of silver coins, thirty pieces of satin as well as seventy other stuffs consisting of under-vests, red- silks, Lousha [perhaps derived from Lucca], Kapki [a kind of velvet], together with five thousand bank-notes ...'.[86] Matteo Ricci observed at the beginning of the seventeenth century that although very few countries were then paying the stipulated tribute, the Chinese authorities had become 'quite indifferent' as to whether it was paid because 'when they come into the country to fulfill their obligation, [they] carry away with them from China more money than they bring in as tribute.'[87] In fact, the system provided a means of conducting trade even when trade was banned, which explains the many examples of countries *requesting* to pay tribute.

In 1751, the emperor Qianlong commissioned an illustrated study of the peoples that paid tribute to his empire. Two-thirds of the entries in the consequent *Qing Imperial Illustrations of Tributaries* concerned non-Han peoples within the provinces of Fujian, Hunan, Guangdong, Guangxi, Gansu, Sichuan, Yunnan and Guizhou. But the first chapter opens with a list of foreign countries rated according to their distance from the imperial capital. First came Asian countries such as Korea, Japan, Tibet, Mongolia, the Ryukyu Islands, Annam (i.e. Vietnam), Thailand, Java, Malacca (Melaka), the Solomon Islands and Burma, followed by European countries including England, France, Holland, Hungary, Poland, Sweden and Switzerland.[88] In effect, the tribute system was a flexible means of regulating contact with the outside world, a rudimentary foreign policy. Thus the Qing records of foreign relations could write in 1880 that once the foreign warships or 'amphibious monsters' had been driven away, the emperor Tongzhi had been able through the sheer force of his imperial dignity to re-establish order and harmony: 'Oxen and horses slept in peace. His Majesty's virtue flowed out to foreign places. For this reason the various barbarians came to be ruled, while others knocked at the open door and offered up ceremonial presents.'[89] This extraordinary document continues as if the emperor believed that he still ruled over *tiānxia* in spite of recent events and the manifest superiority of British and French military forces.

In his view the bringer of tribute was not presenting his gifts and obeisance to a mere man, or even to a mere emperor, but was explicitly acknowledging a system of universal order presided over by the Son of Heaven. To refuse the terms of this ritual was tantamount to rejecting the gods, putting out of joint the chain that passes from god to earth through man (王), so much so that a famous passage from the rhetoric of Shakespeare's Ulysses might be the best way for a Western audience to comprehend the Chinese concept:

> O, when degree is shak'd,
> Which is the ladder of all high designs,
> The enterprise is sick! How could communities,
> Degrees in schools, and brotherhoods in cities,
> Peaceful commerce from dividable shores,
> The primogenity and due of birth,
> Prerogative of age, crowns, sceptres, laurels,
> But by degree, stand in authentic place?
> Take but degree away, untune that string,
> And hark what discord follows![90]

If we substitute tributary states for 'communities', the imperial examination system for 'schools', peaceful coexistence between ethnic groups for 'brotherhoods', then Shakespeare's words exactly express the 'discord' which the Qing feared, and which was shortly to engulf them. For the moral imperative of the Chinese Emperor, as the incarnate link between Heaven and Earth (王 could almost be read visually as the 'ladder of all high designs'), was to maintain order in the entire world.

Lord Macartney as the Bearer of Tribute from King George III

Now we are in a position to understand one of the best-known events in the history of relations between China and the West, the notorious and often-cited episode of the embassy to the Emperor Qianlong headed by George, 1st Earl Macartney (1737–1806).

In brief, as the British version runs, in 1793, an embassy arrived in China bearing gifts from King George III with three main objectives: to enter into an agreement that would help to reduce a huge trade deficit, to create better trading conditions by opening up new ports (at that time legal trade was only permitted in Canton, and only from October to March), and to create a permanent diplomatic presence in Peking. From the British point of view, the royal gifts were considered to be a normal part of diplomatic negotiations. The popular version of this episode is that the mission failed because Macartney refused to kowtow to the Emperor, who dismissed the gifts as worthless trifles, and asserted in an edict that he did not need British goods at all, so that the embassy returned to London empty-handed. With a few variations, and varying degrees of detail, most accounts run something like this.[91]

From the Chinese point of view, the whole matter is entirely different.

First of all, the embassy was recorded as a 'tribute mission' and could not therefore be thought of otherwise by the imperial court and its rigid bureaucrats. Strict procedures were applied as soon as a foreign ship arrived in Chinese territorial waters. Permission to sail from the south to Beijing required written consent from the capital, which took up to twenty-seven days each way to Fuchow and up to thirty-two days to Canton (Guangzhou); this required the presentation of a memorial listing tributary gifts, which had to be formally approved before the embassy could sail north. On arrival in Beijing some months later, when the gifts had been presented to the Board of Ceremonies to verify their value, the ambassador and his retinue needed to visit the Board the day before an imperial audience for a rehearsal of the requisite ceremonies, including the infamous kowtow.[92] Nothing was left to chance.

These rules also applied to Lord Macartney and his embassy. Moreover, although it would appear from later and many present-day accounts that the refusal to kow-tow was the crux of the matter, contemporary Chinese records show that Lord Macartney *did* perform a pro forma kowtow during his audience with the Emperor in the early morning of 14 September. Thus the demands of Chinese culture were satisfied, while modifications in favour of British notions of ceremony, allowing a dignified bow on one knee, were made.[93] There was actually a precedent for a British kowtow, performed almost willingly by a Scottish doctor in Russian impe-rial service, John Bell of Edinburgh, who travelled from St Petersburg to Peking with a Russian embassy in 1720. The Russian ambassador attempted to avoid it, and was first allowed to present his credentials directly to the emperor. But then the ambassador and his retinue were ordered to make obeisance nine times. In Bell's words, the master of ceremonies 'delivered his orders in the TARTAR lan-guage, by pronouncing the words *morgu* and *boss*; the first meaning to bow, and the other to stand; two words which I cannot soon forget.'[94] A few years after the Macartney voyage, the pragmatic Henry Ellis, who travelled to Beijing with Lord Amherst's equally unsuccessful embassy, wrote on the kowtow that 'it could scarcely be deemed advisable to sacrifice the more important objects of the embassy to any supposed maintenance of dignity by resisting upon such a point of etiquette, in such a scene.'[95] All this might seem foolish to us today, and it is easy to joke about the kowtow. But the very notion was central to the idea of the Mandate of Heaven, which is the theory underlying rituals for visiting ambassadors, as the word itself illustrates: we may recall the character 命, meaning mandate, or order. In fact this character is made up of three elements, from top to bottom: first of all 人, *ren*, which means 'man' or 'person'; second, 一, *y*, which means 'one'; and, lastly, 叩, *kou-tou*, which in English becomes 'kowtow'. Thus it was virtually impossible for Qing officials to separate the notion of an ambassador recognising the mandate from his performance of the kowtow. The latter is integral to the essence of the former. The obeisance implicit in the kowtow is essential to the maintenance of order, and the concept cannot be separated from the character representing it.

Secondly, it is nonsense to suggest that Macartney arrived in an isolated country in which Western culture and technical expertise were unknown. China was fully integrated into the world economy at that time: its hunger for silver enriched the Spanish nobility and oiled the wheels of global maritime trade (guns, rum and cloth from Europe to Africa; slaves from Africa to America; sugar, tobacco, furs and bullion from America to Europe; silver from Europe to China; and tea, silk and porcelain from China to Europe). In addition, Western scientific knowledge was no secret for emperors and imperial scholars. There had been an intellectually active Jesuit mission in Beijing since Matteo Ricci arrived in 1601, and already by 1631 343 treatises on non-Chinese subjects had been published, on such varied topics as astronomy, music, mathematics and hydraulics.[96] Astronomy was particularly important for the Chinese emperors, since the Mandate of Heaven needed it to measure 'their cosmological, political and historical worth.'[97] Such a crucial function necessitated the creation of the most accurate calendars possible, capable of predicting and explaining heavenly phenomena like eclipses and meteors that could have significant weight in imperial decision making and planning. For the mandate and its associated cosmic order provided the authority to oversee the events of everyday life. Ricci had studied mathematical astronomy in Rome, introduced logarithms to the Chinese, and translated the first six books of Euclid, published in 1607. In his own words, this new geometry was greatly admired and 'had a considerable effect upon the rearrangement of their calendar.'[98] He created a *Complete Map of the Myriad Countries* (ultimately derived from Mercator's world map of 1569), which ran to eight printed editions and taught the Chinese the correct location of the main European countries. The technical information it contained on such matters as latitude and longitude was adopted by the compiler of the first Chinese map of the world in 1593.[99] Ricci's companion Giulio Aleni (1582–1649), who had also studied mathematics in Rome, wrote books in Chinese to introduce Western culture and history, including *A Summary of Western Learning*.

It should be remembered that in the study of mathematics and astronomy the Jesuits were then absolute leaders, and had produced in their schools mathematicians of the caliber of Descartes (1596–1650) and Christopher Clavius (1538–1612), one of the teachers of both Ricci and Aleni, much admired by Galileo, who devised the Gregorian calendar. In 1700, they carried out a survey of Beijing for the Emperor Kangxi, which was followed over the next twelve years by a survey of some parts of the Great Wall and a map of Manchuria, vitally important as a political tool for defining the frontier with the burgeoning Russian Empire. Whereas earlier Chinese maps had been vague pictures with explanatory text, now the empire had accurate maps drawn to scale; in the emperor's own words, he had 'a precise map which would unite all parts of his empire in one glance'.[100] As a young man, the emperor Qianlong, then known as Hongli, had been a favourite of Kangxi, who recognised his intelligence and took him into the imperial palace to live with him so that he could get to know him better. So it is likely that Qianlong knew of his grandfather's enthusiasm for European knowledge.

In recent times, there had been European painters, architects and scholars in the imperial court. Giuseppe Castiglione (1688–1766) painted portraits for Qianlong and worked together with his fellow priest Michel Benôit (1715–54) as an architect on the European-style palace and gardens at the Old Summer Palace in what are now the northern suburbs of Beijing. This was a kind of eighteenth-century Disneyland inspired by Versailles and the Trianon, with special features like a complex water-clock and *trompe-l'œil* European street scenes, whose ruins are still impressive today. One of the wonders was the hydraulic system for the fountains, probably inspired by those at Villa d'Este in Tivoli.[101] There had even been a Catholic convert, Fan Shouyi (1682–1753), who had spent ten years studying theology in Italy and knew both Rome and Florence, as well as having visited Genoa, Naples, Parma, Milan and Siena. Here was a Chinese scholar who had met and talked with Pope Clement IX and King João V of Portugal, and then shared his knowledge with Kangxi in entire days of conversation.[102] That incredibly curious and energetic emperor himself tells us that he 'often worked several hours a day' with the Jesuits who were translating treaties on arithmetic and geometry.[103] Ignorance of Europe was not a problem.

Neither was China poor. The country's share of world GDP increased from 23.1 per cent in 1700 to 32.4 per cent in 1820, compared to an increase in the same period – at the height of the Industrial Revolution, from 23.3 per cent to 26.6 per cent for all of Europe put together.[104] Since Qianlong reigned for just over half of this period, he must have been getting something right if his realm outperformed Europe in a period of relative prosperity. In fact, life expectancy at that time was good once infant mortality was overcome: in 1784, an official in Beijing noted that amongst candidates for the imperial civil service exam that year one candidate was over ninety, while twenty more were over eighty.[105] In a climate of opulence that filtered down, even peasants began to change from garments made of hemp to those of cotton and silk, and homes were furnished with tables, beds, chests and mirrors to a standard similar to that of Europe. While the embassy took clocks as gifts believing them to be an exceptional novelty, there had in fact been an *Office of Clock Manufacture* in the capital since 1723, with three separate workshops located *within* the Forbidden City. The Jesuits provided eleven European horologists, who in 1752 constructed an elaborate hemicyclical theatre clock with three separate scenes for the sixtieth birthday of the empress dowager.[106] New products from the Americas, such as maize and sweet potatoes, together with increased supplies from the recently conquered south-western provinces of China, meant that the rapidly expanding population had plenty to eat. Food consumption measured as calorie intake was at levels that Europe achieved a century later, while consumption of luxuries such as sugar, tea and tobacco 'met or even exceeded advanced European levels.'[107] Had the emperor been wrong to say he did not need British goods?

Even more significant, in view of the aims of the Macartney embassy, was the fact that China had already signed a trade agreement with another foreign country a century earlier. In 1689, the first treaty ever signed with a Western power was that signed with Russia at Nerchinsk (Nipchu in Chinese), a small town on the left bank of the Nercha River, just above its confluence with the Shilka River. This latter river flows into the Amur, known to the Chinese as the Heilong Jiang, which delimits the Russian/Chinese border almost to Vladivostock. The short treaty, negotiated between an uncle of Kangxi with the assistance of two Jesuit priests, and an ambassador sent from Moscow, Theodor Alexevich Golovin, defined the frontier between the two countries, which granted the Transbaikalia area to Russia and the Amur valley to China. It also explicitly permitted trade in the following words: '… all persons, of whatever condition so ever they be, may go and come reciprocally, with full liberty, from the territories subject to either Empire, provided they have passports, and they shall be able to buy and sell whatever they think fit and carry on mutual trade.'[108] Its terms were further developed in a new treaty signed in 1727 at the frontier town of Kiakhta.[109] As a result, Russia was given permission to establish a language school in the Chinese capital and also an ecclesiastical mission, which effectively served as a 'quasi-diplomatic embassy.'[110] Two trading towns were set up on the border, the most important one being at Kiakhta itself, and the Russians were allowed to send trade caravans to Beijing. Such was its importance that, until sea routes supplanted this trade in the mid-nineteenth century (especially after the opening of the Suez Canal, in 1869), the route through Kiakhta accounted for nearly 20 per cent of customs revenues for the Russian Empire. The main import was tea, some of which was destined for the European market, while the main Russian export was furs from Siberia and Alaska.[111] So valuable was tea, and so well did it hold its value, that brick tea (pulverised tea compressed into brick shape) was used as a monetary unit at Kiakhta until it was replaced by silver in 1854.[112] It is not clear why this precedent for a trade agreement is usually overlooked in accounts of the Macartney embassy.

Thirdly, much of the difficulty for the embassy was due to a total misunderstanding of the Chinese concept of empire and the use of appropriate rites for every important occasion. For the entire tribute system with its ceremonies, banquets, rules for appropriate gifts, dramatic performances and music, was strictly regulated. Indeed the often-cited Edict sent by Qianlong to George III made it very clear that the request to have a diplomatic representative in Peking did not 'conform to the Celestial Empire's ceremonial system.'[113] In the early years of Qianlong's rule, a detailed book of rites known as the 'Comprehensive Investigation of the Five Rites' (*Da Qing Tongli*, 1756) was published as a handbook to the five categories of rites that derived from ancient Chinese tradition. These were the 'auspicious rites' (*jili*), which had 129 ceremonies including sacrifices to Heaven and Earth; the seventy-four 'joyous rites' (*jiali*), which included imperial accession rites and imperial audiences; the eighteen 'military rites', which included troop reviews and ceremonies for the beginning and end of imperial campaigns; the 'guest rites' (*binli*), which specified twenty ceremonies for tributary embassies; and the 'rites of misfortune' (*xiongli*), with fifteen graduated funeral rites for different ranks.[114] Each grand occasion, such as the Emperor's birthday, to be celebrated on Tuesday 17 September during the embassy's stay in Beijing, had detailed rituals to be followed. Yet another book, the *Huangchao Liqi Tushi* ('Illustrated Regulations and Models of Paraphernalia of Our August Dynasty', 1766), specified the ritual vessels to be used on every occasion, the astronomical instruments used to determine the precise dates for the rites, costumes to be worn by everybody present, musical instruments to be played during the rites, and the correct imperial insignia.[115] Nothing was left to chance.

In this case the rites concerned were the *binli*, which had been used at least since Tang times, and in part perhaps as far back as the Zhou dynasty, for the reception of foreign ambassadors. The ceremonies involved were therefore part of an intricate and time-honoured process designed to 'soften those who are far away', with music specially chosen to 'control and pacify' the visitors (an ancient precursor of today's business banquet followed by karaoke). The court mandarins were masters of the art of public relations and political showmanship long before the advent of television and electric lighting effects. An important visiting dignitary such as Lord Macartney would watch performances similar to those of modern Chinese Opera without understanding either their stories or their purpose, dismissing them in his journal as 'wretched drama',[116] while his hosts knew that in the eyes of the indigenous audience the performance was putting the visitors in their place. Titles of the pieces performed for the British visitors are quite explicit: for example, one called

'Ten Thousand States Come to Pay Tribute' would leave no doubt in a Chinese listener's mind as to the purpose of Macartney's presence. The whole process on that occasion involved eight dramatic pieces, lasting for a total of around five hours. Far from being concerned about the foreign presence, Qianlong was delighted that envoys from such a far-off country should come to pay tribute on his birthday.

Another piece played that day was 'Ascendent Peace in the Four Seas' (*Si hai sheng ping*). In this blatantly propagandistic drama, Wenchang Dijun, the God of Literature much admired by the Qing, leads a group of star spirits towards the 'divine god' Qianlong in order to offer their sincere congratulations on his birthday. Phrases like 'the ten thousand states look up in admiration at your magnificent achievements' were spoken by this god-narrator as if Macartney and his embassy were speaking them. In fact, the Wenchang/Macartney character goes on to affirm on the unknowing ambassador's behalf that 'Within the four seas all acclaim your name … and so the country of Ying-ji-li [i.e. England], gazing in admiration at your imperial majesty, sincerely presents its tributes to the court.'[117] Presumably, the gentlemanly foreign guests applauded these sentiments unwittingly, for although Sir George Staunton's son is credited with having learned enough Chinese en route to China to be able to act as interpreter, he could not have comprehended much of an ancient literary language that native scholars took decades to master. If they *had* understood, it would have been clear that the embassy was doomed to failure, and that they could not stay in China longer than was strictly necessary to pay tribute. From the Chinese point of view, theirs was no more than a routine tributary mission. The Wenchang character asserted during this performance that once the embassy had received gifts from the Emperor it would be 'sent back' in the time prescribed by the rites, which was fixed at forty days after a foreign ambassador's arrival. It was an illusion for the embassy to believe that it could have departed earlier, or could have protracted the visit.

Fourthly, it is untrue to say that Lord Macartney was not treated with appropriate dignity, for Qianlong understood very well that this was an ambassador from a powerful country and the protocols specified certain levels of recognition that were scrupulously maintained. Already as the embassy sailed north along the Chinese coast, the Emperor was soliciting his provincial officials to treat Macartney well, because 'the ambassador has sailed far to visit Us for the *first time*; this cannot be compared to Burma, Annam or others who have come for many years to present gifts.'[118] They were to look after the guests with care, and treat them generously. Then, on arrival, when imperial advisors had ascertained the proper intent and sincerity of Macartney by observing his verbal and physical expressions during a meeting with the grand councillors, the Emperor issued instructions to princes and officials to treat the embassy with greater respect and even modified the original plans for an imperial audience.[119] In fact the ambassador himself describes the Emperor as 'dignified, but affable'. He remarks that Qianlong not only offered him a bowl of warm wine similar to Madeira 'with his own hands', but allowed him to pay a long and enjoyable visit to the imperial gardens while he was waiting for a formal audience.[120]

Fifthly, it might be the case that the Emperor understood perfectly well the nature and power of the country that sent Macartney, but was simply too old, on his eighty-second birthday after a long and exhausting life of military campaigns and endless tours around his extensive domains, to engage with such a new and complex situation. In other words, he had neither 'the will or the intellectual energy at that late moment in his life to do more than fall back on traditional attitudes and formalities in the hope of dismissing an intractable problem.'[121]

Another significant factor is the *success* of the embassy from the Chinese point of view. An earlier instance of total misunderstanding might clarify this: in 1342, ambassadors from the papal court presented a large black horse with white hooves to the Emperor Shundi together with other papal presents. The papal envoy, Giovanni de' Marignolli, reported that the Emperor 'rejoiced with great joy, thinking all very good, indeed the best, and honoured us very highly.' The problem here is that he misinterpreted the imperial delight, which was based on the perception that this gift was in the tradition of tribute horses such as the Ferghana stallions, which Central Asian tributary embassies had brought. As a modern scholar of tribute has commented, he was 'completely unaware that the presentation of such a creature to the Emperor of China was perceived as the Pope's acknowledgement of Shundi's suzerainty over the entire west.'[122] Perversely, Marignolli believed he could see a potential convert in such joy, just as the Jesuits later believed that imperial acceptance of their scientific and mathematical knowledge would lead to conversions. As so often in China even today, the 'truth' was exactly the opposite of what it appeared to be to the foreign visitor.

In any case, to return to Qianlong, another myth to be debunked is that the Emperor refused the gifts. It is true that he wrote formally in his often quoted letter that he did not 'cherish exotic things', but he *was* interested in the mechanical and scientific devices that the embassy had brought. So much so that he ordered some Chinese artisans to watch the assembly of some equipment – for example, a planetarium, so that they would know how to repeat the task later, a fact which Macartney himself also observed in his journal.[123] Furthermore, the Emperor later personally wrote a note of admonition complaining that he had not received a report on their activities, which he had requested from these artisans.[124] On this matter too, from the Chinese point of view, the issue was completely different: the denial of interest was nothing to do with the intrinsic value or interest of the gifts, but with the formal necessity that they should be trivialised. They simply could not admit to any virtue or quality in foreign-made products. Qianlong himself wrote of gifts from foreign embassies that 'the only important thing is that they should bring little and are rewarded generously'. This formal requirement can be seen again a few years later, in 1839, when the Commissioner who provoked the first Opium War wrote in a letter to Queen Victoria that whereas 'articles coming from the outside to China can only be used as toys', foreign countries 'could not get along a single day' without Chinese exports such as tea and rhubarb.[125] Whatever the manifest absurdity of such a statement, from Qianlong's point of view gifts from barbarians could *never* as a matter of principle be openly recognised as interesting or superior to those with which the emperor reciprocated. The key point, paradoxically, is that the presence of the embassy, its true purpose and views, was irrelevant. One of the objectives of the imperial court was to maintain the fiction of universal power in the eyes of the emperor's own courtiers and subjects. In a similar way, it is likely that there was no economic or philosophical reason to oppose the creation of a better and balanced trading relationship, since as we shall see China had already traded with Europe for centuries. Britain even had a trade deficit, caused by huge imports of porcelain and tea. The problem was a formal recognition that the political consequences of expanded trade with a powerful country such as Britain risked creating future *discord*. The only defence of an indefensible reality was rhetoric – which was only blasted away, literally, by gun-boats sixty years later.

Or was it?

The Chinese believe in their heart of hearts that whoever comes to conquer or coerce will eventually decline while China itself persists (the discovery in 2007 that the Manchu language is virtually extinct is an excellent example). In the words of a nineteenth-century 'foreign devil' with immense understanding of China, John Otway Percy Bland, it is 'a phenomenon persistent in Chinese history … that the wisdom and diplomacy of the Empire have invariably risen superior to defeat of its naval and military forces, not only nullifying the enemy's success, but frequently deriving solid advantage from the subsequent negotiation.'[126] In reality, as Bland argued, the office of emperor was never more than a politico-religious concept, translated for the benefit of the masses into socio-economic ordinances (more recently, another author has defined the Chinese Empire as a 'tax/office state',[127] which is why, she argues, great wealth was associated with high office). Similarly, the isolation of the Chinese 'empire' undermined its being. In the words of James L. Hevia in a brilliant critique of the tribute system, 'the absence of external challenges was seen to have produced a kind of involution in which law and economic activity collapsed into *culture*.'[128] So the system combined diplomacy and trade without really performing either of them, and provides an excellent insight into the similarly opposite perceptions of diplomatic or business relationships today. It also shows us why there was no need to conquer the outside world, for in the minds of the Chinese court *it was already part of China*

The problem is that a non-territorial empire, an Empire of Mind, can neither be created nor defeated by conventional means; nor need it necessarily decline. It will persist as itself eternally, as Borges said of the tiger.[129]

Chinese Emperors and Western-Style Conquest

From the beginning, the Chinese Empire was conceptually inward-looking rather than outward-looking, partly in order to preserve its uniqueness. Just as, in Gibbon's words, 'the narrow policy of preserving, without any foreign mixture, the pure blood of the ancient citizens, had checked the fortune, and hastened the ruin, of Athens and Sparta', so it was much later with Ming and Qing China. While, on the contrary, Rome 'deemed it more prudent, as well as honorable, to adopt virtue and merit for her own wheresoever they were found, among slaves or strangers, enemies or barbarians',[130] the Chinese Empire was always essentially circumscribed. Yet there were some emperors who practised Western-style attempted conquest, in particular the three whose careers will be summarised in this chapter, with particular emphasis on the way in which their 'conquests' informed the later concept of empire. For there have been three major and lasting expansions of territory in Chinese history.

Qin Shihuang (221–210 BC)

The first of these three emperors brought together the feudal city-states and principalities that had dominated northern China for 1,000 years into a single polity. By some counts, there had been as many as 1,800 of these mini-states in the first half of the millennium.[131] In the third century BC, by a long process of conquest and annexation, this number was reduced to the seven so-called Warring States: the Qi, the Chu, the Yan, the Han, the Zhao, the Wei and the Qin. The warlords who ruled these states still considered themselves to be princes or dukes (*gōng*) of the Zhou dynasty (1122–256 BC), which oversaw them as a figurehead, but the stronger ones gradually began to call themselves kings (*wáng*) in a sign that they considered themselves equal to the kings of the Zhou. In particular, the Qin came to dominate the other six during the third century, and in a series of conquests lasting some ten years subdued their six rivals to create a single state.

King Zheng of Qin, as Qin Shihuang was known before assuming a title equivalent to emperor, was born in 259 BC in Handan, then the capital of the

Zhao kingdom and now in the modern province of Hebei. This town, today an anonymous industrial centre, stands at a strategic site on the main route from Beijing to Xi'an, about half-way between the two cities, at a point where the key ancient provinces of Hebei, Shandong, Henan and Shanxi meet. The family's presence outside their own kingdom was the result of an alliance between the houses of Qin and Zhao, which required his father's presence as hostage to guarantee its success. Zheng himself became King under a regent in 247 BC, and then assumed full powers nine years later. A contemporary described him as follows: 'The King of Qin, with his arched nose and long eyes, puffed-out chest like a hawk and voice of a jackal, is a man of scant mercy who has the heart of a tiger or a wolf.'[132]

The meticulous attention to detail which went into the administration of the first empire was already discernible in the young king's military expeditions. The discipline and bloodthirstiness of his army were legendary, with a few hundred heads cut off here and a few thousand there as he fought each of the Qin's rival states. In around ten years from 230 to 221 BC he devoured them, in a celebrated phrase, as 'a silkworm devours a mulberry leaf'. He was well-versed in warfare and often adopted intrigue and stratagem in place of sheer ferocity, as Sun Tzu recommends in the opening paragraph of the third chapter of his *Art of War*: 'In the practical art of war, the best thing of all is to take the enemy's country whole and intact; to shatter and destroy it is not so good.'[133] In this way, he became the *de facto* ruler of China, although formally he was still the King of Qin. On one of the five imperial progresses that he later made through his new empire, he had the following inscription erected on a mountain in Hebei:

> He has been the first to achieve a single great peace.
> He has demolished the inner and outer walls of cities.
> He has cut through the embankment of rivers.
> He has levelled the bulwarks at mountain defiles.[134]

This stands as an eloquent comment on his military achievements.

King Zheng is conventionally known as the 'First Emperor', although the Chinese had no exact equivalent of the word for emperor. To enhance his own status and show his superiority to other kings, Zheng took the word *huáng* ('August Ones'), which was used to describe the legendary *Sān huáng* ('Three August Ones') who were said to have ruled at the dawn of Chinese history: Fuxi, Shennong and Huang-di. Each of these mythical figures played an important role in ancient Chinese culture: Fuxi was said to have taught his subjects to hunt, fish, and tend animals; Shennong is said to have invented agricultural tools, and to have discovered the medicinal properties of many plants; Huang Di, better known as the Yellow Emperor, is reputed to have invented Chinese medicine and the compass, and his wife to have taught the Chinese how to make silk.

Zheng then added to *huáng* the word *dì* ('God-kings') from the equally legendary *Wŭdì* ('Five Emperors' or 'Five God-kings'). Thus he cleverly amalgamated both sources of ancient Chinese culture to enhance the legitimacy of his rule, combining 'Three August Ones' (三皇) and 'Five Emperors' (五帝) by taking the second character of each phrase to create the single title *Huángdì* (皇帝), that has always been translated into English as 'emperor'. This well-established usage is in fact a little confusing, and it has been suggested that a better translation would be 'Supreme Lord' or 'King of Kings'. [135] The Chinese love puns and epithets with multiple meanings, so the fact that *huáng* also meant 'big' or 'great' and *dì* also referred to the 'Supreme God in Heaven' were added bonuses. Adding the prefix shi, meaning the 'first' or 'commencing', he arrived at the formulation Shihuangdi. Later, after his death, the dynastic name Qin was added to make his name Qin Shihuangdi, and finally the last character was dropped so that the name became Qin Shihuang, by which he is known today.

After subduing the rival Warring States, Qin Shihuang continued his policy of conquest and expansion. His army annexed territory to the south, reaching as far as Guangdong, while on the northern frontiers it was engaged in almost continuous conflict with the troublesome Xiongnu tribes, better known to us as the Hun. The extent of his kingdom may be imagined on a modern map of China as a rough square: on the left a vertical line running from just south of Chengdu, capital of Sichuan Province to the frontier with Inner Mongolia and Mongolia; a horizontal line from this northern point eastwards to the top of the Bohai Sea, and another horizontal line from Chengdu eastwards to the coast of Zhejiang Province. The whole area was approximately 25 per cent of the territory of present-day China, although superficial accounts of his life and of the terracotta warriors often create a false impression that 'his' China was the same. [136]

He built a new capital, Xianyang, on the site of an ancient Qin city just outside modern Xi'an. Within an almost perfectly square wall he built palaces imitating those of the six states he had conquered to make his 'empire', much as Qianlong was to do in the eighteenth century when he built replicas of conquered states in his garden at Chengde. On the opposite bank of the Wei River, a branch of the Huang He that runs through Xi'an, he began a never-completed palace known as Epang whose front hall alone was designed to accommodate 10,000 men. To reach the city from this palace, he built what must have been an extraordinary two-storied bridge across the river; since no representation exists, we might imagine a Chinese version of the enclosed corridor built in Florence by Duke Cosimo I (1519–74) to link the offices, *Uffizi*, designed for him by Vasari, to the Medici residence across the Arno River in Palazzo Pitti. But the Epang Palace remained unfinished at the emperor's death and was soon afterwards destroyed by fire. We must imagine its grandeur from his own rhetoric: 'This palace will have the capacity to entertain one hundred thousand men who will come by cart to drink wine and on horseback to warm their hands by the fire. One hundred thousand men will sing and ten thousand will harmonize. Thus shall we receive the army of heaven.'[137] Had these words not been written by the builder of the mausoleum that housed an army of thousands of terracotta warriors, we might think he was exaggerating. Another pharaonic project undertaken by Qin Shihuang was the creation of the first and partial version of what is now known as the Great Wall, constructed further north than the present one by using shorter stretches of existing walls. This project was undertaken both to facilitate control of the Xiongnu and to protect the new kingdom and its capital. The new emperor's greatest general, Meng T'ien, worked for ten years, between bouts of fighting, with as many as 3,000 men to complete the project. But this wall's stated length of 10,000 *li* is more likely to be a rhetorical expression of great length than an indication of its real dimensions. For the number 10,000 is frequently used in Chinese to indicate great size, weight or length, with no relation to actual dimensions.

The legends of this indefatigable conqueror and builder were recorded a century later by Sima Qian, Grand Historian of the Han court, in a monumental history of ancient China from its mythical origins to his own times in which he narrated the lives and deeds of all past rulers. But the novelty of the new political organisation was already asserted in words inscribed on a stele set up during a royal progress through the new kingdom:

> In his twenty-eighth year the August Emperor made a new beginning.
> He adjusted the laws and regulations, standards for the ten thousand things.
> He clarified human concerns, bringing concord to father and son …

Administrative reforms were employed to reinforce the unity of his new possessions, with such striking innovations as the introduction of a single standard for weights and measures, and the insistence on the use of a standardised script for written Chinese. Until that time, neighbouring states spoke many dialects of Chinese, and possibly other languages, and, although the written form was sometimes similar and wandering scholars could exploit their knowledge in the various states, there were many characters that were not mutually intelligible. Thus the standardised script, supported by the system of radicals that was introduced at this time, was a notable administrative and literary innovation in which the Chinese classics such as the *Analects* of Confucius found their definitive form (in Chinese, he is known as Kong Fuzi). Partly for this reason, in a brief assertion that is eerily prophetic of later dynasties, Sima Qian could write that 'all under heaven are of one mind, single in will.' But most interestingly, Sima, evidently seeking legitimacy for his Han patrons as heirs to Qin Shihuang's unification, provides a clear idea of the extent of the 'empire' in the contemporary mind together with an indication of its political ambition:

> Within the six directions, the domain of the August Emperor,
> West to the flowing sands, south all the way to Beihu,
> East to the eastern sea, north beyond Daxia,
> Wherever human tracks may reach, there are none who
>   are not his subjects.[138]

This is the first, and from an imperial point of view authoritative, statement of the belief that the entire world falls within the 'empire'. What may have been expressed as rhetoric became accepted as dogma. Naturally, the next dynasty saw benefit in demeaning Qin Shihuang's achievement. In the 'Transgression of Qin', the Han author Jia Yi complains that 'he did not change his ways or improve his government,' and that he acted as though he possessed the world in his own person, as the dimensions of his tomb and the number of terracotta warriors would appear to confirm. Worst of all, Jia Yi says, 'he thought there was no difference between conquest and consolidation.'[139]

Yet the unification was real, and the administrative innovations astonishing in their long-term import. The 'empire' was divided into thirty-six provinces ruled over by governors who were appointed on merit rather than inheriting their posts. There was a prescient separation of civilian and military powers, which reflects the dual status of governor/mayor and political secretary in Chinese provinces and cities today, and a system of frequent rotation to prevent governors from building a local power base. There was also an inspector in each province who represented the central government and oversaw the implementation of its policies, his work much facilitated by the use of a single script. To render this complex administration efficient, Qin Shihuang developed a network of roads and canals, also built under the supervision of Meng T'ien, both for the purposes of trade and for swift deployment of troops. Interestingly, in addition to the thousands of terracotta warriors with their weapons discovered at his tomb, there were figures of bureaucrats with *their* tools of labour attesting to the importance of administration in his empire (some of them present at the British Museum's exhibition in 2008). The sinologist Derk Bodde provides an illuminating comparison between his own estimate of the extent of Qin road-building, at 4,250 miles, with Gibbon's estimate of the total length of the near-contemporary Roman road system, which was 3,740 miles.[140] He conscripted 700,000 men to build an immense mausoleum complex of which the area occupied by the terracotta warriors is a small part, and also engaged in other ambitious projects – filling, it is said, 270 palaces with 'curtains and hangings, bells and drums, and beautiful women, each assigned to a particular post and forbidden to move about.'[141] Like Mao in more recent times, he was obsessively secretive about his movements, ordering that anyone in his entourage who revealed his whereabouts to outsiders be executed immediately. Even his death was kept secret. Concubines and artisans were interred with him so that no one would know the exact location of his mausoleum, which is one reason why the warriors lay hidden until 1974.

In conclusion, the short-lived Qin dynasty – which fell far short of its declared ambition to survive for 10,000 years – unified China and establish a centralised kingdom/empire, which endured and evolved in one form or another until the twentieth century (some say into the twenty-first century). It is worth recalling once again that this unification was dramatically different from that imposed on the Mediterranean by the Romans, who unified rule but maintained local languages, customs and laws in their far-flung provinces. Qin Shihuang created an administrative model for enduring and total centralised control, which could be up-scaled as the empire expanded.

Qubilai Khan (1215–94): China as Part of a Larger Empire

It was over 1,000 years later that Qubilai, the grandson of Genghis Khan (*c*. 1162–1227), descended from the Mongol steppes, conquered China, and made his capital as Qubilai Khan in Beijing. In this way, the Chinese 'empire' came to include new domains to the north, while, from the Mongol point of view, China was merely a large if important part of a much greater empire.

In the year of Qubilai's birth, Genghis already controlled much of modern western China, and defeated the Jin, who had ruled northern China since 1152. The Jin capital was at Yanjing (an ancient name for Beijing), which they enlarged and renamed Zhongdu, the 'central capital', located about 3 miles south-west of the present entrance to the Forbidden City.[142] Qubilai drove the Jin from Zhongdu and put their capital to the torch. They retreated to Kaifeng, where in 1233 Genghis' third son and successor Ögödei Khan (1186–1241) completed the task of destroying their power after a siege that saw the first use of gunpowder in grenades hurled by catapults and in flamethrowers.[143] Within four years, Genghis Khan had subdued Transoxiana (roughly, modern Uzbekistan) and Khorassan, in north-eastern Persia. In three great military campaigns over a period of forty years the armies of Genghis and his successors launched invasions of Afghanistan, Pakistan, Russia, Persia, Syria, Egypt, Lebanon, Turkey, and Eastern Europe as far as Budapest in the south and Liegnitz (in Poland) in the north. The second campaign was the first time that a 'Chinese' presence created consternation in Western Europe akin to more recent fears. The chronicler Matthew Paris tells us that in 1238 the fishermen of Gothland and Friesland were so terrified of an imminent Mongol attack that they were afraid to set sail from Yarmouth. The common name in English for the invaders, Tartars, was probably derived from a pun in a letter written by the Emperor Frederick II to King Henry III in which he associated the invaders with Tartarus, which was an alternative name for Hell. Frederick expressed his wish that the Tartars would be driven down to their Tartarus, (*ad sua Tartara Tartari detrudentur*).[144] In an echo of the certainty deriving from a divine mandate, Genghis Khan had replied to papal diplomats that 'the sons of God and of Zingis were invested with a divine power to subdue or extirpate the nations.'[145]

Genghis Khan himself died in 1227, but the conquests continued, so that when Qubilai, Ögödei Khan's nephew, became the fifth Great Khan in 1260, he ruled over much of East and Central Asia, so that China effectively became larger by a kind of reverse conquest. Qubilai completed the conquest of the Southern Song in 1279 and ruled as Emperor of China until his death fifteen years later. In a life-time of constant conquest, his only failures were an unsuccessful campaign into the jungles of southeast Asia and Java, and two disastrous naval campaigns to Japan. Both involved terrain alien to men who lived and breathed horseback warfare.

In 1272, Qubilai issued two key edicts. The first changed the official name of the Mongol dynasty to Yuan, which derives from the *Book of Changes* (*I Ching*) and means 'the origin'. This shift from Mongol to Chinese identity was presumably acceptable to the Mongols because they themselves claimed a Mandate of Heaven that could readily be assimilated to that of the Chinese mandate, and also believed that all other nations were part of a 'Mongolian empire-in-the-making',[146] similar to the concept of *tiānxià*. The second edict decreed that the capital should be renamed Ta-Tu (or Dadu), the 'Great Capital', and that the plan should be drawn up on the basis of the capital city outlined in an ancient Chinese classic of govern-ment, the *Rites of Zhou* (*Zhou li*).[147] Ta-Tu is still discernible beneath Ming and Qing accretions.

The *Zhou li* specifies that the site for the city should be chosen by the emperor himself, using tortoiseshell oracles, and that it should represent the centre of a spatial grid that comprises all civilisation: 'where Heaven and Earth are in perfect accord, where the four seasons come together, where the winds and the rains gather, where the forces of yin and yang are harmonized, one builds the royal capital.'[148] Thus the city was perceived as a cosmic focal point, square in form on a north-south axis:

> The *jiangren* [official responsible for planning] constructs the state capitals. He makes a square nine li on each side; each side has three gates. Within the capital are nine north-south and nine east-west streets. The north-south streets are nine carriage tracks in width. On the left (as one faces south, or, to the east) is the Ancestral Temple, and to the right (west) are the Altars of Soil and Grain. In the front is the Hall of Audience and behind the markets.[149]

Qubilai built three gates on each of the four walls except the north wall (to avoid bad *feng shui*), and his still-surviving *Gǔlóu*, or Drum Tower, at the heart of the city, with massive drums to mark the hours of the day and signal the closing of the gates in the evening. Marco Polo, who referred to it as Cambulac, a variant of the Turkish Khan-baliq, or 'city of the Khan', wrote that the city was so regular, and the streets so wide, that it was possible to see along them from one gate to another. He compared it to a chessboard laid out in a manner 'so perfect and masterly that it is impossible to give a description that should do it justice'.[150] It was a very Chinese city, and shows the degree of assimilation to Chinese culture of Qubilai Khan. But the emperor retained some Mongol customs: his sons often slept in traditional felt tents pitched within the city walls, while he himself imported Mongol grass for his royal altar.[151]

Qubilai was remarkably Chinese in his thinking as well as in his observance of the ancient rituals for capital-building. One of his earliest advisors was a Buddhist monk called Hiayun (1205–57), who travelled to the Mongol capital at Karakorum long before Qubilai became Emperor and explained to him the Confucian concepts of government. Haiyun took with him another monk, Liu Bingzhong (1216–74), who advised Qubilai for thirty years on government and taxation, and on the geomancy of founding new cities (he supervised the choice for the site of Ta-Tu). As a leading Chinese intellectual and expert in philosophy, classical learning and mathematics, Haiyun attracted many others to the court. These figures together constituted a 'Chinese-oriented brain trust, men of varied social and ethnic backgrounds who had in common their fervent devotion to traditional means of governing Chinese society, and to the preservation of Chinese cultural values.'[152] The Emperor's intelligence, curiosity and tolerance are amply testified in the observations of Western visitors to his court like Friar William of Rubruck. Yet his Chinese was 'rather poor', and he always had to use interpreters when discussing with Chinese-speaking scholars (although his son and heir was given daily Chinese lessons, and some later Yuan emperors were proficient in Chinese).[153]

On military matters, Mongols held sway. Commanders were always Mongols, as were the Imperial Bodyguards and the *myriarchs* who controlled the units of 10,000 soldiers; border garrisons were also organised so that Mongols were the dominant force. There were also, however, large numbers of non-Chinese and non-Mongol troops, including a Russian regiment based in Beijing, together with regiments of Alans (i.e., Ossetes), Tanguts, Jurchen, Koreans, Qipchaq, and 'Western Regions People', probably from Turkestan, and a Muslim artillery corps.[154] Trades with potential military applications were tightly controlled: Chinese citizens were not permitted to deal in bamboo, which could be used to make bows and arrows, while Chinese owners of horses were obliged to sell them to Qubilai at an officially established price.[155] With similar regard for ultimate Mongol control, the inhabitants themselves were divided into four classes in descending order of rank: Mongols themselves, Western and Central Asians (*se-mu-jen*), Chin Chinese from the north (*han-jen*), and the former Song (*nan-jen*). So what might be considered the purest Chinese were on the lowest rung. But in fact, as an eminent historian of the Mongols has shown, although there was a centralised rule and 'the provinces were therefore centralized internally … their relationship with the government in Peking might be distinctly loose.'[156] In other words, there was, as in China today, considerable local autonomy.

The Mongol occupation brought tangible and lasting benefits to China. The Yuan dynasty guaranteed peace and stability after several troubled and divisive centuries, and provided China with a basic political organisation and stability that survived through the next two dynasties. Qubilai set up an effective administration under a Central Secretariat, with ministries of Personnel, Revenue, Rites, War, Punishments and Works, each with supporting agencies for specific functions; in addition, there was a Bureau of Military Affairs, which oversaw the continuous military operations and campaigns. One significant innovation that has survived to modern times was the introduction of a provincial level of administration, which later became the *sheng*, or provinces, as in *shi ba sheng*, with the central government ministries and agencies having a branch office in each province. In the *Annals* of his reign written by Ming historians, Qubilai (with his posthumous name Shizu) was praised in the following positive terms, which are designed to stress his assimilation of Chinese values:

> The Emperor Shizu was a man of broadest capacity for judgement. He knew men and was skilled in employing them. He had deep confidence in Confucian methods, and was able to utilize them so that Chinese ways transformed alien practices. He established the basic principles and set forth ruling norms in such a way that the institutions of the age were of vastly encompassing scope.[157]

His government improved road communication, and carried out one of the great engineering works of Chinese history in creating the Grand Canal from Hangzhou to Beijing, over 1,000 miles, to assure supplies of rice to the north and avoid the dangers of coastal transport. It also introduced to China the renowned Mongol postal service, which linked 1,400 postal stations in China by means of over 50,000 horses, 4,000 carts and 6,000 boats. Messages could be delivered up to 250 miles in a single day.[158] In order to facilitate both this system and travel in general, the highway network was improved and extended, while commercial payments were facilitated by the large-scale use of paper money.

Thus Qubilai, in spite of his non-Chinese origins, was an excellent Chinese emperor who reunited north and south, enlarged the empire to its greatest extent until the end of the eighteenth century, and lay the basis for over 600 years of continuity in administration. China, it was true, was merely a part of the Mongol Empire, but for a while the entire area of the Four Khanates – the Kipchak Khanate or Golden Horde (Russia); the Ilkhanate (Middle East), the Chagatai Khanate (Western Asia), and the Great Khanate (Mongolia and China) – was ruled from Beijing. China itself was bigger than ever before. In particular, it was under Qubilai that the province of Yunnan entered into the sphere of Chinese control.

At the same time, it is important to note that the Ming dynasty that followed was not just a resurrected version of the Song dynasty but one of many successor states to the Mongol Empire. The Ming perpetuated existing military and administrative structures, and were able to maintain control over provinces such as Yunnan that had never previously been a part of China. Later, the Qing claimed descent from the Mongols, so the strictly Chinese part of the Mongol Empire, which really was an empire in the Western sense, informed the extent of Chinese territory when the Qing came to power in 1644.

Qianlong (1736–95): The Conquest of Tibet and Xinjiang

While the official mythology asserts, and most Chinese believe, that the extent of their country has remained basically unaltered for millennia, it was in fact relatively recently, under the Qianlong Emperor (1736–95), that China acquired its almost definitive land frontiers (see Map 1, Appendix 1). Chinese historians take for granted that 'Xinjiang "naturally" belonged under the rule of the Chinese state, and that its recovery from the "rebel" Zunghars fulfilled a preexisting definition of national territory.'[159] This is why, in this and in other cases, they always speak of 'unification' (*tongyi*) rather than 'conquest' (*zhengqu*). But it is very much a matter of conquest, as authors such as Peter Perdue have recently shown with exhaustive use of Chinese, Manchu and Russian sources. As Perdue explains, 'Qing expansion was not simply a linear outgrowth of previous dynasties. It represented a sharp break with the strategic aims and military capabilities of the Ming dynasty.'[160] The Qing conquests, and creation of an empire, were similar in many aspects to the conquests of the great western imperial powers.

In fact, at the inception of Qing rule in 1644, what we describe today as 'China' excluded Xinjiang, Tibet, and Qinghai in the west, while the policies of conquest and subjugation in the large provinces of Yunnan, Sichuan and Guizhou in the southwest had not yet been totally successful. An official account of the province of Guizhou written in 1690, for example, stated unequivocally that 'these natives are violent and difficult to tame, but even if they have received some training [in Chinese ways] they easily slip back into their violent way.'[161] There were many pockets of independence and indirect rule, so that in 1700 more areas were subject to indirect rule than direct Qing rule by what were known as a *tusi*, or 'local headman'. So the territory known as *Da Qing* when they came to power was just under half of that constituting the present People's Republic, and even within that territory control was not absolute. Inherent inefficiency and passivity meant that local government representatives enjoyed considerable independence. It was a very different China.

Then, from the second Qing emperor Kangxi (reigned 1661–1722), to his son Yongzhen (reigned 1723–35), and on to the long rule of his grandson Qianlong, (reigned 1736–95), there was a gradual expansion of empire which reached its climax with Qianlong's campaign in Tibet from 1790 to 1792. Ironically, in the latter year George Macartney was created 1st Earl Macartney in the Irish peerage and appointed envoy to the 'weak' China. Indeed, Qianlong was an emperor who 'generally thought and functioned in military fashion,'[162] despite his being remembered today by most Chinese for his calligraphy and interest in painting. Imbued with a strong military ethic, each of these emperors actively promoted military values, and extolled prowess in martial sports such as hunting, horsemanship and archery. Indeed, while one of the Forbidden City myths propagated by guidebooks is that the Ming and Qing 'didn't stray from their pleasure dome unless they absolutely had to,'[163] in truth the Qing emperors spent relatively little time there; some hardly any time at all. In the year 1714, for example, Kangxi spent a total of fourteen days inside the Forbidden City. Most of his time was spent in the Changchunyuan garden to the north-east of the Old Summer Palace in the Beijing suburbs (131 days), or at his northern palace at Chengde, north of the Great Wall on the edge of the Mongolian steppe (139 days).[164] The reason for this may be found in his statement that 'it is when one is beyond the Great Wall that the air and soil refresh the spirit.'[165] This is a thoroughbred nomad speaking. In fact, far from being fixed in a single immutable point such as one palace or another, Qing imperial rule was essentially mobile, with emperors like Kangxi and Qianlong going on lengthy tours throughout the empire as well as their regular visits to the original lands of the Manchu. Until temporary palaces were built in later Qing times, the emperor and his entourage slept in tents during their northern hunting expeditions, another reflection of their nomadic ethos.

Indeed, while Peking was the primary seat of Qing government, the Manchu city of Chengde (Rehe, in Manchu) and their former capital in Shenyang (Mukden) were accorded special status as secondary capitals. So it was quite natural and acceptable for emperors to spend time at those other seats, both of which had, and still have, imperial palaces: in Shenyang a smaller version of the Forbidden City and in Chengde a Summer Palace even bigger than that in Beiing. They sought to create a unique Qing culture that combined the Manchu martial ideals, or *wu*, with the traditional literary and artistic virtues of Chinese culture, or *wen*, and on this base to create a universal emperorship. The idea was to bring different ethnicities such as Muslim, Han, Manchu, Mongol and Tibetan, and different religions such as various forms of Buddhism and Islam, into a single harmonious construct, although it has also been argued that success was due rather to organisational skill than to real military strength.[166]

Military values also informed the rituals of the Qing. For the inhabitants of Beijing, the performance of the military *Dayue*, or 'Grand Inspections', must have been a central experience of their lives: preparations entailed months of work and thousands of men creating temporary stuctures in a park to the south of the city, and intense military drilling. Then, on the day of the inspections, a procession involving the entire imperial family and tens of thousands of other participants in brilliant costumes accompanied by gongs and cannon fire. These Inspections provided public expression of the 'triple mantra of military power, combat-readiness, and devotion to martial ideals.'[167] Two other military rituals underscored Qing military power in the eyes of the Chinese citizens of the empire: the *Mingjiang* ('Dispatching Generals Embarking on Campaign') and *Jiaolao* ('Welcoming a Victorious Army on Return'). The former again involved elaborate protocols and processions in which the emperor rode out of the southern gate of the Forbidden City to a yellow tent furnished with a temporary throne and offered ritual wine to the general who would lead the campaign. The latter were even grander and more impressive since they celebrated significant conquests, such as the return of General Zhaohui from the conquest of Xinjiang in 1760. On that occasion, accompanied as always by ritual music, the emperor performed obeisance to heaven together with his victorious generals and senior officials.[168] Such victories were rendered permanent in celebratory buildings, from the replica of the Potala Palace in Lhasa, which Qianlong built at Chengde, to buildings in Beijing with resounding militaristic names like the 'Hall of Military Achievements', and the even more explicit 'Pavilion for Remembering Military Success' and 'Temple of True Victory' constructed in the military-dominated zone of Xiangshan to the north-west of Beijing (known in English as the Fragrant Hills).

In 1792, Qianlong himself wrote a 'Record of Ten Perfections' in which he detailed ten military campaigns that had defined China. It shows that he fully understood the weaknesses of tribal organisation, and how to exploit the anarchy and divisiveness of the steppe tribes to the advantage of his own empire, through tribute and marriage alliances as well as military campaigns. The list of campaigns, two of which were vital in extending his empire to roughly the dimensions of modern China, provides an idea of the emperor's ambitions and achievements:

Campaign against the Jinchuan tribes in Sichuan 1747–9
Two campaigns against the Dzungar Mongols in NW Xinjiang 1755–7
Campaign against the Turkic Muslims in South Xinjiang 1758–9
Border war against Burma in 1766–70
New campaign against the Jinchuan tribes in Sichuan 1771–6
Suppression of a rebellion in Taiwan 1777–8
Border war against Annan in 1788–9
Two campaigns against the Gurkhas in Tibet, in 1790–2

The territorial consequences of these successes were rendered tangible to the people with a series of maps made to illustrate the extent of the extended empire.

Following his grandfather's example, cartography was one of Qianlong's essential tools of government, conquest and positioning in the world. In fact, the territorial claims and imperial designs of both the Russian and the Chinese empire 'had stemmed largely from the requirements of border defense.'[169] Accurate mapping became vital, and China employed the graticule in map-making to make its national frontiers more precise: the Qing mapped their new territories just as Western imperial powers mapped *their* new conquests in Africa and the Middle East. In the words of a recent historical study of Qing maps, the shape of modern China was 'largely determined through Qing territorial claims communicated via early modern cartography and its international dissemination in the eighteenth century.'[170] They conquered, assimilated, mapped, and created the basis of the territory of the People's Republic today (less 'Outer' Mongolia), which is therefore no older than 200 years.

It was a grand imperial project by a man whose very reign name, Qianlong, meant 'supported by heaven' or 'heaven's support', the central point from which everything radiated, a *shengwang*, or 'sage-king' and a *tiānzi*, or 'son of Heaven': he was a 'grand impersonator, controlling cultures by incarnating them, commanding their moral centers through the conduct of their rituals … through his actions (including the commissioning of literature, architecture, painting, and portraiture) he brought meaning to all cultures.'[171] His long reign and continuous economic success enabled Qianlong to modify the physical fabric of the capital city, rebuilding city gates and walls. Much of what has remained of old Peking for visitors to see today was built or rebuilt by Qianlong. The grandiose, public face of the Chinese Empire was due to him.

He added gardens and pavilions to the Forbidden City, which make its northern end a little less forbidding. He embellished and enlarged the Summer Palace, the Yíhéyuán, in the north-west of Beijing, employing 100,000 workers to increase the size of the lake to its present extent, as well as building European-style palaces at the old Summer Palace not far away. His patronage touched many of the temples in Beijing: the beautiful 'Fountain Compound' of the Biyun Temple, on the eastern side of the Fragrant Hills, was once part of a temporary palace built by Qianlong; at the Wanshou Temple, which was built by Empress Dowager Li, mother of the Ming emperor Wan Li, Qianlong added gardens and a temporary palace to convert it to a suitably imperial venue for his mother's birthday celebrations. After the Sixth Panchen Lama, Badanyixi, visited Beijing for the birthday celebrations of the Emperor and stayed at the West Huang Temple, Qianlong had a *stupa* constructed in the mixed styles of China, Tibet and India to house the Lama's clothes. He carried out renovations at the Fayuan Temple, built in the seventh century as the Minzhong Temple, perhaps the loveliest temple in Beijing today with the finest and most original building in its Scripture Library. His father, Yongzheng, had converted the family's former residence into the Lama Temple known as Yonghe Gong, today the most visited of Beijing's temples, when Qianlong was a boy of eight. Qianlong wished to make Beijing the spiritual capital of Lamaism, and to that end encouraged translations and studies of

Tibetan Buddhism. In the Confucius Temple, just across the road from Yonghe Gong, there is a series of stele known as 'The Stone Classics of Qian Long'.

But in spite of his embellishments, territorial conquest remains his most important legacy. One of the most extraordinary statements of Chinese imperial policy, still valid today, was contained in the 'Proposal to Establish the Western Regions as a Province', published in 1826 by the scholar, poet and reformer Gong Zizheng, to effectively complete Qianlong's process of conquest three decades after his death. In that short work, Gong outlined the measures necessary to guarantee success in newly conquered territories. These were, first, to invest in agricultural reclamation; second, to settle the province of Xinjiang with Han people and Manchu bannermen no longer needed for military purposes in the East; third, to intensify the extraction of mineral resources; fourth, to secure the frontier; fifth, to substitute the traditional rule of the Muslim *begs* with military supervision, in particular by creating fourteen new administrative units; and, sixth, to change all indigenous place names to Chinese names.[172] One of the most interesting features of this process of conquest is the way in which it has been portrayed as a means of bringing harmony. This entailed the use of a 'soft' vocabulary, which emphasises once again the way in which conquest is modulated into assimilation on the basis of a presumed ancient centrality and moral purpose: 'Bandits were "punished", areas were "pacified", and recalcitrant frontier polities were "soothed", "instructed" and "brought to surrender". For the purpose was to ensure harmony by bringing peace, order and harmony.' Not much has changed in the wording of such statements since Gong's day.

Qianlong's ten campaigns created modern China, but probably not in a way that he had anticipated. He argued sophistically in the preface to a multi-language gazetteer, which gave place names and personal names in Manchu, Chinese, Mongolian, Todo (Oirat Mongolian), Tibetan and Turki, that 'once the names are unified, there is nothing that is not universal.'[173] He employed the various scripts on stele and on gates such as those to the imperial palaces at Chengde and Shenyang to make a show of unity. Even the choice of the three 'capitals' employed this symbolism, with Peking in China Proper, Shenyang in Manchuria, and Chengde in Mongol territory. But the nineteenth-century empire was one into which the minority peoples felt themselves to have been coerced, and in 1911 Mongol and Tibetan separatists argued that they had been part of the Manchu Empire, but were not part of China; the reformer Kang Youwei went further in dismissing Qinghai, Xinjiang and Tibet as 'alien waste land' not worth defending.[174] In fact the expression 'China Proper' indicated the area of effective control from Beijing, while the racially and culturally distinct outer provinces of the empire enjoyed some degree of independence. Nevertheless, when the Qing fell, a new Chinese nation was created on the basis of the 'five races', Han, Mongol, Tibetan, Hui and Manchu, originally postulated by Qianlong. The first Republican flag bore the five colours of the races: red for Han, blue for Mongol, black for Tibetan, white for Hui, and yellow for Manchu.

Around the same time, in opposition to the perceived arrogance of imperial powers and in particular to war with Japan, there emerged a single, clear idea of the nation as *Zhōngguó*, which was contiguous with the Qing empire (the modern, and sometimes inconvenient, use of a single time zone for the entire country is presumably to avoid any symbolic separation of the races). It should be added, however, that as late as 1931, a draft Constitution of the Communist Party in line with its basic principles favoured self-determination for minority peoples and stated that 'they may either join the Union of Chinese Soviets or secede from it and form their own state as they may prefer.'[175] But this noble largesse of spirit is long-forgotten.

These three episodes of conquest, under Qin Shihuang, Qubilai and Qianlong, created an imperial mind-set that has lasted to this day. As one scholar of Qing ideology has remarked, 'without an emperor, the cultural similarities, the coexistence of historicized constituencies, had little chance of being coherent.'[176] On this view, we might argue that Mao, and more recently, the Party, maintained this imperial function and used it to hold the opposing forces and factions together. The French diplomat and author Alain Peyrefitte observed in the preface to his book on the Macartney mission, *L'Empire immobile*, that when he went to serve as Ambassador in Beijing in 1971, he found strong parallels between Mao's state and that of the Qing in the late eighteenth century: everything depended on the will of a single man, there was the same concern for the rituals of protocol, the same distrust of foreigners, while Confucian thought and the *Sacred Edict* of Kangxi had merely been substituted by 'Mao Zedong Thought' and the *Little Red Book*.

Mao saw things in the same way and often referred to himself or his actions in terms that may only be described as imperial. One instance of this is the second stanza of the poem 'Snow', written in February 1936, which concludes with a disturbing self-evaluation as superior to the historical founders of five of the greatest Chinese dynasties:

> This land so rich in beauty
> Has made countless heroes bow in homage.
> But alas! Chin Shih-huang and Han Wu-ti
> Were lacking in literary grace,
> And Tang Tai-tsung and Sung Tai-tsu
> Had little poetry in their souls;
> And Genghis Khan,
> Proud Son of Heaven for a day,
> Knew only shooting eagles, bow outstretched.
> All are past and gone!
> For truly great men
> Look to this age alone.[177]

In spite of Revolution, in Mao's view at least, the Empire persisted.

The Persistence of Empire

In the perception of the average Chinese today, the nation they inhabit is merely the territory of past dynasties in new guise, so that indigenous tourists have a strong sense of the way in which imperial artefacts and buildings are part of *their* past, even when they are not. It is commonplace nowadays to speak of 'five thousand years' of civilisation, whether in tourist brochures, television documentaries, or private conversation.

Yet, perhaps surprisingly, this represents a very recent way of thinking, for the presumed antiquity of Chinese civilisation has been increasing steadily over the past century. In the 1930s, it was more commonly said to be 3,000 years old, or the 'thirty centuries' of Malraux's *Human Condition*; by the 1960s, this had been extended to 4,000 years, as in Jules Roy's *Journey Through China*; now, as in *Tales from Five Thousand Years of Chinese History*, we have reached what seems to be the fullest extent of the past, which is constantly quoted both in the media and in private conversation.[178] From a scholarly perspective, the use of the adjective Chinese is anachronistic for a period in which people were known either by the name of their tribe, such as Qin, or by their regional provenance, such as the people 'within the mountain passes'.[179] To avoid slipping into error, or causing offence, we should defend ourselves with a better knowledge of the historical processes behind this change from the Chinese point of view.

In the past, there were two versions of 'history'. The first was the legendary version of the 'Three August Ones' and the 'Five Emperors', who together, as we have seen, created the essential attributes of Chinese culture in the mythological past, including the zither-like *gǔqín* or *qín*, which is considered 'the father of Chinese music'. The second version of 'history' was based on a regnal calendar system, which took the year of accession of an emperor and counted year one from 'the first day of the New Year following the previous ruler's death'.[180] This complex *ganzhi* system of counting past time in sixty-year cycles did not facilitate understanding of either past. Imagine an averagely educated person in, say, 1800, sitting down with a pile of regnal calendars and an abacus, and the sixty-year cycles in his mind, to calculate exactly how many years ago Qin Shihuang had died. It wasn't easy, so probably he or she wouldn't bother. For this reason, historical phenomena like the Great Wall were almost necessarily perceived in mythological terms, while ordinary Chinese learned to measure the events in their own lives by the twelve animal years that are still used today. The regnal system continued in various forms, 'republican years' being used after 1912, until the adoption of the Gregorian calendar in 1949. It seems that the later fixation of what we might term 'cultural nationalism' with the often-quoted 'five thousand years of civilisation' dates from this new chronological arrangement, even though the first recorded date in Chinese history is 841 BC.

It was an American-educated Chinese historian, Lei Haizong (1902–89), who pointed out to his compatriots in an essay written in 1936 that when Chinese history was written up properly, in a narrative with accurate periodisation, they would seen that theirs was the only nation in the world which could boast of such a long and continuous history.[181] At about the same time, during excavations at the site of the ancient Shang capital near Anyang from 1928 to 1937, the deciphering of inscriptions on oracle bones pushed back knowledge of the Chinese language to the second millennium BC. Two years later, another historian, Gu Jiegang (1893–1980), gave voice to an implied racial and cultural continuity when he asserted that the Han people had been the first people to occupy the central plains of China and had been able to 'exhaust their minds and blood, fully utilize their vitality and stamina to diligently manage their circumstances *until this day* [my italics].'[182] Since the Han had occupied Manchuria and Mongolia in the past, he argued, they had legitimate claim on those lands too. Such strong ideological impetus, together with successful periodisation and comparison with tables of Western civilisation, led to reference works such as the 'Chronological tables of Chinese and world history from 5000 BC to 1918' (*Zhongwai lishi nianbiao gongyuan qian 5000 nian-gonyuan 1918 nian*). This was published in 1958, with the clear intention of asserting the glory of China's civilisation and demonstrating it to be not only equal but possible superior in antiquity to that of the rest of the world. Here the impulse was given detailed historical and chronological substance.

The 5,000 years of continuous civilisation had become an incontrovertible historical fact.

The Great Wall as a Paradoxical Symbol of Empire

Not only is the Great Wall a misnomer, since the Chinese themselves use the more literally correct term Long Wall (*Wànlĭ Chángchéng*), or literally 'the Long City/Fortress of 10,000 Li', where the '10,000' is once again not intended to be a precise measurement. But on any rational analysis it must be counted one of the great failures of history. An attacker who could scale a 300ft sheer rockface at less-frequented stretches like Simatai, 70 miles north-east of Beijing, would surely not have baulked at climbing a few extra feet of wall. Besides, Mongol or Manchu cavalry would never attempt to ride over the ridges along which much of the wall is built; it would be much easier to follow the wall seeking a breach, ride round the western end, or, as the Manchu ultimately did, bribe an officer to open a gate. Voltaire wrote of 'that great wall which was not able to save them from the invasion of the Tartars,'[183] and at the end of the nineteenth century the Scottish photographer John Thomson observed more severely that the wall was 'a gigantic, useless stone fence ... a colossal monument of misdirected human labor.'[184] By then it had become redundant as a defensive structure, since the new threat came from the cannon of European warships. Even a patriotic Chinese author like Lu Xun observed that the Wall 'never did more than kill the many workers who labored on it; nor did it stop the northern barbarians.'[185]

Built, we are informed, to keep the northern nomads out, the Wall singularly failed to prevent the Mongol invasion, and, as Lu Xun wrote, effectively created a psychological barrier that hemmed the Chinese people in. Rebuilt and extended by the Ming emperors for the same reason in the fourteenth and fifteenth centuries, it failed to avoid their own demise at the hands of the Manchu. Thus, ironically, China has been ruled for 356 of the past 729 years, from the beginning of the Yuan dynasty to 2008, by tribes that conquered China from beyond the wall. Even odder to a rational observer, around two-thirds of the territory of present-day China lies beyond a feature that is supposed in some way to represent the frontier of the 'continuous' empire.

Until relatively recently, no one seems to have thought much about the Wall. The Persian envoy Hafiz-i Abru, for example, passed through it in 1419 without mention, although he did write about the signalling system between the guard-houses, which he calls *Qarghu*: 'If all of a sudden something untoward were to happen, as for instance the appearance of a foreign army at the point where the frontiers are situated, they forthwith kindle a fire. The next *Qarghu* as soon as it observes the fire-signal acts in the same way.'[186] Thus, he notes in admiration, in twenty-four hours a message could be sent over a distance that would normally require three months travel. One eighteenth-century traveller, the Scottish doctor mentioned above, did observe that when his party first saw the 'most magnificent' wall, 'one of our people cried out LAND, as if we had been all this while at sea.'[187] But most early travellers did not mention it, for two rather obvious reasons: first, because it did not exist in its present form until the late Ming (which makes it odd that its absence from his narrative is used as evidence that Marco Polo never visited China); and, second, since it was far to the north of itineraries based on celebrated cities like Hangzhou. There isn't much else in those mountains except the Wall.

Later visitors were impressed (and tourists still are today) by the false information, based on Jesuit accounts in the seventeenth and eighteenth centuries and perpetuated by tour guides, that the few miles of crenellated and towered wall that are visible just north of Beijing continued in the same form for thousands of miles to the west, and that all of it had been built around 200 BC.[188] Lord Macartney, for example, thought that it was evidently the product 'not only of a very powerful empire, but a very wise and virtuous nation.'[189] But to which empire and to which nation was he referring? He and his secretary Sir George Staunton visited the wall on their way north from Beijing to meet the emperor, and measured it carefully, to the astonishment of the mandarins accompanying them, who had never bothered to stop and look at it.

From the first attempts at territorial expansion, the Chinese always believed in the impression factor of walls. The myriad 'states' and 'principalities' were in the main broad valleys or plains dominated by a walled city in which lived the feudal ruler of the area – very much like northern Italy in the fifteenth century. In fact, as late as the beginning of the twentieth century an American missionary observed that there were still 1,553 walled cities in China.[190] For wall-building was not an isolated or unusual occurrence in ancient times, but what one historian of Inner Asia described as 'the characteristic of an age'.[191] In the south-eastern part of Zhengzhou, just south of the Huang He, there is a surviving stretch of Shang dynasty earthern wall dating from the second millennium BC. Indeed, the word for 'wall' and 'city' is the same in Chinese: *cheng*. At the time of the Zhou, this word was used for the inner wall of a city enclosing the administrative and ceremonial focus of the territory;[192] thus a wall had symbolic as well as practical value. In the case of the northern defensive wall, it followed the highest ridges to ensure that it would be seen from a distance. It served to *impress* nomads.

The Long Wall is usually supposed to have been built by Qin Shihuang, although one of the two original sources for this supposition makes the 'wall' sound more like a defense system created from existing terrain: 'Thus he utilized the natural mountain barriers to establish the border defenses, scooping out the valleys and constructing ramparts and building installations at other points where they were needed.'[193] These early stretches of wall were built quickly, using layers of beaten earth between rows of planks, sometimes mixed with stones or gravel, to create a rapid defense rampart. After an exhaustive survey of ancient Chinese texts and archeological evidence, Arthur Waldron was able to conclude that 'no "Great Wall" anything like our modern conception of it existed in ancient times'.[194] Such walls as existed were modest and local in scale and served specific, relatively temporary dynastic purposes rather than overarching defensive plans. Bricks and mortar would have increased both cost and construction time.

When, then, did the Great Wall as we think of it come into being? The answer falls into two parts, one concerning the physical structure, and another concerning the myth and symbol of modern China.

Nomadic tribes foraging or campaigning from the steppes have represented a constant threat for the rulers of China, and in their manifestation as Huns and Mongols even for Europe, although we were fortunate enough to live at the extreme limit of medieval supply lines. A system of physical barriers to enhance the natural frontier of mountain ranges was one of the key military options against such disruptive forces. From limited sections of wall, and the early attempt to unite them into a single defensive system, the Great Wall might be said to have evolved over a period of 1,500 years to improve upon the natural frontiers and in response to changing concepts of frontier. Wall-building, in Waldron's phrase, 'was thought of as a way of providing boundaries where Heaven had neglected to make them clear.'[195] After Qin Shihuang, the Han dynasty, the northern Wei dynasty, the Sui dynasty and the Liao dynasty all engaged in bouts of wall-building (paradoxically, the Tang dynasty, so much admired by the Chinese, did not build walls; neither did their successors, the equally important Song).

It was the Ming dynasty (1368–1644) that created the system now known as the Great Wall of China, after some earlier half-hearted attempts at traditional wall-building. From the 1540s, they constructed the stone-built, crenellated wall with watch-towers whose restored version we admire today. Most of the brick forts were actually built very late, between 1572 and 1609, but even the much-photographed bricks and mortar section at Badaling, north of Beijing, was anything but consistent in form. Broad enough to accommodate horses and up to 24ft high in some of the flatter parts, it became much narrower and only 3ft high on the more precipitous sections. Moreover, the terrain is such that, as Julia Lovell remarked in her recent book, 'calls for repair came so frequently that the wall could never have functioned effectively as a single unit along its entire length.'[196] There were always gaps, while underpaid and underfed guards often fled or accepted bribes rather than fighting. If we take the example of the eastern end at Shanhaiguan, where the not only restored, but virtually rebuilt wall descends to the Bohai Sea and the Ming retained an important garrison (now a museum), most of the work was carried out in the final decades of the sixteenth century. Fortifications were not even completed at the time of the Manchu conquest, when all these efforts proved to be wasted. For, in late May 1644, the Ming general Wu Sangui betrayed his command and allowed the Manchu army to pass through the putatively impregnable gate known as the 'First Pass Under Heaven', a short ride inland from the point where the wall meets the sea. For the Ming in particular, the Wall was a disastrous and expensive failure.

But the myth has been a huge success, first in its European form and then in its Chinese manifestation. Much of the responsibility for the former lies with Jesuit cartographers who had only visited sections of the wall near Beijing in person, but extrapolated from what they saw a much longer version, which they had never seen. Around the middle of the seventeenth century, Martino Martini (1614–61) began the story with his *Novus Atlas Sinensis*, first published in 1655. In his description of the Wall, he gave the impression that the stone wall north of Beijing continued in the same form throughout its length. He also asserted that the entire wall was built at 'incredible speed' by the man he refers to as Xius Imperator Cinae Imperialis, who he specified lived 215 years before Christ. Thus Qin Shihuang was credited with the entire endeavour, for he built this 'stone wall', in Martini's words 'murum hunc magnum exstruxit', from 'Leaotung' province through 'Xansi' and 'Xensi' to Peking.[197] A decade later his more famous fellow Jesuit, Athanasius Kircher (1602–80), published his richly illustrated *China Monumentis qua Sacris quà Profanis* with a frontispiece that clearly shows a continuous wall running along the northern frontier of China. Moreover, later in his book, in language that suggests he is using the same source as Martini, he repeats the assertion that the wall is a continuous work running through the 'horridi et inaccessi montes' of four provinces, and provides a half-page illustration of a European-looking gate-house with well-faced stonework and what seem to be eight to ten horses galloping in parallel along the top.[198] The massive, elegant and continuous stone wall was now accepted as fact, and in his *Voyages de l'Empereur de la Chine dans la Tartarie*, published in 1685, Ferdinand Verbiest (1623–88) crowned his co-religionists' work with the breathless assertion that 'the seven wonders of the world put together are not comparable to this work …'[199] This was the definitive stamp of approval. Most accounts over the next three centuries, whether by authors who had actually visited the wall or by historians who had never been to China, elaborated on the basis of these descriptions.

In contrast, the Chinese development of the myth is exquisitely political. As we have seen in the case of Lord Macartney's visit, most Chinese had never bothered to look at the wall or think about it; locals used it as a source for good-quality building material up to recent years. It was when Sun Yat-sen was consciously seeking myths of China to reinforce nationalism that he focused on the Wall as one of China's greatest engineering feats, and in his view a key factor in saving the Chinese race. For Sun, it had the added virtue of being a Ming construction, for he often referred to the Republic as a kind of restoration of 'Chinese' values after 267 years of Manchu rule.[200] He argued, sophistically, that the country could never have survived without the Wall and had become so powerful as the result of its presence that it could even assimilate invading peoples like the Mongols and Manchus.[201] Having entered the vocabulary of nationalism on such excellent authority, the Great Wall was there to stay. Sun's sometime fellow revolutionary Mao Zedong also mentioned it in his writings. In a poem written as he travelled north during the Long March, it achieved epic status:

> The Sky is high, the clouds are pale,
> We watch the wild geese vanish southward.
> If we fail to reach the Great Wall we are not men,
> We who have already measured twenty thousand li.
> (Mount Liupan, October 1935)[202]

This famous poem is often sung and frequently misquoted on t-shirts (as if the *tourist* is not a man if he/she doesn't *visit* the wall), and reinforces the confusion found in travel writing.[203] It provides an intriguing comparison between the 'heroic' length of the wall at 10,000 *li* and the even greater march that Mao and his army had covered. Reaching the Wall is represented here as the final achievement of the foundation epic of the People's Republic of China, which is itself odd since most such epics conclude in the capital of the old regime with destructive events such as the storming of the Bastille. In fact the present national anthem of China, 'March of the Volunteers', opens with words that echo the spirit of Mao's poem:

> Arise, ye who refuse to be slaves!
> With our flesh and blood, let us build our new Great Wall!

Thus accepted as one of the founding myths of the country's greatness (although even these words were forbidden during the Cultural Revolution, and their author was imprisoned), 1980s' propaganda asserted that 'loving and repairing the Great Wall will reflect the patriotic feelings of the Chinese people,' and Deng Xiao Ping famously wrote: 'Let us love our country and restore our Great Wall.' As Waldron notes laconically, while the various walls that constitute the myth were never the subject for Chinese painting in the first 2,000 years of their existence, since 1949 it has become a popular theme both for serious painters and for designers.

This myth of the historical continuity and antiquity of the Wall is instilled early in Chinese children. The Middle School history textbook used in all Chinese schools, after a three-line explanation of how the general Meng Tien built the wall for his emperor to 'defend China', turns to much more emotional language in which the Wall is said to represent all the values of the Chinese people: 'The grandiosity of the Great Wall is a unique symbol of the intelligence and labour of the people of our country in ancient times.'[204] But the language of tourism and guidebooks is only slightly less fulsome: a Beijing travel agency relates in a brochure that the 'Great Wall of China was built to ward off enemies in ancient times. Over 6,000 kilometers long, the Great Wall is the symbol of the China'; the *Lonely Planet* guide to China writes of the 'original wall' built 2,000 years ago, and how in Ming times an effort was made to 'rehash the whole project, this time facing it with bricks and stone slabs'[205] – as if it were the same wall which had been restored and reinforced.

Whatever we believe, and whatever the historical facts, the Great Wall now stands for China and is a source of pride to the Chinese people, since few of them know its detailed history. After centuries of ignoring, neglecting, mining for building materials, and dismantling during the Cultural Revolution, it has become the predominant symbol of China as no other. It has also become a ubiquitous brand name for hundreds of disparate products: there are Great Wall jeeps, Great Wall wines, Great Wall hotels, Great Wall optical plastics, Great Wall ceramic tiles,

Great Wall computers – not to mention restaurants from Zhengzhou to Nairobi and from Liverpool to Denver, Colorado, and hundreds in other languages called Grande Muraglia, Grande Muraille and so on. The whole business is absurd, as is the carnival atmosphere surrounding the most easily accessible parts of the wall on major Chinese holidays. It is also striking that, like the other two 'must' sites for foreign and domestic tourists, it is a recent construct: just 100 years ago, the Forbidden City was closed to visitors, the Terracotta Army lay undiscovered, and no one went to see the Great Wall. Other symbols stood for China: music, silk, landscape painting, porcelain and the elite garden culture of cities like Suzhou and Hangzhou. In other words, China was renowned for its southern culture.

The point is that once it came into focus the Great Wall could not be ignored. It is, after all, *there*, potent, tangible, still impressive in the twenty-first century, and when it can be seen snaking across mountain ranges for dozens of miles it is not necessary to see the remaining (imagined) thousands of miles to understand its symbolic value. There is no doubt in the minds of Chinese and tourists alike, in spite of scholarly scepticism in both Chinese and foreign research. Just a certainty that the Great Wall has always been as it is. The fact that is has been heavily restored in the past thirty years is irrelevant. It is simply there.

The Inevitable 'Return' of Hong Kong and Taiwan

The same sense of a-historical immutability informs Chinese ideas about Hong Kong and Taiwan, for in their view these limbs of China were merely 'lost' to British and Japanese imperialism on a temporary basis. This is why the transition of Hong Kong from British to Mainland Chinese rule was much less traumatic than many observers feared and why the Chinese collective leadership feels certain that sooner or later Taiwan will return to the 'Motherland' in the same way. This vision is facilitated by their long-term vision: President Hu Jintao has spoken of 2050 as a probable date for the 'return' of Taiwan. This shows us that his policies are driven by a perception of China as a fixed and permanent entity in the way described above rather than by any attempt to secure his personal legacy as a Western politician might do in a similar situation. For the European concept of empire, and of decline and fall, condition our thinking when we consider such central concerns of recent Chinese policy as Hong Kong and Taiwan.

The island of Hong Kong was ceded to Britain 'in perpetuity' as part of the Treaty of Nanjing signed on 29 August 1842, which brought to an end the Opium War. Not only was this moment the height of British imperial sea power, just a few years into the reign of Queen Victoria, but the Treaty was actually signed aboard the Indian-built frigate HMS *Cornwallis* moored on the Chang Jiang in Nanjing.[206]

It allowed the establishment of the first batch of so-called Treaty Ports (Canton, Fuzhou, Xiamen, Ningbo and Shanghai), for the residence and commercial activities of British merchants, and the opening of consulates in each of these cities. It sparked a series of similar treaties with other European imperial powers, leading to the concession system that later caused so much resentment on the part of the Chinese.

The episode that led to this treaty involved a British fleet comprising sixteen warships, four armed steamers, and twenty-eight transport ships carrying 4,000 men and supplies, sent by Parliament to obtain reparation from the Chinese for a naval blockade and seizures of opium that had been flushed into the sea. It was a classic show of imperial naval strength. As is well-known, Hong Kong became the gateway to China, both for trade and for emigration, until the PRC was created in 1949. With the frontiers closed, there was then an effective hiatus of thirty years. Hong Kong slipped back naturally into its entrepôt role after the reopening of China in 1978. But there were differences that radically changed its function, and turned the colony into a major channel for Overseas Chinese investing in China rather than a base for the international trading community. At the same time it became the preferred destination for investment and listing for Chinese companies, especially after the 1992 'southern tour' of Deng Xiao Ping (which touched Shenzhen, just across the border), made in order to stimulate growth and investment. Interestingly, Deng referred to that trip as his 'inspection visit to the south', exactly the same expression that the emperor Kangxi used of his southern tours between 1684 and 1707.[207] The presence of Chinese companies on the Hong Kong Stock Exchange's Main Board, measured as a percentage of the total market capitalisation, increased from a tiny 4.78 per cent in 1993 to 16.29 per cent in 1997. In September 2006, this figure had increased to 41.78 per cent,[208] and in the autumn of 2007 there were rumours of an imminent Chinese takeover. When Hong Kong businessmen were able to enter China again it was not merely as traders or middlemen for Western companies, but as financiers, investors and factory owners in their own right and integral to China's growth. No longer simply a conduit, Hong Kong became a direct business partner on behalf of the Chinese in neighbouring countries.

Thus as 1997, and the end of a ninety-nine-year lease on the New Territories (which were always technically on the mainland anyway) drew near, the now ex-imperial power knew that it had no way to maintain its role on the once barren island. Given the Gibbonian mindset of British politicians, it was a natural consequence of the 'decline' of imperial power that Hong Kong should be ceded to China. From that viewpoint, the whole story of Hong Kong is one of rise and fall, of a 150-year arc. It is easily forgotten that Hong Kong was already lost to Britain in 1941, when the Japanese captured the colony. The following year, the British government was on the point of renouncing ownership, which would have given a nice symmetry to the occupation of the island, exactly 100 years. Britain held on, and on Japan's defeat British control of the colony was restored. But although there was, in Philip Snow's phrase, 'a dapper resumption of Britishness'[209] when the colony was restored in the autumn of 1945, that interval may also be read as the beginning of decline that led to the return to China. As Snow illustrates, the colony was never the same again, with a lowering of the British profile and greater social and racial integration. Thus Hong Kong has been both British and Japanese, a kind of double nemesis for China. In fact, the eventual surrender of the Japanese brought out pro-Mainland emotions of nationalism, a 'new pride in being Chinese, and a greatly increased disposition to identify with the mainland regime.'[210] After the founding of the PRC, Mao Zedong declared a lack of pressing interest in Hong Kong, 'so long as Chinese are not treated as inferior to others in the matter of taxation and a voice in the Government.'[211] Had Chiang Kai-Shek taken power in 1949, Hong Kong might have returned sooner.

But it was only a matter of time anyway. For the mainland Chinese themselves, Xianggang, as Hong Kong is known in *Putonghua*, has always been part of their nation. One of the reasons it was conceded to the British was that from their point of view it was a barren rock of little apparent value; in fact land more suitable for building like Kowloon and the New Territories was added later. What, after all, is a gap of 156 years in the context of 2,000 years in the past and another 2,000 years in the future? With the death of Mao and the rise to power of Deng Xiao Ping, followed by a rapid acceleration in economic growth, there was a new resolve to reclaim Hong Kong. In truth, however, Britain had long since given up on Hong Kong: in the late 1950s all pretensions to strategic military importance were abandoned, given the cost of creating a garrison strong enough to withstand an attack such as that of the Japanese; then, in 1967, a Treasury review concluded that the colony was no longer a positive asset.[212]

Thus, on the long view, the apparent concession that there would be no change in the political status of Hong Kong for fifty years, made by Deng to British Foreign Minister Geoffrey Howe, together with the ambiguous invention by the former of the principle of 'one country, two systems', is largely irrelevant. So were last-minute manoeuvres on the part of the last Governor, Chris Patten, to force through some measures of democracy. Of course China will maintain the pledge, since fifty years is a very short time for a government nurtured on the *longue durée* rather than brief and unpredictable periods between elections, and because that will allay fears of the same 'one country, two systems' regime being applied to Taiwan one day. Hong Kong, its banking system and its Stock Exchange are useful for the time being, but who knows in fifty years? For the moment, Hu Jintao was able to reassure the Chief Executive of Hong Kong, Donald Tsang Yamkuen, in a Beijing meeting in April 2007, that 'advancing democracy in a gradual and orderly manner' was essential for Hong Kong's prosperity.[213] Certainly it is odd to imagine that meeting: the die-hard communist leader in the leadership compound at Zhongnanhai receiving the bow-tied, British-educated, Catholic Tsang, who before driving to the meeting attended morning mass with his wife at Beijing's Southern Cathedral (which was built in 1703 on the site of Matteo Ricci's house).

The only thing we can be sure of is that Hong Kong is and will always be Chinese. The government in Beijing knows that when 2047 comes, people in Britain will wonder what all the fuss in the 1990s was about – if they can still remember anything about it, if young journalists still recognise the anniversary as significant, and if indeed the story of the British Empire is still part of the school curriculum.

Much the same is true of Taiwan. Although there was some Chinese settlement on the island as early as the seventh century, it was not then considered part of China since the Tang dynasty tended to face west rather than seaward. Indeed, from 1590 to 1662 it was effectively ruled by the Dutch under the name of Formosa (from the Portuguese name *Ilha Formosa*, 'beautiful island'). In the latter year, it was taken by Zheng Chenggong, known to European merchants as Coxinga, on behalf of the Ming, but he subsequently used the island as a private fiefdom and a base for trading and piratical incursions. In 1683, when Coxinga's son was defeated by Qing forces, the island passed under the jurisdiction of Fujian province, although it continued to be the base for pirates and illegal emigration from the mainland for two centuries. In 1887, Taiwan was accorded the status of independent province, with its capital in Taipei, a situation that lasted for less than a decade. In 1895, after the Chinese defeat in the two-year Sino-Japanese War, the island was ceded to Japan as part of the Treaty of Shiminoseki 'in perpetuity', as was the fiction with Hong Kong. Then, when Japan suffered defeat at the end of the Second World War, Taiwan was returned to China as a province, but in 1949 it was taken over by the nationalist government of Chiang Kai-shek and transformed into the Republic of China.

In the past 500 years, Taiwan has been variously a Dutch trading base, the site of Spanish forts, a pirate base, a Chinese province, a Japanese colony, and the bolt-hole of Chang Kai-Shek and the Kuomintang. In fact, on the most generous estimate, Taiwan was part of the 'empire' for just 233 years of the 2,000-odd years that it existed; to take the extreme case, only four years. For it could be argued that Taiwan belonged to China only during the short period between 1945 and 1949, when the Chinese Nationalists occupied the island and killed some 20,000 Taiwanese who demonstrated for democracy. The Qing Dynasty, which ruled parts of Taiwan from 1683 to 1895, was Manchu, not Chinese. At that time, however, China was also a Manchu colony, so that occupation might be said not to count.

Yet for the average Chinese the island is an inalienable part of their country, for which the present government has stated unequivocally that it would be prepared to go to war. But that seems less likely as the political language modulates from 'liberation' to 'reunification'. The statement that China 'will absolutely not allow Taiwan to secede from China under any pretext', made by the Minister of Defence

Cao Gangchun on the occasion of the eightieth birthday of the PLA in August 2007, illustrates China's firmness of purpose.[214] This belief, which began in the early years of Deng Xiao Ping's reforms, was driven by a resurgence in patriotism and nationalism as substitutes for Communism, with economic development portrayed as the means to achieve the twin goals of unification and freedom from international hegemony. Thus, in a paradoxical way seldom explained in the Press, the success of reunification with Taiwan is one of the criteria for judging the success of Deng's reform policies and consequent economic success.[215] That is one reason why such importance is given to the issue of Taiwan.

From these examples, we can see that the Empire of Mind stands outside the Western conventional standards of time and place, in which Taiwan and Hong Kong have always been and always will be a part – even though the former had been part of the 'empire' for such a short time and the latter was no more than a fishing village when it was ceded to Britain. There is no rise, no fall, and no decline. It was, in the words of *River Elegy* ('Heshang'), a television documentary series that will be discussed in the next chapter, 'but a blink'. The Empire of Mind simply exists and always has done, for 5,000 years, in spite of any evidence to the contrary.

Apparent Closure: the Ming Paradox

But why stop at Taiwan and Hong Kong, or on the western frontiers of Tibet and Xinjiang? Why is it that China, in its various manifestations, never attempted to create an empire beyond its traditional boundaries of steppe, sea, jungle, mountains and desert? In the Western sense, empire was the inevitable corollary of voyages of exploration, so that in a work such as *The Wealth and Poverty of Nations* we find it very natural that David Landes should give a chapter the title 'From Discoveries to Empire'. The voyages of Christopher Columbus, Pedro Álvares Cabral, Francisco Pizarro and James Cook led to the colonization of America, Brazil, Peru and Australia respectively. Why did the Chinese not follow up the voyages of the eunuch admiral Zheng He, whose fleets may have reached all three of these continents at least a century earlier, in the same way?

Expansion under Yongle

In the early years of the Ming such an enterprise seemed likely. For Hongwu (1328–98), who founded the dynasty in 1368, was determined to recreate the great empire of the Tang dynasty on the larger canvas of Mongol territory.

Hongwu's first move was quintessentially Chinese: having recaptured Beijing and driven the Mongols back to their northern lands, he reestablished a nominal empire by demanding tribute from neighbouring countries such as Japan, Korea, Tibet and northern Vietnam, and also from others further afield such as Borneo, Java, Sumatra, and Coromandel in India. He sent embassies to the court of Tamerlane at Samarkand and Herat for the same purpose. According to the 'Records of the Ming' (*Ming Shi*) one ambassador, known as An and described as 'one of the most remarkable men of northern China', travelled on to Tabriz, Esfahan and Shiraz, altogether a six-year journey.[216] Another embassy, led by Chen Cheng (Ch'en Ch'eng), returned from the West after visiting seventeen kingdoms.[217] The 'Records' devoted a section of thirteen chapters to foreign countries, indicating a significant opening towards the West in the early years of the Ming, both for tribute and for trade. At the same time, however, Hongwu wished to prevent private or entrepreneurial sea-going voyages and to crack down on piracy, for in 1371 he issued a prohibition on sea trade, which was a blueprint for future regulations. Contraband activities were to be punished by 'too heavy blows' and the building of two-masted ships without permits by beheading, while sentences for trading with Japan ranged from being cast into irons to execution.[218]

It was Hongwu's son Yongle (reigned 1403–24), one of the most extraordinary of all Chinese emperors, who recreated something of the grandeur of the Tang past. Hafiz-i Abru described him in these words: 'The Emperor was of the middle height; his beard neither very large nor very small; nevertheless about two or three hundred hairs of his middle beard were long enough to form three or four curls on the chair where he was seated.'[219] But this provides little idea of the dynamism implicit in his hyperactivity. A contemporary portrait in the National Museum of Taipei shows a man of great interior strength, with penetrating eyes, and hints at the dynamism by means of hands that seem anxious to be doing something. Yongle moved the capital back to Beijing from Nanjing, built the palace complex known as the Forbidden City, repaired and enlarged the Grand Canal both to supply his capital and to facilitate travel to the south of his kingdom, and personally led military campaigns to subdue the Mongols in the north. But while he was prepared to go into combat, and gained his position partly as a result of military success on earlier campaigns, he seems to have preferred using the tools of diplomacy and commerce to extend his influence. Thus he continued Hongwu's policy of sending letters and envoys to countries with which China had tributary relationships. In succession he sent envoys to Japan and Korea in the East, to Siam and Cambodia in the South, and to Herat and Samarkand in the West; soon afterwards he established relationships with strategic outposts such as Champa and Malacca, which acted as staging posts for ships travelling to Borneo, Java and Sumatra. The wealth and power which derived from these embassies and expeditions was transmuted into the great new capital, whose core of the Forbidden City stands today in much of its original form as imperial China's best-known monument.[220]

In another of these initial attempts to establish Ming prestige, Yongle sponsored the maritime expeditions of Zheng He (*c.*1371–1435) in what might be described as the least 'conquest-driven' of all maritime expeditions in world history. Neither were they voyages of exploration in the European sense. Zheng was a Muslim whose father and grandfather both bore the title of *Hajji*,[221] an honorific title granted to those who have made the pilgrimage (*hajj*) to Mecca. Muslim sailors and pilgrims knew the route, and as a young boy he must have heard stories of such an important voyage to the west by his elders. That he was brought up speaking Arabic as well as Chinese hints at profound devotion to Islam and Mecca. Zheng's fleet visited ports and cities familiar to Chinese mariners and sailed with the help of well-known monsoon winds, usually in sight of recorded coastal features. In fact the aim of the seven voyages carried out between 1405 and 1433 seems to have been essentially twofold: first of all, to guarantee the payment of tribute by making a show of Ming power; and, second, to obtain scientific information. Indeed, one author has speculated that the seven voyages were the outcome of an effort to extend the tributary system and 'make it truly the machinery of a world order.'[222] There was, however, yet another possible motive in the new emperor's desire to track down a nephew and rival for the imperial title, Zhu Yunwen, who was thought to have travelled abroad to escape Yongle's wrath and certain execution.

China was not new to maritime exploits, as is often thought. The Song dynasty created an effective navy with eleven squadrons controlling the East China Sea from the coast of Fujian northwards to Korea and Japan, and introduced significant innovations in the design of sea-going junks. Song navigators studied Arabic and Hindu maps and sought to improve on them, and they invented the floating mariner's compass.[223] They experimented with paddle boats and developed weapons like gunpowder grenades for maritime warfare. Later, in spite of being a steppe-based power, the Yuan dynasty also used junks to send envoys to Sumatra, India and Ceylon, and made two failed attempts to conquer Japan. Under Emperor Yongle, even before Zheng He's voyages, fleets of over 3,000 ships sailed to the Ryukyu Islands and Korea.

Seventy years earlier, the Arab traveller Ibn Battuta had described the sea-going junks in these terms:

> The large ships have anything from twelve to down to three sails, which are made of bamboo rods plaited like mats. They are never lowered, but turned according to the direction of the wind; at anchor they are left floating in the wind. A ship carried a complement of a thousand men, six hundred of whom are sailors and four hundred men-at-arms, including archers, men with shields and arbalists, who throw naptha.

He expressed astonishment that the crews of these four-decked junks took their wives, children and slave-girls on board, and grew vegetables and ginger in water tanks. He also notes, as we do today of the inhabitants of apartment blocks in large cities, that due to the immense size of the ships 'often a man will live in his cabin unknown.'[224] Ibn Battuta informs us that even as he wrote these words in Calicut (now Kozhikode, on the Malabar coast), there were thirteen such junks moored in the harbour.[225]

It is curious to note that when, in an imperial edict dated 11 July 1405, Zheng He was ordered to conduct an expedition through the Straits of Malacca into the 'western seas', he had no maritime experience whatsoever. But he was a natural leader, a tall, strong and personally courageous man who had proved his worth on military campaigns, with the charisma needed for command. Above all, as Superintendent of the Office of Eunuchs, he possessed the excellent diplomatic and organisational skills essential to be commander-in-chief of an expedition comprising nearly 27,000 people, including such authoritative figures as seventeen imperial eunuch ambassadors and assistant ambassadors, ninety-five military directors, and over 200 brigade and company commanders. The fleet needed to transport this number of people was of staggering size for the time, with its core being sixty-two nine-masted 'treasure junks', each said to have been 450ft long and 180ft across the beam. One contemporary source, Zheng's private secretary on a later expedition, Kung Chen, tells us that 300 sailors were needed to work the sails, anchors and rudders of one of these treasure-junks.[226] To provide logistical support there were 265 other vessels including seven-masted supply ships, six-masted transport ships carrying food and water, and five-masted warships. The fleet set sail from the treasure-ship yards at Nanjing in the autumn, carrying gifts of gold-trimmed silk for the princes and rulers of countries they would visit; it returned to Nanjing two years later, in October 1407, with tribute-bearing envoys from Calicut, Semudera (northern Sumatra), Quilon, Aru (Eastern Sumatra) and Malacca (Melaka).[227] On this and the later voyages, the practice was to carry out official duties on the outward leg using the monsoon winds from October to March, in a leisurely manner, and then 'make a quick run home during the single period of the south-west monsoon.'[228]

During the emperor Yongle's lifetime there were five more such voyages, although Zheng seems personally to have participated in just three of them and none had as many ships as the first fleet: in the expedition of 1409–11, he sailed to Ceylon; in that of 1413–15, he pushed beyond India to the Maldives and on to Hormuz on the Persian Gulf; in the expedition of 1417–19 he sailed as far as Aden, Mogadishu and Malindi. Altogether, Zheng is said to have visited thirty-seven countries, but he may not have landed in all of them personally since the fleets were often sub-divided into squadrons with separate destinations. Although he brought back rare animals, minerals and plants as gifts for Yongle, and his navigators increased the store of knowledge about the main sea routes and the coastlines between China and Africa, Zheng's most important success in the emperor's view was to increase the number of tributary states. Yet it was more than a flag-showing and public relations exercise, for each time the fleet returned to China bearing rulers and envoys who came to pay their tribute. In 1421, there was an event that brought out the significance of the presence of envoys in the capital. The occasion provides a reason for the voyages which is often overlooked, and which tallies perfectly with the careful long-term planning for major events which still characterises the Chinese leadership.

On New Year's Day, which fell that year on 2 February, the new imperial capital and the Forbidden City were formally inaugurated. Once again Hafiz-i Abru was an eye-witness, and his account points up both the attention to detail and the grandiosity of the ceremony. On the previous day, a message had been delivered to guests ordering them not to wear 'a turban, dress, cap or socks of white colour;'[229] white was the colour of mourning and would bring bad luck to the inauguration.

Then, during the night, the envoys were awoken to find that every city-dweller had 'illuminated his house and shop with torches, candles and lamps that you would have thought the sun had risen already.' There were 100,000 people in the palace from every part of China, twenty-eight kings and princes, and numerous ambassadors, even from 'countries whose names are not known.' The ceremony itself was splendid beyond words:

> He had caused the envoys to be seated just outside his throne-room. Thus a concourse of two hundred thousand men stood with swords, maces, halberds, lances, staves, javelins, battle-axes and other weapons of war in their hands. About one to two thousand men held in their hands the Chinese fans of variegated colours and designs, each being about the size of a shield and slung up across their shoulders. The acrobats and boys danced in ever new fashions, and they wore such dresses with robes and coronets that it is not possible to give an adequate description thereof.[230]

This was followed by a banquet, and although Abru does not describe it we may imagine it to be similar, if grander, to one he attended a few weeks earlier, on 15 December. First, they had been asked to 'ease themselves' because once the banquet had begun it was impossible to leave the hall. Then, when the emperor Yongle was seated on a carved and gilded throne in a courtyard of the Forbidden City, trays were served with 'viands, desserts and bouquets', three trays for noblemen, two trays for slightly lower ranks, and just one tray for the rest. The emperor ate alone, but in view of his guests: 'Whenever food or drink is brought up for the Emperor, the Orchestra begins playing all of a sudden and those seven royal umbrellas at once begin to revolve and moved on with those eatables till they reach close to the throne.'[231] The entire ceremony, set in those magnificent surroundings, the quality of whose stonework made a notable impression on Abru, was designed to legitimise the Son of Heaven's power over *tiānxia*. And to reinforce allegiance.

It was an exercise in what we call today 'soft' power. The *Essentials of the Comprehensive Mirror of History*, compiled in 1767, makes this clear. According to this account, Zheng and the ambassadors 'spread abroad the knowledge of [the emperor's] majesty and virtue. They bestowed gifts upon the kings and rulers, and those who refused submission they over-awed by the show of armed might. Every country became obedient to the imperial commands.'[232] So there was certainly a threat of military action when necessary, but no record of such action. Even the reference here to 'submission' is related to the payment of tribute rather than with military defeat or the establishment of a colony. This is a reflection of Ming policy, based on the specific instructions of a document called 'Ancestral Injunctions' promulgated in 1373. Having listed the foreign countries known to Hongwu, this document goes on to provide a perfect illustration of the pragmatism of Ming foreign policy: 'Their lands would not produce enough for us to maintain them; their peoples would not usefully serve us if we incorporated them into the empire. If they were so unrealistic as to disturb our borders, it would be unfortunate for them. If they gave us no trouble and we moved troops to fight them unnecessarily, it would be unfortunate for us.'[233] This extraordinary document, which also listed fifteen neighbouring countries which were specifically *not* to be invaded, is a cogent negation of the value of either attempted conquest or coerced annexation. It is also an interesting example of the origins of Qianlong's view of foreign powers and their products.

These peaceful intentions seem to be borne out by the detailed narrative of some of the final voyages written by Ma Huan (*c.*1380–*c.*1460), a Chinese Muslim who was appointed as an official translator for Arabic. It reads like the travellers' tales of early Western visitors to China, replete with observations of customs and curiosities. In each country he visits with the fleet, Ma first describes the rulers and their palaces. Then he gives detailed descriptions of the cities, and the clothes, food and customs of their inhabitants, together with information about local fauna such as the rhinoceros and parakeets, which he calls 'hand-upside-down-birds'[234] in a flourish worthy of Sir John Mandeville, and curiosities such as gambling on cock-fights and the practice of suttee. He provides details that indicate that trading, whether by purchase or by tribute exchange, was one of the functions of these expeditions. In Champa, central Vietnam, for instance, he notes that the local people appreciate Chinese blue and white porcelain and hemp-silk (a weave of ramie and silk), and bring gold to purchase them;[235] Ming porcelain is much appreciated everywhere, coloured silk-taffeta particularly in Ceylon,[236] while in Java and Mecca the rulers were also fond of musk.[237] In this light, it is interesting that Ma often notes the use of Chinese copper coins as currency in the countries they visit, which confirms a long history of trading even before these expeditions. In each country, the local products sent as tribute are listed, from rhino horns, elephant tusks and incense in Champa,[238] to sapan-wood and laka-wood in Thailand,[239] precious stones and pearls in Ceylon,[240] pepper from Cochin,[241] and frankincense from Dhufar.[242] In the case of a wealthy city such as Calicut, Ma is more explicit:

> On the day when the envoy returned, the king of the country wished to send tribute; so he took fifty *liang* [60 ounces according to the Translator] of fine red gold threads as fine as a hair; these were strung together to form a ribbon, which was made into a jeweled girdle with incrustations of all kinds of precious stones and large pearls; and the king sent a chief, Nai-pang, to present it to the Central Country.[243]

Once again, there appears to have been no ambition whatsoever, whether explicit or implicit, of conquest in the European sense; indeed, Yongle died on a campaign against the Mongols in defence of his own territories.

We know for certain that Zheng's ships reached India, the Middle East and the coast of Africa, and visited the twenty-eight kingdoms listed. If we accept the hypotheses outlined by Gavin Menzies in his book *1421: The Year China Discovered the World,* based on dubious and circumstantial evidence, some of these ships may have reached Australia and the Americas. In his introduction to Ma Huan's journal, J.V.G. Mills already suggested in 1970 that ships from Zheng's fleet had reached Australia, while Louise Levathes also reviewed similar hypotheses in the early 1990s.[244] The real point is that China had the knowledge, the skills, and the manpower to create an empire that would have dominated half the globe (excluding only the land mass from Central Asia to Europe), but did nothing. So what happened?

One simple answer is that the money ran out.

Worse still, on 12 August 1424, Yongle died. His son and successor, Hongxi, was a sick man who survived his father for less than a year and in that brief period surrounded himself with conservative Confucian scholars. Traditionalist views came into vogue once again, and the finance minister Xia Yuanji, who had tried to advise Yongle against embarking on costly new campaigns, advised the new emperor against the extravagances for which his father had been criticised, and recommended him to renounce further expeditions towards the West. Thus, on 7 September, on his very first day as Emperor and with the recently deceased emperor not yet buried, Hongxi issued an edict that halted the voyages with immediate effect: 'All voyages of the treasure ships are to be stopped. All ships moored at Taica are ordered back to Nanjing and all goods on the ships are to be turned over to the Department of Internal Affairs and stored.'[245] This was a sudden and total reversal of policy. Not only was all building of new treasure ships to cease, but all procurement of shipbuilding materials and gifts too; wherever they were, procurement officials were to return to Beijing. Indeed, all government officials currently overseas on business were summoned to China at once. Such was the reaction to his father's policies that Hongxi even wanted to move the capital back to Nanjing, where he himself had always resided.

The most obvious explanation for this reversal of policy is that with Yongle's death the inspiration and impetus for voyages of expedition were lost. When Hongxi himself died, one of his ten sons succeeded him as Xuande, ruling from 1426 to 1435. But he too was a more traditional emperor than his grandfather. He seemed more interested in poetry and painting, collecting rare and valuable objects, and seeking Korean virgins for his pleasure. His reign passed without notable decisions or events. It is true that he sent one last expedition to the West, from 1431 to 1433, when 100 ships followed the same route to India and the East African coast. But the momentum was lost, and by the time his son Zhengtong came to power three years later, there were new threats from the Mongols. The exploits of Zheng He were forgotten until his story served a new nationalist cause, when Liang Qichao published an article in 1905 on Zheng as 'A Great Navigator of Our

Mother Country', in which he compared the eunuch admiral to Columbus.[246] It is true, as Jonathan Spence writes with Gibbonian splendour in the first sentence of his history of modern China, that 'in the year A.D. 1600, the empire of China was the largest and most sophisticated of all the unified realms of the earth.'[247] But it feels as though it could have been so much more.

Closure under Zhengtong

Renewed pressure exercised on the northern frontier by the Mongols shifted the focus of imperial attention back from the ocean to the steppes. Zhengtong's reign (1436–64) was interrupted by six years of imprisonment at the hands of the Mongol warrior Esen Khan, who had reunited Mongol forces under a single leader for the first time since the collapse of the Yuan dynasty. The emperor returned from his imprisonment burning with resentment against the Mongols. He attempted to eliminate all Mongol influence in Chinese life, from costumes to customs, and even modified statues of Confucius that had been sculpted in Mongol dress. It was as a consequence of further Mongol incursions, a few years after Zhengtong's reign, that the Ming entered on the great phase of wall-building to protect the northern frontier from Mongol invasion instead of financing more overseas expeditions. In 1473, Yu Zijun, known as 'The General Who Pacifies the Barbarians', began the construction of a new 600 mile wall with 800 towers, which 'provided a physical template for the wall-building boom of the sixteenth century.'[248] The Ming had retreated inland.

For our purposes, one of the most interesting facts is that, in imitation of his grandfather, one of Zhengtong's first actions as Emperor was to ban the construction of sea-going junks – clearly under the influence of the same conservative faction, since he was only eight years old at the time. One reason for this was, in a Dutch sinologist's words, that 'the entire business of relations with overseas barbarians became, in the moral and political judgment of the official classes, inextricably bound up with their deep sense of disapproval of the extravagances and usurpation of power of the despised eunuchs.'[249] Zheng and his senior admirals and ambassadors had all been eunuchs, which might also explain why the charts made by earlier eunuch navigators were burned when the eunuch Wang Zhi, recently appointed Inspector of the Frontiers, planned to restore Chinese power at sea in 1477 and asked to see them. Wang complained when his request was refused, only to be informed by the Vice-President of the War Office that their contents were 'deceitful exaggerations of bizarre things far removed from the testimony of people's eyes and ears.'[250]

By that time few large ships survived. It has been suggested that the emperors who succeeded Zhengtong feared the consequences of large ships being in private hands, or that with such ships the distant coastal provinces could make alliances with foreign powers. Be that as it may, edicts against shipping flew fast and furious: around 1500, it became a capital offence to build sea-going junks with more than two masts; in 1525, the destruction of such ships was ordered; much worse, and paranoically, in 1551 it became an arrestable offence simply to sail in a multi-masted ship for any reason at all.[251] The seas were effectively closed to legal shipping and trade, although illegal trade flourished. This closure may have been caused by Confucian conservatism, yet that never stopped maritime trade in earlier centuries;[252] more likely, it was simply that the near-expansion was the result of the personal ambitions of Hongwu and Yongle. When their reigns had passed, the enthusiasm was lost.

Whatever the reason, China was never again a naval power.

Some have considered the closure in positive and admiring tones. Matteo Ricci, for example, observed that:

> it seems to be quite remarkable when we stop to consider it, that in a kingdom of almost limitless expanse and innumerable population and abounding in copious supplies of every description, though they have a well-equipped army and navy that could easily conquer the neighbouring nations, neither the King nor his people ever think of waging a war of aggression.

His answer to the conundrum was that the Chinese were content with their lot, unlike the greedier Europeans who 'are frequently discontent with their own governments and covetous of what others enjoy.'[253] John Bell wrote a century later in similar terms of 'a powerful people, inclined to peace with all their neighbours; and satisfied, as they seem, with their dominions.'[254]

The Chinese today are well aware of the negative long-term consequences of the 'Ming Closure'. A stunning example was a television series broadcast in the summer of 1988, which blamed the problems of contemporary China on precisely that earlier lack of imperial ambition and the failure to capitalise on the success of Zheng He's maritime expeditions. The programme was a six-part series called *River Elegy* ('Heshang'[255]), scripted by the writer and broadcaster Su Xiaokang together with a critic at Beijing Normal College, Wang Luxiang, and directed by Xia Jun. It was written and narrated with real passion, with footage edited from existing documentary material (including a recent film on the Yellow River on which Su and Xia had collaborated) and a dynamic soundtrack composed of traditional Chinese songs and driving rhythms. The series suggested that far from being expressions of the country's greatness, potent Chinese symbols like the Great Wall and the Yellow River (Huang He) were actually holding the country back in what is described as 'Yellow Earth syndrome'. The opening passage speaks mournfully of the decline of a great civilisation, and asks: 'Has our current state of mind been created by our past century of history, in which we were always the helpless victim? Or has it been created by the poverty and backwardness of the past few decades?'[256]

In the course of this complex but arresting series, the Great Wall is dismissed as a 'great and tragic gravestone', which represents 'an isolationist, conservative and incompetent defence and a cowardly lack of aggression' and has 'imprinted its arrogance and self-delusion in the souls of our people'.[257] In a devastating attack on the Wall in the second episode, the narrative stresses than while the fifteenth century was critical for countries throughout the world, China missed its chance because the Ming emperors were fixated with the land. The Wall is excoriated in these terms: 'This truly is the last frontier of an agricultural civilization. Everything is extremely clear: our ancestors would never be able to go beyond the bounds of the soil and of agriculture. Their greatest feat of the imagination and most courageous act could only be to build the Great Wall!'[258] This was in direct contrast to the exhultation of the Wall by Mao and in the National Anthem. It also refuted the argument of a television series broadcast a few months earlier that had spoken of the Wall as an example of man's 'vast creativity' and 'the Chinese people's extraordinary intelligence',[259] and portrayed it as a symbol of China's greatness to which such world leaders as Nixon paid homage.

In the fifth episode, poignantly titled 'Sorrow and Worry', it is observed that the Huang He, usually renowned for nourishing the so-called 'cradle' of Chinese civilisation, is also known as 'China's Sorrow'. Here, the river is condemned for its continued violence against innocent people, with the classical culture of the authors apparent in a quote from the *Book of Odes*: 'Man's life is too short to see the waters of the Yellow River become clear.' Still today, these symbolic floods occur as an act of nature, but, the narrator demands, 'why has our feudal age lasted as long as the Yellow River floods?'[260] The cyclical nature of the river's destructive power is implicitly compared to the cycles of destruction of political turmoil, of dynastic change and revolution (including reference to the recent Cultural Revolution). Ironically, the river that gave life to Chinese civilisation has also carried away the fertility of the land in sediment and left behind an infertile plateau, a process that is graphically compared to 'severe bleeding from the Chinese people's main artery.'[261] The episode ends with an appeal for the end of these sorrows. But the continuing destructive force of the river is emphasised by the visual and sound transition from the fifth to the sixth episodes, marked by dramatic footage of the great river in flood.

Thus, in the view of the makers of *River Elegy*, potent symbols such as the Yellow River and the Great Wall, far from being signs of positive strength, had contributed to a syndrome that handicapped China's full emergence into the world.

The only way to escape this syndrome, the narrative suggested, was to renounce the sorrows of a yellow infertile land in favour of the blueness of the sea: 'The planet of life is a blue planet' and 'the sea … is also blue', as well as being the origin of life. The sixth and last part of the series was given the title 'Blueness' to represent what is called the azure global civilisation of the twenty-first century. It opens with footage that shifts from the Yellow River to the deep blue ocean and includes images of the azure Adriatic in Venice.[262] It is a learned and profound episode, moving from the 'land-bound' philosophy of Confucius to mention of Galileo's *Dialogue on the New Science* (conducted, as the narrator tells us, in a shipyard), to Cromwell's Navigation Acts, Magellan and Adam Smith's criticisms of China in *The Wealth of Nations*, showing how the 'tremendous cultural wealth' derived from Confucianism has become a tremendous burden and obstacle: 'Only when the sea-breeze of blueness finally turns to rain and once again moistens this parched strip of soil will this awesome vitality ... be able to bring new life to the vast yellow soil plateau.'[263] In emphasising the importance of maritime trade in opening up the country, the narrative praises the creation of the Shenzhen Special Economic Zone, and its successors, as a sign that the land-based civilisation of thousands of years had finally turned 'to gaze at the distant ocean.'[264] The time had come to shake off 'the accumulated sentiment of feudalism'[265] by opening to trade and reinvigorating culture and country through maritime engagement with the world. There is fulsome praise for the 'social energy' and 'new vitality' of the 'soft-spoken new breed of entrepreneurs', and for the first signs of some openness towards democracy, which the authors call 'blue transparency'.[266] The series concludes with an aerial view of the meeting of the yellow waters and the blue sea of the open ocean.

The series was seen by some as an attack on the very concept of Chineseness, and therefore provoked a scandal;[267] others saw it as sentimentalising 'the symbolic "azure blue" of the ocean as the direction China must go to reach its vast potential.'[268] Initially, *River Elegy* was a huge popular success; the series was given a repeat screening, and was distributed both as a book and as a video, but when the liberalising faction associated with Zhao Ziyang, who himself appears in two episodes of *River Elegy*, was purged after the events of June 1989, it became anathema to the government. One newspaper is said to have published one article a day for 100 days pointing out inaccuracies, fallacies and distortions in the series,[269] while the main author of the series, Su Xiaokang, was forced to flee the country at least in part for emphasising the importance of opening China's economy to maritime trade. Now, just two decades later, China boasts (vociferously) five of the top ten ports in the world in terms of cargo volume; the prophesy of the series' closing words, that 'after a thousand years of solitude, the Yellow River has finally seen the blue sea', has in a sense been fulfilled.

This is the Empire of Mind asserting itself, first in thought and then in deed. Ricci and Bell were quite wrong; Deng Xiao Ping got it right. There *was* an innate ambition to expand which lack of imperial support could not forestall, and no army or navy could facilitate. In its various forms, China has always sought to create a balance between push and pull, between inside and outside. There is an inner core that reflects a deep cultural identity, and then there is a wider world that is sometimes claimed to be an extension of the 'middle' and is sometimes negated and ignored. Around this inner core there is, and has always been although the form has changed, a buffer zone with ambiguously defined parameters, where the conflicts between identity and ideology have always been evident. Thus, periodically, whether under the Ming or under the People's Republic, the inner core closes for a while as if a dam has been erected; when it reopens the creative and destructive force of the water released – given the size of the territory and its population – can change the world. Yet it is important to understand that these tensions refer to the 'nation', not to the 'empire', which acts according to its own logic and transcends the push/pull tension. There can be no more powerful example of policy shift than the abrupt change from sending envoys on lengthy ocean-going voyages, which touched the furthest corners of the world to the construction of a new wall built as much to keep the empire's citizens in as to keep their enemies out. At the same time, however, there have been few policy shifts that were less effective.

For the Empire of the Mind, conventional boundaries were and are not necessarily a limit. Sixty years ago, Winston Churchill noted in a prescient speech that plans for creating a soft empire through use of a Basic English would offer 'far better prizes than taking away other people's provinces or land or grinding them down in exploitation. The empires of the future are the empires of the mind.'[270] In this sense, China is a geocultural realm within the 'all-under-heaven', which flourishes regardless of geopolitical reality or temporal legislation. On the one hand, there is a visible nation or tangible entity that can be mapped, enclosed by walls or barbed wire, and manned with customs posts; on the other hand, there is an invisible empire that remains elusive, but which we must now attempt to define.

PART II

The Invisible Chinese Empire

… not only is China in a sense unconquerable, but she is eminently a conquering nation. Insidiously, remorselessly and viciously she will subdue apostles of the West who are sent to her, and unless persistently restrained will overflow into adjacent lands and conquer there by cheap labour and unremitting toil.

(Oliver J. Ready, *Life and Sport in China*, 1904)

By discovering the enemy's dispositions and remaining invisible ourselves, we can keep our forces concentrated, while the enemy's must be divided. We can form a single united body, while the enemy must split up into fractions.

(Sun Tzu, *The Art of War*, *c.*500 BC)

The Invisible Chinese Empire

Although China never attempted to build an empire of annexation on the British model beyond what it perceived as its natural territory, there was and is a form of global Chinese empire that we might describe as an *invisible empire*. Paradoxically, the stimulus that initiated this invisible empire was Hongxi's edict of 1424.

For, in spite of the apparent closure of China under the late Ming, and in spite of the formal rigidities of the tribute system, private trade never stopped. The word was out that China had excellent porcelain and textiles, so trade continued surreptitiously or illegally. Former pirates and renegades exploited the new market for Chinese goods created by an explosion of wealth in Europe to transform themselves into legitimate traders; some emigrated from southern China to set up business in neighbouring countries. Within a few years there were also new direct contacts with distant countries, as recorded in the *Ming Shi*. We read that the *Fo-lang-ghi* (foreigners or Franks, from the Persian *farangi*, used here to refer to the Portuguese) were active in the estuary below Canton, that they occupied Malacca in 1511 and founded the city of Macao in 1549; we also read about the Spanish (also, confusingly, called *Fo-lang-ghi*) appearing in the Philippines around 1573. There are accounts of the 'red-haired barbarians' (*Hong mao fan*), as the Dutch were known, during the reign of Wan Li (1573–1620), building settlements on Formosa which included a fort called Zealand on the present site of Taipei. The Japanese also founded settlements on Taiwan at this time.[271] Naturally there is mention of Italy, which was known to the late Ming emperors through Matteo Ricci and his fellow Jesuits. The small trading posts set up by these foreigners, favoured by the merchants of Fujian and Guangdong, initiated the flow of Chinese goods such as porcelain, silk and later tea to Europe. The success and immense profits from the commerce of these products led to the creation of international trading companies like the British East India Company (founded in 1600), which was the basis of the colonial empire that established footholds in Canton and later in Hong Kong.

Neither did cultural and personal contacts cease, for this was the period when the Jesuits established a significant presence in China and developed profound links with the imperial family. John Adam Schall of Cologne (1591–1666), for example, was known to the future Emperor Kangxi (born 1654, Emperor 1661–1722) by the familiar Manchu name of *Ma-fa*, or 'grandfather', and was allowed access to the imperial chambers as if he were an intimate member of the imperial family.[272] Father Schall was permitted to waive the kowtow in the imperial presence, and in the last years of his life saw the young emperor at least once a month, often staying with him until late in the night.[273]

Most fascinating of all, while contact was formally negated and Western writers often speak of China being isolated from the 'world' for centuries, Chinese culture spread throughout the world by more subtle and complex means that we will now examine.

Empire of Language: Japan, Korea, Vietnam

Before international trade, there was language, which was the essential coagulating force that brought together disparate elements into a single state and civilisation during the first millennium BC. The values and norms of this civilisation were encapsulated by Confucius around 500 BC, and worked out further by his pupils to become the Confucian Classics that were the basis for Chinese intellectual endeavour for over 2,000 years. The standardised form of written Chinese imposed by Qin Shihuang became the vehicle to 'record, spread and canonize shared cultural values and norms'[274] beyond the ancestral lands of the early Chinese tribes. This is far more significant than it might seem at first sight. For the language is both the medium and the inspiration of Chinese culture, as we will see in more detail later: painting, through the superior art of calligraphy, ultimately derives from its written form, so that its essential beauty and quality may be found in the brushwork; the melodic line of classical music derives from its sound, so that there is an inherent connection between meaning and melody. As Derk Bodde has observed, it is no accident that 'three of China's greatest inventions – paper, block-printing, and moveable type – are all closely associated with writing.'[275]

Today, China has many spoken languages, of which the best known is the standard form of modern Chinese, *Guanha*, known internationally as Mandarin, which was originally the *lingua franca* of government officials.[276] This spoken language was denominated *Guoyu*, or 'national language' with the founding of the Republic in 1911 (before that, the term *guoyu* was used to refer to Manchu!), and then *Putonghua*, or 'common language', in 1949, the name by which it is known to Chinese people today.[277] A Western scholar defines it as 'a Northern Sinitic language with considerable accretions of loan words from literary Chinese'.[278] The other main languages, each with between 20 and 80 million native speakers, are *Wu* (spoken in Zhejiang Province and the coastal area near Shanghai, including the city, with many variant local dialects), *Gan* (spoken in the southern province of Jiangxi),

Xiang (spoken in the central province of Hunan), *Hakka* (spoken in many areas from Sichuan to Taiwan), *Yue* (better known in the West as Cantonese, and used by most Chinese Americans), and *Min* (spoken in the southern coastal province of Fujian and in Chinese communities in southeast Asia). In addition, there are the minority languages of China's 'ethnic minorities', such as Buyi, Hui, Korean, Miao, Mongol, Tibetan, Uyghur, Yi and Zhuang.

In fact, a surprisingly small number of Chinese use *Putonghua* as their everyday language. According to a report published by the 'State Working Committee of Chinese Language' at the end of 2004, which was based on a six-year survey of 'over 470,000 people in thirty-one provinces, autonomous regions and munici-palities', only 53 per cent of the population were able to communicate in the official national language. Although 42 per cent used *Putonghua* for working and study purposes, a mere 18 per cent used it in conversation with family and friends. Moreover, as we might expect, the percentage of those unable to use the language increased with age: only 31 per cent of people aged sixty to sixty-nine surveyed could speak *Putonghua*. Yet this should not surprise, since classical Chinese was traditionally an elite language, surviving as such until the introduction of a simpli-fied script just half a century ago – when most people still only spoke their local dialect.

The linguist and anthropologist Susan Blum provides an intriguing analysis of the use of language in Kunming, the beautiful and slightly exotic capital of Yunnan where in the older quarters the presence of Muslim and other ethnic minorities is strong. In Kunming, Blum explains, *Putonghua* is used by the media and for teaching in schools, and of course by non-native residents, whereas the most com-monly used language in everyday life is *Kunminghua*. As in all Chinese cities, the native residents make a vehement distinction between themselves and those who have moved in from the country: thus the latter speak *Yunnanhua*, or country dialect, while the word 'Mapu' is used derogatively of people who speak *Putonghua* badly.[279] To complicate matters even more, there are the languages of the twenty-four ethnic minorities that are found in the province, from the well-known Yi and Bai to groups with only a few thousand representatives like the Dulong and Shui. A similar pattern may be found in many cities of southern China. But the charac-ters of written Chinese have always maintained their original meaning regardless of the dialect with which the words are spoken, which means that the same writ-ten script can be used for all of them. Conversely, it is hard to be certain which pronounciation was used for works written in the classical language. Some purists believe that classical Chinese poetry, often composed by poets from the south and west, is more appropriately recited in Cantonese than in what is essentially Beijing dialect.[280]

This 'persistence of meaning' has continued even when the characters have been adopted as the script for the very different languages of Korea, Japan and

Vietnam.[281] Thus, if language is to a certain extent culture, the dissemination of written Chinese to neighbouring countries represents the oldest and most subtle extension of empire, a consequence of the dominating role of Chinese culture in East Asia. In Ming and Qing times, letters from the Chinese Emperor could be read by those who received them in these countries, since the characters had the same meaning in spite of having a different language behind them. Until the twentieth century, scholars from these and other East Asian states who 'looked to China for moral, political, and cultural guidance all sought to master the literary Chinese language.'[282] For the characters bore cultural and moral values deriving from Confucius and his followers that went beyond mere words. Japanese was once written in classical Chinese characters, and even today Chinese morphemes are as common in Japanese as words of Latin and French origin are in modern English, in spite of the fact that after the Second World War the Japanese government attempted to expunge these 'kanji' or Chinese elements from their language. Chinese characters were introduced into Korea as early as the fifth century AD, where the language was known as *hanja*, and used by the mainly Confucian literary elite and aristocracy. The present Korean script was devised by King Sejong in the fifteenth century, but the *hanja* system was used by traditionalist scholars well into the twentieth century; some *hanja* characters still survive, and between 30–50 per cent of Korean words derive from Chinese either as direct borrowings from the old script or as Sino-Korean words invented with Chinese characters. There was a similar situation in Vietnam, where the Chinese script known as *han tu* was used until the fourteenth century and the spoken language was used by government officials until the nineteenth century. Still today, Chinese and Sino-Vietnamese, or *han viet*, words dominate the vocabulary even though the language is now written with a romanised script.

There were other countries that belonged to what we might term the Chinese cultural family even though their language and script were quite distinct. These included Thailand, the Ryukyu Islands and Burma, whose recently changed name Myanmar is in fact derived from the Chinese *Miǎn diàn*. The Burmese refer to the Chinese who live in their country as *paukphaw*, which means 'next of kin', in recognition of their affinity, while the Vietnamese use the colloquial expression *chu khach*, meaning 'uncle guest'. These countries shared for centuries the basic values of Chinese culture, similar food and dress, used the Chinese calendar, practiced Confucianism and even adopted some elements of Chinese bureaucratic organisation.[283] To take the calendar as an example, in Vietnam it was used until 1306 with Chinese reign-names and afterwards with Vietnamese reign-names, while from the seventh century to the beginning of the twentieth century Korea used the Chinese calendar and even Chinese reign-names.[284] Jonathan Spence's explanation of the way in which relationships with these countries were managed by the Ministry of Rituals rather than a foreign ministry, exploiting custom and symbol to 'control these states without excessive military expenditure',[285] serves as a perfect exemplar of virtual uncoerced annexation.

Empire of Inventions

It is commonplace that several of the most significant inventions of modern man were made in China. Conventional wisdom has it that the Chinese invented such things as paper, printing and gunpowder but failed to exploit them – so that, for instance, gunpowder was used for fireworks instead of 'useful' things like accurate cannon. The nineteenth-century British version, in the words of James Bruce, the 8th Earl of Elgin (High Commissioner to China, 1857–61, destroyer of the Old Summer Palace, who knew something about explosives), was that 'the invention of gunpowder has exploded in crackers and harmless fireworks', the compass 'has produced nothing better than the coasting junk', and printing 'has stagnated in stereotyped editions of Confucius.'[286] Fortunately not all Europeans were so obtuse, and as we shall see below many Chinese inventions were recognised as significant, and some of them improved, during the Industrial Revolution by the use of more advanced technology and sources of power. In mitigation for such arrogance, it should also be said that many educated Chinese expressed similar views. For example, the ambassador to London, Xie Fucheng (Hsieh Fucheng), wrote in his diary for 1890 that 'while the Western world steadily seeks to improve on these ancient discoveries, China was content with the early results and ceased to venture any further.'[287]

Although the modern English word 'paper' derives from the Greek *papyros*, paper was invented by the eunuch and Han court official Cai Lun (50–101), perhaps even earlier and, like many products, spread westward from China along the Silk Road in the eighth century. From Samarkand, an Arab chronicler informs us, it was 'exported to all countries'.[288] Marco Polo describes in some detail how the bark from mulberry trees was pulped and made into 'something resembling sheets of paper, but black', which is then 'cut into pieces of of different sizes, representing different values.' These primitive banknotes were then authenticated with a royal seal dipped in vermilion ink.[289] In fact, the first 'Western' paper mill was built in Baghdad in the year 800, and from that time the use of paper spread to Syria and on through the Arab world; it was known in Europe as charta damascene or 'Damascus paper'. The importance of commerce and pilgrimage for the diffusion of inventions can be seen in the fact that in the twelfth century pilgrims brought back pieces of paper as souvenirs.[290] The introduction of paper played an important role in the literary culture of Islam, and in the preservation of ancient Greek texts.

The origins of printing go back to the techniques of wood-block printing used in sixth-century China to make copies of Buddhist texts, one of which survives from the end of that century. While there have been many disputes over the primacy of techniques, for example that of moveable type using clay moulds by Bi Sheng in the eleventh century, there can be no doubt about the spread of printing to Japan and Korea, and the huge libraries of printed books that existed at that time in Asia. So even though it might not be the case that Europeans like Gutenberg actually learned the techniques from Chinese sources, as some scholars have argued,[291] knowledge of printed paper was certainly current in Europe long before the fifteenth century.

Gunpowder first appeared in China during the Tang dynasty, in the ninth century, when an author recommended alchemists *not* to mix saltpeter, sulphur and carbonaceous material because it might singe their beards and burn down the building in which they were working.[292] Ironically, this most military of inventions was not made by imaginative soldiers seeking military advantage but by Taoist alchemists as a chance discovery. In an interesting counter-argument to Lord Elgin, Joseph Needham explains that 'since there was no heavily armoured knightly cavalry in China, nor any aristocratic or manorial feudal castles either, the new weapon simply supplemented those which had been in use before.'[293] For this reason, there was little or no effect on military strategy. In fact the use of gunpowder saw many stages of development, and while we tend to associate it immediately with guns and cannon, it was used initially for incendiary projectiles shot from bows and crossbows. Moreover, since knowledge of these weapons was often transmitted through third parties, such as Persia or Byzantium, the people who learned to use them were unaware of their true provenance.[294]

Another area in which China excelled was measurement. As we have seen, cosmology and the division of time were vitally important for the Chinese dynasties, so we should not be surprised to find that in the eleventh century Su Sung (1020–1101) constructed an astronomical clock, which not only showed the time of day but also provided information about the relative positions of the sun and the moon. The fundamental problem in making a clock was the design of the escapement mechanism that controls movement of the dials, but this had been achieved in China 300 years earlier. There is good circumstantial evidence to suggest that Chinese knowledge about clock-making was transmitted to Europe once again by Persians and Arabs. A book on time-keeping, which included a weight-driven clock with mercury escapement, was published in Toledo in 1277. A researcher into the Eastern origins of Western civilisation notes that 'virtually all the techniques and mechanisms of the European clock, including the automata, complex gear-trains and segmental gears as well as the weight-drive and audible signals' were present in Andalusian clocks of the time and bore a very close resemblance to the clock made by Su Sung.[295]

In agriculture, the Chinese were equally ingenious. Already in the sixth century, for example, a detailed manual on efficient crop rotation had been published,[296] and some of the essential 'inventions' of the early phase of the Industrial Revolution were based on knowledge of Chinese technology. Many key innovations in agriculture, iron and steel production and textiles in the eighteenth century have traditionally been associated with Britain. But research over the past half-century has shown how many of these innovations were in fact adaptations and improvements of Chinese tools and processes. For the Jesuits had been bringing samples and descriptions of many of these technologies to Europe for decades. Sometimes at the request of scholars like Leibniz, and sometimes in the more direct form of the conversion of a leading Chinese author on agriculture, Paul Xu (Paul Hsü; 1562–1633), a Minister of State whose book contained many illustrations of agricultural implements and machinery. One important European text in the transmission of this knowledge was *An Account of the Chinese Husbandry*, translated into English in 1771, which was written by the Swedish author Carl Gustav Ekeberg after spending fifteen months in and near Guangzhou.[297]

One of the most famous names of the Industrial Revolution in England is Jethro Tull, who is credited with the invention of the seed drill in 1701. This was a vital innovation because it enabled farmers to sow seed at a regular depth in three regularly spaced rows, which allowed much better protection and easier weed control for the growing crop, and also reduced the wastage of seeds caused by the technique of broadcasting. Later, in 1733, Tull published a manual called *Horse-Hoeing Husbandry*. Yet the seed drill had been known in China for 2,000 years, and had been described in a book by yet another Jesuit, Alvarez Semedo, *The History of that Great and Renowned Monarchy of China*, published in English in London in 1655. Semedo relates how he observed in China a plough with three shears that dug furrows and planted kidney-bean seeds in them immediately afterwards so that 'at the same time the land is plowed and sown with hopes of a future crop.'[298] Both the system and the wording is so close as to suggest direct plagiarism: one author is tempted to argue that Tull 'borrowed the system lock, stock and barrel from China.'[299] This is more plausible when we consider that Jethro Tull was not an unlettered countryman, but the son of a gentleman farmer who had studied at Oxford, become a barrister at Gray's Inn, and travelled extensively in Europe.

Another agricultural example is the iron mouldboard plough, known as the Rotherham plough. 'Invented' in 1730, this was a lighter and more efficient version of a plough developed in Holland, which was in turn probably based on models brought back from China by Dutch traders. Once again, they were so similar to the Chinese models that it is hard to believe that the European version was not based upon the much earlier Chinese plough. In fact, curved cast-iron mould boards were used in China as early as the Western Han dynasty.[300] One benefit of the iron mouldboard plough was that while European ploughing teams required four, six or even eight animals to draw a plough with a straight wooden mould board, the Chinese could make do with a single animal. Lest we should think these to be cases of special pleading and circumstantial evidence, the case of the rotary winnowing machine, which separates husks and stalks, provides an explicit connection: we know that Chinese winnowing machines were taken to France by Jesuit priests in the early eighteenth century. The 'inventor', Jonas Norberg, who was actually an *improver*, tells us in his own words that three of them taken from Canton to Sweden provided, in his own words, 'the initial idea' for his machine.[301] As Francesca Bray concludes in her review of these influences, 'European mechanized cultivation and sowing methods ultimately derive from the Chinese technology and ideas introduced to Europe in the 17th and 18th centuries.'[302] This, as we saw in the case of Norberg, was well recognised at the time. So much so that a Welsh agricultural improvement society founded in 1753 announced its aim was to make Wales 'as flourishing as China.'[303] Many of the technological improvements in agriculture were therefore borrowed from China, although it is also true that they were soon improved beyond recognition.

In textiles there had been a long tradition of Chinese influence, since the introduction of treadle-operated silk filatures in Italy, first in Sicily and then in Florence, Lucca and Venice, in the early fourteenth century. These were exact copies of Chinese originals invented in 1040. But once again we have learned about such 'inventions' in the second half of the eighteenth century as the spinning jenny of James Hargreaves and the water-frame of Richard Arkwright, which were once again actually improvements on existing models. For technicians working on silk filatures had 'invented all the essential parts for a spinning device' some 500 years earlier, and these inventions for the silk industry were passed on from Italian silk manufacturers and adapted for cotton spinning.[304]

One of the most potent symbols of the Industrial Revolution in Britain is Abraham Darby's iron bridge in Coalbrookdale in Shropshire, which is touted in advertising material in these words: 'Follow in the footsteps of millions of tourists who since 1779 have journeyed here to marvel at the world's first cast-iron bridge.'[305] The great innovation here was the smelting of iron with coke instead of charcoal, a 'secret' that made iron the defining material of the Revolution.[306] In fact the world's first wrought-iron bridge was built in China shortly after the time of Christ, and coke had been used to replace charcoal centuries before that. The blast furnace originated in China, and around the fifth century the Chinese had already developed a 'co-fusion' process in which 'wrought and cast iron were melded together to yield the something in between which was steel.'[307] Once again, the evidence is direct, for Sir William Chambers discussed the Chinese iron bridges in his book *Design of Chinese Buildings* (1757) and even the great bridge and aqueduct builder Thomas Telford knew about them (and knew Chambers personally).[308]

One example is the Pujin Pontoon Bridge in southern Shanxi, over 300yds long, constructed in the Tang dynasty. In 724, the original bamboo cables were replaced by iron chains, and four iron oxen and two cast-iron piers were placed on each end of the bridge to act as anchors, each of the oxen also supported by cast-iron pillars driven into the ground. While this was not a totally iron bridge, it was a great feat of engineering and an 'enormous casting and forging project' carried out 1,000 years before Darby.[309]

Thus Chinese knowledge, first through the agency of the Islamic world and later through that of merchants and the Jesuits, seeped into Europe invisibly, so much so that it is only recently that historians like Joseph Needham, Francesca Bray and John Hobson have been able to make it visible again. What actually happened, as we suggested above, was that this transmission of Chinese inventions led to their *improvement* during the Industrial Revolution with more advanced technology and sources of power. And much of this occurred while according to prevailing wisdom China was *closed* to trade and outside contact.

Empire of Trade

Once again, a closed and yet an open empire. For there has *always* been trade between the mainland and its cultural outposts, and through their agency on to Europe, in spite of imperial edicts. A country with 9,000 miles of often rugged coastline, inhabited in the southeast by a swathe of skilled mariners and congenital traders, cannot prevent commercial osmosis.

The first evidence of sea trade dates from the fifth century BC, although it was limited to coastal trade between the Shandong peninsula and the mouth of the Chang Jiang. Three centuries later, Chinese sailors began trading with what is now Vietnam and it has been suggested that they might have sailed even then as far as the Gulf of Siam and the Malay Peninsula using monsoon winds.[310] Regular trade between China and the coastal regions of the Indian Ocean began during the Tang dynasty (618–907), together with the first small overseas Chinese settlements. This trade was probably conducted at first by Arabic traders, but an increase in knowledge of navigation and charts with information on tides and currents enabled Chinese initiatives during the Song dynasty (960–1279).

The astute Song emperor Gaozong (1127–1162) recognised the importance of the sea for commerce: 'The profits from maritime commerce are very great. If properly managed, they can amount to millions [of strings of cash]. Is this not better than taxing the people?'[311] An increase in the population of the Chang Jiang valley encouraged the inhabitants to look outwards, and higher productivity created a surplus of goods that could be traded. Most of this trade was overland, involving the exchange of livestock, precious stones and exotic products such as frankincense and for silk, spices, porcelain, tea and ginger. But new and larger sea-going junks with iron nails and watertight bulkheads now made longer voyages feasible. Junks could transport up to 600 tons of goods from Fujian to Korea in less than twenty days, but the need to sail to many countries of East Asia with the monsoon winds meant that merchants and crews had to await favourable winds to return home (junks could sail westwards from October to March, and eastwards from April to September). The normal limit was the Malabar Coast of India, but sometimes Song junks travelled as far as the Persian Gulf and the Red Sea. This led to the establishment of permanent outposts in such places as Champa, Tonking, Cambodia, Japan and Korea. At the end of the tenth century there was an 'Office of Monopoly of Trade' in the Northern Song capital at Kaifeng, and an 'Office of Overseas Trade' in Canton, which carried out port inspection and customs duties.[312] Gaozong's words were vindicated, since in the early Northern Song (i.e. around 1000), maritime trade accounted for 2–3 per cent of total government revenues. Sugar was exported to Cambodia, salt to Brunei, and porcelain and books to Japan, while two of the most common imports to China were incense and spices – especially frankincense, pepper and aloes wood.

After the hiatus of the land-bound Yuan dynasty, trade picked up again under the first Ming emperors, Hongwu and Yongle, especially under the impetus of Admiral Zheng's expeditions. Thriving Chinese mercantile communities existed in neighbouring countries, so that Ma Huan could write that in Palembang (in the south of Sumatra, half-way between Singapore and Jakarta), 'many of the people in the country are from Guangdong …, who fled away and now live in this country. The people are very rich and prosperous.'[313] Thanks to these established overseas merchants, and the indomitable mariners, trade between China and its East Asian neighbours prospered throughout the Ming despite Hongwu's prohibition of 1371 and the often-renewed edict of 1424. As one scholar has observed, 'the more restrictive the law was, the more lucrative the trade became.'[314] The route between Fujian and the Ryukyu Islands assumed greater importance in the second half of the fifteenth century, while products from Southeast Asia reached all major cities in China through Canton. Sea-going ships were built illegally in Fujian, smaller than in the days of Zheng He but still adequate for island-hopping in coastal waters. Private, illegal trade between China and Malacca substituted the previous tribute missions, so that Malacca became the leading commercial port in the area and attracted emigrants from Fujian. There were flourishing communities of Chinese in Java and Sumatra, some of them are thought to have numbered in the thousands.[315]

Towards the end of the fifteenth century private merchants – and smugglers from Fujian – increased direct commerce with Southeast Asia, for example with Brunei and northern Borneo, and began to bypass the old route through the Ryukyu

Islands. In one way or another, where there was potential profit there was trade – especially given an ever-increasing demand for pepper, in particular for the imperial court. As one specialist historian has observed, 'the Superintendencies of Maritime Shipping were directed by eunuchs, who were especially interested in obtaining rare imports for the palace.'[316] This in spite of prohibitions and edicts emanating from the palace! It was possible to satisfy this demand because Western appetites for Chinese goods were equally voracious. To give an example of the dimension of this trade, in 1573 two Spanish galleons that had brought cargoes of silver from Mexico returned with a load of Chinese goods 'that included raw silk, silk and cotton textiles, and more than 22,000 pieces of Ming porcelain.'[317]

The numbers are every bit as astonishing as those of Chinese trade today. The size of annual silver receipts by the Ming government at the end of the sixteenth century, for example, has been estimated at 140,000 kilos. But the amounts would certainly be much higher if illegal cargo was added, with some estimates suggesting a total two or three times bigger. When the English corsair Thomas Cavendish captured the galleon *Santa Ana* in 1587 on its return journey from Manila to Acapulco, the cargo of silk, gold, pearls and porcelain on a single ship was worth the equivalent of nearly 60,000 kilos of silver.[318] So extensive was the use of Chinese silks, damasks, brocades and other items that the traditional Mexican female costume of a white blouse and colorful embroidered red and green skirt is known as the 'China Poblana' (Mexican raw silk producers complained about the cheap imports from China much as European and American textile firms do today). As far as porcelain is concerned, already in the 1530s as many as 40–60,000 pieces were arriving in Lisbon each year, with so many other goods that 'the Lisbon elite is said to have been wearing Chinese silks, drinking Chinese tea, and placing special orders for Ming porcelain with Portuguese motifs.'[319] In the first decade of the seventeenth century one Portuguese ship alone carried 1,200 bales of raw silk and 200,000 pieces of porcelain, while the Dutch East India Company could place a special order for 100,000 pieces.[320] So the burghers of Amsterdam also dined off Ming plates.

These numbers, however, should not delude us into thinking that all this porcelain was what we would today call 'museum quality'. There was a huge difference in quality and design between porcelain produced on a small scale according to the standards of technical perfection required by the court, and mass-produced lower quality porcelain intended for export. In fact, there seems to have been a substantial drop in quality as a result of these huge foreign orders, so much so that in 1683 the emperor Kangxi was forced to send a court official named Zang Yingxuan and the painter and calligrapher Liu Yuan to Jingdezhen to reestablish quality production and create new designs worthy of the imperial court. These new products 'accustomed the court to ceramics bodies of unprecedented purity and fineness, glazes in previously unknown colors and textures, and decorative painting, both under the glaze and in overglaze panels, of exquisite exactness.'[321] Some of them also found a ready market in Europe.

How was this possible while China was closed to trade and outside contact? The answer falls into three parts, the first concerning the efficiency of the Chinese junk, the second concerning the lack of effective control of the south-eastern provinces in the Ming and Qing dynasties, and the third concerning the topography of the China Sea.

The junk, a flat-bottomed, high-sterned vessel with square bows and masts carrying lug or square sails often made of matting, at first sight would seem to be unsuitable for sea voyages. But in fact, with a bulkhead to make the hull rigid and provide the watertight compartments mentioned above, and a deep vertical rudder to hold the ship up to windward, it is, in the words of an expert sailor, 'as perfect in its own way as it can well be.'[322] These junks were smaller than those of Zheng He, but usually three-masted. They averaged between 200 and 800 tons in size, the largest ones carrying over 100 crew members, roughly the same number of merchants, and sometimes hundreds of passengers. The junk was ideal as a feeder vessel in the hub system, which involved the transfer of cargoes to ocean-going galleons in Manila and to fast clippers in Hong Kong.

The second part of the answer concerns the relative autonomy of the south-east coastal regions, Guangdong and Fujian. In the section on Lord Macartney's mission, we have seen that in the late eighteenth century trade was only permitted in Canton. But that is a rather reductive 'only'. For 300 years, from tentative trade with the Portuguese and Dutch to the Opium Wars of the mid-nineteenth century (after which Hong Kong assumed the role), enormous quantities of merchandise flowed through the port system of the Pearl River delta, first to Macao at the eastern entrance to the estuary and later to Canton, 65 miles upstream, which was a fluvial port linked to inland trade routes for items such as tea. As long as trade with foreign merchants did not threaten security or peace in southern China, and due taxes were paid to the government in Beijing, these ports enjoyed relative autonomy. The 'Hoppos', or customs superintendents, controlled every aspect of commerce and the foreign presence on behalf of the government; 'compradors', licensed Chinese who provided supplies for ships at anchor and for the voyage home, provided the necessary services while ships were at anchor – often for months, between negotiating fees, clearing holds and laying ballast, purchasing and loading cargo and then awaiting suitable winds for departure. Supercargoes arriving from Europe in early summer could be ready for loading crates of porcelain in October and November, tea in late November or early December, and silk which arrived from Nanjing in mid-December; thus they were ready to depart with the winter north-easterly monsoon winds.[323]

At the time of Lord Macartney's embassy to China, there were around fifty ships each year sailing to Canton, increasing to 300 in the 1840s. This period saw the boom in the opium trade, an 'illegal' cargo carried from Bengal and Malabar on ships bearing the British flag, loaded onto river-boats downstream from Canton and taken into the city with the connivance of Qing officials. The annual trade ranged from 2,000 chests at the time of Macartney's arrival to around 4,600 chests (of one picul each, roughly 66 kilos) in 1828.[324] Profits in silver from this trade, and from illegal rice imports from Manila and Batavia, were used by the East India Company to purchase tea for export to Britain. Other illegal traffic included gold and illegal silk (i.e. quantities over the official quota). By the 1830s, there were 'almost as many smuggling ships anchoring each year at Lintin Island and other harbours in the delta as there were legitimate ships going upriver to Whampoa'[325] (Whampoa was the official port for foreign ships, some 20 miles downstream from Canton). The legal trade was equally impressive. Surviving records show that, in 1845, 327 ships carried nearly 150,000 tons of cargo, mainly porcelain and tea, from China to Europe.[326]

Fujian was equally important, but in a surreptitious way since the greater part of its trade was illegal. It is a large province with a long and rugged coastline, offering excellent harbours for three of China's major southern trading ports, Amoy (now Xiamen), Zhangzhou, and Fuzhou, and many smaller harbours used by pirates. These ports grew with the growth and economic importance of Japan in the seventeenth century, and under the influence of a powerful family, the Zheng, one of whose scions was Zheng Chenggong, known to Westerners as Coxinga. In the 1650s, Coxinga was 'the master not only of a flourishing network of trade with Japan, Dutch Taiwan, Manila, and many Southeast Asian ports but also of a network of revenue-producing estates and commercial nodes on the mainland.'[327] In fact the only way the Qing could control illegal trade from this coastline was by implementing the so-called 'fortify the walls and empty the fields' policy, in force from 1660–66.[328] This entailed evacuating a strip of around 30 *li* in width (around 7 miles) along the coastline, removing the population and devastating homes and crops to prevent pirates and illegal traders from obtaining supplies and to render trade difficult. One unintended consequence was to drive coastal inhabitants onto the sea, so that Fujian became from the beginning one of the great providers of the emigrants who became the Overseas Chinese.

The third part of the answer concerns the convenient disposition of islands in the East China Sea and South China Sea, which favoured the illegal activities of smugglers (and pirates) along the Fujian coastline and facilitated navigation by smaller ships. By using the techniques of coasting and island-hopping, much of the China Sea was open to the junk captains: from Amoy it was two days' sail to Taiwan and with good winds only three days onward to Manila. One of the most contested places in this story are the islands known as the Pescadores (in Chinese, *Penghu*), situated in the Taiwan Strait between the western coast of Taiwan and China. Named by the Portuguese in the sixteenth century, this group of 'fishermen's islands' consists of sixty-four islands with a total area of around 50 square miles. Unimportant in themselves, they acted as a vital half-way point for junks crossing the Taiwan Strait, and offered refuge from tropical storms. The Ryukyu Islands (for the Chinese, *Liu-Ch'iu*), a string consisting of fifty-five volcanic or coral islands stretching in a 700-mile arc from the north of Taiwan to the southern Japanese island of Kysushu, were equally useful. Originally an independent kingdom, the Ryukyus were disputed by China and Japan for centuries until becoming part of Japan in 1879. Given this precarious status, it comes as no surprise that the kingdom maintained ambivalent relations with its two powerful neighbours. In the words of an eighteenth-century Japanese scholar, this kingdom 'subjects herself to both countries and pays tribute to both. She uses the Japanese calendar when she deals with Japan, and the Chinese calendar when she contacts China.' In another ambiguous formulation, the ruling body in Okinawa once said that it regarded China as a father and Japan as a mother.[329] More practically, for centuries the chain acted as stepping-stones for junks plying trade between China and Japan, together with the Senkaku Islands at the southern end. This latter group, known in Chinese as the Diaoyu Islands and to nineteenth-century British seamen as the Pinnacle Islands, acted as the first stepping-stone on the route from Taiwan to Japan.

Further south, in the South China Sea, are the much larger island groups known as the Paracel Islands and the Spratly Islands. The Paracels consist of fifteen islets and a dozen or so reefs and banks, roughly equidistant from Hainan in the north and Vietnam to the west. Although each is tiny, the largest being just over 1 mile long and 700yds wide, their location makes them an ideal reference point and provides potentially safe anchorage in storms on the voyage south from Hainan. Chinese maps of the thirteenth century show them, and China claims that they have been used in navigation for over 2,000 years.[330] A report published in 1928 goes as far as to claim them as China's 'southernmost territory.'[331] The Spratly Islands is a larger group of more than 100 islands, reefs and banks, as many as twelve distinct sub-groups stretched over 600 miles from north to south.[332] Old Chinese maps show these islands too, and they made an obvious point of reference for junks sailing south-east to Malaysia and to Palawan Island, the southernmost extension of the Philippines. Graphic names like Mischief Reef and Fiery Cross Reef suggests the hazards of navigation in the past, but this archipelago could hardly be avoided since it sits on the main ocean route from China to the south and is today traversed by as many as 300 ships a day.

In a sense, all these islands in the East China Sea and South China Sea were an extension of empire, and, as we shall see in Chapter 11, with new potential value deriving from fishing rights and seabed exploration for oil and gas, they are today subject to territorial disputes between China and her neighbours, especially Japan, Vietnam, Malaysia and the Philippines. In the past they were instrumental to trade, and therefore to China's economic success. Nearly a century ago, B.L. Putnam Weale suggested that the empire was essentially a financial mechanism that bound together the various ethnic, racial and geographical components into a single whole: 'Money alone formed the bond of union; so long as questions of taxation were not involved, Peking was as far removed from daily life as the planet Mars.'[333] This was more true for Fujian and the offshore islands than anywhere else in the empire, for they maintained the spirit of *River Elegy* ante litteram and were crucial to the growth and survival of the invisible empire. It remains true today, in 100 small but prosperous cities and towns on the south-eastern coast, such as Wenzhou, a little north of Fujian but part of the same cultural area. Entrepreneurs face outwards to their market in Europe or America, circumventing regulations and avoiding taxes as much as possible; in their spare time they play mahjong or cards with their friends, speaking a local dialect, which to the rulers in Beijing is incomprehensible.

Yet they are indisputably Chinese.

Empire of Culture: Chinoiserie

The novelty of Chinese aesthetic values, together with real knowledge available for the first time in well-informed books about the country and its culture, generated widespread enthusiasm for Chinese products in the eighteenth century and spawned the phenomenon known as *chinoiserie*.

In 1687, there appeared a volume of writings by Confucius edited by Jesuit scholars, the *Confucius Sinarum Philosophus,* which was to have particular influence. The reason for its profound impact on writers and philosophers of the Enlightenment is evident from the following assertions in the Preface: 'One might say that the moral system of this philosopher is infinitely sublime, but that it is at the same time simple, sensible and drawn from the purest sources of natural reason. Never has Reason, deprived of divine Revelation, appeared so well developed nor with so much power.'[334]

This volume contained the first European translations (into Latin) of three of the Confucian Classics, *Daxue* (the Great Learning), *Zhongyong* (the Mean) and *Lunyu* (the Analects), under the title of 'The Learning of the Chinese' (*Scientiae Sinicae*), together with an eight-page biography of Confucius and a portrait of the philosopher in the library of the Imperial Academy surrounded by shelves of books, including his own works. This was followed by a detailed table with the names of the Chinese emperors. Although the implicit purpose of this publication was to gain support for Jesuit activities in China,[335] its success went well beyond such limited ambitions. The works of Confucius were admired by the philosopher Gottfried

Leibniz (1646–1716), then at the height of his powers and Europe-wide reputation, who in a letter referred to the 'excellent thoughts and maxims.'[336] They were also reviewed in learned journals in several languages. During the next century many Europeans, including such influential figures as Voltaire (b.1694), David Hume (b.1711) and Adam Smith (b.1723), became intensely curious about China, so much so that 'they formed a virtual love affair with the world of rococo'.[337] This was fertile ground indeed.

Three years earlier, one of the four editors of the *Confucius*, Philippe Couplet (1623–93), had completed and polished the manuscript as he travelled home from China to Mechlin, in Belgium. He took with him a young Chinese convert from Nanjing called Shen Fuzong, who after baptism was known as Michael Alphonsus Shen. On the way south from Couplet's hometown to Rome, they stopped in Paris and Versailles, where 'Michael Shen' was introduced to King Louis XIV. On the first meeting, the king simply stopped and stared, just as the Chinese in more remote areas still do on seeing Caucasian features; on the second meeting he seems to have been astonished by Shen's attempted performance of nine kowtows, and ordered him to stop such excesses after three or four.[338] The next day there was a more curious incident with one of the first recorded uses of chopsticks in Europe, described by Pieter Thomas Van Hamme, a Flemish Jesuit who accompanied the party in Europe:

> In the presence of all those assembled, the king had M. Shen recite loudly in Chinese the *Pater Noster*, the *Ave Maria*, and the *Credo*. The day before, Madame la Dauphinesse had seen the little ivory chopsticks which M. Shen used to eat with. So she asked the king to watch him eat, and immediately a golden plate with food was ordered, and Michael stood at the table beside His Majesty and demonstrated eating with chopsticks.[339]

We can only imagine how often this ritual, or show, was performed for the curious as Michael continued his journey south through Lyons, Turin, Milan and Bologna, for as late as the 1830s New Yorkers paid to watch a Chinese woman named Afong Moy eat with chopsticks.[340] While in Rome, Michael met Queen Christina of Sweden, who asked him about tea leaves and how tea was drunk in China, and he provided a demonstration with porcelain cups and 'suitable instruments'.[341] The mere presence of this exotic convert helped to stimulate interest in China in the cities he visited. Partly as a result of the meeting at Versailles, Louis XIV, to whom the *Confucius Sinarum Philosophus* was dedicated, was persuaded to finance a group of Jesuit scientists and establish a French mission in China.[342]

In the spring of 1687, Michael Shen visited London. King James II was also fascinated by the young man during an audience at St James' Palace, and asked his court painter Sir Godfrey Kneller (1646–1723) to paint an oil portrait in Chinese dress that he could hang in his private bedchamber; known as 'The Chinese Convert', this delightful painting is now in the Royal Collection at Windsor Castle.[343] The impact of this visit to England was significant in other ways. Michael assisted the celebrated orientalist Thomas Hyde (1636–1703), then Librarian of the Bodleian, both in cataloguing Chinese works and in studying the language. Later, when King James was visiting Hyde in Oxford, he inadvertently revealed for us the feature of Michael that most intrigued him when he observed: 'He was a little blinking fellow, was he not?'[344] Then the king asked Hyde about the *Confucius Sinarum Philosophus*, and was satisfied to learn that there was a copy in the Bodleian.

Fashion followed the court, and the interest of King James implied a royal stamp of approval on the new taste for things Chinese. The urbane English gentleman began to imitate his earlier Portuguese counterparts, in particular in his interest in what became known as chinoiserie, ranging from tea-drinking to wallpaper decorations, and from garden design to collecting porcelain. Some had begun earlier, of course: in 1660, just three years after it is thought to have been introduced to England after Holland and France,[345] after a political discussion with three friends Samuel Pepys (1633–1703) wrote in his *Diary*: 'I did send for a cup of tee (a China drink) of which I never had drank before, and went away.'[346] This was apparently because he believed it would help his wife's cough. A few years later he recorded seeing goldfish at a friend's home: 'Thence home and to see my Lady Pen, where my wife and I were shown a fine rarity: of fishes kept in a glass of water, that will live so for ever; and finely marked they are, being foreign.'[347] But Pepys was an intimate of courtiers and at the heart of fashionable London life, as Secretary to the Admiralty under both Charles II and James II, so it was natural that he should be a precursor. In the eighteenth century, the fashion for things Chinese took Europe by storm.

Chinoiserie had an immense and lasting influence on interior design, furniture, pottery, textiles and wallpaper. The worlds of the Confucian gentleman scholar and the English country gentleman came together in William Halfpenny's *Rural Architecture in the Chinese Taste*, published in four parts from 1750, and Thomas Chippendale's *The Gentleman and Cabinet Maker's Director*, one of the most influential works on furniture design ever compiled and deeply influenced by Chinese designs, published in 1754. The latter offered a new decorative style, with sophisticated lacquers and veneers, which became known as 'Chinese Chippendale' or the 'Director Style'. But Chinese architectural forms were not only transplanted into furniture pattern books. They gradually invaded the new country houses that were being built in the Neo-Palladian style as it became fashionable to include a 'Chinese Room'. These were hung with imported Chinese or Chinese-style wallpaper, furnished with lacquer-ware and 'Chinese Chippendale' desks, tables and chairs and decorated with porcelain. Claydon House, in Buckinghamshire, built by the 2nd Lord Verney in 1768, is one of the most famous surviving examples and offers a glimpse of taste at the heyday of Chinoiserie interiors. Most were simpler than the Claydon House room, sometimes painted imperial yellow, with a few

Chinese-style landscapes and some fine porcelain, and became an integral part of the gentleman's lifestyle.

There was also a fashion for Chinese gardens and garden ornaments as a reaction set in against the rigid symmetry of classical French-style gardens. One fine example may be seen at Shugborough Hall in Staffordshire, seat of the Earls of Lichfield, whose family name is Anson. The park was laid out in 1747 with several Chinese buildings by their ancestor Admiral George Anson (1697–1762), who had recently completed a circumnavigation of the globe in his flagship HMS *Centurion*. During that voyage, the Admiral stopped for five months in Macau; then, after sailing briefly to the Philippines, also spent a summer beneath the walls of Canton, to which he was allowed to make one visit, before returning to England with a huge collection of Chinese objects. The 'Blue Drawing Room' contains the majority of Anson's Chinese collections, while the 'Verandah Room' boasts a 208-piece eighteenth-century dinner service made to commemorate his circumnavigation. In the gardens, a Chinese pavilion and red bridge show how an English gentleman sought to reproduce the scenes of his voyages overseas.

These Chinese rooms were always crammed with porcelain objects, preferably Ming, which had become synonymous with great wealth. But there were plenty of copies for the less wealthy. Just as the Chinese today copy Western styles and brands, so did Europeans in the past freely copy Chinese styles (for there were no Intellectual Property Rights in those days). Imitation blue-coloured porcelain known as 'Medici' was made in Florence as early as 1580, and in Pisa there was a production of blue, floral-patterned porcelain based on Yuan pottery from Jingdezhen. Tin-glazed pottery was manufactured at Delft in Holland from the early seventeenth century, and early ceramic wares at Meissen in Germany also copied Chinese shapes for dishes, vases and tea wares. But the real impact of Ming began when the ban on direct trade with foreign countries was lifted in 1683. Wider availability, and lower prices, made Chinese porcelain fashionable in the homes of the gentry as well as those of the wealthier aristocracy and rich merchants who had been collecting for some time. Not only was decorated porcelain imported. Ming dynasty plain white porcelain known as *blanc-de-Chine*, which was held in great esteem, was imported into Europe to be hand-painted with scenes inspired by French and Italian landscape artists. At the same time, several English factories, notably in Plymouth and Bristol in the 1770s, made porcelain that for a non-expert was almost indistinguishable from the Chinese original.

But the most celebrated Chinese feature of all, which inspired innumerable imitations, was the pagoda built at Kew Gardens by William Chambers (1723–96). Chambers was born in Sweden of Scottish parentage in 1723 and then educated in England. He returned to Sweden at the age of sixteen to join the Swedish East India Company, with which he travelled to India and China for nine years. On one occasion he stayed in Canton for several months and became interested in Chinese architecture, making architectural drawings of traditional buildings. Inspired by his Chinese experience, at the age of twenty-six Chambers decided to further his studies and become an architect. He studied in Paris and Rome, and on returning to England in 1757 published his Canton drawings in book form as *Designs of Chinese Buildings*. The Kew pagoda, construction of which began in the summer of 1761, represented his studies and theories in synthesis. Its ten-storey octagonal structure, reaching a height of nearly 50 metres, was at that time the most accurate imitation of a Chinese building in Europe. Originally, the roofs were covered with varnished iron plates, with an iron dragon sitting at each edge. Each of the eighty dragons was covered in coloured glass and had a bell in its mouth. The Pagoda was opened to the public in the 1870s, a vitally important fact in the dissemination of Chinese influences because for the rest of the century any middle-class or gentry member of the public could visit the pagoda on one day each week.

Thus, at first slowly and then with greater impetus, from around 1680 to the end of the nineteenth century, Chinese motives, forms, colours and taste exercised the role of cultural ambassadors for the invisible empire.

Empire of Food

The Chinese are often surprised to see that foreigners can eat efficiently with chopsticks, but of course theirs is the most globalised of all cuisines and the use of chopsticks has grown with the spread of Chinese restaurants, especially in recent years with those seeking to provide 'authentic' Chinese food. This process has been longer than we might imagine, from the first 'invisible' invasion of tea in the seventeenth century to the creation of Chinatowns in London and San Francisco in the nineteenth century, from thirty-six restaurants in Britain, for example, in the 1950s to over 8,000 today.[348] The food, red lanterns, porcelain spoons and puzzled waiter faces all indicate the presence of an invisible empire.

So do the famous dishes: dim sun, chop suey, chow mein, spring rolls, sweet and sour pork, which all derive from Cantonese food – so that a visitor on his first trip to Shanghai or Beijing is often disappointed to see that there are no spring rolls or prawn crackers on the menu. Early Chinese food in San Francisco was described as 'mostly curries, hashes and fricassee',[349] in which the lack of distinguishable ingredients presumably helped the formation of prejudices. Iris Chang relates a well-known legend in which some drunken clients in San Francisco were served a concocted mixture of leftovers of fried vegetables, meat and gravy, which the restaurateur called 'chop suey' (from Putonghua *za sui*, 'bits and pieces', pronounced in Cantonese as *cha sui*). Another story relates that it was linked to the visit of a senior Chinese official to New York in 1896.[350] In either case, it became known as an invented Chinese-American dish. But Lynn Pan points out that that chop suey is a bona fide Chinese dish based on chicken livers fried with mushrooms, bean sprouts and pig's tripe, which was gradually modified to suit American taste. In any case, she observes, it represents an authentic Chinese tendency to avoid waste, and the dish soon became popular. She even reports a 1940s' sign in Shanghai offering 'Genuine American Chop Suey'.[351] In fact, however, the early prejudices were soon overcome, since food imports from China were such that in the 1860s duties on foodstuffs reached half a million dollars annually.[352]

The first Chinese restaurants in the West frequented by non-Chinese were in the United States: in 1918, there were in New York alone fifty-seven restaurants of which more than half were outside Chinatown, thus also catering to non-Chinese customers; in San Francisco five years later there were twenty-eight, some of them touted as attractions for native tourists in Chinatown.[353] Most major cities had Chinese restaurants by the 1930s, some of them already selling a combination of Chinese and Western food in a sign that they were adapting to the new customers, and by 1941 there were around 700 in New York. In Britain, apart from a temporary restaurant built for the 1884 Health Exhibition in London, which served delicacies like bird's nest soup, sharks' fins, lotus roots, lychees and Shaoxing wine to an elite public, the Tanhua Lou in Piccadilly set the fashion in the early 1920s. A decade later, the Ly On in Wardour Street, still the site of many Chinese restaurants, became popular with non-Chinese Londoners. In Cambridge in the late 1930s there was a cheap and friendly restaurant popular with students called the Blue Barn, which served only chop suey, chow mein and fried rice.[354]

The real boom came after the Second World War, partly because of the new influx of Chinese immigration and partly as a consequence of returning soldiers from the Far East having acquired a taste for oriental food (including, of course, Indian food). A little later, as the result of immigration from Hong Kong before the Commonwealth Immigrants Act became law in 1962, the number of Chinese restaurants in London shot up from 300 to 800.[355] Gradually, Chinatowns became tourist attractions, gentrified streets in once poor inner-city areas like Gerrard Street in London with Chinese gateways, pavilions and postcards. At the same time, the Chinese takeaway became as much a part of the urban landscape as fish and chip shops or milk bars, and Chinese supermarkets selling both Chinese and indigenous products became common in America and Britain.

The Chinese were shrewd enough to adapt their cuisine to local tastes, one of the best examples of which is the ubiquitous 'Chinese ravioli' in restaurants in Italy, adapting the northern *jiaozi* to Italian taste and shape and serving them as a first course. Over the next two decades there was a futher change as these businesses evolved from cheap chop suey houses to restaurants selling regional cuisines, mainly that of Guangzhou for obvious reasons, but also the distinctive cuisines of Beijing, Shanghai and Sichuan. The partial opening of China after 1972, and greater change after 1978, increased knowledge both of the country and of its food, and profited from the more general interest in ethnic food in the same decade.

In 1983, the *Yang Sing* restaurant in Manchester won the annual award of the Good Food Guide,[356] an event that brought Chinese restaurants and dim sun into the mainstream of British dining. Chinese restaurateurs began to move decidedly upmarket. To take London as an example, *Yming*, located just outside Chinatown in Greek Street, began a trend in the mid-1990s towards more elegant restaurants with a wider range of dishes from beyond Guangdong, and a champagne menu that marked its shift of gear. The more elite area of Mayfair now boasts several high-quality Chinese restaurants, such as *China Tang*, in the Dorchester Hotel, and *Kai*, in Audley Street. In 2003, the London restaurant *Hakkasan* – well away from Chinatown in the area known as Fitzrovia – was awarded the ultimate Western respectability of a Michelin star, usually given to French and Italian restaurants; in this case, the name of the restaurant clearly betrays its origins, as does its speciality dish, dim sun. Two years later *Yauatcha*, in Soho, with the same owner and the same chef as *Hakkasan*, also gained a Michelin star.

Another index of the fashionability of Chinese cuisine, and the way in which it can be fine-tuned to the trend of the moment, may be seen in the huge range of specialised cookery books published in Britain. To take a random selection of titles without value judgements, they range from general books like *The Complete Chinese Cookbook* by Jacki Passmore and Daniel P. Reid (1998) to celebrity cookbooks like Ken Hom's *Quick Wok: The Fastest Food in the East* (2003) and works on regional cuisine such as *Land of Plenty: A Treasury of Authentic Sichuan Cooking* by Fuchsia Dunlop (2003). But they go beyond mere cooking and eating, as in the wordy *Low-fat No-fat Chinese Cooking: Over 150 Low-fat and No-fat Chinese and Far Eastern Recipes for Tempting, Tasty and Healthy Eating* by Maggie Pannell and Jenni Fleetwood (2006), to health, as in *The Healing Cuisine of China: 300 Recipes for Vibrant Health and Longevity* by Zhuo Zhao, George Ellis, and Zhuo Zhao (1998). Then, last of all for the serious foodie, there are books on culture such as *Food Culture in China*, by Jacqueline M. Newman (2004). This is a stunning demonstration of the power of the invisible empire, compared to only twenty or thirty years ago when books on Chinese cooking were rare: just over twenty books had been published in English throughout the world in 1966.[357]

It is also fascinating to observe how the spread of Chinese cuisine in the West mirrors the changes in mainland China and the parallel extension of an invisible empire. The first chefs followed the break-up of the Qing empire, bringing a mainly Cantonese and cheap version of Chinese food with the earliest immigrants. There was an escalation in the number of restaurants, and of their quality, in the 1960s as restaurateurs fled from Hong Kong. Then, after the reforms of 1978, a further impulse that brought increased awareness of regional China and the introduction of diverse cuisines. In the 1990s, as China grew wealthy and bilateral trade accelerated, the restaurants moved upmarket in terms of locale and food quality, and away from the Chinatowns. Now, in the first decade of the twenty-first century they begin to accumulate Michelin stars, which represent culinary recognition akin to that of China's acceptance into the world community.

For Chinese cuisine has become part of our lives in an almost imperceptible – that is to say, *invisible* – way. At the turn of the Millennium, a survey found that 59 per cent of British people counted Chinese cuisine as 'among their favourites', and as many as 65 per cent of households owned a wok.[358] At about the same time, the then British Foreign Secretary, Robin Cook, declared *chicken tikka massala* to be the 'true British national dish'.[359] In the twenty-first century, that dish will probably be surpassed in popularity by pot noodles.

The Overseas Chinese

The foot-soldiers of the invisible empire have always been the Overseas Chinese. As a consequence of the trends outlined in the previous chapter, today, according to a database maintained by Ohio University Library, there are 34 million people constituting what we have described as the invisible Chinese Empire,[360] while some estimates run to 55 million[361] (see Map 2, Appendix 1). Even the lowest of these figures would make the 'overseas Chinese community' the thirty-third largest country in the world by population, with more people than Canada and Morocco and just less than Argentina and Poland. Moreover, since so many are engaged in commerce, the relative weight of the overseas Chinese in countries like Thailand or Malaysia is far greater than their physical number. More strikingly, while the author of *The Bamboo Network* could write in 1995 of the vibrant Chinese business activities in Hong Kong, Taipei, Singapore, Bangkok, Kuala Lumpur, Jakarta, Manila and Saigon,[362] now the Taiwanese have shifted operations and often themselves to Shanghai, which boasts its own Taiwanese quarter, while the businessmen of Hong Kong commute to Shenzhen and the manufacturing agglomeration of the Pearl River Delta.

But the effects of sustained economic growth reach beyond China itself. Apart from the consolidated and historical communities of East Asia, the USA and countries like Australia and Britain, there has been an explosion of investment and emigration to Africa, where, to take Zambia as an example, there has been an increase in the Chinese population of Lusaka from around 3,000 in the mid-1990s to around 30,000 today. A further change is the emerging power of Chinese influence in, say, the traditional Tuscan textile manufacturing cluster of Prato, where for years now the local banks have had bilingual signs. In Prato, there were fifty-three Chinese-owned companies exporting fashion garments to France and Germany in 2004, with combined annual revenues of 56 million.[363] The Chinese now represent around 20 per cent of the population, with bars, tobacconists, traditional Italian grocery shops along the main street now owned by families that have reinvested their earnings from the textile industry.

In the older emigrant destinations, there has been a substantial social and educational shift. No longer are Chinese immigrants confined to manual labour as cooks and laundrymen, since they tend to be highly educated and aspirationally middle class. There is a growing army of academic researchers in English-speaking universities. An 'Analysis of Overseas Chinese S&T Talent', published in a Chinese journal in 1999, estimated that there were then already 600,000 scientists and technicians working around the world, of whom 45,000 were in the United States.[364] Many are today in key positions in universities and research institutes, and by a process that has been described as 'flexible circulation' effectively act as a two-way channel for the long arm of the invisible empire, returning to China regularly as visiting professors, advisors and consultants even when they choose not to return permanently. The process is fuelled by still-increasing numbers of students travelling abroad for advanced education, especially to the US and Britain – where there are currently nearly 60,000 Chinese students in institutions of higher education. This phenomenon is also an excellent example of what has been called a 'beneficial brain drain', in which 'the return migration of "brains" who have acquired new skills abroad (possibly at foreign taxpayers' expense)' is added to the more traditional advantage of cash remittances.[365]

Once Chinese, always Chinese: loyal, the country hopes, to their *zǔguó*, or 'motherland'. There are few countries where race, culture, nation and personal identity are so profoundly integrated, and none as large as China (although Frank Dikötter has compared the term 'Chinese' to the Victorian notion of 'Anglo-Saxon' in the sense of a race, language and culture dispersed throughout the world).[366] It is obviously true that in such a huge country there are significant regional differences, between, for example, in caricature terms, rice-eating southerners and noodle-eating northerners. In his book *My Country and My People* (1935), Lin Yutang wrote of the northerners as 'acclimatized to simple thinking and hard living', of those south of the Chang Jiang as 'inured to ease and culture and sophistication', of the enterprising natives of Guangdong 'where people eat like men and work like men', and of the 'loud-swearing and intrigue-loving' people of Hubei who 'think pepper not hot enough to eat until they have fried it in oil.'[367] But once abroad, they are all Chinese – and famously indistinguishable for most Westerners.

The most obvious physical manifestation of this fact is the large number of Chinatowns. The first evolved in Manila in the 1580s, when there were said to have been 10,000 Chinese residents, compared to 2,000 Spaniards. Already in 1590 the 'domination of local trade and artisanal production by the Chinese was striking, and included everything from breadbaking to book-binding, tavern-keeping, and stone-masonry.'[368] Other early Chinatowns were *Nankinmachi* in Nagasaki and Yaowarat Road in Bangkok, both over 200 years old. Later, the model was adopted in San Francisco and the East End district of Limehouse in London, although strictly speaking these Chinatowns were really 'Cantontowns'. The *putonghua* word for Chinatown, *Tángrénji*, meaning '*Tang* people streets', was used because the Cantonese, who make up a large proportion of immigrants, were only fully brought under imperial control under the Tang dynasty; the Cantonese themselves speak of a *Tong yan fau*, meaning 'Tang people town'. Since early arrivals came mainly from Guangdong and Fujian, Cantonese was the most commonly used language and cooking style. It is appropriate that the present Chinatown in San Francisco was once known more accurately as 'little Canton'.[369]

In the past, there were two commonly used words for emigrants: the *huashang*, or trader, and the *huagong*, or labourer. To these were added the negative back-formation *kuli*, from 'coolie', and *huaqiao*, or sojourner, meaning originally someone who works abroad for a temporary or indefinite period.[370] The category of sojourners included the majority of the maritime traders who fled from the Mongol conquest, and later from the Manchu trading restrictions, to set up home in the neighbouring countries of Southeast Asia. It also included pirates, for many of the earliest 'emigrants' were perceived as rebels or political criminals. Thus in 1712, the emperor Kangxi, in a continuation of Ming policies, ordered that 'those who stayed overseas permanently are liable to capital punishment, and will be extradited from foreign countries by the provincial governors for prompt beheading.' Fifteen years later, his son the emperor Yongzheng asserted not only that 'I believe that the majority of those who go overseas are undesirable elements', but that the longer they were allowed to stay abroad the more undesirable they would become.[371] Similar fears of emigrants, whose loyalty to the *zǔguó* was potentially tarnished by contact with outsiders, persisted at least until the 1970s.

Today, *huáqiáo* is normally used of overseas Chinese who were born in China, and *huáyì* of someone of Chinese ancestry, who is considered an 'overseas Chinese' even if he or she has never been to China and does not know the language (which is the case of many second- and third-generation family members). A more explicit popular expression is *qiaobao*, or 'bridge compatriots'. But in the government's view all are Overseas Chinese, and all have an unspecified but somehow precise moral duty to the 'motherland' regardless of their private beliefs or background. Thus, while British emigrants or their children eventually became American or Australian citizens, and their descendents are proud to call themselves American or Australian, the umbilical link of a Chinese emigrant to the 'motherland' is never broken.

One noticeable feature of Chinese emigration has always been the remarkable success rate of emigrants, especially those from Fujian and Guangdong, which confirms another of Lin Yutang's generalisations, that 'the northern is essentially a conqueror and the southerner is essentially a trader.'[372] The fact that the Cantonese will eat anything is proverbial, but so is another saying that the *Wenzhouren*, or people of Wenzhou (just a little north of Fujian), will make money from any business enterprise they choose to set up. A missionary of the nineteenth century with a profound knowledge of the Chinese wrote that it was 'certainly most fortunate for the peace of mind of that portion of mankind which is not Chinese, that this people does not as a whole take to emigration on a large scale.'[373] In fact those who did emigrate at that time came from a relatively small area, and mainly from four river deltas, two in Fujian and two in Guangdong: from north to south that of the Min River at Fuzhou (known to Westerners as Foochow), that of the Jiulong River at Xiamen (Amoy), the Han River, which rises in Fujian but reaches the sea at Shantou (Swatow), and the Pearl River at Guangzhou (Canton).

The Hakka people, many of whom came from this area and form significant communities in Hong Kong, Singapore, Taiwan and Bangkok, have contributed immensely to the overseas community. Their very identity hints at their prime vocation, for the *Putonghua* name, *kejia*, means 'guest family',[374] a reference to the fact that although they have a strong ethnic background they do not belong to any particular city, as the Cantonese obviously belong to Canton. This powerful ethnic group has had enormous influence on Chinese history, both at home and overseas, and includes such influential men as Mao's companion and the founder of the PLA, Zhu De, Lee Kuan Yew in Singapore, and more recent political figures such as former General Secretary of the Communist Party Hu Yaobang and the former premier Li Peng. Another prominent Hakka was the entrepreneur Charlie Soong, two of whose daughters married Sun Yat-sen and Chiang Kai-shek, with more recent exemplars being the shoe designer Jimmy Choo, the founder of the London restaurant Hakkasan, Alan Yau, and the former prime minister of Thailand and present owner of Manchester City football club, Thaksin Shinawatra. Can it be a coincidence that the man responsible for the recent reforms and opening up of China's economy, the man who understood *River Elegy*'s message better than most of his fellow cadres, was the most prominent Hakka of all, Deng Xiao Ping?

But apart from the Hakkas, within a distance of around 230 miles there are four mutually unintelligible languages with quite distinct cultures, which formed separate communities of overseas Chinese. In particular the ferociously loyal Teochiu speakers have common ancestors in just seven villages near Shantou and maintain a close and closed network throughout the world. This extended clan of several million is the most successful of all overseas communities, constituting the majority Chinese population in Thailand and the second largest group in Canada, Hong Kong, Malaysia, Singapore, the United States and Vietnam.[375] Relationships are based on absolute trust, which implies much more than simple membership of the community by birth or ancestry (an anthropologist who worked in rural Guangdong in the 1980s noted that the people there 'excel in cooperative ventures that, by dint of hard work, mutual trust, and faith in the future, almost invariably succeed').[376] The second wealthiest group is that of the Hokkien speakers from Xiamen, who are in the majority in Indonesia, Malaysia, Singapore, Taiwan and the Philippines. The Chinese government is well aware of this. Whenever we read of Deng's celebrated 'southern tour' of 1992, where he travelled to legitimise and bolster the new capitalism and 'get rich' philosophy, the main object of attention is the Special Economic Zone at Shenzhen. But from the start there were four such Special Economic Zones, and it is noteworthy that two of the others were at Xiamen and Shantou, while the fourth at Zhuhai bears even greater historical resonances in standing on the Pearl River just north of Macao.[377] Each of them had ancient connections with piracy, opium and of course Overseas Chinese financial networks (Fuzhou and Guangzhou were included in the ports accorded the privilege of special trade zones). Investments flowed in immediately, often to the ancestral hometown of the investor.

The emigrant set out to make his fortune. He therefore concentrated on businesses that required a low capital input relative to labour and built a business that was always labour-dependent. He exploited the labour pool available in his immediate family, facilitated by the fact that often he lived in or above the premises of business. The original businesses were, therefore, 'low capital, low-skilled, owner-operated, family-based' enterprises,[378] often dealing in specialised goods and offering services to ethnic niche markets. The grocer's shop, family restaurant and textile sweat-shop all fall into this category. Each could be driven to success like a force-fed goose by endless working hours, but each also offered the possibility to build larger enterprises. The hard-working nature of the Chinese that spurred this progression is proverbial. An early twentieth-century American traveller to China wrote of 'toil that knows no beginning, for it begins before the toilers have begun to think; toil that never ceases, for without it there would be an end to life; toil that would be heroic were it not utterly unconscious of itself.'[379] This toil was supported by Confucian values, which emphasised socialisation within the family unit, sobriety, education and the acquisition of skills. They also provided a strong moral base, inculcating a tendency to help the group, the acceptance of hierarchical rules, and a sense of complementarity in relationships, which enhances perceptions of fairness and equity.[380] It is clear that such a strong cultural base and networks favoured success, as compared with the individual and competitive nature of traders from other cultures working far from home. Links with the hometown reinforced the network, completing a virtuous circle with fresh blood from new emigrants. We often hear of the way in which a chance meeting, on a plane or in a holiday resort, or on a home visit, can be enough to ignite a new business relationship on the basis of a profound but, until that instant, invisible relationship. A certain degree of trust is instant. These relationships always exist in potential, but remain invisible until serendipity or a business opportunity draws them out into the open. But they are vitally important, since the underpinning of trust enables the entrepreneur to act decisively when the opportunity occurs without the need for prolonged due diligence procedures or permission from a distant corporate headquarters.

If we add together the population of Mainland China to the millions of overseas Chinese, and around 50 million unregistered children and farmers on the mainland, and bear in mind the relative importance of the overseas Chinese in both East Asia and countries such as America, this virtual economic area comprehends something like 2 billion human beings, fully one third of the global population. Moreover, the role of the Overseas Chinese has been vital in the decades since the reopening of trade in 1978 in terms of growing nationalism. For, in the words of Prasenjit Duara, 'the intensification of economic ties with overseas Han Chinese from other nation-states in East and Southeast Asia has led to a renewed confidence in Han ethnicity.'[381] This has been seen first in Hong Kong, and in the past two or three years in Taiwan.

The greater the invisible web, the greater the strength of the spider at the centre. Economic growth is both global and exponential. It has been argued that in the world after nation-states the world economy will be dominated by 'global tribes', defined as 'cultural groups whose members are geographically dispersed, maintain worldwide business and cultural networks, and share a strong sense of a common origin as well as important values on the primacy of science and knowledge in general'.[382] If this is the case, then the Global Tribe of Chinese will dominate the world economy.

The Asian Empire

In countries where assimilation and inter-marriage were easier, the Chinese communities have had more success in entering mainstream politics, so that Thailand has had two Prime Ministers of Chinese origin, Chaun Leekpai (1992–5; 1997–2001) and Thaksin Shinawatra (2001–6), Myanmar a dictatorial head of state in Ne Win (1962–88), while the family of Lee Kwan Yew has driven the economic miracle on Singapore since his election in 1959. At the same time, political change and repressive policies had often disrupted the Chinese business communities, for example in Malaysia, Indonesia and Vietnam, creating a mini-disapora within the diaspora. Thus there are Vietnamese-Chinese in America, Philippine-Chinese in Taiwan, and Indonesian-Chinese in Hong Kong, each with a set of previously existing relationships and assumptions that can suddenly spark into new business. There are many examples of business collaboration and co-investment between the Chinese in such disparate political and economic environments as Indonesia, Malaysia and Thailand. In these cases, the usual bonds of kinship and hometown are sometimes substituted by long-term personal friendship, while today's relationships are just as likely to begin at the prestigious universities in Britain and America where the scions of such families are sent as if to finishing schools. Alumni-style networks are therefore added to existing dialect and business networks as another layer. In an echo of the British transition from Empire to Commonwealth, the latter term has been used of this various but subtly linked community:

Not based on any one country or continent this commonwealth is primarily a network of entrepreneurial relationships. From restaurants to real estate to plastic-sandal makers to semi-conductor manufacturing – from a staff of five to six family members to a factory of thousands – the Chinese commonwealth consists of many individual enterprises that nonetheless share a common culture.[383]

Perhaps the best way to give some idea of its importance will be to take the examples of three prominent Overseas Chinese families as short case studies.

The first case concerns the Indonesian entrepreneur Liem Sioe Long. Liem was born in Haikou in Fujian in 1916, and emigrated to Indonesia in 1938 to escape the political turmoil of the time. He began by working in the shop of an uncle selling peanut oil, before starting his own business selling coffee powder. While he was supplying goods to the army he met a young officer in charge of supplies and finance called Suharto (who is himself rumoured to be of part-Chinese descent), with whom he developed a deep friendship. Suharto's sons called him Uncle Liem. As one wrote, 'I remember when we were younger, me and Bambang and his other friends would go over to Uncle Liem's house.' A friend of his second son recounted to *Time Magazine*, 'Uncle Liem would always give us a package of money wrapped in newspaper.'[384] Apparently these packages often contained more than $1,000. When Suharto supplanted Sukarno as President of Indonesia in 1965, Liem, who was already involved in the textile, trading and banking businesses, entered into essential industries such as flour milling, cement and car manufacture. But while his friendship with Suharto was instrumental to the success of his multifarious ventures, the typical Overseas Chinese virtues of hard work and an eye for the main chance also played a role (in the early days, Liem was said to have covered 70 miles a day on a bicycle selling coffee). A Malaysian peer, Chew Choo Keng, founder of a biscuit empire that covers Malaysia, Thailand and Indonesia, expressed the key requirements in an interview: 'There is an old Chinese saying "Tien See, Tah Ki, Jin Ho" (the timely opportunity, the geographical advantage and the harmonious relationship). A person cannot succeed in his business unless he has these three conditions.'[385]

Liem clearly had them. He boosted the geographical advantage by changing his name to the more Indonesian-sounding Sudono Salim (although he named his son Anthoni, albeit with an 'i'), and exploited the Suharto relationship so successfully that by the mid-1990s he had built an industrial group with nearly 200,000 employees, which was thought to produce around 5 per cent of the entire GDP of Indonesia.[386] The Salim Group included Indocement, the biggest cement producer, and Indofood, the biggest flour producer, Indomobil, then the sole importer for Mazda, Nissan, Suzuki, Hino and Volvo, and was organised into twelve industrial sectors, which provide some idea of the scope of its business: Agribusiness,

Automotive and Shipping, Banking and Financial Services, Chemicals, Computers and Communications, Construction Materials, Food and Consumer Products, International, Multi-industry, Natural Resources, Property Development and Leisure Industry, and Trading and Distribution.[387] At that time, the main focus of expansion was in a series of international chemical operations in East Germany, West Germany, the Philippines, Vietnam, Australia, the Soviet Union and also Mainland China, creating vertical integration on the basis of Indonesian raw materials.[388]

The collapse of the Asian economy in 1997 and the overthrow of Suharto in 1998 led to a downturn in the Group's business. But Liem's son Anthoni Salim, who took over the business at that time, managed to rebuild the empire in part by looking away from Indonesia to India and China. One of his first moves in this new strategy was to invest in China and India. In 2002, for example, the group acquired a 45 per cent stake in COSCO Property Co., a Chinese state-owned real estate company. COSCO, which was founded in 1961, is one of China's most important corporations, with a turnover of $17 billion. Together, they created a joint venture called COSCO Salim, with interests in property management and consultancy, food supply, shopping malls and conference centres. It is one of Shanghai's most prominent property companies, in that city of booms, and boasts amongst other projects a residential zone on the Suzhou River in Shanghai, a conference centre on Hainan, and the Asian Forum Center in Boao. Assets are reported by the Chinese company to be 'more than RMB 15 billion'.[389] It is therefore an excellent example of capital entering one of the best businesses in China, arriving in 2002 through the son of an emigrant from Fujian in the mid-1930s.

The second case concerns Chin Sophonpanich (c.1914–1988), who together with nine other Teochiu investors entered into a partnership in 1944 that resulted in the creation of the Bank of Bangkok, which was appropriately located in Chinatown. Chin was Chairman from 1952 to 1977, and following a non-family interregnum his son Chatri Sophonpanich became Chairman in 1980, while his other son Robin, who called himself Robin Chan, took over the Commercial Bank of Hong Kong, which the family also controlled. After another brief non-family interregnum Chatri Sophonpanich's eldest son Chartsiri Sophonpanich became Chairman in 1994, a post that he holds to this day. During Chatri Sophonpanich's chairmanship, the Bank of Bangkok became the largest company in Thailand and was listed among the top 200 banks in the world.[390]

At the moment of the financial crisis in 1997, the Bank of Bangkok was one of the ten ethnic-Chinese-controlled commercial banks that dominated the Thai banking scene. It weathered the storm and is today the largest commercial bank in Thailand, with an overseas network of twenty-one branches and approximately $30.5 billion in total assets.[391] It declares on its website that 'Our Vision is to be the leading financial service provider in Thailand, and to be the leading international bank in South East Asia.'[392] Its 'Chinese Relations Department' offers banking services for Chinese clients in all Asian countries with a strong Overseas Chinese presence. In China itself, the location of the four branches speaks strongly for the Bank's ethnic origins: apart from the politically necessary representative branches in Beijing and Shanghai, the other two are located in Shantou and Xiamen. That one of the five major services is 'remittance' speaks volumes for their business logic.

Family links with their origins and with Hong Kong remain strong. In 1959, Chin Sophonpanich founded together with other prominent Chinese businessmen a company called Asia Insurance based in Hong Kong, which is now a subsidiary of Asia Financial Group, incorporated in 1990 and registered in Bermuda. Chartsiri Sophonpanich's uncle, the younger brother of Chatri, Robin Yau-Hing Chan, is currently the chairman, and holds a third of the group's shares through an investment vehicle called Cosmos Investments.[393] He is a director of PICC Life Insurance Company Limited, a joint venture company established in the People's Republic of China in which Asia Financial Group has a 10 per cent shareholding. With paid-up capital of 1 billion Yuan (US$123 million), PICC Life is based in Beijing. This might explain why Robin Chan, in his capacity as the president of Hong Kong Federation of Overseas Chinese Associations, Robin Chan Yau-hing, gave his pragmatic support for the Taiwan Anti-Secession Law passed by the 10th National People's Congress in 2005: 'It serves the fundamental interests of the Chinese people,' he stated in an interview, 'and tallies with international laws.'[394] Certainly his standing in China is demonstrated by the fact that he is also a deputy in the Chinese National People's Congress. He is also an Honorary Chairman of the Chinese General Chamber of Commerce in Hong Kong.

Robin Chan's son, Bernard Chamwut Chan, is the president of Asia Financial Group and a director of Asia Insurance, as well as being a member of the Hong Kong Special Administrative Region's Government's Executive Council and Legislative Council. He is also a director of City e-Solutions Limited, Peaktop International Holdings Limited, Pioneer Global Group Limited, Yau Lee Holdings Limited, Chen Hsong Holdings Limited and New Heritage Holdings Limited, an adviser to Bangkok Bank Public Company Limited, Hong Kong Branch. In addition, he is Deputy Chairman of Lingnan University (which praises its fund-raising prowess in a 2006 campaign on its website),[395] a member of the Insurance Advisory Committee and the Greater Pearl River Delta Business Council. Robin Chan's nephew, more recognisable from his name as Choedchu Sophonpanich – without an English name even though he studied at the LSE – is a non-executive director of Asia Financial Group and also Chairman of the Executive Board of Directors of Bangkok Life Assurance Company Limited.[396]

These two cases, of the families of Liem and Chan, come together from time to time and in different places in a way that illustrates the power of these Overseas Chinese networks, since the men were long-time friends and business associates. A couple of examples will illustrate this.

When, in 1957, the first President of Indonesia Sukarno effectively nationalised all Dutch-owned companies and ordered the army to take control of them, the army was unable to raise the necessary capital. Liem went to his acquaintance Chan, and quickly obtained credit from the Bank of Bangkok. Again, in 1973, it was the Bank of Bangkok that enabled him to build cement kilns for Indocement and set him on the way to making it the biggest cement producers in the world.[397] Moreover, Liem and Chan find common cause in the move into insurance. For in 1975 Liem Sioe Liong and his son Anthoni created a life assurance company, which began operation the following year under the name of P.T. Asuransi Jiwa Central Asia Raya, now known as ACA Asuransi.[398]

Thus investments and relationship flowed back and forth between the Chinese communities of South and East Asia. In 1981, when Liem himself was in a stronger situation, he invested US$100 million in a bank created in Hong Kong by Manuel V. Pangilinan, an American Express investment manager, known as First Pacific. Today First Pacific, whose Chairman is Anthoni Salim and CEO still Manuel Pangilinan, owns 51.5 per cent of Indofood. Liem, listed as Soedono Salim, was Chairman until 1999 and is now, ninety-two in the 2006 *Annual Report*, Honorary Chairman and Advisor to the Board. He is also still Chairman of the Salim Group.[399] The old links are strong, since Professor Edward K.Y. Chen, a non-executive director of First Pacific, is, among other roles, president of Lingnan University, where we have just seen Bernard Chamwut Chan is Deputy Chairman.[400] The main investments of First Pacific are listed as 51.5 per cent of Indofood, Liem's old company in Indonesia, and holdings in three Philippines companies: 76.1 per cent of a real estate company called Metro Pacific, 24.6 per cent in PLDT, the leading telecoms provider, and 24.6 per cent in Level Up, the leading online games provider. One of the most interesting things about this company is the way in which the composition of the Board reflects long-term loyalties typical of the Overseas Chinese. The authors of a paper on the 'the economics of connectness', who take the Salim Group as an example, write that: 'By the end of the 1960s Liem had formed a coherent group of investors which included the Djuhar family, Sudwikatmono (cousin and stepbrother of Suharto) as well as a local businessman, Ibrahim Risjad. These people were called the "Liem Investors" and were later complemented with sons of Liem and Djuhar.'[401] They write in the past tense of these figures, but as of 2006 (the last available in late 2007), three of them still sat on the Board of First Pacific: Stutanto Djuhar (aged seventy-eight), his son Tedy Djuhar (fifty-five), and Ibrahim Risjad (aged seventy-three); while Sudwikatmono (aged seventy-three) is listed as an Advisor to the Board.[402]

The third case of complex inter-relationships concerns the Chia family of Bangkok. The 'Thai' founders, the brothers Chia Ek-chor and Chorncharoen Chearavanont, were Teochiu emigrants from Chenghai, near Shantou.[403] The business was carried on by Chia's son, Dhanin Chearavanont or Xie Guomin (his father's original name was Xie Yichu), and in the mid-1990s controlled more than

280 affiliated companies, fourteen of which were listed in Hong Kong, New York, London, Jakarta, Taipei, Shanghai and Bangkok.[404] In 1997, the Chiaravanon family holding company, Charoen Pokphand (CP) Group, was the biggest foreign investor in China with nearly 130 joint ventures.[405] In that year, like the Salim Group, CP suffered from the financial crash, but restructured and through a combination of mergers and sales of businesses that were losing money in both Thailand and China withstood the financial consequences.

After the opening to foreign investment, the first official investor in China was Charoen PokPhand, which obtained investment certificate No. 0001 in the Shantou and Shenzhen Special Economic Zones. In China it is known as Zhengda Group, which contributed much of Charoen PokPhand's mid-1990s revenues of $7 billion and from initial investments in agriculture diversified into motor cycle manufacture, retail, property, oil refining, telecommunications and banking. In 1997, it was the biggest foreign investor in China with nearly 130 joint ventures.

Today the Group describes itself as 'Asia's leading globally committed conglomerate,'[406] with two main business areas: Agribusiness and Food Industry and Telecommunication and Multimedia Services (which they call 'Food for the Brain'). It has investments, operations and trading in twenty countries and in 2005 had a turnover of over $13 billion. It is still an intensively family company, in spite of its size. Dhanin Chearavanont is the Chairman and Chief Executive Officer, his brother Sumet Jiaravanon is the Executive Chairman, while two other brothers, Jaran Chiaravanont and Montri Jiaravanont, are Honorary Chairmen. The Boards of Charoen Pokphand, Chia Tia Group in China, and other companies like Chia Tai Enterprises and CP Pokphand, both quoted on the Hong Kong Stock Exchange, are populated with members of the second and third generations bearing three variants of the family surname – Chearavanont, Chiaravanont and Jiaravanont (it is not at first obvious that Benjamin Jiaravanont is the nephew of Xie Guomin, or even of Dhanin Chearavanont). Even the un-Thai sounding Michael Ross, who joined the Board of Chia Tai Enterprises in 2006, turns out to be the son-in-law of Dhanin Chearavanont (whose three sons are all board members). This tendency to maintain control by the family while non-family professionals manage the companies, together with the fact that the Hong Kong companies are registered in the Cayman Islands, are hallmarks of the successful Overseas Chinese business.

In China, the company is known as the Chia Tai Group. This mainland conglomerate controls over 200 subsidiaries and has over 80,000 employees. Beginning from the traditional basis of agribusiness and telecommunications, it now lists its subsidiaries under nineteen industry sectors and includes well-known companies like Chia Tai Feed, Dayang Motorcycles, Lotus Supercenters, Chia Tai Pharmaceutical Group and the Business Development Bank.

Other similar case studies could be cited from the Philippines, Malaysia, and obviously Singapore and Taiwan. The picturesque phrase used by Kukrit Pramoj, who was Prime Minister of Thailand from 1975 to 1976, that each successful Thai family had a Chinese 'hanging somewhere on their family tree',[407] could apply to any of the other Asian countries. The Widjaja family from Indonesia, originally the Oei family of Quanzhou in Fujian, after creating Indonesia's second largest conglomerate, returned to invest in forty-one state enterprises in their native city.[408] The Kuok family, from Fuzhou in Fujian, after building an empire in Malaysia through a friendship with the Sultan of Johore parallel to that of Liem with Suharto, diversified into Singapore and Hong Kong, and returned to China with investments in the Kerry Centres and the Shangrila hotel group. A glance at the *Forbes Rich List* for Southeast Asia in 2006 reveals Robert Kuok at No.1, Dhanin Chearavanont at No.15, a symbolic sequence of Chatri Sopohonpanich, Liem Sioe Long (as ever close together!) and Eka Tjipta Widjaja at Nos 25, 26 and 27, and Eka Widjaja's son Oei Hong Leong at No.36.[409] The only thing most commentators would agree on is that these men probably have more wealth that remains invisible to *Forbes*. But the details that links them is that all of them were poor emigrants from mainland China, or sons of poor emigrants, who earned their vast wealth in the business networks of Southeast Asia and later made significant and successful investments back into China.

Yet in fairness, we should for a moment forget the sensationalist reporting of newspapers and business magazines, which focus on success stories, and recall here the observation of Wang Gungwu that not every Overseas Chinese is a millionaire or a born business genius, and that they do not by themselves create economic miracles. As he says, 'the story of the millions who remain poor is rarely reported on.'[410] The gold rushes of California and Australia, the sugar plantations of Cuba and railways from America to Africa would not have been maintained or completed without Chinese labour. Not to mention the stories of the coolies in Cuba and the cockle-gatherers and prostitutes still shipped illegally to Europe by Chinese 'snakeheads'.

The Beginnings of a More Distant Empire

For obvious reasons, success has not been so rapid and massive beyond Asia. There was a notable acceleration in Chinese emigration to the United States in the middle of the nineteenth century, given the fortuitous combination of the pull of the Californian Gold Rush in 1849 and the push of political turmoil in China, which began with the Taiping Rebellion in 1851. Three years earlier, when gold was first discovered in California, there were probably no more than fifty Chinese residents in the entire country;[411] in 1852, there were already 20,000. For most, it was a hard life of deprivation, difficult working conditions, discrimination and even torture by thieves who wanted to find their hidden gold. But even in this desperation the Chinese showed signs of their ingenuity and capacity for hard work (it must be said that they were luckier than victims of the 'coolie trade' after the abolition of slavery, when Chinese were cynically substituted for African slaves in Australia, Cuba, Hawaii, and Peru). One charming example is that of a man called Ah Sam who invested $20 in a log cabin bought from a group of gold prospectors because he was convinced that he could wash sufficient dust from the dirt floor to make a profit: the results proved him correct, as he managed to salvage gold dust worth $3,000.[412] A similarly attractive legend from the gold-mining town of Weaverville in California, which boasts a nineteenth-century Chinese temple, concerns a laundry-man who was ridiculed because he washed miners' clothes free of charge but was later found to have become wealthy from the gold dust he managed to retrieve in the process.[413]

Many others were successful in a more conventional way. A few years later, a business directory listed five Chinese restaurants, thirty-three shops and fifteen Chinese medicine shops amongst many other flourishing businesses. In the 1870s, there were 5,000 Chinese business owners in San Francisco alone, owning half of the city's cigar factories, most of the slipper factories, and involved in sectors as diverse as agriculture, retail and mining (with one entrepreneur employing 900 people). They also acted as labour contractors for factories and construction companies, exploiting their language knowledge and networks to draw on the Chinese labour pool.[414] By that time the total number of Chinese in California was around 50,000.

As the gold fever cooled, there was a shift in Chinese business patterns, first from mining to laundries, and then to railway construction. The second was the result of quintessentially Chinese entrepreneurship. The Chinese noticed that people in California were prepared to pay for laundry services, which involved shipping to the East Coast, Honolulu and even Hong Kong, which were all both costly and took time. It was obviously beneficial for customers to pay $5 for a dozen shirts rather than $12, and to receive the shirts in a few days rather than up to four months.

But the railways were the major employers, and they paid for muscle and toil rather than creating entrepreneurial possibilities. From 1862 to 1869, thousands of Chinese, of whom around 10 per cent died in work-related accidents, worked on the transcontinental railway, which linked east and west coasts. Overland journey times were reduced from four to six months to six days. At first, the railway companies were reluctant to employ these short, light and apparently weak men, but by the end they were so impressed by their productivity and low cost that one executive said it would be better both for the railway company and the state of California if half a million more Chinese could come.[415] Without Chinese labour and know-how, especially of explosives used to blast tunnels and rock faces, the job might have taken much longer.

The industriousness of the Chinese in America may be summed up in an observation by Mark Twain, who wrote in *Roughing It* that:

> A disorderly Chinaman is rare, and a lazy one does not exist. So long as a Chinaman has strength to use his hands he needs no support from anybody; white men often complain of want of work, but a Chinaman offers no such complaint; he always manages to find something to do.[416]

Twain was an admirer and sympathiser, and wrote an amusing sketch of the travails of an imaginary immigrant named Ah Song Hi in a series of magazine articles for the New York-based *The Galaxy* called 'Goldsmith's Friend Abroad Again', where Ah Song recounts in his putative letters how he was cheated and unfairly beaten as he dreams of his new freedom and wealth.

Following the Chinese Exclusion Act (1882) there was a big fall-off in the number of new immigrants, a series of negative court decisions against allowing even those born in the United States to claim citizenship, and widespread instances of prejudice and personal violence. In 1887, the total number of immigrants dropped to ten, and a distorted social make-up of 100,000 men and only 5,000 women could not generate a natural increase in the community. Later, even an American-born Chinese woman would lose her citizenship if she married a native Chinese; anti-miscegenation laws impacted on them as much as on the black population. The Chinese became an invisible community, quietly developing new laundry businesses, and, after the 1906 earthquake destroyed all birth records, quietly infiltrating new immigrants into California by claiming they were born in America or were the children of American citizens (who then had the right to claim citizenship for children born elsewhere). But, according to the 1920 Census, there were only 45,000 predominantly male Chinese, with about a third working in laundries.[417] Invisible, as it were, in the steam.

Yet silently, tenaciously, in spite of prejudice and barriers to study and employment, the Chinese-Americans prospered. In the post-1929 years of economic depression they in fact suffered less than many Americans, since their savings and internal credit systems were less affected by the financial crisis and their money was not invested in banks and stocks. In 1943, the Exclusion Act was abolished following a tour by Chiang Kai-shek's charismatic and articulate wife Meiling Soong, who was invited by President Roosevelt, and, an often overlooked fact, as many as 20,000 Chinese fought in American uniform during the Second World War against the common enemy, Japan.[418] As a result, restrictions on employment of Chinese by public and state companies in California were lifted, and the 1945 War Brides Act allowed a Chinese-American veteran to marry a Chinese woman and bring his bride to the United States. After years in which the numbers of female immigrants had numbered in double figures, there was an influx of 6,000 women – with a consequent long-term boost to the community, whose numbers increased from 77,000 to 117,000 in just a few years.[419] Then, in 1965, the new Immigration and Nationality Act, which abolished racial discrimination in the United States, opened the floodgates: from that year, the number of Chinese-Americans, then just over 236,000, doubled every ten years, including a significant flow of Taiwanese, as many as 20,000 graduate students each year to prestigious universities. After Mao's death in 1976 and the rise to power of Deng Xiao Ping in 1978, an immigration quota of 20,000 each year was fixed for mainland Chinese, with no limit on students and tourists. The Overseas Chinese in all their ramifications moved into the mainstream of American life, and made notable contributions to academic research and the work of government laboratories – with awards like that of the Nobel prize for Physics to Tsung-Dao Lee and Chien-Shiung Wu in 1962 crowning these achievements, and senior executive positions gained in companies like Honeywell and Intel.

Today, the community of 2 million Chinese-Americans plays an important role both within the country and in its business relationships with the Mainland. Famous Chinese-Americans include a batch of creative talents in authors Bette Bao Lord, Amy Tang and Iris Chang, the actor Brandon Lee and the architect I.M. Pei, while there have been some significant figures in the computer industry, from the Cray supercomputer designer Steve Chen to An Wang, co-founder of Wang Laboratories, the unrelated Charles Wang, founder of Computer Associates, and Jerry Yang, the founder of Yahoo. Chinese-American academics and entrepreneurs were integral to the success of Silicon Valley, and a distinct professional class has emerged in many cities. But there have been few prominent politicians, for example the first and only Chinese-American Congressman David Wu from Oregon, elected in 2001, and the un-Chinese-sounding third-generation Gary Locke, who was the state governor of Washington from 2000–05. It is interesting to note that they both come from areas in the northwest where the first Californian emigrants moved (although Wu himself immigrated to the US with his family at the age of six in 1961),[420] so that the process of achieving national prominence has taken well over a century.

In Britain the first Chinese immigration took place about half a century earlier than in the United States. Originally it mainly concerned employees of the East India Company living in the docklands of Liverpool and London. Other immigrants offered basic services such as shops and eateries for this core population, so that towards the end of the nineteenth century there were nearly 600 Chinese in Britain (582 according to the 1890 Census), mainly in the Limehouse area of East London, which was given the name Chinatown by the journalist George Sims.[421] The main activities were work connected to ports and shipping, in London and in Liverpool, and laundries.

Immigration increased after the Second World War, with ethnic Chinese from Hong Kong, Singapore and Malaysia who after the 1948 British Commonwealth

Act gained the right to residence in Britain. But the Chinese were still tainted by the connection with opium dens and the white slave trade – and the inscrutable characters found in the stories of Fu Manchu and Sherlock Holmes. Since Limehouse had been badly damaged during the war, the growing Chinese community moved to what was then the low-rental area of Soho. The 1991 Census recorded 156,938 persons of ethnic Chinese origin legally resident in Britain,[422] with as many as 90 per cent involved in the catering business. But only 11.8 per cent of them came from Mainland China, with the rest having been born in the United Kingdom itself (28.4 per cent) or the Commonwealth.

It is fascinating to compare fiction to reality in the British case. Let us consider, for example, this passage from the story 'The Chink and the Child' published by Thomas Burke in 1917:

> Now there lived in Chinatown, in one lousy room over Mr. Tai Fu's store in Pennyfields, a wandering yellow man, named Cheng Huan. … He had come to London by devious ways. He had loafed on the Bund at Shanghai. The fateful intervention of a crimp had landed him on a boat. He got to Cardiff, and sojourned in its Chinatown; thence to Liverpool, to Glasgow; thence, by a ticket from the Asiatics' Aid Society, to Limehouse, where he remained for two reasons – because it cost him nothing to live there, and because he was too lazy to find a boat to take him back to Shanghai.[423]

It is a condensation of prejudice, from the yellowness and the crimp to the laziness and the deviousness. By way of contrast, we might take an example that in a sense goes beyond fiction, the extraordinary, restless intelligence and ability to make the best of any world which characterised the life of Samuel Chinque, who died in London at the age of ninety-six in 2004. This improbable figure was born in Jamaica, became a merchant seaman, and since he had British citizenship moved to Liverpool and became the representative of the China Seaman's Union and a member of the British Communist Party. During the Second World War he worked as an auxiliary fireman. An autodidact, he studied Marx in English, developed a network of like-minded Chinese and contacts with trade unions, and at the end of the war set up the first overseas branch of Xinhua, the official Chinese news agency – making him, in the absence of any other representation, his country's *de facto* ambassador. In 1962, he was expelled from the British Communist Party on a matter of principle, and joined the Chinese Communist Party, continuing to work as a journalist in England until he was seventy-four years old. The raw energy of the man emerges from the words of an obituary in *The Guardian*:

Samuel Chinque remained a formidable and charismatic figure well into his old age. Even in his late 70s, he was capable of flooring, with one blow, a racist skinhead who had assaulted him on a London tube train. He is survived by his wife, and 11 children whose birthdates span 60 years and who live as far afield as Hong Kong, Canada, the US and Switzerland, as well as in the UK, plus numerous grandchildren and great-grandchildren.[424]

Laziness is the last word that springs to mind as one reads these words. He was in fact an archetypal Overseas Chinese foot-soldier, born outside China and never resident there but always loyal to 'his' country, willing to turn his hand to any activity, physically courageous and wily, with an eye to the main chance and a large multi-generational family scattered across the globe.

Coming Back: The 'Sea Turtles'

The expression *hai gui*, or 'sea turtle', a creature that is born on land, swims out to grow in the sea, and then returns to the same place on the shore, is used to refer to students who return to their homeland and use foreign-acquired expertise to further a political career or set up a business. It is an old tradition, for the *hai gui* of the past who rose to prominence after studies abroad include such figures as Sun Yat-sen (Hawaii, Hong Kong and London), Zhou Enlai (France), Deng Xiao Ping (France) and Jiang Zemin (Russia). Nowadays, there are two main ways that a *hai gui* returns to mainland China: first, as a physical person, and second by investment.

First, let us consider the physical transfer.

As many as a million students have left China on government scholarships to do study for graduate degrees since the government began to provide support for overseas study in 1978. Around 30 per cent of these return to work in China, usually equipped with advanced degrees in good universities. The reentry of the 'turtles' has been facilitated by financial and fiscal incentives, and by the creation of what are known as the Overseas Pioneer Parks situated within the major science parks – known rather grandly in Chinese as 'High-Tech Parks for Returned Students Making Great Industry and Business'. In 1997, the Business Incubator Center of Haidan Science Park in Beijing created an 'Overseas Students Pioneer Park' intended for 'enterprising overseas returnees', and provides a full range of services and 'standard incubation units' in which they can set up business. In addition to standard incentives such as zero corporate tax for the first three years, returning students enjoy extra privileges such as initial funding from the Ministry of Science and Technology (MOST) and from Zhongguancun Science Park, and later low-interest bank loans.

They also enjoy personal benefits such as preferential housing and special schools for their children.[425] In 2007, there were more than 200 companies in this Pioneer Park, and over 100 successful exits as a result of growth and with a wide variety of businesses including a seed technology company, which has been listed on Nasdaq. The model has been replicated elsewhere in China with success.

The call home to the sea turtle is not a new phenomenon. In 1898, after the so-called Hundred Days Reform, officials in many Chinese consulates around the world made appeals to successful 'local' Chinese entrepreneurs to invest in China and open new avenues of trade. One such was Chen Yixi (1844–1928), who at the age of twenty left his home village of Langmei in the Doushan district in Taishan, southwest Guangdong, which was the major source of early Chinese emigrants to the West Coast. He began work as a labourer at Seattle railway station, rising to become a foreman and a leader in the Chinese community, and then a successful labour contractor and merchant. As general agent for all transcontinental lines that ended in Seattle, he understood how railways could generate economic growth, and on his return to his hometown in 1904 initiated a project to build the Xinning Railway, from Taishan to Jiangmen, naturally passing through Doushan. He raised funds from other successful Chinese-Americans from the area on a lecture tour, amounting to nearly $3 million for the first stage.[426] It became an 80-mile privately-owned railway using American rolling-stock and German locomotives, which Chen planned to link to port facilities and extend to the manufacturing centre of Foshan to create a modern transport network. But bribery, extortion and attempts by local authorities to wrest control meant that his ambitious project was never completed, and Chen died, depressed in Langmei in 1928.[427] The railway itself was dismantled ten years later with all other local railways, to avoid them falling into Japanese hands. Sadly, recognition that his railway might be of strategic importance for the Japanese was a tardy recognition of the quality of Chen's project.[428] For the vision that took two decades of his life and much of his wealth was correct, since Taishan is situated within 100 miles of the three major ports of Guangzhou, Hong Kong and Macao.

A more recent example is that of Shi Zhengrong, the founder of Suntech Power Holdings. Shi was born in Yangzhong, a town on the Chang Jiang between Shanghai and Nanjing, and studied physics in the optical sciences department of the University of Jilin and in the Shanghai Institute of Optics and Fine Mechanics. In 1988, he travelled to Australia to study for a PhD at the University of New South Wales, after which he worked for some time in an Australian company. Then he returned to China and set up his own company, and with a gesture befitting the tradition of returned 'turtles' set up a factory in his hometown. Within a few years, Suntech Power Holdings became one of the world's largest producers of photovoltaic equipment, which converts sunlight into electricity, and is quoted on the New York Stock Exchange. One of the interesting things in his story is that

Shi decided to return not because he read of the boom in China in newspapers or learned about it from broadcast media, or even from personal visits, but heard from a businessman from his hometown of Yangzhong whom he chanced to meet while he was in Australia on business. This again is typical of the trust pattern; had the businessman been from another province, he might never have returned to take a look for himself.[429]

The Empire Strikes Back

One of the problematic phrases that best points up the discrepancies between China the 'nation-state' and China 'the empire' is foreign direct investment (FDI), for the latter is a misnomer. In the 1980s, investment on the mainland by Overseas Chinese companies like Charoen PokPhand took off, much of it flowing through Hong Kong, so that by 1995 as much as 59 per cent of all Foreign Direct Investment to China came from Hong Kong, 11 per cent from Taiwan, 3 per cent from Singapore, and a further 2 per cent from Southeast Asia, which may be assumed to be chiefly Chinese in origin, thus accounting for three-quarters of all FDI, while Hong Kong was also the largest foreign investor in Vietnam, Thailand and the Philippines.[430]

If we look at detailed figures for investment in Fujian, the emphasis is clear: over the period 1979 to 1993, when most FDI went into hotel construction and/or energy extraction, 65.7 per cent came from Hong Kong, 16.5 per cent from Taiwan and 4.6 per cent from Singapore – with, for example, only 1.4 per cent from Japan and 3.1 per cent from the USA and Canada together.[431] But even more striking is the precise correlation between investment and ethnic origin. Analysing the data from a survey of entrepreneurs in Guangdong and Fujian in the mid-1990s, this turns out to be consistently very high and in one case even 100 per cent. In a table showing the ethnic origin of 'foreign' investors, the average percentage of ethnic Chinese investors from Hong Kong and Taiwan in four cities (Nanhai, Panyu, Quanzhou and Xiamen) is 98.5 per cent. As far as language is concerned, these supposedly foreign investors put their money where they speak the local dialect: Cantonese speakers from Hong Kong represent 70 per cent of investment in Nanhai and 88 per cent in Panyu, while Hokkien speakers from both Hong Kong and Taiwan represented an extraordinary 100 per cent in Quanzhou, and 54 per cent and 98 per cent respectively in Xiamen.[432] Although in succeeding years there has been an increase in FDI from other parts of the world, in particular from the USA, in 2006 inward investment from Hong Kong, Taiwan and Macau was still about 40 per cent of the total.[433]

This leads to some interesting conclusions. First of all, that such high levels of FDI would be unsustainable without the Overseas Chinese, whose role is therefore vitally important in the global economy since China itself is now a major factor in its stability. Secondly, that such sustained investment from Taiwan necessarily implies closer engagement. In fact, in 2001 the Vice-Director of the 'Mainland Affairs Council' in Taiwan explicitly recognised in a statement that: 'China takes cross-strait economic association as a means to integrate Taiwan's economy in to itself. So gradually, Taiwan will lose its economic autonomy and its sovereignty in dealing with cross-strait affairs.'[434] Independence becomes ever less likely, while the integration of the wealth of Overseas Chinese and the economies they dominate with the Mainland represent a much larger share of economic power than is usually recognised.

The 'Third Wave' of Migration

Traditional Overseas Chinese communities are now receiving a boost from what is often referred to as the 'third wave of migration': no longer the poor who went to sugar plantations in the nineteenth century or traders from Fujian and Guangdong developing businesses in nearby countries like Thailand and the Philippines, but Mandarin-speaking entrepreneurs.

There are significant differences between the emigrants of the first two waves and these new arrivals. They are mostly Mandarin speakers and come from a country that is diplomatically and economically much stronger than in the past; they are proud of their heritage, and often openly nationalistic. There was an example of this in the summer of 2007, when the Chinese community in Milan revolted against what they saw as unfair pressures by municipal authorities restricting access for loading and unloading in the street at the heart of Milan's Chinatown, Via Paolo Sarpi (himself, ironically, a great Venetian patriot and civic hero). A riot broke out, with five Chinese residents finishing in hospital, and fourteen policemen injured (*feriti*).[435] Whereas similar protests in the past have been quiet and purely local, in this case local shopkeepers brandished large PRC flags in front of cameras, and the incident led to official declarations by the Chinese Consul-General, Zhang Limin. Previously, the sense of identity of 'Milanese Chinese' was strongly linked with Wenzhou, the city where many of them came from, rather than with Beijing. This is a sign of new confidence, and an omen for the way in which the 'Third Wave' of immigration might act as another spearhead for the Stealth Empire.

The same confidence was displayed during the contoversial progress of the Olympic torch throughout London and Paris in April 2008, when patriotic students demonstrated in large numbers in opposition to Western and Tibetan activists who attempted to monopolise the event to highlight political suppression and abuses in Tibet. These youthful protesters are profoundly different from their silent, labouring, 'invisibile' forebears.

Scenarios for the Future

Should we worry about this spreading Chinese influence in the world? Perhaps yes, if we consider the implications of a comment by Liang Qichao when he noted that in the fifty years before he was writing (in 1922) overseas emigration had 'established some real foundations of economic power' in America and Australia. His conclusion was that 'Racial expansion is a matter worth celebrating; and because of this, it can be proved that our race is just in its age of youth ...'[436]

In his magisterial work *The Shield of Achilles*, Philip Bobbitt traced the evolution of what he termed the 'market state': although to synthesise a 900-page book in one paragraph is impossible, he showed how after hundreds of years of development in the twentieth century the nation-state entered a 'long war', which lasted from 1914 to 1990 (i.e. the First World War, Second World War, the Korean and Vietnam Wars, the Cold War and innumerable other wars such as the China-Japan conflict, which shaped modern China, all seen as a continuum that broke up the old world order – and, we might add, whose death-throes are still visible in countries like Iraq). Out of this turmoil and destruction, there emerged the new model of market-state. The main difference with the past is that in the new global marketplace 'nation' does not necessarily tally with 'market'. There are transnational entities or networks, which sometimes effectively control commerce and finance. Large multi-national corporations are one obvious example, while the main stock exchanges are another – just consider that more cash transits on the electronic financial network every day than the annual GDP of most countries, something the 'nations' do not control. Unfortunately, as Bobbitt's book presciently understood, a terrorist network like Al Qaeda also fits into this category, and is likely to be a model for future disruption and conflict – no longer war between nations but war between markets (with Islam considered here as a 'religious market' pitted against the United States as a 'financial market'). Having defined three models of the market state – entrepreneurial, mercantile and managerial (roughly corresponding to Britain, Singapore and Germany respectively) – Bobbit expresses hope that in the twenty-first century, 'informal private networks that cross international lines ... will supply the links necessary to prevent the growing divergence of the three models of the market-state.'[437] As examples of these networks he cites multinational corporations, global non-governmental organisations, and the social network of the overseas Chinese. Thus in his view, the role of the latter will increase in importance in this century. It is for this reason that while David Landes' description of the overseas Chinese as 'the leaven and lubricant of Southeast Asian trade'[438] is so apposite, its weakness is that it delimits the sphere of influence excessively. For it is now obvious that there is a significant misfit between the territorial concept of China and the social and economic impact of what we might call the 'non-territorial China' or the invisible empire.

Estimates of the financial power of the overseas Chinese community vary widely, but they are unanimous in providing very big numbers. In 2002, for example, the *Asia Times* of Hong Kong reckoned them to have a combined estimated wealth of over US$1.5 trillion, and to be arguably 'the third-largest economy in the world after the gross national products (GNPs) of the United States and Japan.'[439] Yet this 'economy' remains invisible because it is not measured or reported in global statistics, which are compiled by nation-dominated organisations like the World Bank or the OECD on the exclusive basis of 'national' figures. Moreover, its significance is likely to increase rather than decrease in coming decades. Yet there is one sense in which we need not worry, as the French, for example, worry about the cultural impact of American 'imperialism', for Chinese culture is notoriously intractable. This means, as we shall now see, that the 'soft power' that accompanies military or economic power as seagulls accompany ships will have much less influence – although, ironically, this fact contributes to the 'invisible' nature of a very real Chinese empire.

Why Chinese Culture Stops at the Border

Chinese culture can be immensely attractive to Westerners. The early and universal desire for silk products and porcelain provides an early example of the diffusion of 'soft power', defined by Joseph Nye as the ability to get other countries to accept a culture and ideology, or for one country to obtain that other countries '*want what it wants*'.[440] As China expands its economic strength and builds a modern military force, it would dearly like to add 'soft power' to these elements of 'hard power', to compete with the pervasive influence of American soft power. Yet it is difficult to write of all Chinese culture as attractive. There are several obvious barriers to its dissemination, and reasons why it would be difficult for the Chinese to export cultural values. There is, as yet, no Chinese Winnie-the-Pooh or Mickey Mouse, although China has sought to soften its image by lending pandas to foreign zoos. Four 'Chinese' have won Nobel prizes (including three Chinese-American scientists), but the only one of cultural significance is the Literature prize awarded in 2000 to Gao Xingjian, who lives in exile in Paris and is not even named in the periodic laments of cultural officials on the mainland that Nobels are never given to Chinese.[441]

Moreover there are certain quixotic features of Chinese culture that derive from ancient needs for harmony and symmetry, forcing nature to conform to an ideal conception of the world but at odds with what we call common sense. One such feature, which sets the Chinese apart, is the measurement of time. The solar year has since ancient times been divided into twenty-four fortnights: to respect ancient needs for symmetry, the year was divided into halves based on the winter and summer solstices, and then halved again in accordance with the spring and autumn equinoxes. These quarters were further divided into eighths, and then two dates were inserted between each of the spaces between these eight sections to create the twenty-four fortnights. This need for symmetry means that the beginning of the seasons must fall exactly half-way between solstices and equinoxes, while for Westerners they occur six weeks later.[442] Thus, since the summer equinox must be exactly in the middle of two forty-eight day sections, summer begins on 6 May and ends on 8 August, which – when Beijing is ferociously hot, and summer fruit at its prime – local people insist on calling the beginning of Autumn. This also explains why on 5 February or thereabouts the Chinese celebrate their 'Spring Festival', much to the bemusement of many foreigners in Beijing who associate spring with daffodils and warm sunshine rather than skating on frozen canals. But no amount of discussion can shake these historical certainties.

Such apparently minor irritants are typical of many cultural features of everyday Chinese life that create separateness and make it hard to imagine a soft culture combining with a harder economic, military and technological culture to create a truly global power. Indeed there are several specific barriers to the deployment of 'soft power', which we will now review in language, the visual arts and music.

An Intractable Language

Chinese is notoriously a difficult language: Westerners accustomed to similar-looking languages and scripts receive a rude shock when they begin to study Chinese. Not only is there no relationship at all between Chinese and any European tongue, but learning is complicated by the fact that each morpheme or syllable needs to be memorised twice: once for its sound, and once for its visual form.

One of the oddest features of Chinese, especially the classical literary language, is the fact that in a culture in which the memorisation of texts was so important for learning, a literary scholar listening to the recitation of a text that he had not previously studied would be unable to understand it. The spoken word is not sufficient to distinguish one written character from another since there can be dozens of characters – all with utterly different meanings – with a single pronunciation. Matteo Ricci, who came from a scribal culture in which dictation was an important tool, made the interesting point that 'one could not write a book in Chinese from dictation.'[443] The best illustration of this is a virtuoso performance to prove that classical Chinese script could not be reduced to alphabetical form by Zhao Yuan Ren (1892–1982), a distinguished scholar who lectured at Yale, Harvard and Hawaii (as Y.R. Chao) as well as at Peking and Tsinghua universities. Zhao is known as the father of Chinese linguistics, and was one of the designers of the National Romanization System (*Guoyu Luomazi*). To illustrate the difficulties of transcription from Chinese characters to Roman script, he wrote a story in which every one of ninety-five different characters had exactly the same sound. It began 施氏食狮史, which, when transcribed in the officially proposed phonetical alphabet became *shih, shih, shih, shih, shih* (pronounced as the first syllable of 'sher*b*ert') and so on for all ninety-five characters.[444] The piece ended with a provocative challenge: 试释是事! ('Go on, check that it's true'), whose four characters were transliterated, obviously, as *shih, shih, shih, shih!* Thus a meaningful, if contrived, story became totally deprived of meaning in the process of transliteration and provides an insight into the otherwise puzzling notion of the 'inability of *any* [sic] extended passage in Literary Chinese to remain intelligible when romanized.'[445]

There were also language problems with modern technology. It was impossible, for example, to send messages over the first telegraph lines because there was no phonetic alphabet. By 1920, all the provinces in China were connected by telegraph, and English messages could be easily transmitted. But Chinese messages had first to be translated into a sequence of numbers, and then retranslated into language on reception.[446] Likewise, the difficulty of developing typewriter and computer keyboards or other input devices hampered the introduction of modern business practices. It was the development of a successful Chinese-character system by Ni Guangnan of the Computer Institute (part of the Chinese Academy of Science) and later of Legend Computers, which from its completion in 1985 spurred the latter company's growth. It took Ni and his team of researchers ten years to develop the system. Now it is relatively simple to input Chinese characters by using their Pinyin spelling, with several systems available. But it is far more difficult than using a purely alphabetic language since each Pinyin word causes a pop-up menu to appear with several characters to choose from (thirty-two in the case of *shih* in the system on the computer on which this is being written, fewer than those available to Professor Zhao but still enough to make life complicated). Clicking on one causes the chracter to appear in the text on the screen. It is laborious, but possible.

There is ambivalence in the attitude of the Chinese themselves, most of whom love their language but cannot read its classical form. Lu Xun, in an essay called 'An Outsider's Chats about Written Language', expresses this ambivalence neatly. Having asserted that the heritage of the language is something modern Chinese should be thankful for, he adds: 'However, at the present time, when pictographs no longer resemble the objects they are supposed to resemble, and when symphonetic graphs have gotten out of tune, our thanks cannot be but a bit hesitant.' He then goes on to stress how important it is to make literature available to the masses and discusses various proposals for simplified Chinese. After praising the romanisation system pioneered by Professor Zhao, he remarks that even that is too complicated and another system called 'New Latinisation' is possibly better. It would enable, in Lu Xun's words, even a 'lazybones or an imbecile' to read and write. Having said this, and stressed the fact that latinisation allows one to write fast, he then goes on to make a perfect literati conclusion: 'The Americans say, "Time is money." But I think that time is life. To squander other people's time for no reason is, in fact, no different than robbing and murdering them. However, those like us who sit idly chatting in the cool evening breeze are exceptions!'[447]

Classical Chinese is tough even for the native-born, now that they learn their language at school in its recent simplified script. The sinologist Derk Bodde stressed the deleterious 'burden' of memorisation, especially the triumph of what he calls 'quotationism', the need to remember quotations and allusions and recognise them when they occur in historical compilations or encyclopedias.[448] An excellent memory was essential for the celebrated 'Eight-legged essay', which from 1487 until 1905 was a crucial part of the civil service examination. It was a daunting system, which progressed from three exams at prefectural level to a provincial exam that took place once every three years, to the metropolitan exam in Beijing that took place the year after the provincial exam, and finally to the 'palace exam' overseen by the emperor. In order to have the slightest chance of success a young boy needed to have a good knowledge of characters at five, and to be able to compose classical poetry by eleven. Lu Xun's curriculum at the school known as the 'Three Flavour Study', just across the canal from his home compound in Shaoxing, provides an idea of the classical education of an eleven-year-old boy at the end of the nineteenth century. The sequence was as follows:

> The *Hundred Surnames* (*Bai Jia Xing*, a book of Chinese surnames written in verse during the Northern Song Dynasty).[449]
> *Poems on Child Prodigies* (an anthology from the same period).
> The *Four Books* (the *Great Learning*, the *Doctrine of the Mean*, the *Analects of Confucius*, and the *Book of Mencius*).
> The 'Five Classics' (*Book of Songs*, *Book of History*, *Book of Rites*, *Book of Change*, and the *Spring and Autumn Annals*).
> *Three Hundred Tang Poems*, an anthology of Tang dynasty poems compiled by Sun Zhu in the eighteenth century.[450]

This was just the beginning, since preparation for the examination entailed studying commentaries on these classics and many other related works. This was the same curriculum that the young Mao Zedong began just twelve years later than Lu Xun, which explains the frequent allusions to classical literature in his *Works*.

There was a huge pay-off for successful candidates. A good pass in the provincial exam guaranteed an official position and sought-after status as a scholar, while success in the metropolitan and palace exams led to the highest government offices. Given that most men managed to achieve the ultimate accolade, if ever, in their thirties or forties, examination success entailed spending decades memorising as many as 500,000 characters. Unthinkable nowadays.

Although the format varied slightly through the centuries, in the nineteenth century the provincial and metropolitan exams consisted of three sessions: the first with questions on the 'Four Books', based on three quotations, and a poetry question; the second based on the 'Five Classics', with one quotation from each book; and the third on Policy Questions, with five required essays.[451] The system had a practical function as a filter, guaranteeing at least a good level of literary scholarship and creating a group of learned men whose opinions could act as a counter-balance to those of the emperor. As Elman observes, this 'carefully balanced and constantly contested piece of educational and social engineering' actually worked quite well as a system until the middle of the nineteenth century.[452]

Emperors sometimes used the exam sessions to seek fresh ideas for policy issues. In 1371, for example, Hongwu set this question for the final 120 candidates: 'In past dynasties, the personal policy questions all invoked the duties of "respecting heaven" and "working diligently for the people". Of those kings and emperors who in antiquity respected heaven and diligently worked for the people, which of them can we use as models today?'[453] In 1649, the Qing emperor Shunzhi sought suggestions as to 'how Manchu and Han Chinese could be unified so that their hearts were the same and they worked together without division.'[454] Here, the most brilliant men in the empire, weaned from several tens of thousands by a ferocious process of selection and deeply steeped in the greatest works of ancient Chinese thought, are effectively being asked to function as a think-tank on the pressing problems of the day.

But the stresses were hideous. In the provincial exams, perhaps one candidate in 100 had a chance of success; then at the metropolitan level, one in ten. One analysis has shown that 'the odds for success in all stages of the selection process were only slightly better than one in 6,000'.[455] So it is not surprising to see cases of candidates taking exams every year for decades, and even failing yet again at the age of 104, as happened to one scholar in 1826.[456] We can only imagine the atmosphere suffered by scholars after years of study as they found themselves in a market or 'cultural prison' where they were locked into a cell for the three days of the exam together with 'thousands of other candidates, examiners, copyists, woodblock cutters, guards, cooks, and doctors surrounded by a market fair atmosphere and popular urban culture within which dreams, fate, and karma mattered to candidates as much as the classical curriculum.'[457] We can sympathise with the mother in the novel *The Scholars* by Wu Ching-Tzu (1701–54), who is so overwhelmed with shock to learn that her son Fan Chin (aged fifty-four) had passed his exam that she dies on the spot.

The American sinologist John K. Fairbank, discussing late nineteenth-century reforms, observed that 'the Chinese written language, rather than an open door through which China's peasantry could find truth and light, was a heavy barrier pressing against any upward advance and requiring real effort to overcome – a hindrance, not a help, to learning.'[458] Derk Bodde expressed a similar idea with respect to the acceptance of foreign ideas: '… the Chinese script has long proved a major deterrent to the free entry of foreign ideas and values into Chinese culture, because it meant that those ideas and values, when put into writing and translated into Chinese, could reach the Chinese consciousness only through the filter of the characters.'[459] This, for example, was a problem when it came to translating Christian texts: first, because the characters chosen were pervaded by Confucian and literary allusions that influenced the concepts translated and, second, because

Chinese was 'relatively poor in resources for expressing abstractions and general classes or qualities',[460] which are essential for the transmission of the Christian message. Paradoxically, the script that was such a powerful tool in the dissemination of Chinese values in East Asia became a hindrance when it came to cultural interchange with the West.

The Chinese government has announced the creation of around 100 Confucius Institutes around the world, on the model of the Goethe Institutes, for the dissemination of Chinese language and culture, while tens of thousands of foreigners are now studying the language in China itself. Most of them will acquire sufficient language skills to deal with the basic needs of business and everyday life, and perhaps enough characters to read a newspaper (at least 3,500). But few will master the classical language and script, and none will reach the level of the old imperial scholars. It would be possible to argue that the real classical literary culture of China is dead.

To conclude, written Chinese is a powerful poetic medium, as it plays on lost etymologies and complex references in both the visual and aural elements of a word, and can be beautiful to look at in fine calligraphy. Although it lacks many of the virtues of an alphabetic script it may be seen as 'an embodiment of simple and final truth … invulnerable to storm and stress' and above all 'solid, square, and beautiful, exactly as the spirit it represents.'[461] But it is just too difficult for facile acquisition, with a need to learn 4,000 or 5,000 characters to be reasonably literate (about twice as many as are needed in Japanese),[462] and therefore alien to the easily acquirable popular culture, which soft imperialism must nourish to succeed.

An Alien Language of Visual Arts

Visual culture is an essential concomitant of economic hegemony, as demonstrated by the projection of American values by Hollywood films. Here again, Chinese culture faces an obstacle. For the lexicon of myth, human beauty, religious imagery, colour and perspective that we have absorbed from ancient Greece and Rome through the Renaissance does not facilitate the enjoyment of Chinese visual arts.

To begin with, the idea behind a Chinese painting, even in a genre superficially analogous such as landscape, is fundamentally different. In Western art we have the imagined landscape as decorative background in a Raphael portrait, the composed landscape based on 'real' elements in a Poussin landscape, or the impressions of reality of Turner and Monet. But the purpose of a Chinese landscape was determined during the Tang dynasty by the very word that translates the concept, *shanshui*, which means literally 'mountain-water' (it is worth noting here that *shui* is never understood in this phrase as 'sea', only as 'river'; there is no tradition of seascape in Chinese painting). The objective of the painter was to express an emotion together with the rhythm of nature, each within a precise symbolic system. In the words of a Song dynasty writer, 'pictures are not simply produced by the practice of artistic skill, they must also correspond to the *I Ching*.'[463] There is always meaning in the decorative forms, in a brush stroke, in an inference rather than in a precisely rendered detail. A late Tang theorist, Ju Jing Xuan (Chu Ching-hsüan), explained the quality of the greatest painters in these terms:

> The ancients called the painters Sages, because they reached by their creative activity the very limits of heaven and earth and made manifest the brightness of the sun and the moon. By moving the brush (made of finest hair) they could represent all the innumerable things, which take their origin in the mind, and unroll within some square inches thousands of *li* so that they may be held in the palm of the hand. Both the shifting spirit and immovable matter may be rendered by some light touches of ink on the silk either through forms or by suggestion without forms. That is the beauty.[464]

The translator of this passage observes that the object of such painting was 'to open up vistas into the realms of a world beyond intellectual definition.' Indeed, in the refined and deliberate blandness and empty spaces of many landscape paintings, there might be, as François Jullien has expressed it, nothing that 'strives to incite or seduce … or compel the attention' and 'no decorative, or merely pleasing, touch.'[465] Chinese paintings might charm us by their quaintness or by exquisite detail, but they are unlikely to draw us further into their world, for only those 'who have acquired great learning can distinguish the coarse ones from the fine.'[466] It is an art for the learned, in symbiosis with literary culture.

To complicate matters further, some of the great innovations of the Italian Renaissance are dismissed out of hand by Chinese painters, who achieve similar effects by different means. When the Jesuits tried to teach perspective and *chiaroscuro*, they were informed that such techniques were no more than clever tricks. One of their students remarked that while Western-style painting 'shows skill and technique, it cannot be considered as true painting.'[467] From their point of view, distance should be rendered by the sophisticated use of blurred outlines, or mountain slopes that disappear into mist or cloud, while a key element in any Chinese painting is the 'rhythmic vitality', which can be described as 'the spiritual expression which emanates from a painting.'[468] Moreover, the true excellence of a painting is often measured by non-painterly qualities, such as the affirmation of Taoist or Buddhist harmony between man and nature.

This is made clear in a famous *Essay on Painting* written by Wang Wei, a gentleman painter who lived in the fifth century AD, in a passage in which he explains the difference between observed nature and the content of a painting:

Eyesight has its limits, hence what I see is not the whole. Therefore, with one reed brush I simulate the embodiment of the Great Void, and with fragmentary shapes I paint the intelligence of inch-wide pupils. With sweeps I render the heights of Mount Song; with a dash I create the hermit's hut. With upswept lines I mark Mount Hua, and with slanting dots show the prominent nose. The brow, forehead, chin and jaw are as if in a peaceful smile. The lonely cliffs, luxuriant and flourishing, seem to spit forth clouds … This is the achievement of painting.[469]

This anthropomorphic vision of painting is similar to the Chinese idea of music, which is never far from nature, and appears in titles such as 'A flock of crows complaining about cold'. Ming guide-books and travel literature praised similar aspects of Beijing, focusing on 'the greenery and shade, the vistas across a lake or from a peak or of a temple in the distance, pools and springs and the taste of the water, the evening or nighttime sounds, dark caves, and the trees, especially old or flowering ones.'[470] The creators of the 'scenic spots' beloved of Chinese property developers today are obviously inspired by the same criteria, although often in a clumsy and haphazard fashion – from our point of view.

From their point of view, painting looks different. Many of Giuseppe Castiglione's paintings are well regarded by the Chinese, but for some critics it seems just too much that he might be compared to his indigenous peers. One commented that 'if we compare the horses painted by Giuseppe Castiglione with those of Han Kan, Li Kung-lin and Chao Meng-fu we immediately observe that Giuseppe Castiglione lacks *hsi-lien* [purity and training] and that he is ignorant of the specific procedure of Chinese painting.' In an equally dismissive vein, another critic observed in a lecture during an exhibition of Castiglione's work in Taiwan in 1969 that 'the horses and flowers painted by Giuseppe Castiglione are exactly like what they are in reality: it is a photograph and that is all; there is neither the spirit not the rhythm of Chinese painting.'[471] In a similar vein, Sir George Staunton, secretary to Lord Macartney's embassy, mentioned an instance of the Chinese considering the shadow of a nose in a portrait to be a 'great imperfection'. All shade, he explained, was thought by them to be 'an accidental circumstance, which ought not to be carried from nature to a picture, from which it takes a part of the éclat and uniformity of colouring.'[472] This runs against the grain of an artistic culture in which shading is an integral part of drawing lessons.

The two main stumbling blocks to full appreciation are the *colophon*, or inscription, and the *seal*. The juxtaposition of an image and a poem or short prose text is rare in Western art, the notable exception being William Blake. In fact, study of Blake's visionary use of the relationship between words and images in *The Marriage of Heaven and Hell* provides an excellent way to understand Chinese painting, which often includes a poem. The colophon can also provide information about the creation of the painting, the patron who commissioned it, or even comments added by a later owner. Some of these comments are very personal, and provide insight into the way painters worked, such as this one by the poet Su Dongpo: 'Originally I did just the tree, but some exhilaration was left over, so I did the bamboo and stone on another piece of paper.'[473] These usually red squares might be best thought of as personalised book-plates.

Even more problematic is calligraphy, which for the Chinese is one of the highest forms of art but for us is well-nigh incomprehensible. A reading of the ancient texts, which describe calligraphy in terms of nature, both animate and inanimate, illustrates how far we are from being able to enjoy this art. The following, for example, is taken from a description by Cui Yuan, written around 107 AD:

> Here, there are dots and dabs that resemble a string of pearls which, though broken, remains intact. With anger and frustration contained inside, they display themselves with abandon and create marvelous forms. There, there are tremulous strokes perilously elongated, like a withered tree that stands on the edge of a cliff. The slanting strokes and dots off to the side are like a cicada clinging to the branch. Where the brush stroke ends and the configuration is terminated, the dangling threads are tucked in and knotted away, it resembles the scorpion that has inflicted its venomous bite and darts to a crack or crevice, or a hurtling snake that dives down a hole, its head has disappeared but the tail trails behind.[474]

In an age in which handwriting, such as a good italic hand, is little appreciated and we are reduced to a handful of commonly used computerised fonts, this passage appears almost meaningless (in Britain, it could be a candidate for *Private Eye*'s 'Pseuds Corner'). But for the Chinese, calligraphy aspires to reach the 'profound cosmic essence' of things.[475]

For this reason, everywhere in China, whether in a temple or a factory, hosts will show their visitor examples of the excellent calligraphy of emperors and recent political leaders, who cultivate calligraphy as a means of demonstrating intellectual superiority. Since there is little real oratory in Chinese political life – speeches are composed in advance, carefully checked, and read in an extremely mannered way – it is often calligraphy that distinguishes politicians, and allows them to convey honour. To take a random example, the Industrial and Commercial Bank of China announces among the important achievements of its history the fact that, in January 1994, 'General Secretary of the CPC Central Committee Jiang Zemin, prime minister of the State Council Li Peng wrote an inscription to celebrate the 10 anniversary of ICBC foundation.'[sic][476] In fact, there was once so much respect for the written word that it was an offence to throw away paper bearing written characters. Still today, one of the most elegant presents is a boxed writing set with brush, inkstone, ink and some rice paper (the so-called 'Four Treasures of the scholar's studio', to which pigment is added as the fifth treasure for the painter). Even for a foreign visitor, who can neither write Chinese nor imagine what to do with it. It is one indication of the gulf between the aesthetic canons of East and West.

Architecture, on the face of it, is more immediately comprehensible and enjoyable. The forms of Chinese architecture are familiar from books, magazines and film, not to mention the survivals of chinoiserie, so that the Forbidden City, the imperial Summer Palace, or the great temples evoke ready admiration, sometimes without the viewer quite knowing the reason. For it must be said that admiration is often expressed in terms of grandiosity, the sheer scale of things, rather than in the quality of individual structures. Lord Macartney recognised this paradox when he wrote of Chinese architecture that:

> It has certain principles from which it never deviates; and although, when examined according to ours, it sins against the ideas we have imbibed of distribution, composition and proportion, yet upon the whole it often produces a most pleasing effect; as we sometimes see a person without a single good feature in his face, have nevertheless a very agreeable countenance.[477]

It is the 'principles from which it never deviates' that cause a problem, from the apparent sameness of imperial palaces, temples and the grand family compounds of identical-seeming buildings. For the architecture is essentially modular, based on the three elements of a foundation platform, a timber frame and a decorative roof. These could be assembled according to dimensions established by the building's 'rank' and multiplied in accordance with the prestige and the pocket of the owner.[478] This explains why a former imperial residence like Yonghe Gong in Beijing, Qianlong's childhood home, could easily be converted into a Lamaist temple: it was merely a matter of rearranging some non-supporting walls and changing the furniture. Even 'non-Chinese' structures, such as the Great Mosque in Xi'an, conform to this pattern, with some slight variants. Sometimes, this can result in monotony as one visits temple after temple, but the system had many advantages. Modular construction allowed for constant substitution of damaged parts, and greatly facilitated rebuilding after a fire or a cultural revolution. One disadvantage for the Western observer is that since these wooden structures are frequently repainted it can be hard visually to assign a date to a building from the early Ming to the late Qing. There is little obvious difference in style, say, between a building of the date of King's College Chapel in Cambridge (1446) and one of the date of the Natural History Museum in London (1873), which are as different in style as we can imagine.

Few short-term visitors can take the trouble to understand the symbolism of colours and decorative motifs, or the subtle variations of multiple eves. Even the use of pavillions and pagodas in eighteenth-century gardens involved the very specific adoption of decorative rather than functional features. Most of all, in terms of soft power it is difficult to imagine the forms and motifs of Chinese architecture being used in new building elsewhere in the world, with the exception of the arches, roofs and decorative features in Chinatowns. Local styles of great fascination, such as the circular Hakka courtyard houses of Fujian, are never likely to be imitated outside their cultural environment.

'Discord of Discords'

Perhaps the most difficult aspect of Chinese culture is its lyrical culture as expressed in popular song, propagandistic song, and the various forms of traditional opera of which the Peking Opera is the best known. The Chinese love both song and singing (from classical opera to drunken karaoke), but foreigners often find the objects of this love very strange.

They have always sounded so. In his introduction to the first systematic study of Chinese music and musical instruments in a European language, the Jesuit priest Jean-Joseph Amiot (1718–93) noted that some Chinese musicians said to him that 'Our tunes ['nos airs'] are not made for their ears, nor their ears for our tunes.'[479] Other early observers were even more dismissive: another Jesuit father, Nicholas Trigault (1577–1628), writing around 1620, observed that Chinese music was 'nothing but a discordant jangle',[480] while Matteo Ricci made a diary entry in Nanjing in 1599 recording a performance of 'bells, basin-shaped vessels, stringed instruments like a lute, bone flutes and organs played by blowing into them with the mouth' together with 'other instruments also shaped like animals, holding reeds in their teeth'. When they were all played together, he writes, it was a result 'that can readily be imagined, as it was nothing other than a lack of concord, a discord of discords.'[481] The Macartney embassy took with it a certain Herr Hüttner, a 'good judge of music' in Sir George Staunton's words, and five German musicians. Hüttner's expert judgment of Chinese music was that 'their gamut was such as Europeans would call imperfect, their keys being inconsistent; that is, wandering from flats to sharps', and that 'the Chinese, in playing on instruments, discovered no knowledge of semitones, nor did they seem to have any idea of counterpoint, or parts in melody.'[482] Indeed, the gravest defect for the German expert, brought up on the counterpoint of Bach, was that in Chinese music there was always only one melody.

Hüttner was spot on. For the single greatest difference between the European classical tradition and Chinese classical music is that the former is based on harmony, and the latter on melody. We admire the musical genius for the elaboration of harmony, and the very word 'composition' derives from the Old French verb 'composer', meaning 'put together' or 'arrange'. That its first recorded use, in 1597, should come when the 'principe della musica' was Giovanni Pierluigi da Palestrina (1525–94), whose polyphonic techniques lay the foundation for the art of counterpoint, is no accident (the young Matteo Ricci, an accomplished musician and madrigal composer, must surely have heard his music and its famously 'smooth' harmonic style when he was a theological student in Rome during Palestrina's prime). In that tradition, composition means the art of arranging, developing and accompanying melodies and themes, and in doing so create harmony, which Aristotle, in the *Poetics* (Book IV), defined as 'instinctive'.

In Chinese music, on the contrary, not only is melody the essential part of the music, but, in the words of one early student and practitioner, John Hazedel Levis, who was born and brought up in Beijing at the beginning of the twentieth century, the melody itself 'is composed'.[483] Indeed, China was for him 'the birthplace of the oldest and perhaps only developed art and science of melody extant.'[484] The very language is melodic. Levis suggests that early sinologists were mistaken to translate *sheng* as 'tone', a word that students of Chinese still today find on the first page of their textbook. For 'tone' means, to use a definition from the *Oxford Dictionary*, 'a musical or vocal sound with reference to its pitch, quality, and strength', in other words a single pitch of sound, whereas the main characteristic of *sheng* is melodic movement – moving in an upward or downward direction ('tone' might correctly be used of the first of them, *ping*, translated as 'level'). Since in a musical composition each note must necessarily be followed by another that rises, falls or remains constant, this constitutes the basis of musical melody, which is then distributed in time to create rhythm (which should itself both follow the nature of the words and the melody).[485]

In other words, to simplify a complex musicological argument, complete with diagrams and historical examples, there is in China an 'inherent connection between melody and meaning' so that 'the slightest reference made to the tonal uses in everyday speech is helpful in enabling us to discover more completely their uses in music.'[486] This means that when a composer sits down to write music for a poetic text, his work is already partly done because there is melody inherent in the words; and, conversely, that on hearing this piece of music an educated listener is made aware of implicit meaning by associations deriving from the melody. One classic text says that 'Poetry expresses intention. Singing extends speech, and sound follows that extension',[487] and another that 'song is nothing but words, yet words prolonged.'[488] Thus the classical Chinese poetic line of five or seven words provides five or seven units of tonal movement and rhythm, which influence musical composition. Here, then, the problem for non-Chinese is akin to that of calligraphy, for full appreciation of the music requires the immense effort of entering into the poetic language and its aesthetic values. Conversely, many Chinese, on hearing a piece of Western classical music that they find attractive in its sound, ask: 'What is it about?' For they assume that the mood and beauty of the music must be derived from ideas expressed in language.

In fact, the most refined Chinese music is that written for the *qin*, a seven-stringed zither-like instrument beloved of Confucian literati, because of the strong association between words and music, between melody and meaning. This is further strengthened by the emphasis in the *Book of Rites* on music and ethics ('Gentlemen of moral excellence alone can truly understand and appreciate music'), and also between music and rites ('The knowledge of music is close to the knowledge of rites').[489] The *qin* is mentioned in ancient texts like the *Book of Documents*, and was considered to offer 'the true tone of heaven and earth' and 'harmonize the powers of the spiritual forces.'[490] Two of the main genres of *qin* music are that of depicting natural scenery by using different musical pitches and instrumental sonority, and that of reflecting the human element in the natural environment. An example of the former might be 'Mists and Clouds over Dongting Lake', with descriptions of fishermen singing in their boats, and of the latter 'Elegant Orchid', which has been attributed to Confucius and expresses his wordly insuccess by comparing himself to an orchid in a lonely valley which the world cannot enjoy.[491] These are pieces typical of the 'Way of Qin', a philosophical system in some ways similar to the engagement of a Thoreau or a Wordsworth with nature, where the *qin* is played in a forest glade or beside a lake. Such scenes are often the subject of paintings, and obviously represent a rarified view of art. The *qin* is an intensely private instrument, 'at its most expansive a parlor music and more particularly for only one or two' where one of the most essential elements is the 'interplay of visible hand movements and sound'. There are even moments when 'the performer's hands dance through a series of complex shapes and motions, rendering nothing audible, especially to the ears of the non-initiate.'[492] The instrument itself has an exceptionally low volume when unamplified, making it more a private pleasure for the mind than for public performance. It is not a music of soft empire.

Neither is the Peking Opera, a feature of many organised tours to China. Many Westerners are fascinated in anticipation by the masks and costumes, but the harsh, strident, falsetto and nasal voices tend to be less appreciated. The *Jing*, or 'painted face character' seems to shout rather than sing, while gongs, cymbals and clappers accentuate the melodrama of the plots and a modern Chinese love of excessive amplification often renders performances deafening. Even a sympathetic critic like George Bernard Shaw, in the days before amplification, asked the great singer Mei Lanfang why the 'noisy drums and gongs' were necessary.[493] Once again, without knowledge of the structures, plots, and the intricate reasons behind its rhythms and melodies, together with the extremely stylised gestures, postures and of course painted masks, it is hard to enter the spirit of the genre. At its best, Peking Opera is a marvellous amalgam of voice, instruments, acrobatics, face-painting, gesture, costumes and masks. But aspects of performance such as exaggeration, which are key to much of its stagecraft, such as the upward painted eyebrows, costumes and to our eyes absurd artificial beards, can verge on the ludicrous. Most young Chinese today find the opera unappealing, as a glance at any audience will show. Already in 1936, Levis could write that the 'cheaper variety' of Chinese music 'with its din and its clatter and raucous instrumental music, the very reverse of the ancient classical music' was unfortunately the only music to which normal Chinese were exposed.[494] Since most performances of classical music were private, as was that of the classical string quartet in Haydn's day, even fewer foreigners managed to hear it.

There are other approaches to the enjoyment of Chinese music (the character for 'music', *yue*, 乐, is the same as that for 'enjoyment', *le*, 乐). For example by means of the *erhu*, an upright fiddle with a skin-covered resonator played rather like a *viola da gamba*, whose viola-like pitch and nostalgic melodies make it perhaps the easiest Chinese instrument to appreciate. The programme style of music for *erhu* and Chinese orchestra, such as a piece for the lower-tuned *tuoyin erhu* like 'Moon Over the Mountain Passes' from the Tang period, can provide an entry point for someone who enjoys the melancholy viola of Berlioz's *Harold in Italy*. There are also mellower forms of Chinese musical drama, such as the *Huang Mei* opera style from Anhui and the *Yuè Jù* musical theatre of nearby Jiangsu, in both of which there are cross-dressing and gender confusions worthy of Shakespeare. In an example of the former, 'The Emperor's Female Son-in-Law', the heroine, Féng Sù Zhēn, wants to marry her love, but her father has greater social ambitions and forbids the union; she travels to Peking disguised as a boy and is so successful in the civil service examination that the emperor decides she would make an excellent husband for one of his daughters. In the *Yuè jù* style, where in a reversal of the practice of Elizabethan drama all characters are played by female actors, a popular example is 'Liang Shanbo and Zhu Yintai', in which a young girl (Yintai) disguises herself as a boy in order to study and becomes the closest friend and 'blood brother' of her classmate Shanbo. Lines such as 'If you were a girl, I would marry you', spoken to a girl disguised as a boy, could easily be spoken by Orlando, in Shakespeare's *As You Like It*. But apart from the plots, the singing and musical accompaniment in these two very different works are beautiful and never strident.

Yet it is hard to imagine this music becoming as popular in the West as Western music has become in China in past decades, with a concert hall in the grounds of the Forbidden City and a competent China National Symphony Orchestra. It is equally difficult to imagine a young European or American gaining the same fame on the *erhu* as Lang Lang on the piano – or even Yo-Yo Ma on the cello, for although he was born in Paris and studied at the Jiulliard School and Harvard he is considered in China to be Chinese.

What is Chinese Culture?

These considerations are important because the success of traditional Western empires has always depended on elements of their culture being attractive to the 'conquered' – baths and Roman roads to the British, Napoleonic administration to the Italians, American fast food and music to global youth today. The status of superpower requires other countries and peoples to desire to mimic the lifestyle and customs of the imperial power, to accept cultural values together with military hardware or cash. Yet in the case of China, this is unlikely.

Another reason Chinese culture cannot spread is that, paradoxically, it is very hard to explain what exactly it consists in today. This is partly because it has been much destroyed, from the determined Maoist attempt to destroy the 'four olds' (old customs, old habits, old culture and old thinking), to the destruction in the past by both international and internecine warfare, to the ravages of the Cultural Revolution, and to what might be termed the creative destruction of most Chinese cities by zealous modernising administrations. The defining symbols of Chinese culture, Wall, Warriors, Forbidden City and Chang Jiang, cannot be exported. Confucianism is equally problematic: William Theodore de Bary noted that in the twentieth century alone it 'has been successfully buried (in the May Fourth Movement); disinterred and either desecrated or made a museum piece (during the Mao era); and now revived as a live subject of sociological study (for example, the East Asian work ethic) or as a moral philosophy.'[495] Part of the reason for this is explained in a brilliant metaphor by Tsiang T'ing-fu (1895–1965), a graduate of Columbia University and ambassador to the United Nations. In an address at Chatham House in 1935, he suggested that 'Confucianism torn apart from monarchy is like a flying buttress without the cathedral walls to make it functionally useful.'[496] The real problem is how to conciliate past culture and present lifestyle in a more profound way. Yet, when asked to specify what Chinese culture is, and what exactly the tangible elements of the 5,000 years of culture so often touted are, most Chinese, even the educated Chinese, are often at a loss. Their culture is a new middle-class lifestyle culture of leisure, with coffee houses for the adults and American fast-food outlets for the children, and a few titbits of Chineseness to add a touch of local flavour. In some provincial cities, the opening of a KFC franchise is seen as a significant local event. This middle-class lifestyle is increasingly presented as a worthy goal to pursue, but the notion of worthiness is heavily based on Western stereotypes. It is a lifestyle based on images of luxury cars, Western-style homes, and imported leisure activities thought to represent stylish living such as wine-drinking and golf – the latter an enthusiasm that has been adopted with the speed of the introduction of mass motoring. One example was the advertising campaign by SAIC (Shanghai Automotive Industry Corporation) in the summer of 2007 to sell the rebranded Rover 75 as the Chinese-made Roewe 750 with reference to the lifestyle of the 'traditional English gentleman'. Sometimes the advertisements are reminiscent of the foreign-dressed men and women who were mocked by traditionalists at the beginning of the twentieth century.

Yet, once again, little has changed: 'At present, the daily concern of the poor is food and clothing, while the rich are never satisfied. All their leisure is taken up with amorous adventures and material acquisitions …' Thus Beijing just over 200 years ago, according to Cao Xueqin in the best known of modern Chinese novels, *A Dream of Red Mansions*.[497] The new Chinese rich indulge in both pastimes with the same enthusiasm, and it is good to see them enjoy themselves after decades of appalling living conditions. But there is little here to export, and the psychological barriers against language, visual arts and music discussed above seem insurmountable.

PART III

The Stealth Empire: Positioning China for the Twenty-First Century

It is true of the Chinese, to a greater degree than of any other nation in history, that their Golden Age is in the past.

(Arthur H. Smith, *Chinese Characteristics*, 1895)

It seems indisputable that the Chinese, under wise direction, are destined to dominate the whole of Eastern Asia, and, maybe, to play a leading part in the affairs of the world.

(Demetrius Charles Boulger, *China*, 1893)

Finance, Brand and Sport:
Fundamentals and Image

China's new empire will be a Stealth Empire, acquired surreptitiously as an extension of the Invisible Empire of the past. As this book was being completed, *The Times* of London reported that China may have been secretly using a special fund to build a stake in the Hong Kong stock exchange. The title of the piece began: 'China may be conducting stealth attack on …'.[498] It is an adjective that appears increasingly in such reports, and which sits well with the secretive – or, as the old prejudice has it, inscrutable – way in which the Chinese go about politics and business. We will see much more of this in coming years and even decades as China seeks to expand without upsetting the sensibilities of those who see every diplomatic move or investment as a threat to the status quo – which of course they are.

Forecasts about China have always been wildly contradictory. Just as Boulger and Smith reached opposite conclusions 100 years ago, today we can follow a good read like the disturbing *China Threat* with the more reassuring *Coming Collapse of China* (published within twelve months of each other); or in terms of foreign policy we can compare an American view in *Hegemon: China's Plan to Dominate Asia and the World* with a softer Chinese view in *China's 'Peaceful Rise' to Great-Power Status*. Given such a huge terrain, population and historical presence, such contradictions do not surprise, neither do failed predictions such as that as that of Jack Goldstone's 1995 paper on 'The coming Chinese collapse'.[499]

The optimists have been anticipating the boom for half a century. To take one example from many, in 1956 the American journalist Julian Schumann wrote that China would soon be 'a first-rate power, with a lucrative consumers' market awaiting the breaking down of trade taboos and with export products of which some nations are already availing themselves, while others gaze wistfully at them across artificial barriers.'[500] Today, the barriers have been largely removed, as a result of diplomatic success, economic pragmatism and WTO membership. But the 400 million customers of Carl Crow's 1937 memoir and the 3 billion (including India and the ex-Soviet Union) of Clyde Prestowitz's 2005 rhetoric have yet to materialise. The other side of the coin is what the leadership calls 'going out': Mainland companies buying up well-known brands like IBM's PC-manufacturing division, or seeking to create new markets with products such as domestic white-goods or low-cost motor vehicles.

The prospect of Chinese companies increasing global reach alarms Western executives and politicians. Such fears are by no means new, for there have always been fears of the Chinese applying their enthusiasm and hard work outside their country, as can be seen in these lines from a poem entitled 'John Chinaman', published in *Punch* on the occasion of the arrival of the first Chinese ambassador to London in 1877. Having pointed out that the Chinese will 'outdo our doos', and be successful by dint of hard work even where we fail, the poem continues:

> If all this he has learnt without leaving home,
> What will it be now that he deigns to roam,
> And from civilized Christians learns to plan
> From dodges undreamed of by John Chinaman?
> If in fits we would throw John Chinaman,
> Stock Exchange-wards show John Chinaman,
> Where promoters he'll study, financiers scan,
> And go home an improved John Chinaman.[501]

Now that over fifty Chinese companies are quoted on the London Stock Exchange and nearly as many in New York, the previously irrelevant Shanghai Stock Exchange attracts global attention, and giant Chinese IPOs steal the headlines of the financial media, Punch's humour has come true with a vengeance. The 'improved John Chinaman' has learned indeed.

The *De Facto* Financial Empire

China's foreign-exchange reserves exceed $1.5 trillion, or around 30 per cent of global reserves. This sum would be, in a nice analogy from *The Economist*, enough to buy almost all of London's residential property.[502] That in itself is an invisible empire. Since much of this huge sum is invested in dollars, it is effectively sustaining the American currency. The real problem is that Americans spend too much and save too little, but they are held afloat by Chinese savings, which have allowed global long-term real interest rates to decline from around 5 per cent to around 3 per cent in less than a decade. China is effectively subsidising American consumers, or, as Will Hutton expressed it a few years ago, 'the American economy rests on an enormous confidence trick' supported by foreign investors and domestic consumers.[503] At present, the key investor is China, which in a sense already exerts imperial influence over the global economy by means of its influence on the American economy (oddly enough, a survey of educated Chinese found that only 14 per cent of Chinese know that China loans more to the United States than vice versa, while 30 per cent believe the contrary).[504] In early 2007, around 60 per cent of Chinese reserves were invested in US Treasury bonds, although steps were being taken to diversify future investments into Euros and other currencies. At the end of September, a new government fund known as the China Investment Corporation (CIC) began operations with $200 billion available for long-term investments overseas, although one-third might be used to purchase assets from the investment vehicle that holds controlling shares in the big state banks. Direct political control was evident in the choice of the chairman, Lou Jiwei, who is also Deputy Secretary-General of the State Council. The dollar is however likely to remain the favourite currency, and dollar investments are preferred by the new agency. For, apart from its influence on American interest rates and consumer spending power, if China began to sell large numbers of bonds, the dollar would probably collapse and take with it those currencies that are pegged to it. Such self-flagellation is unlikely, for China itself would in this case see its own reserves diminish. This situation is extremely beneficial to America, in spite of the negative views of congressmen and opinionists. In 2004, Morgan Stanley estimated in a report that in the previous eight years cheap imports had saved American consumers more than $600 billion and had lowered costs across the spectrum of industry for American manufacturers. That, in turn, enabled the then chairman of the Federal Reserve, Alan Greenspan to 'keep interest rates lower for longer, making it easier for America's consumers to buy houses and for its companies to invest.'[505]

At the end of February 2007 there was an interesting illustration of China's new role as a major player in global financial markets when the Shanghai Composite Index fell 8.8 per cent and the Shenzhen Exchange 9.29 per cent in a single day. The knock-on effect of these unexpected corrections not only caused the Dow Jones Index in New York to drop 416 points and lose 3.3 per cent, and the FTSE 100 in London to lose 2.28 per cent, but created havoc in smaller exchanges scattered around the world such as the Mexican Bolsa (5.8 per cent) and the Argentinian Merval (7.5 per cent). As a result of this China-induced shock, the month ended with forty-five of the fifty-three key stock markets in the world lower than at its beginning. As a reverse consequence, the UNCTAD report on the *World Economic Situation and Prospects 2007* estimated that in the event of a collapse in the US housing market the growth of China's GDP could drop from an anticipated 8.5 per cent to 7 per cent. Furthermore, since 'about 60 per cent of China's exports are categorized as "processing trade", this in turn would mainly harm exports of intermediate goods by many other Asian countries that are part of the same global production chain.'[506]

China is thus an integral part of the global economy, and already impacts on the individual economy of households all over the world in many invisible ways. In the past few years, especially since joining the WTO in 2001, it has become the world's low-cost technology manufacturing centre for electronics and for much else, especially as Taiwanese producers and the big international contract manufacturers have set up factories on the Mainland. Most products with a chip inside are now manufactured in China. In 2005, an OECD report indicated that China had for the first time overtaken the USA as the world's top exporter of laptop computers, mobile phones and other information and communications technology devices, exporting $180 billion worth ICT goods compared with US exports of $149 billion. Yet in spite of appearances it is predominantly a low-tech industry. On the one hand there are Chinese OEM manufacturers assembling computers, mobile phones and flat-screen televisions, which are assembled from high-value imported components: to give two brief examples, chips from Intel and AMD in the USA and LCD panels from LG and Samsung in Korea. On the other hand, there are companies like Dell and Motorola, and the big Taiwanese companies now manufacturing in mainland China like Quanta, which manage their own manu-facturing.[507] In fact around 60 per cent of Chinese exports are actually produced by foreign-owned factories, often in the 'processing trade', which processes and assembles imported intermediate goods for export.[508] One of the biggest of all the 'exporters' is the extremely low-tech Wal-Mart. At the time of writing, Wal-Mart uses a total of nearly 20,000 suppliers in China, both for exported items and for supplying its Chinese stores (seventy-three in early 2007, with as much as 95 per cent of goods on sale being locally produced). The company itself reckons its total annual exports from China to be around $18 billion, half of this sum being in the form of direct imports and half going through third-party suppliers.[509]

This in itself is a remarkable success story, and it is a commonplace that China has become the world's factory. Yet there are also signs that China is moving up the value chain, becoming a viable alternative to Japan, Korea and Taiwan in providing strong design capabilities as well as cheap manufacturing conditions. Thus investment opportunities in the coming years are likely to be in the areas such as semiconductor design, enterprise software for business automation and operations management, communications infrastructure, software for financial services, and high-tech building infrastructure. A brief visit to some of the semi-conductor or telephone equipment manufacturers is enough to dispel the notion that Chinese development is all about cheap textiles. One factory in Tianjin can produce up to 90,000 mobile phones a day with only 300 employees: components arrive from Asian suppliers by sea, are assembled on automated lines, and shipped out to Western contract customers within a matter of hours. In this case, it is logistics and supply-chain management that create the competitive advantage, not the usually-cited drivers of China competitiveness such as the nine listed by Peter Navarro in his rant against 'the China price': low wages, minimal worker health and safety, lack of environmental controls, FDI, clustering, counterfeiting, undervalued currency, government subsidies and protectionism.[510] Visit the automated warehouse of the Lenovo factory in northern Beijing, and you will see no workers at all, simply a high glass-enclosed observation post from which visitors can watch the conveyor belts, automatic packaging machines, and loading operations performed by computers and robots. The same is true of the contract manufacturers and Taiwan-owned factories that now assemble most of the computers, PDAs, flat-screen televisions, mobile phones and other sophisticated electronic goods in the world (with percentages ranging from 70 per cent to 95 per cent for the various sectors) for Dell, Hewlett Packard, Motorola, Nokia, Toshiba and most other global 'manufacturers' who comprise the major share of China's exports. Indeed, one researcher has put the percentage of high-tech exports as high as 85 per cent.[511] As China overtook the USA as the largest exporter to the European Union countries in 2006, 191.5 billion against 176.2 billion (although it should be observed that EU exports to China also increased by 24 per cent),[512] the largest increase was in fact in mechanical and electrical machinery. In large measure, it is the 'supply-chaining', as Thomas Friedman calls it in his book *The World Is Flat* in a section on Wal-Mart,[513] which makes all this possible, rather than slave labour (this is not to deny that it exists, but that it is a declining part of the story). In this, China is as misunderstood as Wal-Mart: operating in tandem, they are unbeatable, perfecting supply-chain efficency into what Friedman calls 'global optimization'. Nowadays, this goes beyond the traditional function of suppliers, since the source factories are fully integrated into the final customers' business: rather than simply loading pallets into containers, leaving the customer to sort everything out in his own warehouse in Europe or the USA, goods for customers like Wal-Mart and Tesco are shipped already prepared on separate pallets for distribution to individual supermarkets; articles can even be priced, or arranged on a display stand ready to be unwrapped and placed directly in the shop. Morever, pressure by major global firms on Chinese manufacturers of electronic goods to comply with the Electronics Industry Code of Conduct (EICC) means that these factories, often in fact foreign-owned or foreign-managed, are far from the conventional image of the sweat-shop.[514]

Good, well-educated technical management – in the case of the Tianjin factory, having studied engineering in Britain – and skilled workers also play a key role. Thus China has been able to leapfrog Western companies in some technologies. This is evident in the fact that Chinese companies going to IPO abroad are often Internet, wireless, or value-added telecommunications firms, while Chinese political leaders constantly stress in their official pronouncements the importance of science and technology related development.[515] The government's support for Lenovo's acquisition of IBM's personal computer division, and encouragement of 700 foreign-invested R&D centres now operating in China, are also examples of this.

But success is by no means a foregone conclusion. China has been trying for a long time, but the results have so far been relatively meagre in terms of genuine high-tech innovation. Top-down approaches have not succeeded in creating the necessary eco-system in which innovation flourishes; neither have they managed to generate an overall sense of quality in China brands (as several quality scares concerning toy and food exports evidenced in 2007). A book published a few years ago opened with a distinction between brand-name products manufactured in China and Chinese brands.[516] A group of people identified among the personal belongings taken for a weekend retreat some thirty items made in China, but no one could think of a Chinese brand name. Not even the white-goods company Haier, which is rapidly developing a brand in the Western world, or Tsingtao, whose beer is familiar to lovers of Chinese restaurants everywhere.[517] The authors suggest that it is likely that at least one Chinese brand will in the future enter the list of the world's top ten most valuable brands, but which one could it be? It is difficult to imagine today, when customer service levels are quite inadequate. A more profound problem is the lack of 'country brand'. Once again, a top-down approach has been attempted with the 'Chinese Brands Promotion Committee', organised by the State Bureau of Quality and Technological Supervision,[518] but truly excellent brands derive from the expertise and management of products and services rather than from bureaucratic fiat.

It has never been clearer that in this shrinking world, countries and regions and cities have to compete with each other for tourism, inward investment, aid, membership of supranational groups, buyers of their products and services, and for talent. So countries as well as companies must emphasise brand and develop realistic strategies for communicating and promoting themselves, their culture and their policies contribution to the global community. In the past few decades, the wealth of developed countries has grown as a result of marketing, both of individual products or services, and of the country itself. Indeed, country branding possesses such intrinsic value that it can become more important than other reputation building factors. If we read that a new, extremely expensive and technologically advanced car will be built in Germany, we will not be surprised but simply curious; implicitly, we know it will involve superb engineering and design quality, and we know that it will be both expensive and solid. But if we were to learn that such a car would be built in Portugal, or Morocco, we would immediately be sceptical, for our assumptions are inspired by the perceived personality of the country of origin (with no disrepect for those countries and the excellence of individual companies, Portugal and Morocco do not have global reputations for quality engineering). Yet it is also true that a country can build a new brand, as Finland has managed to do: whereas ten years ago Finland was associated with abstract concepts like 'cold' and 'midnight sun', today it is the land of technological innovation and design in mobile communications led by a one-time manufacturer of lavatory paper and wellington boots. In similar fashion, the smoky industrial Britain of Dickensian legend has reinvented itself as a centre of finance, tourism and sport.

Creating the China Brand: the Olympic Games

One good move is to begin with the image of sporting success. As this book is being written the big event on everyone's tongue in China is the 2008 Olympics, from government officials and businessmen to local market-stall keepers and schoolchildren. There is genuine national enthusiasm as the Games are seen as the culmination of China's rise to world recognition and a return to the pre-1989 status quo in terms of international respectability. In this, China is following the entry into the OECD and global acceptance of Japanese products after the 1964 Olympics, and the emerging economy growth that accompanied the 1988 games in Korea. And when the naysayers emerge to complain about Beijing bulldozing slums, beautifying the city falsely, and removing beggars from the city centre in a cosmetic attempt to show off the city, we should remember that similar processes are not new to Olympic venues. These consequences, 'evictions of low-income communities; criminalization and arrests of homeless people; and reinforcement and acceleration of ......'s gentrification process', could well be describing Beijing but actually refer to Atlanta in 1996 when as many as 30,000 people were 'displaced' from their homes. Similarly:

> state and city authorities, together with the tourism industry, regard the Games as a gigantic public relations exercise to showcase .... as a major tourist destina-tion for the next several decades. Any intrusion by the homeless – one of the most visible signs of the city's immense social problems and inequality – will damage the advertising image

These words were written of Sydney in 2000.[519] Thus there is nothing new or risible about the Beijing organising committee's boundless ambition: the Beijing Games, they assert with confidence, 'will fully express the common aspiration of the Chinese people to jointly seek peace, development and common progress with the peoples of the world,'[520] and the 'most memorable Games in history' will provide 'corporate partners with an opportunity to invite the world in and introduce China to the world.'[521] According to the Mayor of Beijing, over 95 per cent of the population of China supported the Olympic bid because they believed that hosting the Games would 'help raise their quality of life.'[522] These are no different from the aspirations of the citizens of Atlanta and Sydney.

What is different for China is that this enthusiam for sport is quite new. Until the twentieth century, it had never been known as a sporting nation and even in that century for its prowess in a limited number of fairly minor sports such as table tennis and gymnastics. In the more distant past, contact sports were rare and spectator sports inexistent. There can be no comparison in modern sporting traditions with Australia, for example. It is true that pursuits such as archery and chariot-driving were two of the 'Six Arts' practiced by the Confucian gentleman, but as martial training rather than as spectator sports for their own sake. The Qing were keen on hunting and related martial sports, but practised them in the privacy of imperial hunting reserves. There are references in historical documents to a kind of football played during the Warring States period, perhaps with a leather ball filled with hair. But there are no details of rules and tactics. In Tang times there was a variation in which players attempted to score a 'goal' by kicking a ball through a hole in a piece of cloth held up by bamboo poles, but there seems to have been no action with players simultaneously involved and no physical contact.[523] Other participatory sports occasionally played include dragon-boat racing (an annual event, with its origins in ritual sacrifice), tug-of-war (also ritual, with the aim of bringing rain) and wrestling. There was some cock-fighting and dog- and horse-racing, but they were aristocratic pastimes; in fact, none was a team sport, and the human element of participation was minimal. All this was, presumably, linked to the basic idea of non-competitiveness found in Confucius, who asserts that 'The gentleman competes in nothing' (*Analects*, 3.7).

There were physical difficulties for Chinese sportsmen before the twentieth century: imagine playing sports with a queue (aka as a pig-tail)! Some athletes cut them off on their way to the first national athletics competition in Nanjing in 1910, and one is said to have removed his in desperation after it pulled down the high-jump bar. There was also an incident that must have been both amusing and acutely embarrassing when the young emperor Guangxu was learning to ride a bicycle in the Forbidden City. It was said that 'his queue had become entangled in the rear wheel, and that he had had a not very royal tumble.'[524] Then there was the problem of 'face'. At the beginning of the twentieth century, as Carl Crow explained, the 'fetish of face provided what appeared to be an insuperable obstacle to the development of athletics in China, for the loser in a contest, whether a team or an individual, felt such a humiliating loss of face that it was impossible to maintain regular sports schedules.'[525] Once defeat seemed inevitable, a team would be likely to walk off the field before the game was finished. It was only due to official promotion of sports, and ceremonies in which both winner and losers were cheered, that this ancient 'fetish' was overcome.

The earliest use of the Chinese word for sport, *tiyu*, was in 1895 in an essay on *Strength* by the moderniser and translator Yan Fu (1853–1921), who had studied in London and knew England well.[526] Yan based his essay on the concept of moral, physical and intellectual education developed by Dr Thomas Arnold of Rugby. He understood how the duty of the individual was above all a commitment to the survival and growth of the society of which he was a part. Physical culture represented for him the importance of the human body in the new China of which he dreamed, in which this new strength would be unleashed. Yan wrote that:

Today, if we want to talk about the wealth and power of nations, the basis must be the physical strength of the people ... if we look at the lessons left us from Chinese and Western history, of the fifty to sixty nations that exist in the five continents today, there is not one that did not arise out of this physical strength. Greece of the Zhou, Rome of the Han, the Turks of the Tang – these dominant groups of each age have all grown to be strong and beautiful, able to withstand suffering and capable in war, ruling over their era.[527]

He might well have mentioned the British Empire, which was consciously built on the same foundation – on the famous playing fields of Eton, in the Duke of Wellington's phrase. The Social Darwinism promulgated by Yan Fu set the stage for the rise of competitive sports in China on the basis of the English public school ethos, although it was also spurred by contemporary phenomena like the damage to national pride and recognition caused by the disastrous Sino-Japanese War of 1894–5. Only an emphasis on personal strength and physical health would make China strong enough to overcome such disasters in the future, it was argued.

In 1902–3, Liang Qichao made the link even stronger in his series of essays *On the New Citizen.* In these, he argued that the weak Chinese body was due to the absence of concepts of progress, public morality, and duty in the country, and that it was vital to be physically strong as well as morally and intellectually strong. This was true of women as well as men: foot-binding was condemned because it weakened the children born to women who practised it. Liang even suggested specific types of physical training, maintaining that there was no European nation that did not promote fencing, horsemanship, soccer, wrestling, marksmanship, swimming, and boat races.[528] His protégé Cai E coined the slogan 'strong citizens, strong nation' with reference to the same sports and to the great sporting and military state of ancient Sparta.

The modern Chinese scholar Wu Wenzhong has identified the first modern sporting competition as an athletics meeting held at St John's College in Shanghai in 1890, organised by a Canadian missionary,[529] while an American Board missionary suggested that the earliest competitive events were those held between Christian institutions fourteen years later.[530] But there is no dispute over the period: around the same time, the first YMCA in China was opened in Tianjin, using sport as a focus for its proselytising, and British missionaries built a soccer field in the village of Noufu, in Yunnan.[531] From its origins in London in the post-Arnoldian climate of 1844, the YMCA emphasised the importance of sport, and its members invented several well-known sports: in 1891, James Naismith invented basketball at the International YMCA Training School with elevated goals to avoid the physical clashes of rugby; in 1895, Volleyball was invented by William Morgan at the YMCA in Holyoke, Massachusetts by blending elements of basketball, tennis and handball into a game that he first called mintonette; and, in 1926, softball was invented at the YMCA in Denver. Thus it was natural that basketball should be introduced to China in the 1890s at the Tianjin YMCA. Soon sports textbooks were being published in Chinese and the first gyms and swimming pools were built in major cities. Fittingly, it was the director of the Shanghai YMCA, who, in 1908, as he showed slides of that year's London Olympics on his new 'projectorscope', asked rhetorically when China would be able to 'invite all the world to come to Peking for an International Olympic contest …'.[532] Now, exactly a century later, his question has been answered.

The first attempt at Olympic participation involved sending a single athlete, the sprinter Liu Changchun, to the Games in Los Angeles in 1932, although he was eliminated in the preliminary rounds in his two events, the 100m and 200m. But this meagre participation may have inspired the 1934 silent film *Athletics Empress*, in which one of China's best-known actresses, Li Lili (1915–2005), played the role of a talented teenage sprinter. The ideas of Liang and Cai inform the film. Li Lili's wonderfully sympathetic character Yin Ling is brought from the country to live in her merchant father's mansion in Shanghai, where she reveals a natural talent for sprinting. She notes in an early scene that 'Father, I know why China is not strong. The first reason is that the body is too weak'; later, her father observes that 'you always say athletics will make the country strong.' In order to achieve this, and to foster her natural talent and exuberance (she climbs up the ship's funnel to celebrate on arrival in Shanghai), Ling enters the Jinghua sports training school for women, where her teacher insists that the 'self-renewal' of any race requires a sound body. Through several episodes with her main rival, Ai'zheng, the viewer is led to understand that everyone can lose sometimes. In the closing sequence, her good friend Xiao Qiuhua suffers a heart attack in the 100m final of a national competition, and Ling is distraught at such consequences of competitive spirit. That afternoon, she is scheduled to run in the 200m final against Ai'zheng, and her family and friends are preparing for her coronation as the Empress of Athletics. A gold crown has been prepared, but Ling decides that it is not worth the trouble and runs slowly so that her rival can win both the race and the crown. The final message, made explicit in the subtitles, is a synthesis of the values of Confucius and Baron de Courbertin: it is the success of the sport and the competition that matters, not individual victory and glory.

As Liu Changchun's participation in Los Angeles may have inspired the film, so the film itself may have inspired the decision in 1935 to provide proper financial support and training facilities for the upcoming Berlin Olympics. For in 1936 there were sixty-nine Chinese competitors in athletics, swimming, basketball, football, weightlifting, boxing and cycling, and a delegation of thirty-nine observers. Only one athlete, the national pole-vault champion Fu Baolu, passed beyond the preliminary rounds, and even he did not win a medal. An official report by the delegation complained that on their return to China 'we were ridiculed as

China Central Television's new headquarters building in Beijing, designed by Dutch architect Rem Koolhaas and due for completion in 2008

Modernity in the provinces: the entrance to an Internet Café in Nanchang (Jiangxi Province)

The First Pass Under Heaven, at Shanhaiguan, on the coast north-east of Beijing, where in 1644 the Qing army entered Ming China from Manchuria b[ ] bribing the commander, Gener[a] Wu Sangui (Hebei Province)

Entrance to the Golden Resources Shopping Mall, Beijing, claimed to be the larg[e] shopping mall in the world

Interior of the Golden Resources Mall: 1,000 shops, 230 escalators and 200 restaurants

Inside the 'Egg': the spectacular new Opera House and concert hall complex in Beijing, by French architect Paul Andreu, a stone's throw from Tiananmen Square

A fighting Buddha at the shrine of Chinese martial arts, Shaolin Temple (Henan Province)

Ladies preparing dried Tofu on the pavement, Zhangzhou (Fujian Province)

The Long Corridor in the
Summer Palace, Beijing

淄博压力容器厂

Mao still revered on a
factory entrance in Boshan
(Shandong province)

The 'impression factor of
walls': the Ming dynasty
walls of Xi'an (Shaanxi
Province)

A believer at prayer in the Great Mosque at the heart of the bazaar in Xi'an's bustling Muslim quarter (Shaanxi Province)

Old habits die hard: a modern pawnshop in Beijing, on the 3rd Ring Road in the wealthy district of Chaoyang

A traditional pawnbroker's shop inside a secondary entrance to the home of the head of the village of Luo Tian Cun (Jiangxi Province); it was customary for the great landlords to offer 'banking services'

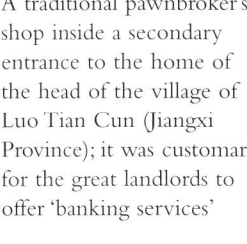

Ruins of the Emperor Qianlong's European-style Palace, designed by Jesuit architects led by Giuseppe Castiglione (the Old Summer Palace, Beijing)

Sunday afternoon in the park: spontaneous music-making in the park of the Temple of Heaven in the south of Beijing

The ruins of a small neglected temple amidst the building frenzy of Beijing (near the Niujie Mosque)

Traditional bridal chamber in the ancient village of Shui Nan Cun (Jiangxi Province)

Traditional houses awaiting demolition in Zhangzhou (Fujian Province)

A treacherous section of the Great Wall at Simatai, north-east of Beijing

Athanasius Kircher, frontispiece showing the Great Wall (1667), scanned from a copy in the Beijing Centre Library with the kind permission of the Centre Director, Dr Ron Anton

having brought back nothing but a "duck's egg".[533] Then, after the 1930s, there was a prolonged period in which for reasons of war, the emphasis on economic development, and the travails of the Cultural Revolution, in which less importance was given to sport – with the exception of sports that could be used in a political context like that of the famous 'Ping-Pong Diplomacy' of 1971, when a visit by an American table-tennis delegation paved the way for President Nixon's visit and the reopening of diplomatic relations.

Only in the past decade or so has there been widespread interest in popular global, and televised, sports like soccer and basketball. Traditionally, sports strategy followed the military concepts of Sun Tzu. The emphasis was on sports like badminton and table tennis, which involved moves that put the ball in an impossible position for the opponent rather than lead to hard physical contact. Thus the Chinese have also excelled at diving and gymnastics, but have found little enthusiasm for contact sports like rugby (except in Hong Kong). But in spite of thousands of training centres, and hundreds of golf courses, there have as yet been few major success stories. Soccer has fallen flat, in spite of Huang Jianxiang's prowess as an excitable (Brazilian-style) television commentator who became briefly renowned, and then lost his job, for his hysterically partisan support for Italy and disparagement of Australia during the last World Cup. At the time, various websites, including the Italian daily newspaper *La Reppublica*, offered downloads of his Chinese language excitement at a goal.[534] Corporate soccer sponsorship has also not taken off as expected, despite attempts by soccer enthusiasts like Lin Ming San, founder of the motorcycle manufacturing company Lifan.

It has been a gradual rise to success. China has gone from the single athlete at Los Angeles to the large delegation sent to Berlin four years later, then from fifteen gold medals at Los Angeles in 1984 to twenty-eight at the Sydney Games in 2000 and thirty-two (and second-place overall after the USA) at Athens in 2004 – which included the 110m hurdles gold for Liu Xiang. Lobbying to hold the Games in Beijing grew in force parallel to this increased athetics success, but first it was necessary to readmit China to the Olympic community as the People's Republic of China while the previous 'China' – namely Taiwan – changed its name to Chinese Taipei. This occurred in 1979, after Deng Xiao Ping announced that China would soon be prepared to make a bid; that China did so in 1991 in the aftermath of international opprobrium for the events of 1989 meant that the first attempt to host the Games in 2000 failed. Then, in 1999, with the country gathering strength as an economic power and increased respectability in international organisations such the United Nations and the World Trade Organisation, the successful bid was launched. Celebrations took place in July 2001 with a crowd of over 400,000 people in the same Tiananmen Square that had seen unhappier events just twelve years before. The great hope for 2008 is to win more medals overall, and possibly also more gold medals, than the USA. More than a handful fewer would be perceived as disastrous failure; a greater number would drive investment in sport for the foreseeable future.

Nothing has been left to chance, with events like the Asian Games in Doha in December 2006 serving as competitive training sessions. Each sport represented in the Olympics has a precise target for the number of medals it should win, with as many as 20,000 athletes in full-time training for a team in which only a few of them will participate. The quality of training has been assured by the best foreign coaches, who were hired to ensure success in this 'nationalistic' enterprise: an American for the women's softball team, a Serbian for men's soccer, a Lithuanian for men's basketball, South Koreans for men's and women's hockey, and a Japanese woman for synchronised swimming, with dozens more at lower levels.

In China, for all major sporting events selection comes early and training is ruthless. From early childhood, small-hipped children are pushed towards gymnastics, strong-thighed children towards weightlifting, and children with good coordination between eye and hand towards table tennis. Sometimes the selection begins at birth, as in the case of China's most famous athlete, the basketball player Yao Ming. In this case the birth was closely observed, since his parents were both unusually tall and themselves well-known basketball players. News of the newborn child's height and weight (23in, 11.2lbs) was immediately sent to the Shanghai Sports Commission. Such was the fervour that Wang Chongguang, who had coached Ming's grandfather and father and was to coach Ming himself, wanted to call the baby boy Yao Panpan, meaning 'Long Awaited Yao'.[535] It was as if a messiah had arrived. Yao appeared in his first feature story in the Shanghai newspaper *Xinmin Evening Post* when he was only four years old. Put together this obsessive long-term planning together with slogans that emphasise the pride of being part of a great national achievement, such as 'Put your Motherland in your heart as you cast your eyes to the world' and 'Practise your skills and bring back something for your country', and it is easy to see why even an expert such as Jim Scherr, CEO of the American team for 2008, perceives China as the biggest threat to US medal aspirations.[536]

One sporting name is now recognised in most places in the world, that of Yao Ming. But this is mainly the result of his enormous height (7ft 6in), the fact that he plays for the Houston Rockets and is successful in advertising as a global brand ambassador for McDonald's. Two other Chinese players, Mengke Bateer and Wang Zhizhi, participate in the NBA. Then there are other rising sports stars such as Liu Xiang and Li Na, who have the advantage of relatively simple names to remember and in the second case to pronounce. Liu equalled Colin Jackson's 110m hurdles world record in the 2004 Olympic final, and in 2006 broke Jackson's record in Lausanne. Li was the first Chinese tennis player to win a WTA tour title when she won the Guangzhou International in 2004 and in 2006 reached the quarter-finals at Wimbledon. Among the 10,000 junior Chinese players seeking to emulate her, it is a safe bet that some will eventually follow her into the list of the top twenty players in the world. Chinese sportsmen excel in the favourite Mongol and Manchu sport of archery, in particular He Ying, fourth in the women's individual event and winner of a silver medal with the women's team at the 2004 Olympics together with Lin Sang and Zhang Juanjuan. In diving there is Fu Mingxia, who won several world championships and three Olympic golds (in Barcelona and Atalanta), and even a skiing champion in Han Xiaopeng, who by winning a freestyle gold at the 2006 Winter Olympics in Turin become the first ever Chinese medalist at the Winter Olympics. More visible in Europe are Chinese soccer players like Li Tie of Everton and Sun Jihai (who with Fan Zhiyi was the first Chinese player in Britain at Crystal Palace in 1998) of Manchester City. The youngest recent success and one of the best-known faces on British television is the snooker player Ding Junhui, who became the first non-British player to win the UK Championship in 2005.

This boom augurs well for future Chinese sporting success. It is striking how many school-age children of both sexes can now be seen on the streets of the major cities dressed in track-suits and carrying brand-name sports bags, and how they tower over the parents who come to collect them. What is certain is that substantial success in the Olympics, finishing first in the medals tables or at least surpassing the 2004 numbers, will generate greater sporting achievements. It will also provide a fresh impulse to the new nationalistic fervour.

9

Nationalism, Militarism and Technology

On the foundation of the People's Republic of China as a modern nation-state in 1949, ideas and concepts that had been floated for a century coagulated in a clearly defined concept of the Chinese nation. Its main traits were delineated by one of the foremost Chinese historians, the British-educated Fu Sinian (1896–1951), in an unpublished manuscript entitled 'A Revolutionary History of the Chinese Nation'. In extreme synthesis, he defined them as follows:

- the Chinese nation is peace-loving, cherishing peaceful relations with neighbours;
- even if the Chinese nation was sometimes occupied by foreign nations, national awareness could never be destroyed and would re-emerge when necessary;
- the Chinese nation would never forget territorial losses to enemies;
- although there could be problems and weak moments, the Chinese nation would always see a resurgence with new and effective leadership.[537]

Still today, these principles can be seen to inform both Chinese nationalism and foreign policy, and can be used to explain the mindset behind events and actions that might at first sight seem inexplicable to a non-Chinese observer. Indeed, we can also see how Communism and Nationalism went hand in hand, to use the phrase of Zhou Enlai, in 'state nationalism' (*guojiazhuyi*),[538] which is why it is possible to suggest that a form of nationalism, which we might define as 'state patriotism', is currently replacing Communism as an ideology without any need to change the structures of power. The most recent evidence of this is the way in which enthusiasm for the Olympic Games has been subtly transformed into nationalistic protests abroad and support for Party policies in Tibet at home.

New Nationalism

In the 1980s, nationalism nearly disappeared as a result of the failures of the Cultural Revolution. Intellectuals sought to place blame for this and other failures on Chinese culture and the nation, and advocated the total destruction of their country's culture. This view was also advocated by the authors of *River Elegy* when they argued that Chinese civilisation was doomed to disappear like that of the Maya and the Inca and like 'all the river valley civilizations in the world'.[539]

This tendency saw a dramatic reversal in the 1990s, as the Party exploited nationalist sentiment to bolster its legitimacy after the events of Tiananmen Square. One way of doing this was to shift the ideological focus from class struggle to patriotism. Thus nationalist sentiment was officially described as 'loving the state' (*aiguo*) or 'patriotism or love and support for China' (*aiguozhuyi*).[540] As the diplomatic historian Michael Hunt has observed, 'by professing *aiguo*, [the] Chinese usually expressed loyalty to and a desire to serve the state, either as it was or as it would be in its renovated form.'[541] The shrewd part has been to transfer patriotism in the sense of nationalist feeling for the nation or state into loyalty towards, or at least support for, the Communist Party. There is yet another useful term that helps us to understand the shift, coined in English by an anthropologist who has lived and worked in China: 'Great Han Chauvinism', which as he defines it is a hotpotch of 'nationalism, ultrapatriotism, traditionalism, ethnocentricism and culturalism.'[542] These sentiments were nurtured through programmes of indoctrination in the workplace and exemplary stories in school textbooks (sponsored by the 'Policy Outline for Implementing Patriotic Education', 1994), with such success that those who went through them are often unaware that what they assume to be 'facts' about the past are little more than propaganda. Their influence may be seen today in the historical costume dramas that are broadcast on major television channels throughout the day, and through patently chauvinistic computer games. Nicolas Chauvin would have been at home in China at the turn of the twenty-first century.

The Chinese scholar Zhao Suisheng has shown how the rise of nationalism in the nineties operated on three separate levels: state, intellectual and societal. At the state level, the main influence was a patriotic education campaign initiated in 1991 emphasising Chinese tradition and culture, the *guoqing* ('national essence'), with key elements such as the celebration of the virtues of the Great Wall, the revival of Confucianism and the emphasis on traditional costumes, music and dance. This top-down campaign was bolstered by military exercises against the putative 'enemy' of a separatist Taiwan, and concerted attempts to enter the WTO and host the Olympic Games. At the second level, around the same time Chinese intellectuals began a more critical stance towards Western culture, and what they perceived as excessive Western influence in the previous decade, that is to say between 'opening up' in 1978 and the summer of 1989. The resonance of influential Western books such as Francis Fukuyama's *End of History* (1992) and Samuel Huntington's *Clash of Civilizations* (1996) generated in China a 'geopolitical-based intellectual discourse critical of the West' parallel to the impulse towards cultural nationalism, while the argument of an earlier book, Edwaid Said's *Orientalism* (1978), was used to invent the term 'occidentalism' to define the historical 'other' against which China defines itself (usually Japan, in its recent 'Western' guise).

The third level, societal, was identified with bottom-up populist sentiment, although in a paradoxical and very Chinese way the 'bottom-up' is at least partly driven 'top-down'. Spurred by official propaganda, there was a flourish of best-selling anti-Japanese books in the mid-nineties with explicit titles like *The China That Can Say No*, *The China That Can Still Say No* and *How China Can Say No*, which drove popular support for headline events such as naval exercises in the Taiwan Strait, and protests against a right-wing Japanese group that built a lighthouse on one of the disputed Senkaku islands – which provoked a new book with the title *Be Vigilant Against Japanese Militarism!*[543] This simmering nationalist sentiment prepared the ground for popular protests against the Belgrade bombing incident of 1999.

Thus in cultural terms nationalism and the new national identity were forged from two significant threads: anti-Westernisation (building on the historical victim narrative against China's century of shame and 'humiliation' by imperial powers), and the revival of traditional Chinese civilisation (more or less loosely based on a revival of Confucian values) after Mao's attempts to destroy it. These two threads are brought together in the propaganda and beliefs concerning some innate form of Chinese superiority, which manifest themselves most obviously in the well-known slogan 'socialism with Chinese characteristics'. This phrase is not as meaningless as some people like to portray it. As Bruce Gilley has written of 'Chinese' democracy in the future, it will be different 'not because China is unique but because democracy is always heavily colored by the culture in which it operates.'[544] This contemporary Chinese nationalism is based on a variant of John Stuart Mill's utilitarian principle of the greatest good for the greatest number, which might be expressed as follows: 'as long as you don't seek to undermine the Party, and eulogise Chinese culture at every opportunity, you may do as you wish.' Such pragmatic nationalism, which lays behind the wish to extol Chinese virtues in the Olympic Games, may be stoked into flame on demand by references to 'humiliating' events such as the Nanjing Massacre. It is a key element in what political leaders refer to as their 'strong country dream', which in synthesis means substituting the decaying Communist ideology with a new form of nationalism.

This new nationalism is projected through two main channels, military power and technological excellence, which are intimately related in the Chinese mind and which we will now review.

Chinese Military Power in the Twenty-First Century

The element of national pride is evident in the growing openness in the Chinese Press about military exercises and public satisfaction in the success in the design and production of advanced indigenous weapons and spacecraft.

According to American analysts, China has been escalating military expenditure significantly in the past few years because it wishes to take centre stage as a world power. In particular, according to the *Annual Report to Congress* in 2005, the PLA is 'emphasizing preparations to fight and win short-duration, high-intensity conflicts along China's periphery.'[545] That is to say, against Taiwan. But preparations now go beyond this. Just two years later the tone had modified and the target changed, with the PLA said in the 2007 *Report* to be 'pursuing comprehensive transformation from a mass army designed for protracted wars of attrition on its territory to one capable of fighting and winning short-duration, high intensity conflicts against high-tech adversaries.'[546] This, translated, means the United States, at least in its Pacific Ocean ramifications. Since leading military planners realised how vulnerable China would be in a modern war after the collapse of Iraq during the 1991 Gulf War and again after the 1998 Desert Fox operation in Yugoslavia, the PLA has been rapidly updating and modernising for air warfare. For a country whose traditional military power and strategy has always been land-based, this represents a major shift in thinking. Officially, China's development and modernisation strategy for the PLA is articulated in three steps: first, 'to lay a solid foundation by 2010'; second, 'to make major progress around 2020'; and third, to 'reach the strategic goal of building informationized armed forces and being capable of winning informationized wars by the mid-21st century.'[547] Put bluntly, even in their own terms, the PLA is unlikely to be a threat beyond its immediate territorial claims for some time, while the likelihood of a land invasion of China by one of its neighbours seems even more remote. That is just as well, since even with the improvements in organisational training, better education, new weapons and modernisation, which impress many observers, the blend of old and new 'has yet to prove effective in battle'.[548] Yet in military planning terms, given the long planning cycle of complex weapons such as advanced fighters and aircraft carriers, the middle of the twenty-first century is not so far away, and the ambitions of the PLA cannot be taken lightly.

There is another possible explanation of increased military expenditure concerning the relationship between the Party and the PLA. Until the late 1990s, the personal prestige and charismatic leadership of Mao Zedong and Deng Xiao Ping, and their indisputable military accomplishments, guaranteed the full support of the leading generals in implementing policy. Mao could 'intervene freely in military affairs' as he saw fit, knowing he had the PLA's unconditioned support, while in a later decade Deng was secure enough in his long-term vision to freeze military expenditure and even decrease it in terms of the overall budget.[549] This was possible in spite of transparent need for modernisation, and Deng was still able to obtain the PLA's loyalty in a key moment like June 1989 – when senior generals may have privately disagreed but did not disobey. But neither of their successors as President, Jiang Zemin and Hu Jintao, has a military background, and one shrewd way in which both have gained the support of the military leadership is to increase military spending.

China's goal of regaining its old prestige necessarily entails greater defence spending, which is now thought to be running at about $100 billion annually, over twice the Chinese government's declared level ($45 billion in 2007), and is expected by America to rise to between $250 billion and $350 billion by 2025.[550] Even the official Chinese figures admit that in 2007 there was a 17.8 per cent increase over the previous year. Explaining these figures at the Tenth National People's Congress in March 2007, which formally approved the budget, government spokesman Jiang Enzhu (using figures from two years earlier for comparison) pointed out that China's military expenditure was 6.19 per cent of that in the United States, 52.59 per cent of that of a much smaller country like Britain, and 71.45 per cent of that in France, representing 1.35 per cent and 4.02 per cent of GDP for China and the United States respectively.[551] More interestingly, in a formal speech made in the Great Hall of the People during the ceremonies for the eightieth anniversary of the foundation of the PLA, President Hu Jintao linked military expenditure to the growing economy. 'Economic growth,' he argued, 'is the basis for enhancing defense capability, which is, in turn, an important indicator of overall national strength.' He also made an explicit link between military power and technology investment when he added that the PLA will be better positioned to defend the nation by 'putting in place a comprehensive scientific, technological and industrial structure.' While this is in line with Maoist thinking, the notion of gradually increasing 'input in national defense as the economy grows' reads as a real threat, given the predictions for China's economic growth in the twenty-first century.[552]

To this end, using the so-called 'Three Ways Policy', China employs its new-found wealth to purchase weapon systems and military technology from Russia and Israel (in the period 2001–5 China purchased 120 aircraft, eight submarines, and 200 aircraft engines from Russia),[553] develops and builds aircraft in cooperation with other countries, such as the Su-27SK/F-11 Flanker fighter built under Russian license. It is also producing its own advanced fighter known as the Jian-10, or Fighter-10, which went into service at the end of 2006 with the first home-made turbo-fan engine.[554] This was an exceptional media event, which displayed nationalistic pride in the development of the fighter in widespread coverage in newspaper reports, in published photographs, and in clips broadcast on state television networks. Both the fighter and the Taihang turbofan engine were developed by China Aviation Industry Corporation, whose vice-president, Geng Ruguang, took the unusual step of holding a press conference at which he announced that 'China has become the world's fourth country to develop its own advanced fighter planes, engines and missiles.'[555]

Another striking example of technological advance was the successful launch of an anti-satellite ballistic missile just a few days later – perhaps encouraged by positive reactions to the Jian-10 – to knock out an orbiting weather satellite. Western intelligence sources announced that a missile, probably a KT-2 ground-launched rocket introduced in 2002 for launching purposes, launched 'from or near' the Xichang Space Center in Sichuan, had destroyed a Feng Yun 1C (FY 1C) polar orbit weather satellite, which had itself been launched in 1999, early on 12 January at an altitude of 530 miles.[556] No explosives were used, simply a collision, or what the experts term 'kinetic impact', in what was in effect a 'low-tech' attack. But, in theory, this means that China is now capable of attacking American spy satellites, something that previously only the United States itself and Russia could do, although no similar tests have been carried out since the mid-eighties. It could also destroy the satellites that Taiwan uses to monitor the deployment of Mainland missiles. Apart from the concerns of space environmentalists about thousands of pieces of debris floating in space for years to come, this successful mission brought simmering Western fears briefly to the boil. Since the first war in Iraq, satellites have played a vital part in American surveillance and battlefield communications and the new 'National Space Policy', promulgated in late 2006, asserted that 'freedom of action in space is as important to the United States as air power and sea power.'[557] This attack may indeed have been an effective reply to the threat implicit in the Space Policy that the United States 'will deny, if necessary, adversaries the use of space capabilities hostile to U.S. national interests', and 'oppose the development of new legal regimes or other restrictions that seek to prohibit or limit U.S. access to or use of space.'[558] Be that as it may, that China possessed the capability to target satellites, and could demonstrate it, a few months after provocatively illuminating an American satellite by a laser beamed from the ground, reinforced worries about China's arms build-up expressed in successive reports to Congress. It is unlikely that the PLA or Second Artillery performed such a test without the knowledge of the Central Military Commission, as some commentators suggested, and much more likely that it was a typically Chinese way of sending a strong diplomatic signal concerning the use of space. A few days later, when the news became more widely known, the *International Herald Tribune* quoted a Harvard astronomer as saying 'this is the first real escalation in the weaponization of space that we've seen in 20 years', while in London, *The Times* ran the headline 'Star Wars' missile test heralds new arms race in space'.[559] Whether or not this was pure rhetoric, these two events taken together certainly marked a significant achievement by the PLA.

Sixteen ambitious technological projects were announced in 2007, of which the most significant from a commercial point of view is a wide-bodied passenger jet, and the most important from a scientific point of view is a proposed Deep Submergence Vehicle (DSV) capable of diving to 7,000m – even though there are no such depths in Chinese territorial waters. The implication of such technological advances is, however, not limited to China itself. For, as if in retaliation for arms embargoes against itself, China sells weapons and provides military assistance to countries such as Iran, Sudan, Zimbabwe and Myanmar, which are also under embargo from the European Union.

But how big, and how effective, are China's armed forces?

It is no surprise to learn that China has the largest armed forces in the world, with around 2.3 million members of the PLA, which is organised into the Ground Forces, the Navy, including marines and naval air force, the Air Force, and the Second Artillery Corps, the strategic missile force (see Figure 4, Appendix 2).[560] In addition, there are 660,000 paramilitary personnel in the People's Armed Police (PAP), whose main tasks include internal security, anti-terrorism, guarding gold mines, forests, water and electricity supply, and communications, border security and firefighting,[561] and more than 10 million members of the Reserve and Militia Forces. The main PLA forces are increasingly well armed, although American Intelligence believes that it will take at least five years before its modernisation programme results in a force that defeats a 'moderate-size adversary.'[562] One problem, however, as David Shambaugh notes in his detailed analysis of China's military forces, while the air force – essential to a Gulf-style conflict – has changed its policy so that its leaders are both younger and have a flying background, this means that the PLAAF has no leaders with combat experience.[563] Nonetheless, the latest *Quadriennial Defense Review* reported that 'of the major and emerging powers, China has the greatest potential to compete militarily with the United States and field disruptive military technologies that could over time off set traditional U.S. military advantages absent U.S. counter strategies.'[564] One major difference between Western armed forces and the PLA is the latter's explicit political function: it is expected to ensure the success of economic reforms and modernisation of the country and guarantee the 'nature of the people's army under the absolute leadership of the Party politically, ideologically and organizationally'.[565]

Perhaps the most worrying aspect is the growing nuclear force, incuding silo- and vehicle-based missiles and five new missile Jin-class submarines, which will each have twelve missiles with a range of 5,000 miles. But it has been argued recently that China does not maintain tactical nuclear forces and that unlike most other nuclear powers the country bases its nuclear strategy on the minimum force necessary for deterrence. Its eighty or so operationally deployed nuclear warheads (compared to nearly 200 in Britain and 350 in France) are 'assigned exclusively to ballistic missiles that are kept unfueled and that are stored separately from the war-heads.'[566]

The Navy is also acquiring more credibility. In addition to its nuclear submarines, the PLA Navy possesses sixty-four surface warships and between sixty and seventy attack submarines, which makes China's submarine fleet the largest in the world in terms of quantity and a key player in the waters surrounding Taiwan and Japan.[567] In addition, there are over forty medium and heavy amphibious transport ships, and around fifty coastal missile patrol craft. Although Chinese ships now venture into the open ocean, or blue water as the specialists call it, the development of the PLA Navy is at present envisaged in terms of dominating the coastal territorial waters up to 200 nautical miles and gathering Intelligence. But some experts believe that by around 2020 China will be able to focus on 'the greater periphery', meaning the Strait of Malacca, the Indian Ocean and the Persian Gulf.[568]

In some ways, the PLA's organisational structure is well suited to modern warfare, since the separation of air force and navy is increasingly difficult. In fact, in terms of defence it has moved from the protection of key military, industrial, and political targets to a doctrine based on an integrated system combining aircraft, surface-to-surface missiles, artillery, special operations forces, naval forces, and guerrilla units. Newer and more advanced aircraft, including AWACS, a new supersonic bomber, and the Jian-10, provide China with forces that are technological similar to potential regional adversaries.[569] The *Report to Congress* from which some of these details are taken concludes that 'over the long term, if current trends persist, PLA capabilities could pose a credible threat to other modern militaries operating in the region.'[570] This latter phrase comprehends American bases within range of China's weaponry, such as Okinawa, and prompts sinologist-hawks such as Arthur Waldron, Michael Pillsbury and Bill Gertz to advocate a more explicit military stance against China as an aggressive and unstable nation.

Defence Culture

Such fears do not square with the 'defence culture' that has dominated Chinese strategic thinking since ancient times. This is based on three basic principles: that the Chinese people are by nature peace-loving, that they only resort to force in self-defence and that they are neither aggressive nor expansionist in nature. In the last case, as if to underscore the weight of history in Chinese thought, the example of Zheng He's 'peaceful' and non-colonial voyages is often cited. In 2005, a government *White Paper* cited Zheng's expeditions in these terms: 'What he brought to the outside world was peace and civilization, which fully reflects the good faith of the ancient Chinese people in strengthening exchanges with relevant countries and their peoples.'[571] One expert suggests that there has been no change in attitudes towards violence in over 2,000 years,[572] for they are assumed to derive ultimately from Confucian precepts, such as the statement in the *Analects* that to 'lead an uninstructed people to war, is to throw them away',[573] or Sun

Tzu's dictum that 'supreme excellence consists in breaking the enemy's resistance without fighting'.[574] Such thinking led to Mao's enunciation of four operational principles around 1930: when the enemy advances, we retreat; when the enemy camps, we harass; when the enemy tires, we attack; when the enemy retreats, we pursue.[575] His own military writings usually begin from the concept of the strategic defensive,[576] and his successors speak as if China has never been to war. Yet the history of China, like the history of most countries, abounds with wars, warriors, and Warring States. Minor conflicts along the Chinese frontier are not usually widely reported in Western media, but there were as many as forty-seven 'planned organized military actions' against neighbouring countries between 1949 and 2002.[577]

One interesting feature of the way that China has historically viewed defence policy, especially in terms of the concept of 'non-territorial defence thinking', is the way in which in which the basic rationale behind defence was that of moral principles.[578] Why, we might ask by way of example, did China's massive manpower advantage and the possession of Krupp cannons not allow the imperial army to defeat the tiny Westerrn forces involved in the Boxer Rebellion of 1900? The superficial answer is that the Dowager Empress's real fear was of internal rebellion: hence she fled to Xi'an after putting up a token show of resistance to the foreigners, but ruthlessly executed court officials she believed had betrayed her. As a modern commentator remarks, 'the contrast of the reluctant attacks on the Legations and the resolute execution of one's own loyal officials revealed most vividly where China's enemy resided.'[579] There was a comparable event in 1860, when the emperor Xianfeng fled from Beijing in the belief that it was better to suffer military defeat at the hands of the British and French than to concede them the right to open diplomatic missions in his capital. For that would entail recognising the power and legitimacy of these foreign barbarian countries as in some measure equal to the power granted by the Mandate of Heaven. It was part of the same non-territorial logic that enabled China to cede a large chunk of land to Russia, and Hong Kong to Britain, since bits of physical territory were less important than face or principle. Beyond this, however, are more profoundly Chinese concepts such as *shih*, 'a dynamic power and integrated force that combines the effects of material things, natural forces and human factors in some action.'[580] The logic of this may be seen in otherwise inexplicable statements of Sun Tzu in *The Art of War* such as 'Hence those who use fire as an aid to the attack show intelligence; those who use water as an aid to the attack gain an accession of strength.'[581] It was the astute combination of natural forces and human factors that led to Mao's unexpected success during the Long March. Still today, *The Art of War* and Mao's concept of 'People's War' (*renmin zhanzheng*) inform the basic thinking of military planners.[582] There is more to warfare than man-made weapons.

The concept of *shih*, which in this context we might also define as 'stealth warfare', also informs the Chinese policy of deception and disinformation that Western observers perceive as military opacity. For in this way, China can use Intelligence to confound enemies by policy changes and the introduction of new weapons in peacetime, and by unexpected attacks in war. One high-level American official has lamented that 'We are caught by surprise by the appearance of new systems that suddenly appear fully developed.'[583] There is little reason for China to change this distinctly stealth empire approach in which tactics such as those of Sun Tzu and Mao still condition strategy. Scenarios of future conventional wars of aggression against neighbours like Korea and Japan, or of China sparking a global war over oil, make good light reading,[584] but seem inherently improbable given the Chinese way of approaching problems.

The nineteenth-century diplomat Sir John McNeill, referring to the way in which Russia professed to have no desire for 'conquest and aggrandizement' and would drain its resources before succeeding in military conquest of Persia and Turkey, wrote of 'successive encroachments' as a strategy superior to that of actual conquest. In this way, he wrote, 'no violence is thus called for – no collision need take place; and *if there is no collision, there is no opportunity for other powers to interpose*' [italics in the original]. In fact, similar successive encroachment is one of the key components of China's stealth empire, and it is a concept that puts a completely different spin on the phrase 'peaceful rise'.[585] In this light, it is fascinating to observe that a phrase like 'peaceful strategy' is actually something of an oxymoron in Chinese since the character for 'war': 战 (*zhan*), appears as the first of two characters used to write 'strategy': 战略 (*zhan lue*)

As one modern Russian military advisor noted of the Chinese in the 1960s, their view of strategy has always been different: 'Unlike Europeans, they did not construe it as a matter of striking with force, but as an art of stratagem, trickery and outsmarting the enemy.'[586] Rather than wiping out an enemy force, they would by preference force it to flee, or attempt to trick the enemy into conflict with another force. Joseph Needham makes the same point in another way when in a discussion on gunpowder he notes that the 'belief in action at a distance' is a 'cardinal feature of Chinese technology and science.'[587] Hence the widespread use in the past of toxic smoke, smoke-screens, incendiaries as well as the use of gunpowder in cannon, rockets, grenades and guns, and the basic traditional strategic doctrine of 'active defense' or *jiji fangyu*. The emphasis is on seeking the weaknesses of the enemy rather than his strengths. In the words of a recent detailed analysis, 'the Chinese stress intentions, while Westerners focus on capabilities.'[588] The cultural difference is substantial. But it would be unwise to underestimate the Chinese military. Harold R. Isaacs noted how, in a single decade, the American perception of the Chinese army as a 'pulpy and ineffectual mass' before the Korean War was transformed during the conflict into that of a body of key strategic advisors deploying sophisticated equipment. It was the fact of facing the army in the field that made the difference.[589] Vague reports and prejudices became tangible soldiers and weapons.

In his review of China military strategy, Scobell concludes that while Chinese 'elites' think of China as a defensive power, this 'does not mean that China will shy away from conflict.'[590] In a moment of crisis, China is capable of switching unexpectedly and rapidly to the use of force. Just as China used 'calibrated force' in Korea in 1950–3, against India in 1962 and against Vietnam between 1965 and 1973, so it might resort to force – spurred by nationalistic impulses – in order to defend what it perceives as issues of sovereignty in the China Sea and against neighbouring states. But it must be said that in the new century the famously opaque PLA has become surprisingly open in allowing foreign military observers to visit military installations and participating in joint military exercises. Beginning with the presence of twenty-seven foreign observers, from Asian, African and European countries, at exercises in Inner Mongolia in 2003, several similar groups have been invited – in particular a group of sixty Asian observers at a live-ammunition exercise involving 10,000 troops, a mechanised division and the air force.[591] In spite of all this 'peaceful' activity, however, the hypothesis of wider-ranging military initiatives cannot be ruled out in the long-term.

Military Build-Up and Taiwan

In the short-term, the most likely initiative concerns Taiwan. This is the one conflict for which China prepares assiduously in terms of military hardware, and has publicly described as a potential reality. A *White Paper on Defence* published in December 2004 stated bluntly that 'the situation in the relations between the two sides of the Taiwan Straits is grim.'[592] Then, in case there was any possibility of ambiguity, it was made absolutely explicit: 'Should the Taiwan authorities go so far as to make a reckless attempt that constitutes a major incident of "Taiwan independence," the Chinese people and armed forces will resolutely and *thoroughly crush it at any cost* [my italics].'[593] China could hardly go further than this. Moreover, in the following year the Anti-Secession Law, promulgated in the National People's Congress on March 14, reinforced this concept, in particular in Articles 8 and 9. The former states that the State Council and Central Military Commission will employ *non-peaceful* means to protect China's sovereignty if 'secessionist forces … cause the fact of Taiwan's secession from China,' if there are 'major incidents entailing Taiwan's secession', or if 'possibilities for peaceful reunification' are exhausted. The latter adds the softener that China will 'exert its utmost' to protect the lives of Taiwan civilians in the event of conflict. This is made clear also in Chapter III of the *White Paper*, when it assigns priority to 'Strengthening the Navy, Air Force and Second Artillery

Force', the last of which is 'responsible for deterring the enemy from using nuclear weapons against China, and carrying out nuclear counter-attacks and precision strikes with conventional missiles.'[594]

The Second Artillery was created in 1966 to operate all ground-based strategic missiles in China, with the commanders of missile bases reporting to the Artillery's headquarters in Beijing rather than to one of the nine regional military commands. Described as a 'technology-intensive military force' with a high proportion of engineers and university graduates.[595] Each of its eight bases has between two and four launch brigades with nuclear or conventional missiles kept in highly secret undereground bunkers. The Wannan Base, known as Base 52, located in the mountains between Anhui and Jiangxi provinces, has around 800 missiles trained on Taiwan from launch sites in Jiangxi, Fujian and Guangdong provinces. This was the base that launched live missiles across the Taiwan Strait in 1995 and 1996. Soldiers of the Second Artillery are amongst the most highly trained and screened in the world. They are required to make a lifetime commitment to the force, after which they are never allowed to travel abroad; even domestic travel and contact with family members are 'rigidly monitored'. They enjoy little contact with the outside world: even their own families live as much as 60 miles away, and their children are not allowed to study at university.

The Second Artillery operates on a four-stage alert system for its nuclear missiles, with all orders issued directly by the Central Military Commission, whose chairman is the President of China. Since the PLA airforce is not yet ready to enter into combat with potential enemies such as Taiwan or Japan, with inexperienced combat pilots and aircraft 'at least a generation behind' these 'enemies', the Central Military Commission depends on their short- and medium-range missiles in the event of a high-tech local war.[596] This is the unit that would fire the missiles, and it is worth noting that while personnel in the Army has been reduced by 1.5 per cent in recent restructuring that of the Second Artillery has been increased by 3.8 per cent.[597]

Military escalation of the Taiwan issue is actually fairly recent. It began after the collapse of Western Communism in 1989, when China no longer needed to maintain large numbers of troops and weapons along the Soviet frontier. The rapid increase of forces facing the island, and the purchase of Su-27 fighters from Russia, led in turn to President George Bush authorising the sale of 150 F-16 fighters to Taiwan in 1992.[598] Then the deployment of conventional missiles targeting Taiwan accelerated after the visit of Lee Teng-hui to America in 1995. That year, the Second Artillery had its baptism of fire with the launch from Base 52 of five tactical missiles, which landed near the harbour of Keelung, in the north of Taiwan. In March the following year, one missile landed in the sea 19 nautical miles east of Keelung.[599] Since then, the PLA has conducted almost annual exercises 'on and near' Dongshan Island off the coast of Fujian, with Dongshan playing the role of Taiwan in what are as much visible political statements as military exercises. The 2001 exercises were noteworthy. They lasted through the entire summer from May to August and were overseen by the Vice-Chairman of the Central Military Commission. They are thought to reflect how the Commission imagines such a conflict will evolve in three phases, following the guidelines for an amphibious assault: 'Strive for quick resolution, prepare for a sustained war.'[600] The first phase was one of electronic warfare designed to 'paralyse Taiwan's communications systems.'[601] The PLA employed technological devices to emit false signals, jam electronic signals and coordinate attacks on command, communications and Intelligence centres. The second phase employed live cruise missile launches and aircraft sorties to simulate a cross-straits attack; in a throw-back to the days of Coxinga and junk warfare, this phase also simulated an airborne landing on the Pescadores Islands. This would be feasible because, according to American military analysts, in addition to the mobile CSS-6 and CSS-7 short-range ballistic missiles deployed by the Second Artllery there are more than 700 aircraft within unrefuelled operational range of Taiwan, while around two-thirds of Chinese naval forces are deployed to the East and South Sea fleets.[602] The final phase simulated engagement with foreign military units that might come to the aid of Taiwan, such as American aircraft carriers.[603] Naturally, the Chinese hope that there would be no third phase in the event of a real attack, but that might not be enough to deter them from trying.

For Taiwan is integral to China's coastal defence system, acting, in General Douglas McArthur's picturesque turn of phrase as an 'unsinkable aircraft carrier and submarine tender',[604] which as a base 100 miles offshore would offer freedom of access to the China seas and the Pacific Ocean. Yet the real present purpose of those exercises was 'to avoid conflict in the future by deterring Taiwan from pursuing independence', or, as military sources expressed it in a typically Chinese turn of phrase, 'resorting to force to press for peace.'[605] A full-frontal attack would smack too much of a 'conventional' empire.

As we have seen above, the attitude of the PRC to Taiwan is a matter of cultural or even spiritual rather than territorial reunification. Once again, Sun Tzu provides the best illustration in his section on 'Attack by Stratagem': 'Thus the highest form of generalship is to balk the enemy's plans; the next best is to prevent the junction of the enemy's forces; the next in order is to attack the enemy's army in the field; and the worst policy of all is to besiege walled cities.'[606] It is an issue of moral suasion, of such importance that it must be backed up by the threat of military action – however unlikely that may be in reality. For this reason, it is likely that an eventual naval blockade is much more plausible than an amphibious assault or even a missile attack.[607] It would be less bloody, and America would be forced to call its bluff.

Stealth Scenarios for Attack

So what, we might ask, are the twenty-first-century equivalents of traditional tactics and weapons? For it is generally accepted that while ballistic missile capabilities are impressive, the conventional warfare capabilities of Chinese armed forces are around 'twenty years behind the state of the art, with the gap widening,'[608] with much antiquated equipment still in use, some even dating back to the 1950s. The point is that technology permits the leapfrogging of conventional capabilities. An interesting article by a retired American-trained general compared warfare to acupuncture, and sought to identify the appropriate points, or Achilles' heels, in the United States.[609] Some of the 'acupuncture points' enable us to consider possible scenarios, and consider the kind of attacks that a 'stealth empire' could carry out, such as an electro-magnetic pulse (EMP) attack, a cyber attack or an interdiction of foreign oil supplies.

China is capable of delivering an electro-magnetic pulse attack, which could be launched from an intercontinental ballistic missile, a submarine-launched ballistic missile, a long-range cruise missile, or an orbiting satellite armed with a nuclear or non-nuclear EMP warhead. The *Report to Congress* cited above suggests the possibility of an electro-magnetic pulse attack against Taiwan. The fascinating if slightly disturbing hypothesis is that of using a high-altitude nuclear burst to generate a high-altitude electromagnetic pulse (HEMP), which would cause a change in the ionisation of the upper atmosphere and lead to 'the degradation of important war fighting capabilities, such as key communication links, radar transmissions, and the full spectrum of electro-optic sensors.'[610] The attraction of this for China is that such an action might not be considered by the United States to be a full-out nuclear attack; thus Taiwan would effectively be disabled without the fear of nuclear retaliation. The problem is that the effects of such an action might also impact on Japan, the Philippines, commercial shipping and air routes, and even key areas of the Chinese mainland itself. Worse still, however, such an attack could be delivered against the United States itself. A single nuclear burst of one or more megatons 4km over one of the central states like Nebraska or Kansas could cover the entire continent with electro-magnetic pulses in less than a second. This would damage electrical grids, and immediately disable computers and all other devices containing microchips. The economy would grind to a halt as businesses and entire industries shut down.

A cyber attack could have similar consequences, without the inconvenience of having to launch such a complicated array of weapons. It can be launched 'at home'. China's growing expertise in computer technology and ability to manipulate and exploit the Internet would make it relatively easy to disable much of the Western world's technological infrastructure. In 2007, there were several incidents assumed to have been caused by Chinese government hackers in US government offices, military suppliers and think-tanks, in one case entering computers in the office of Defence Secretary Robert Gates in the Pentagon. Although such attempts are probably common on both sides, the Pentagon attack caused particular concern because it suggested that the PLA could disrupt systems at will. In the words of one official, it showed that they had the ability 'to conduct attacks that disable our system ... and the ability in a conflict situation to reenter and disrupt on a very large scale.'[611] Other reports spoke of further plans to disable America's aircraft carriers – obviously useful in the case of a strike against Taiwan – and of a detailed plan to achieve 'electronic dominance' over rivals such as the US, Britain, Russia and South Korea by 2050.[612] Similar hacker attacks were carried out against British and German government offices in the same year. The problem was, and will be in the future, that there are many ways of disguising the origin of the searches or attacks, using proxies, simulating false IP addresses, or launching the assault from outside Chinese territory, to take three simple examples.

Blocking foreign oil supplies would involve a more complex military operation, but since the United States now imports about 75 per cent of its oil needs, and a quarter of that comes from the Persian Gulf, it could be an attractive option. The threat of such an action could also be exploited in diplomatic terms as a counter-measure to a possible American blockade of supplies to China through the Malacca Straits. Alone or in partnership with regional rogue nations, China could mine the Strait of Hormuz or block it with cruise missiles; this would have the double advantage of preventing supplies from reaching Japan. China's modernised navy, especially when it acquires greater deep-water experience, would be capable of such action. At the same time it would compromise the fleet of super-tankers that China itself is currently building, with a target of around ninety due to be in operation by 2012. But one of the potential sources of US-China conflict, whether military or diplomatic, in future decades is likely to derive from pressing demand for oil supplies. While even a China-basher concedes that it is unfair for a country like the United States, which consumes 25 per cent of global oil production to satisfy the needs of 5 per cent of global population, to criticise a nation that currently consumes only 7 per cent of global oil for 20 per cent of the population,[613] it is equally clear that China's demand is increasing rapidly while oil stocks peak and diminish. If car ownership continues to develop at the present rate, and no truly viable alternative emerges, Chinese oil imports could equal those of the United States by around 2020.

These ideas are fascinating first of all in their potential, and secondly because they force a shift from the traditional Chinese mindset captured in the phrase *zhong dao qing qi* ('attach importance to self-cultivation but neglect technology'), which long influenced military thought and still figures in debates on strategy, to a more modern acceptance of technology.[614] At the same time, from a Chinese point of view there has been a important change in the mentality of the PLA. Since the demise of the second generation of leaders, in particular Deng and his cohorts, the role and scope of the PLA in internal affairs has been greatly diminished. It has, in the words of one expert, morphed from 'the tool of revolution to the guardian of national security'. It is now an increasingly professional force, indeed 'professionalism, as embodied in the slogan of winning the next major high-tech war, has been set as the ultimate goal for military modernization.'[615] Both these changes can be seen in the 2004 *Defense White Paper*, which spoke of the new doctrine of 'local wars under conditions of informationalization'[616] and in the American assessment two years later that much of China's current investment is in 'high-end, asymmetric military capabilities'.[617] The problem here is that such doctrines turn an uncomfortable spotlight on the country's technological deficits. China is well aware of this, and if there is a single area in which the Chinese will admit to being behind any other country, it is in terms of the United States and its advanced technology. Military expenditure is one way in which the gap could be narrowed, thus Chapter VII of the *White Paper* asserts that while China's defence-related science, technology and industry is focused on military applications of technology it also 'vigorously develops dual-purpose technologies and actively participates in the development of the national economy.'[618] This provides an insight into the way in which the Chinese have absorbed the need to develop technologies that can serve military and civilian purposes, in particular in the broad field of microelectronics and ICT (Information and Communications Technologies). Future wars, as the United States has shown in recent years, will be fought through technology rather than through infinite supplies of disposable soldiery.

The Coming Technological Supremacy

Apart from the United States, where the invention of the Internet and advances in satellite technology provide excellent examples of dual-purpose technologies, China looks to Japan and South Korea as models. This is justifiable when a report on what the Korean government designates as the '99 core technologies' stated that on average China was only 2.1 years behind that country's position.[619] But the gap with the US is narrowing rapidly too as nationalistic fervour requires that China develops it own capability to drive technological innovation – even if, in contradiction to an expressed desire for indigenous development, that entails purchasing technology licenses, inveighing against foreign companies to provide technology transfer as a bargaining chip for entering the Chinese market, and exploiting industrial espionage. This can be seen in the desire to delay the introduction of 3G mobile phone systems until Chinese engineers could perfect the indigenous TD-SCDMA standard in which most intellectual property is Chinese. In the typically grandiose Chinese style of an online forum dedicated ambitiously to 'promoting the global uptake' of the technology, the standard is extolled in the slogan 'Promote TD-SCDMA, Create 3G Glory'.[620] But which country with over 500 million mobile phone users would not prefer the 'glory' of developing its own standard and at the same time save money on purchases from the multinational equipment vendors? Certainly companies like Siemens and Nortel were happy to sign research and development agreements with Huawei and China Putian Corporation respectively.[621]

They may have forgotten the EVD (Enhanced Versatile Disc). This new standard was designed in 1999 to be a purely Chinese competitor to the DVD format after Sony and other electronics companies had demanded retroactive royalties on DVD players that had been made in China. This, plus the desire to enhance the country's reputation in technology, was the main reason behind the new format. According to Xinhua new agency, the new discs would 'shake off dependence on foreign technologies in production.'[622] The discs would have better quality and much more storage space. With full government support it was announced as a product in 2003; the first players were expected to arrive on the market the following year. The leading proponent, Beijing E-World Digital Technology, the business arm of the EVD Industry Alliance, whose shareholders included various government bodies and ten domestic DVD-player manufacturers, saw itself as competing with the Blu-ray format. The players were launched with great fanfare, with the *People's Daily* lauding the fact that they featured 'players featuring the core technology of China's own intellectual property rights.'[623] In 2006, it was said that the electronics chain store Gome would have 150 sales areas in its shops, while the number of franchised retailers would reach 1,200 by the end of the year. Zhang Boaquan, Secretary-General of the Alliance, declared that nineteen of twenty-one DVD manufacturers would cease making them and produce only EVD players by 2008.[624] As yet, as 2007 draws to a close, although they exist on the market, EVD discs and players have failed to take off.[625]

In fact, although supposed to be a Chinese standard, with exclusively Chinese Intellectual Property Rights, the video codec was provided by the American company On2 Technologies, which entered into litigation with the Chinese developer over failed payments, while the audio codec was provided by the German company Coding Technologies. These companies supply many multinational and household name companies, from Facebook to Intel and Warner Bros (and also Coding Technologies) in the former case, and from AOL to Nokia and Samsung in the latter case. In late 2007, On2 Technologies lists China Netcom and another Chinese company, Nanwang Multimedia, among its customers but not the EVD partner Beijing E-World, or any of the DVD manufacturers,[626] while Coding Technologies lists no Chinese customers at all. Amidst all the bombast, perhaps the Alliance forgot that if the new EVD players were to be compatible with existing

DVDs, the Chinese manufacturers would in any case have to to pay for foreign licenses.

Another vital sector in which there is much catching up to be done is aviation. But here the signs are more promising. In March 2007, the State Council gave formal approval for a long-term plan to design and manufacture a wide-bodied jet for over 150 passengers in competition with Airbus and Boeing, with 2018 as a possible date for the first flight.[627] This makes good business sense in a market for new aircraft estimated as around 1,600 large jets by 2020, and as many as 3,000 more by the middle of the century.[628] Sales are guaranteed in a country where the largest airlines have the government as the majority shareholder. In addition, a military version of such an aircraft would be an important asset for the PLA Airforce: the civilian version will be manufactured in Shanghai, and the military version at the hub of the Chinese aerospace industry in Xi'an. There is, of course, a certain amount of hubris in this ambition, since this 'indigenous' aircraft will in fact be less than 50 per cent Chinese. For, rather like 'Chinese' computers, which are assembled from key components manufactured elsewhere, vital components such as the avionics and engines will be imported or at the very least produced under license in China. Yet, when pushed, in a straw poll most acquaintances admit privately to feeling safer on an Airbus or Boeing.

Technological excellence is thus a matter of national pride, but also difficult to achieve. But in some areas, such as military applications, homemade technology is an imperative, especially in the presence of embargoes and Western reluctance for technology transfer in sensitive areas.

Around twenty years ago it was recognised that military security, economic prosperity and social welfare required leadership in science and technology, and that 'self-sufficiency in high technology' could both sustain development and help to achieve China's rightful place in the world order.[629] The investments initiated at that time have already born fruits in success stories such as that of Lenovo, and in the strength of China as a manufacturer of technological goods. In the next ten years or so, China will upgrade from low-cost manufacturing to genuine innovation – especially in fields such as nanotechnology, chip design and medical robotics. There is a strong argument on the basis of present-day shifts that China will become a technological superpower on or near to parity with the United States by mid-century. This tallies with the observation in the 2006 *Report to Congress* that the PLA is transforming itself from a mass infantry army designed to fight wars of attrition to a high-tech professional force capable of fighting high-intensity wars beyond China's borders.[630] Since most future conflicts are likely to involve either 'local limited warfare' with neighbours like India or Vietnam or low intensity 'armed conflicts' deriving from border disputes, it is obvious that China needs to focus more on technological warfare and less on land-bound forces.[631] Until 1991, China believed itself to be as invulnerable as the Iraqi army had believed. The lesson was not lost on the PLA generals.

This transformation, and the development of China's high-tech industry, dates back to a decision taken in 1986. In March of that year, four leading scientists wrote a personal letter to Deng Xiao Ping urging greater investment in new technologies and the creation of a National High-Technology Development Program. From the date of this letter, the plan that Deng approved and pushed into being was known as the '863 Plan' or *Baliusan* (from the Chinese year and month of initiation, *ba*=8; *liu*=6; *san*=3, hence '86 March'), which aimed to 'pool the best resources' to bridge the gap between Chinese and international high-tech development. In extreme synthesis, the key objectives of the 863 Plan were as follows: first, to monitor international high-tech developments, seek to narrow the gap between foreign and Chinese technology, and seek breakthroughs where China is strong;[632] second, to 'train and cultivate' the future workforce; third, to commercialise and industrialise technological achievements in order to create a new high-tech industry by 2000; and, fourth, to play a leading role in the promotion of high-tech development.[633] The impetus behind the programme was military, from weapons experts, but the implications were much broader since its seven designated sectors included areas where the non-military applications were also important such as information technology, biotechnology and energy. It proposed a concerted solution to the problem of high-tech deficiency in terms of development, ideology and organisation. In other words, it represented a total solution, which overturned the Maoist concept of science as elitist and emphasised the economic and social importance of science and technology.

One area in which China has made immense technological progress under the 863 Plan is in fact in space technology. This bore its first tangible fruits with the eight-day flight of Shenzhou (one of the alternative names for the country, 'the Spiritual region', as we will recall), a spacecraft that 'combines features of the American Gemini vehicle, launched in 1964, with the Soviet Soyuz of the late 1960s.'[634] It has since been used for the first Chinese manned flight in October 2003, and the more recent four-day flight of Shenzhou 6 with two astronauts in 2005. The political and nationalistic thrust of the Shenzhou project was evident both in the presence of President Hu Jintao at the launch-site at Jiuquan in the Gobi Desert and in the pre-launch declaration of China's first astronaut, Lt Col. Yang Liwei, who said: 'I will not disappoint the motherland. I will gain honor for the People's Liberation Army and the Chinese nation.'[635] Now, in 2008, a new and more powerful launch vehicle denominated Long March 5, with capabilities similar to those of the European rocket launcher Ariane 5, is ready for use. Chinese experts have begun to speak about colonies on the moon and the possibility of manned exploration of Mars. The eleventh Five-Year Plan for space development approved in the summer of 2007 emphasises manned space flight, lunar exploration, and high-resolution earth observation. This includes the launching of a 'breeding' satellite for agricultural experiments and research into short-term manned and long-term autonomously orbiting space laboratories. In addition, on the ground, research in space astronomy, space physics, micro-gravity science, and space life science, in which it is hoped China will make 'important and original achievements'.[636] A longer-term plan known as Project 211 entails a soft landing on the moon in 2010, and a return mission by 2020.[637]

A less militaristic development was the creation of a country-wide system of Science Parks. Already in 1984, spurred by visits by city officials and scientists to Silicon Valley and Boston in the USA, and Cambridge in the UK, the district government of Haidian, a suburb in the northwest of Beijing, held a conference to discuss future development and in a subsequent report stated its ambition to create 'China's Silicon Valley.'[638] Four years later, Haidan Science Park, now usually known as Zhongguancun (Haidian) Science Park after the road that leads from the Third Ring Road to the Park, was created as the first science park in China. Now, having grown at a uniquely Chinese rate of around 30 per cent for many years, this vast area includes dozens of universities, hundreds of research institutes and over 6,000 companies. But it must be said that most of this growth is the result of government investment: if we look at the example of the year 2002 (data for later years are not readily available), we find that of the total number of 863 programmes in China, 34.59 per cent were in Beijing, and that they absorbed 48.6 per cent of the overall 863 expenditure.[639]

This was in part the result of another initiative known as the Torch Programme, launched in 1988 with three objectives: to establish high-tech zones throughout the country, to create service centres for development and training, and to establish projects in areas such as new materials, biological engineering, electronics, opto-electronics, energy saving and environmental protection. Thus by 1994 there were fifty-two recognised high-tech development zones sponsored and financed by the state, covering much of the country except the far western provinces (today there are fifty-three). In 1996, an updated plan known as Super-863 extended the technology tracking programme to 2010, while in 1997 another programme called the National Key Basic Research Programme, or 973, was introduced. In 2006, all these programmes were brought together in the 2020 Science and Technology Plan, which outlines the official objectives for that year.

According to this Plan, from now until that date 2.5 per cent of GDP will be devoted to research and development (slightly more than the present level in Britain, and slightly less than the USA), and by then the numbers of patents and scientific papers are expected to rank in the first five countries worldwide. It is believed that scientific and technological progress will contribute to 60 per cent or more of GDP by 2020, while China's dependence on foreign technology will decline to 30 per cent or less. In a break with past weapons-focussed objectives, the key industrial sectors listed include 'population and health' and 'urbanization and urban development', while the environment and research into diseases are also given priority together with advanced scientific research areas such as nanotechnology and protein. The Guidelines state unequivocally that, by 2020, 'China will have developed a number of frontier technologies in sectors such as biology, information industry, materials technologies and advanced manufacturing technology.'[640] These are ambitious, but realistic, goals. But the top-down planning approach remains in place: statements such as 'China will push enterprises to spend more on research and development', for example, suggest the difficulty of the spontaneous investment and innovation that characterise other technologically advanced countries.

As always in China, the numbers are staggering: for example, in the Five-Year Plan for the years 1991–5 the government promised financial support for as many as 20,000 research projects, and by the end of the 1990s the so-called Basic Research Plan created then was responsible for funding as many as 3,000 new research projects each year.[641] At the same time, important steps were taken to improve both the quality and the quantity of university education after a disastrous period of total closure during the Cultural Revolution, with a series of reforms introduced in the late 1970s, which gradually improved their quality. In fact, as recently as 1978 only 400,000 students were enrolled in Chinese universities, of whom only 10,000 were graduate students (before the 1970s this was a category that did not exist).[642] Then in 1997, a project known as the 'National 211 Project' was launched to focus on the improvement of 100 selected universities. According to the Ministry of Education, in line with the implementation of Project 211 and the focus on key universities and disciplines, by 2010 the total enrolment of Higher Education Institutions will increase to 6.5 million students, of whom 3.5 million will be university undergraduates and the others in specialised schools and vocational education. But the most interesting objective is to have 200,000 postgraduate students each year, with an annual growth rate of 6.6 per cent.[643] The universities now produce large numbers of technically trained people, although many described as engineers might best be described as technicians since their level of attainment is not always exceptional.[644]

Some universities produce a stream of good graduates, such as the oldest of Chinese universities, Peking University (founded in 1897) and Tsinghua (1911), both in Beijing, or Jiaotong (1896) and Fudan (1905), both originally founded as schools in Shanghai. Yet the quality is obviously very uneven with over 1,000 institutions of higher education in the country. Many are characterised by enormous classes, little practical work, and much rote learning and memorisation of texts. An often-quoted McKinsey report on the potential of high-tech off-shoring found that 'while 50 per cent of engineers in Poland or Hungary are suitable to work for multinational companies, only 10 per cent of Chinese ones and 25 per cent of Indian ones would be suitable.'[645] Among the main reasons for this figure were inadequate English skills and the low quality of many of the universities, particularly their inability to teach practical skills. Expressed in another, more graphic, way, 'even though China's population is 16 times the size of the Philippines, for instance, its pool of suitable young professional engineers is only 3 times the size of the Philippines.'[646] Another consequence of this investment and development of universities, and the emphasis on technical subjects, is that according to an authoritative American report as many as 40 per cent of Chinese undergraduates study engineering compared to only 6 per cent of American undergraduates.[647] America is justly proud of the fact that a nation that counts only 6 per cent of global population has in recent decades produced 'more than 20 per cent of the world's doctorates in science and engineering';[648] but not only is that likely to be overtaken in the future, as the report argues, but a good proportion of those doctorates are probably awarded to Chinese anyway. It is this group that is most likely to lead genuine innovation and outward investment in coming decades.

But what are the tangible results of all these ambitious technology programmes and investments in education and in the first decade of the twenty-first century? And what is the likelihood of the objectives now in place being realised by 2020?

Silicon Valley is often quoted in the brochures of Chinese science parks, from the 'Silicon Valley of Beijing' to the 'Silicon Valley of Western China' at Jiaotong University in Xi'an, and more ambitious claims in lesser-known cities like Hefei. Yet if we consider the key elements of the Silicon Valley eco-system, we find that most of them are lacking in all these claimants. The first, historical, element was the presence of a world-class university, Stanford, which has provided company founders from Bill Hewlett and William Packard in 1939 to Sergey Brin and Larry Page in 1998. Although Tsinghua is touted as China's Harvard, and is certainly one of the oldest and most prestigious universities in China, it is not quite up to the level of a world-class university in terms of measurable output – papers, books or prizes recognised by the international peer community. Zhejiang University in Hangzhou boasts on its brochures that Joseph Needham called it the 'Cambridge of the East' during a visit in 1944, but that may almost certainly be taken as a generous and polite compliment of a visitor rather than reality in the terms mentioned above. It is enough to recall that Cambridge's first spin-off companies included the Cambridge Scientific Instrument Company in 1881, and W.G. Pye and Company, which emerged from the Cavendish Laboratory in 1893 before there were even science courses in China. Similarly, the flexible infrastructure of accounting services, or specialised legal services in areas such as patent protection and intellectual property, do not exist except at a fairly rudimental level in centralised, government-sponsored service centres. But perhaps most of all there is a distinct lack of genuine entrepreneurial spirit – although it is increasing – and genuine local venture capital; most new high-tech companies get off the ground with government funding, especially inside the Science Parks, and most venture capital firms are wholly or partly government funded. The Silicon Valley paradigm is still very much wishful thinking. At least for the moment. Innovation needs more than gleaming new buildings and cash.

The funding is real enough, though, and the results are slowly becoming tangible. It is true that twenty years after the introduction of Plan 863, though there have been many changes, the approach is still top-down. The state still plans and develops broad policies, which are then implemented by universities and research institutions, and eventually companies emerge to exploit the results commercially. Then, in turn, the companies have a ready market in state-owned enterprises and the enormous machinery of government. An example of this is the series of Golden Projects: the Golden Bridge Project was designed to link 'ministries and commissions of the State Council with 30 provinces and autonomous regions, 500 cities, 12,000 large and medium-sized enterprises, 100 leading busines conglomerates, and keypoint industrial projects involving large-scale capital construction.'[649] Here the sequence of policy > finance > research > production > market creates a form of technological monopoly in which the companies at the end of the line are necessarily successful. With such a huge country and populace to modernise, and so many commercial and financial systems to digitise, this approach evidently has merits. But the problem is that there is little spontaneous innovation, little that can be taken abroad as the spearhead of Chinese technology. What actually happens is that the pressures of going to market and seeking profit means that many university laboratory 'spin-offs' produce no more than 'cheaper versions of technologies that are widely available in the West.'[650] Others prosper on copies with slight modifications or sleight of hand to avoid copyright and patent issues. Ironically, then, the huge internal market for low-cost technology militates against genuine innovation.

Yet the state has created a formidable apparatus for technological development, backed up by an increasingly well-educated techno-workforce and supported by a dense network of overseas and returning researchers and entrepreneurs. Visiting the incubators in science parks and the innovation centres, the sensation of much copying and incremental technological advance is accompanied by a feeling that a slight change of mindset or a tweaking of the business model could quickly unleash a torrent of genuine technological innovation. It will not happen this year or next year, but when the moment comes it could really lead to the equality with the United States that the Chinese aim for, and even eventual technological supremacy.

In 2004, it was estimated that within ten years China would develop a significant number of competent reseachers in such fields as life sciences, nanotechnology, new materials and optoelectronics once the current output of graduates from the top universities have passed through doctoral and post-doctoral research programmes.[651] In the meantime, here has been an increase emphasis on IPR protection, particularly as the Chinese government recognises that developing its own nation's IP is vital for continued economic growth. There have been strong signals in this direction, for example the government order in mid-2007 that all State-Owned Enterprises must use genuine software in their computer systems, and a ten-point Action Plan on IPR Protection, which was promulgated in April and will lead to improved legislation (*Part I*, Paragraph 3 concerns improvements in the patent law, and *Part I*, Paragraph 5 deals with new regulations for IP protection). An increased awareness of the value of patent protection means that in the first six months of 2007 alone, according to the State Intellectual Property Office, there were 216,467 applications for domestic patents (the majority from enterprises) and 52,453 applications for international patents, compared to a year-end total for 2004 of 278,943 applications for domestic patents and 74,864 for international patents. During this period, spending on Research and Development has been increasing at an annual rate of about 17 per cent, much higher than the 4 per cent to 5 per cent annual growth rates reported for the USA, Japan and the European Union in recent years. There are no signs of a let-up, since China's share of global R&D was expected to increase from 12.7 per cent in 2005 to 14.8 per cent in 2007. In the same period, the USA would see a gradual decline from 32.7 per cent to 31.9 per cent.[652] The gap is still wide, but it is closing.

For all these scientific areas, the right question would appear to be not if, but when. Success in this quest for technological supremacy will be the ultimate test of China's rise to power.

Stealth Foreign Policy

Until 1860, it was possible to argue with Confucius that 'those distant people have nothing to do with our great land; those wild tribes must not be permitted to create disorder among our flowery States.'[653] Then the effects of steam-powered globalisation and modern weaponry reduced the distances, increased the threat, and made the elaboration of a foreign policy indispensable.

Post-tribute foreign policy might be said to begin with the creation of the *Zongli Yamen* or 'Office for the Management of the Business of all Foreign Countries' in 1861, although an office called the *Li-fan yuan*, the 'Mongol Superintendency' or 'Barbarian Control Office', had been created two centuries earlier to manage relations between the Qing and their Mongol neighbours.[654] The new office was divided into five bureaus that reflected the priorities of China in mid-century: American, British, Coastal, French and Russian. Although it was presided over by Prince Gong, the emperor Tongzhi's uncle and then the most powerful man in China, it was thought of as a temporary measure to deal with current problems. Given the Confucian mindset and innate superiority complex of senior government officials, it was difficult to find adequate staff. One candidate complained that no gentleman of honour could bring himself to learn anything about foreign affairs, while another is said to have burst into tears of shame on learning of his appointment to the *Zongli Yamen*.[655]

The Communists who were later to rule the country had no formal foreign policy until the completion of the Long March. They were to all intents and purposes isolated from the world, except for direct links to Stalin and other foreign fellow travellers. They understood the need to create an international front against Japanese aggression, but the real 'opening' came with the famous visit to Yan'an by the American journalist Edgar Snow and his subsequent book *Red Star Over China* (1937), based on long conversations with Mao Zedong.[656] Snow gained his scoop, and Mao achieved his purpose of making his policies known to the world. His aim was to create an anti-Japanese alliance with the United States, the Soviet Union, Britain and France. Mao told Snow that one of the three conditions that would guarantee China's success against Japan was 'the formation of a World Anti-Japanese United Front'.[657] Later, he affirmed in a speech to the Sixth Plenum of the Communist Party that 'China could not sever its connections with the world and expect to achieve victory in the War of Resistance,[658] which he perceived as an integral part of a global fight against fascism. In other words, the Communists were now positioning themselves in terms of the whole world rather than exclusively in terms of the Soviet Union.

From 1950, guided by Zhou Enlai, the 'cornerstone' of Chinese foreign policy was the 'Treaty of Friendship, Alliance, and Mutual Assistance' signed with Moscow in that year, and the need to maintain that alliance without antagonising the United States – given their military presence in nearby Taiwan and Japan. This worked both ways, as when the United States declined to attack Chinese military targets during the Korean War to avoid escalating the conflict into a nuclear war with the Soviet Union.[659] In fact, Zhou's forte lay in his skill at the balancing act: 'leaning to one side' for Soviet support against the United States in the 1950s, and to the other side when he sought rapprochement with the United States in the 1970s to counteract a perceived Soviet threat. In 1956, he was able simultaneously to berate Moscow for not recognising the independence of Hungary (which he visited in the following year), and to support Moscow's puppet János Kádár in his crushing of the so-called counter-revolution. These were modern variants of the ancient practice of 'using barbarians to control barbarians'.

Since the earliest formulations of contemporary foreign policy, the Chinese people have been motivated by a single obsession: 'How to join the world community as an equal member.'[660] Today, this means a focus in three main directions: first, maintaining carefully balanced relationships with the major world powers, especially at present in economic terms the USA and the EU and its most important member countries; secondly, developing close relationships with energy-producing countries (such as Venezuela and Russia) and with countries black-listed by First World powers (Iran, Sudan, and smaller states in Africa and South America); and, thirdly, building tighter relationships with states in which the Stealth Empire is advancing most rapidly. From 1996 this was achieved as a 'dialogue partner' with ASEAN (Brunei, Cambodia, China, Indonesia, Laos, Malaysia, Myanmar, Philippines, Singapore, Thailand and Vietnam), which was originally created as a bulwark against Communism. Then, to the West, as a founding member of the Shanghai Five (with Russia, Kazakhstan, Kyrgystan and Tajikistan), which became the Shanghai Cooperation Organization with the addition of Uzbekistan in June 2001. This web of alliances and friendships, for the Chinese all foreigners are denominated 'foreign friends' until they prove to be otherwise, may also be seen as what one expert calls a 'stealthy strategy toward global dominance', integrating military, economic, and diplomatic instruments and aiming to displace the United States as the world's preeminent power.[661]

The general principles of present Chinese strategy and foreign policy were set out succinctly by the late Deng Xiao Ping in these words: 'Observe calmly; secure our position; cope with affairs calmly; hide our capacities and bide our time; be good at maintaining a low profile; and never claim leadership.'[662] These cryptic remarks may be translated in policy terms to a few basic hypotheses that underly most foreign policy decisions: policies with broader appeal are more likely to be adopted; with the passage of time, long-term goals tend to recede; steps that reinforce each other tend to be adopted; and consistent policy can be built of apparently contradictory goals provided the goals are not both to be realised in the short term.[663] But here it is important to understand that even apparently innocuous words like 'appeal', 'long-term' and 'consistent' can have very different meanings for a Chinese politician or strategist. It depends what is meant by planning: setting a goal, and taking the necessary steps to achieve the goal, as we in the West tend to think of it, or assessing the general flow of events and shaping actions in such a way as to benefit from it. In the words of François Jullien, that means 'to rely on the inherent potential of a situation and to be carried along by it as it evolves.'[664] At present, the emphasis is on what the Chinese refer to as their 'peaceful rise' (*heping jueqi*) or 'peaceful development' (*heping fazhan*).

Peaceful Development

Anti-war sentiment runs deeps in the Chinese consciousness. Confucius' successor, Mencius (Meng Zi), wrote that 'if the ruler of a state loves goodness, in all-under-heaven he will have no enemies.'[665] The present government built on this sentiment in a document published in 2005 with the title 'China's Peaceful Development Road', in part to allay fears about China's dramatic economic growth and its potential effects on the global polity. Starting from the Mencius-like affirmation that 'Peaceful Development Is the Inevitable Way for China's Modernisation', the programme is defined in utopian terms as 'sticking to peace, development and cooperation, and, together with all other countries, devoting itself to building a harmonious world marked by sustained peace and common prosperity.' The document stresses, reasonably enough, China's membership of inter-governmental international organisations (130) and its commitment to international multilateral treaties (267), but with a little too much insistence on examples such as the International Atomic Energy Agency and the Treaty on the Non-Proliferation of Nuclear Weapons. But whatever doubts or suspicions we might harbour, it is difficult to quibble with the notion that in order to achieve the 'moderately well-off society', which is the country's declared long-term aim, China 'cannot develop independently without the rest of the world.'[666]

One tangible consequence of this policy is a radically different approach to international diplomacy over the past decade or so, as China has exercised quiet soft power throughout Africa, Latin America, Central Asia, Southeast Asia and the Middle East. The first requirements to gain China's favour, and aid, are recognition of the 'one China policy' and breaking off relations with Taiwan. These are followed by agreements on energy supply and debt-financing; in exchange for this recognition, China can offer future use of its veto powers in the United Nations. This is why from a hostile stance towards the United Nations that endured until the 1980s China has modulated to a constructive attitude, which obtains more favours and support in international diplomacy. This may be seen in China's increasing participation in peace-keeping forces, from its earliest contribution of twenty civilian observers of Namibian independence in 1988 to the more dangerous deployment of riot-police in Haiti and military personnel in Lebanon in 2004. Negotiations over possible actions in Darfur during 2007 saw China playing the role of the responsible world citizen – its favourite role when it can be seen as counterbalancing unilateral actions by the United States.

Another of the tangible consequences of this peaceful rise policy is an attempt to increase the use of 'soft power' through non-diplomatic means. To this end, the 'Chinese Bridge Project' was announced in the same years as the 'China's Peaceful Development Road' document. This project consists of a series of government measures to encourage the teaching of Mandarin overseas in order to popularise Chinese culture. The first measure was to accelerate the process of opening Confucius Institutes throughout the world, around 100, for the teaching of language and culture. Others included the production of better-quality multi-media teaching materials for schools, and the introduction of an Advanced Placement exam (AP) for American high-school students. In addition, the government announced that it would provide assistance for foreign universities building Chinese libraries and donate books to schools that give Chinese language courses.[667] As we have seen above, the essence of soft power is creating cultural artefacts that make the country attractive to others. One of the best examples is the successful exportation of American culture, and especially its Californian sub-culture, through popular music, film and food. Broadcast media such as the Voice of America and BBC World Service radio and television have also worked towards the fostering of cultural and political values. China has taken the cue from these much-criticised stations, and now offers a CNN-inspired state television programme in English via satellite, although its main focus seems to be on inward tourism rather than on exporting ideology and propaganda as in the Maoist past.

Now, bearing in mind both the emphasis on military build-up discussed in the previous chapter and the focus on peaceful relations, we shall consider some of the salient features of present foreign policy. But rather than survey the whole panoply of international relations, we will simplify by building out from the centre in concentric circles with a few comments on each of the following categories with particular reference to their role in the Stealth Empire: Neighbouring Countries, Coastal Policy, Africa, and Key Trading Partners.

Neighbouring Countries

China shares a frontier with fourteen nations and also has an extensive coastline, so the range of real and potential territorial disputes goes well beyond the tussle for Taiwan. Today, it is relatively open, with numerous land and sea entry points together with several international airports (see Map 3, Appendix 1).

The underlying objective of relationships with neighbouring countries is to become the dominant player in Asia without ruffling too many feathers or generating fear of either military action or economic imperialism. This entails seeking to resolve border issues with countries such as Russia, India and Vietnam, to improve economic relations as China overtakes the United States as the main trading partner of countries such as Japan and Korea, and to exercise influence through regional institutions such as ASEAN (the Association of Southeast Asian Nations), APEC (the Asia-Pacific Economic Cooperation Forum), the Greater Mekong Subregion Economic Cooperation Program, and new Chinese creations such as the Shanghai Cooperation Organization.

During the past half-century, the countries of East Asia have made several chronologically unrelated attempts at 'rising': first Japan, then the four 'Tigers' (Hong Kong, Singapore, South Korea and Taiwan), and later countries like Thailand and Malaysia, and most recently China itself. Today, regional experts define East Asia as ASEAN + 3 (the three being China, Japan and South Korea). Putting these thirteen countries together, we arrive at 30 per cent (1.9 billion) of world population and nearly 25 per cent ($18.450 trillion in 2006) of global GDP measured at purchasing power parity, much of it linked, as we have seen by the community of Overseas Chinese. Let us imagine for a moment these thirteen countries as thirteen tectonic plates linked together. So far, since the 'rise' of Japan in the 1960s, these plates have moved independently of each other and in different time frames. Now let us imagine for a moment that all rise simultaneously, with the propulsion of China at the heart of a regional system. That will truly generate an 'earthquake' in the global system.

Politicians and business leaders in the other twelve countries are becoming aware of this. When the survey that has been quoted above looked ahead to the next half-century, few respondents in all three Asian countries (China, India and South Korea) believed that the United States would be surpassed in terms of world power. Oddly enough, however, on the question of whether China would catch up with the United States economically, Americans and South Koreans were more confident than the Chinese themselves. More interesting, a majority in all three

Asian countries (68 per cent, 60 per cent and 53 per cent respectively), and even in the United States (55 per cent), believed that 'another nation' would be at least as powerful as America by the middle of the century.[668] That would already be quite an achievement for either India or China, but the support of the Stealth Empire would appear to make the latter a stronger candidate. Some economists predict more dramatic results in the future. William W. Fogel calculates that in terms of purchasing power parity China's GDP, which in 2000 was $5 billion compared to $10 billion for the USA, will in 2040 be three times that of the USA at ($123 billion against $42 billion).[669] He also sees annual growth in China at around 8.4 per cent until that time, compared with an average of 3.8 per cent for the United States.

The relationship with India, or a future virtual economic union as 'Chindia', could play a significant role in the Stealth Empire. In the past, the relationship has been characterised by continuous bickering over borders, which escalated into the forty-day Sino-Indian War of 1962, and more recently by India's successful nuclear tests in 1998. But in recent years both countries have realised that there is so much at stake in economic terms that minor border disputes are not worth a war. They share similar objectives (economic growth, a stronger military role in their respective regions), and face similar challenges (wealth gap, potential religious and ethnic unrest). For this reason, reciprocal high-level visits have accelerated in recent years. In 2006, Wen Jiabao made an observation that would appear to encapsulate China's current objective, and illustrates how once again a major country can be exploited as a tool against another 'Asian' power, the United States, when he stated that 'strong bilateral ties [between China and India] will usher in a true Asian century.'[670] What he really meant was a Chinese century.

China is already India's third largest trading partner, which is one good reason to avoid diplomatic scuffles over borders. It also explains why so much media attention was devoted to the reopening of the Nathalu Pass between Tibet and India forty-four years after the Sino-Indian War forced its closing. The Indian Press greeted it as a moment of 'the banter of merchants replacing the military speak of soldiers', but noted the symbolic importance of the reopening as firmly establishing 'China's recognition of Sikkim as part of India'.[671] The Chinese view, with references to the medieval Silk Road, emphasised the economic aspects of a 'major event for the two countries to expand and deepen trade and economic cooperation and exchanges', and the fact that it 'would also eventually help the two countries leave the border row behind.'[672] Officials estimated that border trade through this pass alone could grow to as much $3 billion by 2015 (from $100m in mid-2006). Overall, bilateral trade between the two countries grew from $332 million in 1992 to $13.6 billion in 2005, while on the occasion of Wen's visit in the latter year targets were set of $20 billion by 2008 and $30 billion by 2030.[673]

From the point of view of the Stealth Empire, apart from the *de facto* integration via Overseas Chinese with the economies of Indonesia, the Philippines, Malaysia and Thailand, the most interesting aspect of Chinese foreign policy in Southeast Asia today concerns Myanmar. China is by a long stretch Myanmar's principal trading partner and arms supplier, and has provided loans and development aid. Myanmar may rank equal 179th and last together with Somalia on Transparency International's index of corrupt countries in 2007 (China comes in the mid-rank, equal 72nd with India),[674] but there are three very good reasons why China should develop good relations: first, because it shares a 1,300 mile frontier; second, because this convenient neighbour has reserves of 3 trillion cubic metres of gas and 3 billion barrels of oil; and, third, because Myanmar offers direct access to the Indian Ocean. While the media and international opprobrium focus on Taiwan and Tibet, economists and the business world on revaluation of the yuan, and foreign policy experts on US-China relationships, China has been literally building bridges and seeking alternative routes to market in what can ony be described as a stealth strategy. While another neighbour like Thailand is interested in obtaining inward-looking benefits from Myanmar, such as water and electricity from hydrodams on the Salween River, China covets the outward-looking advantage of building deep-water ports directly on the Indian Ocean.[675] A new deep-water port suitable for both cargo and military vessels under construction at Kyaukpyu, on Ramree Island, will eventually mean a sea journey to India or the Middle East of nearly 2,000 miles less than from the southern Chinese ports of Guangzhou and Shenzhen, and completely circumvent the Malacca Straits problem. There will also be a Chinese trade zone, known as the Shanghai Jingqiao Export Processing Zone, at the port of Yangon (Rangoon, which was the capital until 2005 when it was moved north to Naypyidaw).

The process may be said to have begun in 1991, when an agreement was signed by the two countries to build a new border bridge at Ruili over the Shweli River, which rises in China and flows south-west into the Irrawaddy. This effectively reopened the famous 700-mile 'Burma Road' from Chongqing to Mandalay, which linked the two great river transport systems of the Chang Jiang and Irrawaddy rivers during the Second World War. In yet another example of historical precedent, just as the Chinese originally built this road in 1937-8 to transport war supplies when Japanese invading forces cut off routes to the south-eastern ports, so it could be utilised as a way of circumventing an American naval blockade of the Malacca Strait or the South China Sea. The old bridge at Ruili, known as the 'Gun Bridge', since it was used for years for arms shipments, was closed in 2005 and replaced by a new and broader one. Further north, at Myitkyina, the Chinese have built an even bigger bridge over the Irrawaddy, which could be an essential component of a more direct new road from Tenchong. Thus Myanmar will become a strategic transit point for Chinese goods, which can be shipped from Yangon to India, and on the Middle East and Europe. This will be a particular boon for exporting companies in the western cities of Chengdu and Chongqing, located far from the southeastern ports.

But the 'gateway' has many conduits. Agreements have been signed to build oil and gas pipelines from the Andaman Sea to Kunming, and then onwards to other neighbouring provinces. This would also serve to circumvent eventual naval blockades of sea routes from the Middle East to China. At the same time, the three main Chinese oil companies (Sinopec, CNPC and CNOOC) are involved in direct exploration for further oil and gas deposits off the Myanmar coast. Investment by companies in other sectors has also been intensive, especially in Lashio, Mandalay and Muse, each with noticeable Chinese communities, since as many as a million Chinese citizens have moved into Myanmar in the last few years to add to an ethnic Chinese minority, which already constituted 3 per cent of the population. Myanmar, for all its faults and problems, is rapidly becoming a south-western extension of the Chinese 'empire'. This is why during protests against the regime led by Buddhist monks in late 2007, China found itself in the ironic position of advising the military government against a violent crackdown on dissidents. There are investments to protect and strategic projects to complete, and fear of massive reverse immigration in the case of country collapse. The stealth empire imposes economic imperatives that overrule the political imperatives of the past.

Coastal Policy

The coastal ramifications of foreign policy are the only part that might in future add physical territory to the 'empire'. For although China has a long coastline, access to the open ocean is effectively blocked by three large islands or island chains: from north to south, Japan, Taiwan and the Philippines. The situation is complicated by the fact that each of these has its own territorial claims, and further exacerbated by the presence of many smaller islands between them. We have seen the historical importance for maritime trade routes of the Senkaku, Paracel, and Spratly islands, each of which falls into the so-called 'dotted line' or 'U-Shaped Line' drawn by China in the 1930s.[676] Today, all of these are disputed territories, especially since the probability of there being oil and natural gas deposits beneath the archipelagos became apparent. The U-shaped line may be readily pictured as running due south from Taiwan to the Philippines, then turning south-west along the coast of Palawan and Malaysia; about half-way down Malaysia it turns west to circle the Spratly Islands and then north along the Vietnamese coast to run between the Paracel Islands and Hainan, and then follows the 200-mile territorial limit parallel to the coast of Guangdong and Fujian to rejoin Taiwan (see Map 4, Appendix 1). China lays partial or total claim to all three island groups, in two particular aspects: first of all, the jurisdiction of resources, in terms of the continental shelf and an exclusive economic zone; and secondly, sovereignty.

The nearest island group within the 'U' is the Paracels, with important fishing grounds and potential oil and gas reserves. Here, China's claim is disputed by Vietnam, although in the past France also claimed sovereignty and Taiwan has more recently done so. The dispute is long-standing, and merges into the history of other disputes and wars: France annexed the islands in 1932 and set up a meteorological station that passed to Vietnam in 1954, when France, defeated by the Viet Minh, retreated from Asia. In 1974, China took a South Vietnamese garrison holding the western islands and has held them since then; it maintains a token military force there, and in 1997 announced plans to develop tourism on the islands.[677] In this case, after a detailed historical and legal review, Greg Austin, an Australian international affairs expert who has written a detailed study of China's 'Ocean Frontier', comes down in favour of China, although careful phrases such as 'would appear to suggest'[678] show that his opinions are not definitive. In fact, Vietnam, with over 2,000 miles of coastline stretching along the main shipping lanes, is the biggest obstacle to Chinese control of this vital area of sea.

The case of the Spratly Islands is more complex, especially since they are scattered over an area of 400,000 square kilometres of the South China Sea. In the past, islands within the group have been annexed or claimed by Britain, France, Germany and Japan, mainly as a source of guano and phosphate. Today, three countries – China, Taiwan, and Vietnam – claim the entire group, while Malaysia and the Philippines lay claims to limited areas of the group and tiny Brunei claims a fishing zone in the south. In 2007, as many as forty-five islands in the group were occupied by small military forces from one of the five disputing countries.[679] In this case, Austin argues that China has a claim to the entire group 'at least equal' to the other principal claimants, and suggests three ways of resolving the claims: 'judicial arbitration to which all parties agree; long-term abandonment of insistence on sovereignty in favour of a multilateral cooperative regime; or use of force to expel rival claimants.'[680] It would be hard to decide which of these 'resolutions' is most unlikely; none seems likely, given the presence of rich fishing grounds and potential gas and oil deposits.

The most controversial of China's claims is that to the Senkaku Islands, five tiny uninhabited islands with a total area of seven square kilometres, situated midway between Taiwan and the nearest of the Ryukyu Islands (the Japanese name derives from 'Pinnacle Islands', given by the British in 1845). In China, they are known as the Diaoyu Islands. In the past, they were a vital navigational aid for junks sailing from the mainland or Taiwan to the Ryukyus and on to Japan. For this reason, an official organ like *People's Daily* argues, China has 'indubitable sovereignty over them'.[681] Once again, rich fishing grounds, and oil reserves discovered in 1969, are the underlying cause of the dispute.[682] For China did not lay claim to these islands until 1971, but now argues that they were part of the Ming coastal defence system and were lost as islands belonging to Taiwan as a result of the Treaty of Shimonoseki in 1985. Japan disputes this, and insists that they were 'an integral part of the Nansei Shoto Islands which are the territory of Japan' and have never been part of Taiwan.[683] Taiwan itself also formally laid claims to the islands in 1971, a few months before China. In this case, Austin argues that the Chinese connection with the Senkaku Islands before that date 'were so few and such a nature that it would appear difficult for the PRC to support its claim that China possessed a valid title to the Islands at that time.'[684] International law in this case would probably be in favour of Japan, but amidst attempts at flag-planting, clandestine landings, lighthouse building and vociferous media campaigns, the dispute is yet another thorn in the briar of relationships with Japan.

In the long-term, however, the main coastal issue is Taiwan, not merely for the island in itself but because east of Taiwan lies direct access to the Pacific Ocean for large ships, unhampered by the need to navigate through scattered islands and reefs. Moreover, if China then added Taiwan's claims on the Spratly and Senkaku Islands to its own, and intensified its naval presence from bases in its new province, it would have a much stronger case in all the above disputes. These coastal issues may be decades away from definitive resolution, but when China absorbs Taiwan it will not only 'conquer' the land mass. Given the recent extension of rights over internal waters to 200 nautical miles of Exclusive Economic Zone, an 'empire' that traditionally faced inland towards mountains and steppes will conquer a valuable area of ocean and sea-bed.

Africa

Further out, the area in which China has invested most political capital in the past few years is Africa. Links with the African continent are long-standing and solid. The earliest Chinese emigrants went as traders, shopkeepers and railway workers to Mauritius and Madagascar in the second half of the nineteenth century. Later, they worked on railways all over the continent and also in the gold mines of the Transvaal, where expert miners travelled from the province of Shandong. In the early years of the twentieth century as many as 50,000 Chinese arrived in Durban alone.[685] It was, as always, a hard life for immigrants, and they must sometimes have ruefully acknowledged the truth behind their language's name for Africa, *fei zhou* (非洲), the 'wrong continent'.

The first diplomatic contacts between the PRC and African countries took place in 1955 at the Asian-African Conference in Bandung, Indonesia. From initial trade with Egypt following that conference, and an increasing number of African delegations to Beijing, already in 1966 diplomatic relations had been established with twenty countries and the continent accounted for 3.6 per cent of imports and 5.9 per cent of exports.[686] The gradual loosening of European colonial ties created opportunities that China was quick to take as much for revolutionary aims as for new possibilities for trade, for example in providing $10 million of aid for the Front de Libération Nationale in Algeria in 1959, and aid to the Congo two years later.[687] Such aid fitted into Mao's scheme of building global Communism.

The most significant technical assistance was that provided for the Tanzania-Zambia railway, to create access for Zambian copper to the Indian Ocean, but there was also extensive agricultural assistance, the building of mills and factories, and the provision of training in China for African students. An expert on Sino-African relations was able to conclude that 'in large measure China's economic aims appear to be simply those of normal commerce.'[688]

More recently, Africa has become the focus of a new kind of Chinese entrepreneur and investor. While the continent tends to be associated in the Western mind with extreme poverty and aid programmes, the Chinese see it as a vital source of much-needed raw materials such as copper (Congo, Zambia), iron ore and platinum (South Africa), timber (Gabon, Cameroon), and above all oil (Sudan, Angola, Nigeria), and as a land where the political correctness and moral suasions of Western powers leave commercial gaps to fill in countries like Sudan, Zimbabwe and Sierra Leone. The above raw materials, in descending order of importance as a percentage of exports to China, were in 2004 oil and gas (62 per cent), ores and metals (17 per cent), and agricultural raw materials (7 per cent), while the main Chinese exports to Africa were textiles and footwear (36 per cent), machinery and transportation equipment (33 per cent), and manufactured materials (18 per cent).[689] Much of this export is achieved by the use of debt relief and concessional loans from the Chinese government, with the bulk of the finance going to five countries – Angola, Mozambique, Nigeria, Sudan and Zimbabwe – and concentrated in sectors such as power, telecoms, construction and utilities.[690]

At the same time, Chinese companies have been officially encouraged to make commercial investments in Africa. To take one example, in Angola, apart from the energy sector investment has been concentrated in infrastructure projects such as roads and a new airport for the capital, while ZTE Corporation is investing $400 million in both military and civilian telecom projects, which include the setting up of a training school. Yet even this pales in comparison with the oil industry, for in 2006 Angola was the largest exporter of crude oil to China, and the state-owned oil company Sinopec has shares in four offshore oilfields in the country, which Wen Jiabao visited on his African tour in the summer of 2006. Everywhere in Africa, the extreme pragmatism of the Chinese finds ample space to operate, and the 700 companies now active there feel little pressure from shareholders about such issues as human rights. As a result, in the decade from 1995 to 2005 trade between China and Africa increased from $3 billion to $32 billion, including about 25 per cent of the oil exported from Angola and 60 per cent of that from Sudan, which alone supplies 12 per cent of China's oil needs. In 2006, trade exceeded $50 billion, with a declared target of $100 billion by 2010.

An event that crowned all this diplomatic activity came in the first week of November 2006, when senior representatives from forty-eight African countries, forty of them Heads of State, met for the Third Forum on China-Africa Co-operation. Participating leaders included international pariahs such as Robert Mugabe of Zimbabwe and Omar Hassan al-Bashir, President of Sudan. President Hu announced in a press conference two days before the opening that 'we will look back at the development of the China-Africa friendship and devise a blue-print for future partnership.'[691] More colloquially, newspapers wrote of the 'three 50s': fifty years of Sino-African cooperation, fifty-three African countries and $50 billion in trade. To that end, there was a conference in Beijing for nearly 2,000 entrepreneurs, an African product exhibition, and discussion about large-scale proj-ects in agriculture, infrastructure, energy and natural resources, transportation and pharmaceuticals. The result was an 'Action Plan' adopted at the end of the Forum, intended to 'strengthen cooperation in politics, economy, international affairs and social development' over the period 2007–2009. On a more pragmatic level it stated that China will build thirty hospitals and provide $37 million for providing anti-malaria drugs to African countries and building thirty demonstration centres for prevention and treatment of malaria in the coming three years. It will also help African countries set up 100 rural schools, and increase the number of scholarships for African students in China from the current 2,000 a year to 4,000 by 2009.[692] Towards the end of 2007, China announced loans of $5 billion to the Congo to build roads and railways, and to provide social infrastructure such as universities, hospitals and healthcare centres. If these projects are completed on schedule within the three years that were described as the target, and the Congo linked successfully to existing Chinese-planned infrastructure networks in Zambia and Angola, it will bring significant economic advantage and order to a chaotic region whose natu-ral resources have never been adequately exploited. It will be an excellent test of China's ability to repeat elsewhere policies that have been so successful at home.

While most media focused on economic matters, a fascinating insight into Chinese diplomatic thought processes was provided in a leading article in *People's Daily*, the official government newspaper, outlining the political advantages China has gained from its generous aid in over 800 African projects:

> For their part, African countries have always lent a helping hand to China at criti-cal moments. It was with the support and help of the country's African brothers that China had its seat at the United Nations restored; defeated Taiwan's attempts to return to the United Nations and join the World Health Organization; rejected an anti-China draft proposed by western countries at a meeting of the UN Commission on Human Rights; became a formal member of the WTO; won the right to host the 2008 Olympic Games and the World Expo; pushed for a reform of the United Nations and more.[693]

Thus three of the most fundamental trappings of global respectability – WTO membership, Olympics and the Shanghai Expo in 2010 – were obtained with the help of 'African brothers', while the diplomatic thwarting of Taiwan is here seen as equally important. This is something the Western media did not mention, a crucial fact that indicates the success of China's stealth empire and billions well spent.

Naturally, there are problems with this ambitious policy. Already the rapidly increasing communities of small businessmen and investors from Tanzania to Gabon are creating frictions and fears. In a country such as Zambia the increased Chinese presence had a significant impact, since the country provides 48 per cent of imported African copper and 63 per cent of imported base metals to China. In 2005, protests resulted in a shooting incident that killed forty-six men in the mining community of Chambishi, and a further six were shot dead the following summer, when some people claimed that Chinese managers had been responsible for the killings. Then, during presidential elections in October 2006, artisans and shopkeepers protested against the Chinese presence: Michael Sata, leader of the Patriotic Front, took 28 per cent of the vote on the basis of a campaign directed against 'Chinese exploitation' and making Zambia a 'dumping ground for their human beings'.[694] Further protests against Chinese companies, focussed on low salaries and poor working conditions, forced President Hu to cancel a ceremony in Chambisi to inaugurate a new copper smelter during his visit to Zambia in February 2007.

There is also an underlying fear in some of the more democratic African countries of a new colonialism. One tangible problem is that on the massive engineering and construction projects the manpower is often predominantly Chinese, sometimes as much as 70 per cent; they are very visible.[695] Then there is the sensation of yet another superpower stripping the continent's assets. In the words of the South African president's brother Moeletsi Mbeki during the Beijing Forum in 2005, 'Africa sells raw materials to China and China sells manufactured products to Africa. This is a dangerous equation that reproduces Africa's old relationship with colonial powers.'[696] It also raises fears that the new Chinese influence could 'derail international attempts to foster good governance in Africa.'[697] This is of particular concern, since it was only with the adoption of a strategic framework document in 2001 that the Organisation of African Unity created what is known as the New Partnership for Africa's Development (NEPAD) to emphasise the importance of political governance for African development.

The resolution of these problems, and the overall fulfillment of the African policy, will require all the diplomatic and economic skills that China possesses. It will also answer the unspoken question: is China's foreign policy a series of vacuous platitudes about peace and harmony, or is the country really prepared to assume the responsibilities that its global economic role imposes? Events in Africa over the next decade will be a key indicator of the success of the Stealth Empire.

Key Trading Partner and Nemesis

Once again, pragmatism rules, with one eye on present needs and one eye on the long-term future. That means dealing with the world's most important markets, in particular the USA, which is China's most important trading partner.

In 2006, trade between China and the United States was worth $263 billion, an increase of 24 per cent over the previous year. But while the US was the principal destination for Chinese exports, in terms of imported goods into China it ranked fourth after Japan, South Korea and Taiwan. This reflects China's position as a low-cost assembler rather than a genuine manufacturer, with, as we have seen, around 60 per cent of exports being goods assembled by foreign-owned companies on the mainland. Thus a flat-screen LCD panel or cell-phone component arrives from Japan, Korea or Taiwan, and departs from China to the US in a finished product for sale at Wal-Mart or similar retail outlets. The main import items, in descending order of importance, are electrical machinery and equipment, power generation equipment, toys and games, apparel, furniture and footwear.[698]

This imbalance has led to the ugly face of protectionism appearing in the country of free trade, in spite of obvious benefits to the American consumer. According to the authors of a survey article in *Foreign Affairs*:

> [The] 109th Congress introduced 27 pieces of anti-China trade legislation; the 110th introduced over a dozen in just its first three months, and in March 2007 the Bush administration levied new tariffs on Chinese exports of high-gloss paper – reversing a 20-year precedent of not accusing nonmarket economies of illegal export subsidies.[699]

There is plenty of statistical evidence to show that protectionist sentiment is on the rise, and also evidence of popular support. One long term poll found that from December 1999 to March 2007, 'the share of respondents stating that trade agreements have hurt the United States increased by 16 percentage points (to 46 per cent) while the "helped" share fell by 11 points (to just 28 per cent).'[700] It seems likely that tariffs and trade barriers will be raised, or that more subtle means such as quality standards may be used to reduce the trade deficit (something akin to emissions requirements on automobiles). This, of course, makes the task of Chinese economic expansion tougher. But it might also have the consequence of making it stealthier, and thus more difficult to legislate against.

Yet meticulous preparation, in which the Chinese are masters, can obviate problems, secure local support, and placate industrial lobbies. An early example of this was seen after the opening up of the country under Deng Xiao Ping. In December 1978, the Third Plenum of the Eleventh Central Committee of the Communist Party laid out the requirements of the 'four modernizations' in industry, agriculture, science and technology, and national defence. Shortly afterwards, on 19 December, Boeing announced the sale of three 747s to Air China, and Coca-Cola announced on the same day that it would open a bottling plant in Shanghai. These two initiatives paved the way for the announcement of full diplomatic relations on 1 January 1979, quickly followed by a visit made by Deng to Washington at the end of the month. The timeframe of these events smacks of secretive late-night meetings and detailed planning.

The same pattern was repeated in early 2006. Just before President Hu Jintao was due to arrive in Washington for an official visit, Vice-Premier Wu Yi, then the most powerful woman in China, flew to America with a group of officials and over 100 businessmen on what was widely described in the Press as a 'shopping spree'. The whirlwind tour began in Hawaii and included visits to thirteen states, with multibillion-dollar orders for Boeing aircraft (again!), automobile parts, computer software, telecommunications equipment, grain, cotton, soybeans and other products. President Hu's own trip began with a stay in Seattle, where he was photographed at the Boeing factory wearing a cap with the company logo and attended a dinner hosted by Bill Gates at his private home. Naturally, with such a wave of lobby support preceding him, the Washington leg of his trip went off smoothly.

These trips twenty-five years apart offer identical evidence of Chinese prepared-ness, how nothing is left to chance. China-bashers and protectionists in thirteen states and in Washington were effectively silenced by such big orders on their own turf, and the visit could be trumpeted as a huge success. But such diplomatic ges-tures rarely generate lasting success, even if they are passed off as such; they often create false impressions of success. But the Chinese know that memories, except their own, are short. It is usually forgotten, for example, as we see the smiling faces in pictures on the Great Wall, that the famous Nixon-Kissinger/Mao-Zhou meetings in 1972 were a total failure in their primary objectives: to end the Vietnam War, and to return Taiwan to China. To portray that visit as a 'week that changed the world'[701] is merely to view China from the narrow perspective of the United States. Indeed, it would be easy to argue that the real 'opening' of China in diplomatic terms came with the 1955 Asian-African Conference in Bandung and the consequent flurry of diplomatic activity. By 1971, China already had diplomatic relations with fifty countries, mainly in Asia, Africa and South America but including France (1964, officially considered to have 'smashed a keylink in Western Europe of the U.S. attempt to isolate China')[702] and America's neighbour Canada (in 1970). In that year too, China became a full member of the United Nations General Assembly, before Nixon's visit. The popular narrative is false, but it doesn't matter.

The stealth empire moves according to its own logic.

The Stealth Business Empire

China's business imperative in the next decade is to shift from low-margin manufacturing for overseas companies to the production, marketing and sales of high-margin products (inventing, for example, a Chinese equivalent of the Gucci business model that takes the Western world by storm). Yet it is a curious fact that this is exactly what China has always done very well. For centuries it has taken low-cost natural 'components' such as raw silk, bamboo and clay and converted them into high-margin products – in the case of two of these, products that have been profitable in the global market for over half a millennium. Ming was the first truly global brand.

In fact, the recent 'rise' of China is hardly a surprise, except in its timing. It has been coming for decades. As long ago as the eighteenth century Adam Smith noted, in words that echo those of the Song emperor/economist Gaozong 600 years earlier, that an opening of the Chinese market would be immensely beneficial for the country. After remarking that the domestic market was about the same size as that of all of Europe, he wrote that adding the global market by creating a 'more extensive foreign trade … could scarce fail to increase very much the manufactures of China, and to improve very much the productive powers of its manufacturing industry.'[703] Opening up the economy, he added, just a few years before Lord Macartney set off for China, would enable the Chinese to learn from the practices of other countries and improve their own industries. Then they would be ready to take on the world.

It has taken a little longer than Adam Smith imagined, but now China seems ready to follow his advice.

'Going Out'

The 'going out' policy (sometimes referred to as 'walking out') was developed in the early 1990s as a successor to an earlier 'open door policy'. In 1992, the then president Jiang Zemin explained that 'we should encourage enterprises to expand their investments abroad and their transnational operations.'[704] At first a 'national team' of 120 state-owned companies or groups was selected to accelerate internationalisation, with financial incentives and support from the government. Excellent management would, it was said, enable these industries to become competitive in the global market. Later, as part of the efforts to meet WTO requirements, and following the 'suggestion' of Jiang Zemin at the 16th National Congress of the Communist Party in 2002, this policy became a formal strategy known as 'going out', as the logical counterpart to the older strategy of 'bringing in', which was devised to promote 'the continual development of the economy through energetically importing capital, technology and management.'[705] The emphasis on 'energetically' in this quotation from a government minister provides an insight in the official view.

Much of the growth and export success of Chinese exporting manufacturers to date has been based on clusters adopting the 'Original Equipment Manufacturing' (OEM) model. One example may be seen in Shunde, a city of around 1 million inhabitants in the Pearl River Delta with seemingly endless roads lined with factories. Shunde describes itself as the 'Kingdom of Household Electrical Appliances' and 'the Capital of Household Electrical Appliances'.[706] Already at the beginning of this decade, the cluster had an annual production of over 2 million refrigerators, 3 million air conditioners, 30 million electric fans, 8 million rice cookers, and produced 30 per cent of the world's microwave ovens.[707] Although it does have well-known domestic brands like Midea and Kelon, much of the manufacturing is contract work for non-Chinese firms such as Philips and Bosch. Elsewhere in China the story is the same. Manufacturers have been successful to date, but margins are shrinking and the OEM model means that the greatest part of the total margin is earned outside China. An excellent example of this was provided by an American journalist who visited the Tianjin Jiahua Footwear factory in 2006 and did the sums for a pair of boots. This foreign-owned factory produced boots with leather imported from America; the finished boots, complete with price tags, were then sent back and sold for $49.99 a pair. The problem for China is that 'of the roughly $46.50 the U.S. retailer spends to get the boots to market, at least $29 circulates entirely within the United States, paying the salaries of advertisers, Web site designers, truckers and salespeople.' The cost of labour for each pair was a mere $1.30 a pair, or about 2.6 per cent of the American retail price.[708] The same story, and similar figures, can be told of any product.

Accession to the WTO and global markets is changing the game. Companies in industries that are open to global competition, such as the household appliance manufacturers in Shunde, are now faced with a pressing need to enter the home markets of their major international competitors. For although the Chinese domestic market is potentially enormous, the big profits lay elsewhere: in household appliances the US profit pool is worth more than $2 billion, nine times that in China; in consumer electronics, it is worth more than $1 billion, ten times more than in China. But to succeed in these markets requires a combination of attractively priced products, good service, and sophisticated marketing, skills that many Chinese companies must yet acquire at the international level.

To overcome this deficiency, around fifty 'national champions' were created from key industrial sectors including internationally known companies like Baosteel, CNOOC, Haier, Huawei, Lenovo, PetroChina, Sinopec and TCL. Most of these companies are motivated, apart from government incentives and local political pressure, by three main factors: locating new markets (for example, domestic appliance manufacturers, like Haier in Pakistan); securing resources (for example, the major oil and mining companies, towards Russia, Australia and Africa); and acquiring technology and brand names (for example, Lenovo in the USA). Others, such as the major national banks, have gained global notoriety by means of massive and successful IPOs. Since they are mainly companies whose business and services are concentrated on the Mainland, however, this does little in terms of creating a global brand, although they are now beginning to offer specialised investment services outside China. While many of the 8,000 or so Chinese companies said to be active 'abroad', perhaps a third are located in Hong Kong: there are now around 800 with operations in the USA and nearly 500 in the European Union. Path-breaking acquisitions by Chinese companies included that of Schneider Electronics by TCL in 2002 and of IBM's personal computer manufacturing division by Lenovo in 2004. Other notable acquisitions have been made by Qianjiang Group, the largest Chinese motorcycle manufacturer (which bought the Italian maker Benelli), by Shenyang Machine Tool Group (the German machine tool-maker Schiess), by Wanxiang Group (Schiller, Universal Automotive Industries and Rockford Powertrain), and the headline-grabbing purchase of Rover by Shanghai Automotive Industry Corp (SAIC) and MG by its competitor Nanjing Auto. The latter, with the Chinese company now producing the MG7 and MGTF, was referred to in the Press as adopting a cautious 'stealthlike approach' to winning international brands in contrast to the earlier and louder approach taken by Japan and South Korea.[709] There have also been failures, mainly in the face of economic nationalism, such as Sinopec's offer for the Russian company Slavnet in 2002, followed by China Minmetals' attempted takeover of the Canadian company Noranda, and the offer by CNOOC for the American company Unocal, both in 2005.

The tough question is, are Chinese companies good enough to go global? When Huawei Technologies began to sell telecommunications network equipment in Europe, the biggest problem was overcoming the perception that their goods were inferior in quality. Huawei was founded in 1988, and is based in its own company town on the outskirts of Shenzhen with groomed lawns, gleaming white apartment blocks for its employees within walking distance of offices and the R&D centre, and a sense of military perfection in the streets befitting the company's origins. The company describes itself as a research-focused organisation, proudly announcing that 'at the end of 2006, Huawei has over 61,000 employees, of whom 48 per cent are dedicated to R&D.'[710] But this was not enough in a mature and sceptical industry where quality and near-absolute reliability are paramount, even though the company had early sales in Asian, African and Middle Eastern markets. One telecoms expert could write that: 'There is still a snobbishness among Western manufacturers on quality. As soon as the Huawei's can show they can compete on quality then that will have to be addressed.'[711] Indeed, some operators exploited low-cost offers from Huawei as a means to extract lower prices from established European equipment suppliers like Alcatel. Even when quality seemed to have improved, there were problems such as copyright disputes with Cisco, and consequent legal action, over the allegedly illegitimate use of source code in routers. The company also suffered an unsuccessful bid for the British telecoms equipment manufacturer Marconi in 2005, which was later acquired by Ericsson.

But Huawei learned some valuable lessons. It established R&D centres in Sweden and Holland and set up training programmes in several target markets. In 2008, Huawei is an approved supplier to Vodafone, and also provides optical transmission and network equipment to BT and Fibrenet in Britain, Telfort in Holland, Neuf in France and QSC in Germany. It has set up a subsidiary called FutureWei, with headquarters in Texas, but it still lacks major American clients. However, the company is enjoying increasing success in the advanced world, and claims to serve twenty-eight of the top fifty global telecoms operators. It is a perfect example of 'stealth success', in the sense that the end-customer using an operator's service knows neither the name nor the brand of the switch or router but is satisfied with the service of the network provider without needing to know Huawei.

Many medium-sized enterprises have also found sufficient motivation to seek new markets abroad. A survey carried out as early as 2003 amongst fifty-one companies in the Shanghai area found that as many as 45 per cent of the companies had invested or intended to invest in Asean countries, 35 per cent in Hong Kong, and 33 per cent in Japan.[712] Beyond that area, there had been some investment in textiles in Latin America (for example Shanghai Textile Group, Hua Yuan Group), and in R&D centres in Silicon Valley (SVA, Holley Group, Shanghai Electronics), and several attempts at building international sales networks. Since 2003, the process has accelerated, with the latest available figures showing a steady annual increase from $2.9 billion of external investment in that year to $16.1 billion in 2006, mostly from the highly developed provinces of Shanghai, Zhejiang, Shandong and Guangdong. These investments touch several industrial sectors, with 20 per cent in wholesale and retail activities, 15 per cent in mining, 12 per cent in transportation, and smaller percentages in real estate, construction and telecommunications.[713]

But it must be said that the policy is not yet as successful as China hoped. There are two ancillary reasons for this: first a tendency to generate a proliferation of new products and enter as many markets as possible without sufficient planning; and, second, the haste of Chinese companies to achieve in two or three years what their often-cited role models like Samsung managed in twenty.

An example of the former is Haier, an excellent company that has gained a worldwide reputation as a white-goods manufacturer, especially for its refrigerators and wine coolers (the latter especially in the USA). It is now the fourth biggest in the world. But a visit to the company's circular headquarters building in Qingdao and the vast array of products in its brightly-lit showrooms leaves one bewildered. Company documents speak proudly of '15,100 varieties of items in 96 product lines'.[714] But in fact, these are reduced to five real areas: refrigerators, freezers, washing machines, microwave ovens and televisions. It is very hard to find even a Chinese consumer with a Haier mobile phone or computer, and instinct suggests that it would be better to concentrate on a core range of products rather than try to make everything in hit-or-miss fashion. But this is a very Chinese entrepreneurial approach.

It pervades the automobile industry, as could be seen at the Beijing Auto Show in late November 2006. In that year, Chinese manufacturers like Chery, Great Wall, Red Flag and Geely had 27 per cent of the domestic market, which means they manufactured around 1.5 million cars. According to the Chairman of Great Wall, Wei Jianjun, in 2006 Great Wall exported 27,505 sports utility vehicles, mainly to Russia and the Middle East.[715] Moreover, the vehicles on show were not just low-cost and slighty flimsy cars for the local market, but prototypes and concept cars for the luxury market styled by international designers. New models already proliferate on the streets of the large cities, yet Chinese manufacturers displayed over 180 further models at the Beijing Fair. They are nothing if not ambitious. Chery, for example, which was founded in 1997 in Wuhu (Anhui province), announced in 2007 that it alone would produce 1 million cars a year by 2010, 400,000 of which will be for export. The company already has factories in Egypt, Indonesia, Iran, Russia, Ukraine and Uruguay, and plans new ones in Argentina and India. It has signed production agreements to build engines for Fiat and to distribute small cars in Europe and the USA with Chrysler. Such fervent optimism is distant from the woes of most Western manufacturers.

Many observers believe that the industry is moving too fast, that it is impossible – or at least inadvisable – to build a durable, market-oriented car industry on the basis of state support and copied technology and designs – or purchased technology and designs in the case of SAIC, which transformed the Rover 75 into a 'Chinese' car known as the Roewe. Again, if it took the Japanese and the Koreans twenty years each to enter Western markets with real success (understanding different distribution systems, the car-buyer's psychology, and the necessary service quality), how is it possible for the Chinese to do it in less than five years? The basic problem is quality, which is still insufficient for mature overseas markets but acceptable in, say, emerging markets like Vietnam. Cost reigns supreme, and Chinese buyers have yet to go through the sequence of new car > serious repairs > residual value; as many as a third of drivers in a city like Beijing did not even have a licence three or four years ago, within the lifespan of a single new car. As an article on the Beijing Auto Show in *The Economist* observed, Chinese car companies have been able to grow so rapidly due to government support and cost-conscious consumers rather than technological know-how. But the inherent lack of quality and reliability, not to mention robustness and safety in an accident, 'may yet prove costly tomorrow'.[716]

These problems are of course widely recognised. Li Dong Sheng, Chairman of TCL, recognised them explicitly when he observed that: 'In the future, Chinese companies have a choice of three routes. The first is where the Chinese company is obliterated by the growing competition. The second route is where the Chinese company is subsumed into a world-class company. The third route is where the Chinese company becomes a world-class company itself.'[717] Mr Li believed that in fact most Chinese companies will follow the second route, but for TCL his ambition was to navigate what he calls the 'coveted' third route. Unfortunately it was more difficult than he imagined. In 2004, he created a joint venture called TTE Europe in order to enter the global television sales market with the leverage of the Thomson brand. Just one year later, the Chief Financial Officer announced that the plans for profitability had been moved forward, and in the first nine months of 2006 net losses reached 159 million euros.[718] The pressures were too great, and the learning curve too steep. In November 2006, TCL announced that it would close down most of its operations in Europe, sell its factory in Poland and close five of its seven European offices in what was euphemistically described as a restructuring operation.[719]

One problem was Chinese irritation at the European work ethic. Mr Li was frustrated because his French managers refused to answer their mobile phones on Sunday, which is inconceivable for a Chinese entrepreneur, and could not understand the psychological and physiological importance of Sunday. The same reaction even occurs in Africa, where Liu Ping, the general manager in Lusaka for China's largest construction company in Zambia, the state-owned China National Overseas Engineering Corporation, expressed it in these terms: 'Chinese people can stand very hard work. This is a cultural difference. Chinese people work until they finish and then rest. Here they are like the British, they work according to a plan. They have tea breaks and a lot of days off.'[720] Like Mr Li, and many other Chinese entrepreneurs, he simply could not 'get' the need for weekends and holidays. Or even for rest: I once travelled from Europe with a Chinese factory owner on an overnight flight to Shanghai. On arrival at Pudong Airport, I assumed that he would go home to see his wife and baby after ten days' absence, but his driver was waiting to take him to check the production lines in Nanjing – a three-hour drive – before going back to Shanghai late that evening. The problem is that sooner or later this ferocious work ethic will pay dividends abroad as it has in factories on the Mainland.

One consequence is that many Western companies are being forced to reconsider their strategies and business models, if not their 'holiday strategies', to reinvent themselves by doing something the Chinese cannot do. An American author, Reed Hundt, has gone so far as to argue that the best way to face the challenge of China's growing economic power is to recruit better-quality people to government and actively encourage entrepreneurship and funding so that American companies can compete better against the new Chinese global firms. Although it might be unpalatable advice for companies accustomed to being industry leaders, it might also be wise to learn from the Chinese. Hundt quotes John Chambers, the dynamic CEO of Cisco Systems, on the need to develop a strategy of 'becoming a Chinese company' so that Cisco can remain a big American employer and combat Chinese competitors like Huawei in the pro-duction of routers.[721] Ironically, therefore, the 'going out' policy could have a positive effect on Western government and business.

We will now consider the three main strategies for 'going out'. The first is to find new markets outside China for successful products or companies (it will be some time before Chinese services will be good enough); the second way is to list on a foreign stock exchange; and the third is a government-sponsored method entailing the creation of overseas trading hubs and industrial areas.

New Markets

An example of the first way is the case of Lenovo, previously known as Legend. The computer industry in China may be said to have begun in 1956 with the creation of the Computer Institute of the Chinese Academy of Sciences, which was later placed under the Scientific Industries Commission of the Ministry of Defence as 'Jing Troop 116'.[722] That is where Liu Chuanzhi, the future founder of Lenovo, began his career in 1970, already in the area that later became Zhongguancun Science Park and which Lenovo's factories and offices now dominate. Then, in 1984, coincidentally the same year that Michael Dell began selling computers in Texas, with ten colleagues from the Computer Institute, Liu founded the company known after a series of compromises and nods to authority as the 'Chinese Academy of Sciences Computer Technology Research Institute New Technology Development Company'. It was situated in a single-storey guardhouse that was China's equivalent of a Californian garage. Later, in 1989, the name was simplified to *Liangxiang* in Chinese and *Legend* in English.

The initial capital and brainpower came by way of the Chinese Academy of Sciences, a government institution. Early revenues derived from trading and services, and a series of events in the late 1980s showed how Legend operated in a 'stealth' manner similar to the Overseas Chinese companies. In a classic move to improve profits on trading, the company decided to cut out the middlemen by importing directly into China. This required a presence in Hong Kong. So partnerships were formed with two companies, one of which was a state-owned company called China Technology Licensing Ltd, the Hong Kong investment arm of the China Council for the Promotion of International Trade. Liu Chuanzhi, who was now formally the General Manager of Legend, stressed in a meeting that the new partner had access to large amounts of funding, but neglected to mention that the chairman was his own father, Liu Gushu, a successful banker who introduced his son into the world of Overseas Chinese finance.[723]

Legend assembled its first computer from imported components in 1990, and sold 2,131 that year.[724] At that time, the major foreign makers held 70 per cent of the market for computer sales in China, but by 1996 this market share had decreased to 40 per cent.[725] The following year, having become the leading company in China, Legend began its own process of 'going out' by exporting small numbers of computers to Mongolia and eight countries in Eastern Europe and Africa. But before accelerating the process, the company needed to change its English name, which was protected by trademarks in many countries, such as Japan, where it was owned by Honda. In 2002, it became 'Le-gend novo', the new Legend, truncated to Lenovo. By then, it was one of the top ten global computer manufacturers, but the problem was that over 90 per cent of sales revenue still came from China. Worse, still, the company was ineluctably losing market share to Dell, especially in the profitable notebook sector. The process of 'going out' needed a kick-start.

It came with a signal that suggests a way forward for other Chinese companies. For at the end of 2004, Lenovo and IBM announced that the Chinese company would purchase IBM's PC Division for $1.25 billion, roughly half in cash and half in stock, and assume about $500 million of IBM debt. As a result, IBM would become the second largest shareholder in Lenovo after the Chinese government. Although the PC division had declined from its heyday and only accounted for about 15 per cent of company revenues, the acquisition was symbolically significant for China.

There are few more illustrious brands than IBM. American politicians and institutions immediately protested at the planned acquisition, but formal approval was given, partly because IBM itself had made the initial approach. Furthermore, the deal was evidently favourable to them because it would have been hard to find another suitable buyer for a loss-making division. But Lenovo's management saw possibilities of turning losses into profit, and above all the possibility of acquiring a global brand – at least for five years. Moreover, the IBM link was almost as old as Lenovo itself. For IBM-related activities were critically important in its inaugural financial year: first, the company secured a service contract for 500 IBM personal computers acquired by the Chinese Academy of Sciences (which represented around 30 per cent of revenues); second, with typical Chinese vagueness, the annual results reported 'US$70,000 in gross profit for various things done on behalf of the Beijing Central Agency of IBM.'[726] Even the predominant blue of Legend corporate design was homage to 'Big Blue.'

Thus in 2008, two threads of China's rebranding of the country image come together in a display of patriotic zeal, as Lenovo, which was the first partner to be announced, provides its computers and logo for the Olympic Games, replacing IBM itself, which had been the computer industry sponsor of the two previous summer Olympics (Lenovo already gained practice as sponsor of the 2006 Winter Olympics in Turin). In the proud if exaggerated words of the Vice-Chairman of the Olympics Preparatory Committee, 'the Liangxiang Group has come up with a new model for taking Chinese enterprises out into the world.'[727]

Another prominent example is that of Haier, which, with its impressive American headquarters on Broadway in New York, is one of the most visible Chinese companies abroad, with a wide range of products available at well-known supermarkets and department stores like Best Buy, Costco, Home Depot, Sears and Wal-Mart. In this case, brand acceptance was at least partly facilitated by a non-Chinese-sounding name, which derives from a joint venture in the 1980s with the division specialising in commercial freezers and drinks refrigerators of the German group Liebherr. In Chinese transliteration, the German name became four syllables, 'Li-bu-hai-er', of which the last two were maintained as the new company name after the joint venture and licensing agreements were dissolved. In terms of brand, the name has been excellent: in Chinese it contains the meanings 'sea' (*hai*, appropriate since its headquarters' city Qingdao is renowned as a seaport and holiday destination), and also 'child' (*hai er*, which enabled a logo with two boys, Chinese and Caucasian), while in English it allows puns with 'higher' – as in the slogan 'Haier and Higher', and in a *Harvard Business Review* article entitled 'Raising Haier'.

The group later created another joint venture, since also dissolved, with the Italian white-goods manufacturer Merloni (owner of the Ariston brand) to make washing machines. In terms of growth and prestige abroad, the symbolic turning-point was the failed acquisition of Maytag, one of the most famous consumer brands in America, for even though Haier was out-bid by fellow national champion Whirlpool the resulting publicity put the company firmly on the global map as a serious player. That had always been the objective, with its declared mission to become 'a global top 3 white goods manufacturer'. Founder and CEO Zhang Ruimin has sought to imitate his heroes Jack Welch of GE for management methods and Akio Morita of Sony for product diversification (Liu Chuanzhi of Lenovo once did a course at GE's management training centre at Crotonville).[728] Another company that provided a model is Hewlett Packard. As explained in the hagiographical book *The Haier Way*, which explicitly invites comparison with the more famous 'HP Way', the policy of globalisation was based on the HP formula of 'three one-thirds', meaning that one-third of Haier's products should be made and sold in China, one-third made in China but sold elsewhere, and one-third produced and sold overseas.[729] To this end, the company first set up joint-venture factories in the

Philippines, Malaysia, Iran and Algeria, and then acquired plants in its own name in northern Italy, producing air-conditioning units for the European market, and in Camden, South Carolina, producing refrigerators, washing machines, wine coolers and air conditioners for the American market. With a current total of fifteen overseas factories, Haier is also a truly global group in the sense of corporate and tax structures, with holding companies in Qingdao, Hong Kong, Bermuda and the British Virgin Islands. The group comprises a total of over 240 subsidiaries, including the many operating companies in target markets, and listed companies on both the Shanghai and Hong Kong Stock Exchanges.

However, as of 2008, in spite of these success stories and with all the policy support, infrastructure and research support, access to foreign technology both licit and illicit, and financial incentives provided by the government, there is no truly global Chinese company with an instantly recognisable and wholly Chinese brand. But that is surely a matter of time.

Stock Markets

An example of the second way of 'going out' is what was then the biggest listing in the world when Industrial and Commercial Bank of China (ICBC) raised $19 billion on 20 October 2006, in spite of the history of non-performing loans and scandals that had characterised the big Chinese banks in previous years.

ICBC was established in January 1984, the same year as Lenovo. It has since become the largest corporate banker in China and has 145 million bank cards issued to personal customers, having been the first bank to create a card business in 1989. The bank introduced Internet-banking services in 2002, in a technological partnership with Microsoft. In preparation for listing and in order to gain international respectability, in 2004 it invited PricewaterhouseCoopers to plan for corporate governance and a risk-management system. Then, in 2005, it changed from being a state-owned commercial bank into a shareholding company, although its principal, and equal, shareholders remained the Ministry of Finance and Central SAFE Investments Limited. A year later, in an important deal for the Chinese banking sector, three significant foreign investors, Goldman Sachs, Allianz and American Express were allowed to buy shares in the bank, the biggest holding of 7 per cent going to Goldman Sachs.

The period 2005–2007 saw a dramatic rise in the number of stocks quoted on foreign exchanges, especially London.[730] This was partly due to stricter requirements for entering Nasdaq imposed by the Sarbanes-Oxley rules, and partly a consequence of the relatively simple rules for going to IPO on AIM (the Alternative Investment Market), which had no requirements for a trading record or minimum market capitalisation. In the first eight years of its existence, from 1995 to 2003, only three Chinese companies chose to enter AIM, with Nasdaq being the preferred market for often US-educated entrepreneurs. In 2004, this number crept up to four, since the new requirements of Sarbanes-Oxley were not yet fully implemented. Then, from 15 November 2004, according to the notorious Section 404, public companies with a market capitalisation of more than over US $75M faced new requirements in year-end fiscal reports and all quarterly reports thereafter (smaller companies had until 15 July 2007). This opened the door for AIM: in 2005 there were eleven Chinese listings, and in 2006 twenty-six, bringing the total to forty-four. Meanwhile, on Nasdaq, listings dropped from nine in 2005 to five in 2006. The companies came from a wide variety of sectors, although most were finance-related companies (eight), mining companies (seven), and software companies (four).

Yet simple rules can be a double-edged sword. Perhaps it was just too easy, and in the rush to bring Chinese companies to AIM there were inevitable problems. In fact, while this market was created to meet the needs of growth companies and provide a focus for investors who follow growing companies, some Chinese companies perceived listing as a means of shifting assets abroad. For this reason, many of them failed to grow after listing. Among the worst-performing Chinese stocks in the 2006 listings was Bodisen Biotech, a manufacturer of liquid and organic compound fertilizers, pesticides, insecticides and agricultural raw materials, which was listed in AIM in February 2006 (BODI.L) after listing in New York two years earlier. A month before the UK listing, Bosiden was said by *Forbes China* to be the sixteenth fastest-growing company in China. Due to some rather ambiguous relationships in the past with consultants and advisers, the American authorities censured Bosiden for alleged disclosure, and the share price saw a constant, steady decline from 950p on the first day's trading on 6 February to around 52p in September 2007. This corresponds to a drop in market value over that period from £146m to £9m. In 2007, the company's website still proclaimed it to be one of the fastest growing companies in China, but from the perspective of London things are rather different. On the whole though, the Chinese companies on AIM have performed in line with newly-listed companies from other countries. In 2008, over 50 are listed.

There was one further intriguing sign of 'going out' through the stock market early in 2007, when a consortium of three Chinese companies (the gold-mining company Zijin, the state-owned copper mining company Tongling, and Xiamen Construction and Development), made a successful takeover bid for an AIM-listed British company, Monterrico. The main interest was in a potentially important copper mine in Peru, in line with China's strategy of investing in mineral resources to guarantee future supplies. This could be a sign of things to come, especially as China becomes more widely accepted in the global market.

There are also six larger companies on the main London Stock Exchange (Air China, Datang International Power Generation, Jiangxi Copper Company, Sinopec,

Zhenjiang Expressway Company and Zhejiang Southeast Electric Power), half of which listed as long ago as 1997. However, these companies are all secondary listings with depositary receipts rather than normal shares; these Global Depositary Receipts (GDRs) are in effect groups of shares owned by institutions rather than individual shareholders, and are not therefore subject to trading.

To date, the scramble to list in London and New York has not resulted in the success that was hoped for, but the listings continue and that means, together with the enormous growth of the Hong Kong and Shanghai indexes, that Chinese-owned companies are destined to play an increasingly important role in the world's leading exchanges. Soon the success of Chinese companies listing abroad will unleash new waves of protectionism.

Trading Hubs and Industrial Areas

A further government-sponsored strategy for 'going out' has been the creation of trading areas and industrial zones.

An example of the former is the Dragon Mart in Dubai, described as the 'largest trading hub for products from China outside the Chinese mainland', which opened in 2004. Consisting of a dragon-shaped structure over a kilometre long, this market houses 4,000 companies together with restaurants, warehouses, and business services. It also has a conference centre and exhibition spaces, and a nearby residential development, which effectively creates a new-style Chinatown as part of Dubai's ambitious tourism project. The market itself has sections devoted to industries such as textile and garments, home appliances, interior decoration, sports and leisure goods and electronics. For European buyers, it is closer and has good services.

A similar official approach may be seen in recent plans to create industrial areas outside China on the 'Special Economic Zone' model used in Shenzhen in the 1990s. Towards the end of 2006, for example, Hu Jintao made the first visit by a Chinese president to Pakistan for over a decade and, following an increase in the previous year of 40 per cent in bilateral trade, signed a broad, multi-sector, five-year economic and trade development programme, which was an absolute precedent with any country. There will be two special zones for Chinese companies, one to be located in Lahore and to be known, tellingly, as the Haier-Ruba economic zone,[731] and a special textile zone in Faisalabad. Eventually, these zones will be linked to China by new railway routes over the Karakorum Pass, which are currently under discussion. In diplomatic terms, however, such strategies can easily backfire. A comment in the Indian Press illustrates the importance of this venture as marking a 'qualitative transformation of Chinese economic presence in the subcontinent' from another neighbour's point of view. In creating these zones, Beijing might be seen to be 'outflanking India in its own natural hinterland', so that India 'will soon have to reckon with the fact that Chinese money might soon rule the roost in its neighbourhood.'[732] This is a perfect example of the ancient technique playing off enemies against each other, what in the terms of this book might be called a 'stealth wedge'.

A similar strategy was initiated in Africa during Hu Jintao's 2007 tour. The first example will be the Zambia-China Economic and Trade Cooperation Zone, which he formally inaugurated together with Levy Patrick Mwanawasa, the President of Zambia. The Chinese government has pledged to make investments of $800 million in the zone over a three-year period. At the same time, President Hu announced the creation of 'three to five' further trade and economic cooperation zones in Africa in the next three years.[733] Conditions are reminiscent of those in the domestic economic zones. The Zambian finance minister Ng'andu Magande announced that China will offer Zambia tariff-free market access for its products, and has increased the number of products that can be imported from 192 to 452. In another unusual move, Zambians will also be able to borrow investment capital from the Bank of China, which has a Zambian branch that previously provided services only to Chinese investors, to facilitate their entry into the Chinese market. Helped by generous tax exemptions and other incentives, the hope is that by 2010 around sixty Chinese companies will set up production facilities in the new economic zone and create as many as 60,000 new jobs for Zambians.[734] Success in such zones, in Africa and elsewhere, will certainly lead to the creation of many more as Chinese businesses continue to pursue international expansion.

The Stealth Business Empire

Put together, these elements – new markets, foreign listing and trading hubs – constitute a stealth business empire in formation. The 'going out' strategy has faced many difficulties to date, but the Chinese government insists on its importance. At the end of 2006, the State Assets Supervision and Administration Commission (SASAC), which was set up by the State Council in 2003 to preserve and enhance the value of key State Owned Enterprises, reiterated that by 2010 between thirty and fifty large business groups should emerge from this category.[735] That sounds very optimistic in such a short time, but certainly it will happen eventually. Due to the boom in the Shanghai Stock Exchange, in September 2007 three Chinese companies featured in the top ten global companies measured by market capitalisation: the Industrial and Commercial Bank of China (No. 3, following Exxon and General Electric), Petrochina (4), and China Mobile (6). So they certainly have the financial wherewithall, if the bubble doesn't burst.

But brands? These are today the measure by which reputations are judged. China lacks brand aura. '*Made* in China' is fine if the article is supported by a European brand name, but 'made in China' with a Chinese brand is more difficult to accept – especially in the short term. As we saw in an earlier chapter, brand building can be a very slow and arduous activity: Cerruti started out in 1881, Coca Cola in 1886, Salvatore Ferragamo and Gucci in 1923, and even upstart Microsoft is over thirty years old. It is true that modern technology has accelerated the process, so Amazon, Yahoo and Google have achieved similar recognition in a decade. But they were nurtured within a strong regional high-tech brand that the Chinese do not possess. This is vital for future success, much more than most Chinese companies and entrepreneurs realise. The first strong Chinese global brand might be Lenovo, Huawei or Haier, but is more likely to be a company as yet neither imagined nor founded, a Google in the sense of a company that comes from nothing to the status of a global brand within a few years.

The real question is, remembering predictions about China overtaking the USA in economic terms by the middle of the twenty-first century, when will China succeed in having a substantial proportion of leading companies that count amongst the top 100 global brands? The realistic answer must be, probably not in the first half of this century. But perhaps the question itself is wrong. The true strength and success of China's 'going out' may never be quantifiable in numbers of global brands, and will in all likelihood be difficult to measure precisely in conventional terms. For it will be predominantly a stealth business empire, different from the traditional empires of Europe- or US-based multinational corporations and unlike any we have seen before.

The New Chinese Mindset
and the Stealth Empire

Can China's leadership conquer the world? Had we asked that question nineteen years ago, the answer would have been a resounding negative. For the events of 1989 amply demonstrated the archaic mindset of the gerontocracy that then ruled the country: 'As products of the Long March generation, with a lifelong experience of sabotage, class struggle, civil war, foreign war, and endless mass campaigns of one sort or another, they had become highly sensitive to the question of safety, security, and, above all else, survival.'[736] Power was synonymous with life, and life without power would have been meaningless for them. Deng Xiao Ping was eighty-five years old, Yang Shangkun, the President of China and an ex-general in the PLA, was eighty-two, while Wang Zhen, the Vice-President, was eighty-one; around these key figures gravitated many influential octogenarian politicians and generals, and even the nonagenarian veteran Marshall Nie Rongzhen. From their point of view, their lives, the future of their families, and their privileges, all depended on the maintenance of social and political order at any cost. As Ulysses said in the passage quoted above, 'Take but degree away, untune that string/And hark what discord follows!' They would do whatever was necessary to keep the string tuned, however harsh that might seem to an outsider. Better a few days of shooting, however unpleasant or against the grain, than long term discord. A few hundred deaths have never been a major problem.

But in the two intervening decades, much has changed. There is more power-sharing and a greater willingness to look beyond China, with up-and-coming leaders who know European languages and have often studied abroad. Another significant change is that the leadership is much younger, with key figures still in their fifties like the hyperactive Party Secretary of Chongqing, Bo Xilai (fifty-eight), and three men who have been touted as possible successors to the current president: Li Yuancho (fifty-seven), the Governor of Jiangsu province; Li Keqiang (fifty-three), recently elevated to the Standing Committee of the Politburo; and Wang Yang (fifty-three), Party Secretary of Guangdong Province. All these men are well positioned for greater future power. In fact, the average age of the nine members of the Standing Committee of the 16th Politburo when they assumed power in the spring of 2003 was 62.4, while that of the sixteen new non-standing-committee members was just under sixty (59.8), with the eldest being Cao Gangchuan at sixty-seven and the youngest Zhang Lichang at fifty-three. Hu Jintao himself enjoyed one of the most remarkable careers of all, becoming a member of the Standing Committee of the Politburo when he was only forty-nine years old.

One of the most interesting changes in the leadership is that from a strictly military background in earlier generations to engineering in the current 'fourth' generation, and on to the humanities graduates appointed as provincial leaders by Hu Jintao's Politburo since 2003 and who will be the backbone of the 'fifth' generation from 2012. This is a little-noted but significant trajectory: of twenty-nine appointees in the first year of Hu Jintao's presidency, six were graduates in economy, three in philosophy, two in history, and five others in humanities and social sciences; by way of contrast, only five were engineering graduates (six members of the Standing Committee of the 16th Politburo were engineers; three held technical degrees). Most were born after the PRC itself, and the youngest, Lin Jinzao, Vice-Governor of Hubei, as late as 1958.[737] Another striking fact, which concurs with the impression on meeting senior officials, is the increase in educational achievement. The proportion of county-level cadres with a university education increased from 16.4 per cent in 1981 to 87.9 per cent in 2002, while in the Communist Party's central committee the increase went from 23.8 per cent in 1969 to 55.5 per cent in 1982, and on to 98.6 per cent in 2002.[738] Few countries in the world can boast such levels: indeed, this emphasis on choosing and nurturing future leaders with care is one of the positive aspects of Chinese leadership culture that Hundt advocates as a model for the United States – stating forcefully that 'The Chinese Communist Party cannot be the only government that trains its leaders.'[739] At ministerial level, it is rare in other countries to find such a high level of preparation for the brief.

So the leadership is changing in its formation and outlook. But what of the populace?

Some interesting light was thrown into the contemporary mindset of the Chinese in the latest biennial survey published by The Chicago Council on Global Affairs in 2006, based on surveys carried out in China, India and the USA, with additional surveys involving countries such as South Korea and Australia.[740] It furnished insights into how Chinese adults perceive their country's role as a Great Power, and the future of the world in terms of the triangular relationship between China, India and the United States. One of the most intriguing findings is that the Chinese who were interviewed were not alarmed 'by potential threats to vital interests except for the spread of epidemic disease'.[741] In other words, they were so confident of their country's growing power in the world, they they feel no military threat. Indeed, they considered foreign policy goals to be related to economic issues rather than to diplomacy or military security. Most believed that within ten years China would overtake the countries they currently perceive as numbers two and three, Japan and Germany respectively.[742] They also thought that their economy would eventually catch up with that of the United States, but doubted that they could equal America in developing new products and technology. They were not obsessed with the trappings of global power, and world power status was of relative importance. Their main concerns were economic security and quality of life, which is understandable after a century of turmoil and hardship. The three dominant 'foreign policy' goals of these interviewees were protecting the jobs of Chinese workers, promoting economic growth and securing adequate supplies of energy.[743] Building superior military power was ranked the penultimate of eleven goals.

So much for the relatively sophisticated adults. One key driver of change is of course youth, which in this case means hundreds of millions of young people (nearly 400 million under eighteen alone) who have never known the travails of revolution and food shortages. Most Chinese citizens born after 1978, the year of 'opening up' and reforms, have lived through continuous economic growth both in the country and within their extended family. They inhabit a world of fashionable music and dress that bears no relationship to propaganda songs and Mao suits, and are as brand-conscious as their Western peers; those born after 1990 are even further removed from the past, fattened on KFC and Pizza Hut, in the large cities often driven to school by parents, and in perpetual contact with friends through a mobile phone or Internet (70 per cent of the 200 million Internet users are under thirty). Even the poorest teenage girl can look attractive and feel good beyond the imagination of her forebears with clean well-combed hair, painted nails, a brightly-coloured teeshirt and ribbons, one fashionable pair of shoes, and a mobile phone dangling from her neck.

Teenagers have a sense of individuality in dress, behaviour and thinking that is quite new, and their culture is markedly international and mediatic in its formation: 'We talk like the way of Hong Kong/Taiwan stars, dress following the fashion of South Korean stars, wear the expression of European or American stars and fall in love like what Japanese movies and TV series describe.'[744] They are physically different to their elders, taller and visibly healthier, often plump. They eat meat every day, enjoy cheese on their pizza, and drink milk, and to watch them leave a high school in a major eastern city dressed in tracksuits and listening to i-pods reminds us of the great social change more tangibly than the building sites. They too tower over waiting parents, and even more so over grandparents. Their ideology is consumerism rather than communism; their conversation is about blogs and fashionable sports like skiing. Their greatest aspiration is foreign travel and overseas study. The need for cash to pay for clothes, telephones and entertainment for the new lifestyle trumps traditional values like saving money for marriage. The attitudes that emerge from a detailed survey are distinctly pragmatic, verging on cynical. In fact, as many as 43 per cent believed that 'human relationships are entirely profit-oriented', while 63 per cent expressed the view that life should be fun.[745] Their Western counterparts might complain of their political complacency, but from another point of view any teenager who has heard the horror stories of relatives in the Great Leap Forward and the Cultural Revolution is being entirely rational in avoiding politics. They look forwards and outwards, and they will be the political and business leaders as China approaches mid-century (see Figure 5, Appendix 2).

Looking a few years further ahead, a survey of 10,000 university students found substantial changes in value orientations and political attitudes, which could be categorised on four dimensions.[746] The first was a significant shift from the old idea of students as an élite, since competitive pressures have forced them to view themselves in a different way and understand that entering the job market is by no means simple even with a degree. My personal experience is that in the past few years there has been an increasing number of graduates even from prestigious universities who are content to accept positions beneath their original expectations, and often seek unsalaried internships in order to gain experience. The second dimension in the survey found a shift from unified to diversified choice, in other words a desire to exploit the new possibilities of the market economy in a new way: 'They are no longer content with the present situation or with an ordinary life, but seeking for development, for establishing their own business, for a full display of their potential in order to realize their own value in the fiercely competitive environment.'[747] The third dimension concerned a shift away from ideals to pragmatic needs, dismissing 'Communist' values, respecting the interests of China but not at the cost of truncating personal development or realising their own interests. Finally, there was a shift from the acquisition of pure knowledge to that of practical skills that can find an outlet in the employment market.

Most interesting of all, in terms of our present argument, was the fact that while the vast majority understood and appreciated the role of the Communist Party and its leadership in bringing about the reforms and changes that made their lives different, very few expressed interest in participating in political activities. They see themselves as protagonists in the future development of the country, but in the sense of entrepreneurship or salaried work rather than political activity. They seem to be, in a sense, beyond politics.

Will an Absence of Democracy Impede the Steath Empire?

Observers have long been predicting that China's encounter with market forces and the liberal institutions of the West, together with the use of new media technologies like the Internet, would spur inevitable democratic change. Such a view is typified by the argument of Bruce Bueno de Mesquita and George W. Downs in a recent article on 'Development and Democracy',[748] – although they note that economic growth, at least in the short term, stabilises and legitimises authoritarian regimes more than it undermines them. Similar ideas inform the bestselling *Writing on the Wall*, where Will Hutton proclaims on the second page of his Preface that the 'central argument of this book is that if the next century is going to be Chinese, it will only be because China embraces the economic and political pluralism of the West.'[749] But why should that necessarily happen? What seems more likely is that China will continue to be led by what has been called 'market preserving federalism', which 'limits the central government's control over economic decision making, promotes creative competition among local governments, constrains rent seeking, and provides an array of incentives to induce creative local enterprises.'[750] It also maintains fiscal federalism, which is used to prevent taxation from diminishing growth, and it is noteworthy that after the 2002 Congress as many as 42 per cent of the enlarged Politburo was composed of provincial leaders. There is no reason why a democratic regime should necessarily be able to improve on this, especially since one of the often-noted advantages of China is to be able to carry out long-term projects and policies that are not drastically truncated or cancelled after elections bring in a new party or faction.

Another author has devoted an entire book to the question what if 'China becomes fully integrated into the world's economy, yet it remains also entirely undemocratic?'[751] Yet from a Chinese, non-individualistic, perspective, this is an odd question. They retort: why shouldn't it remain undemocratic? As Samuel Huntington has wisely observed, 'Economic exchange brings people into contact; it does not bring them into agreement.'[752]

There is indeed an opposite point of view, succinctly explained in a *Foreign Affairs* article by the Israeli political scientist Azar Gat. He suggests that authoritarian capitalist states like China and Russia may represent 'a viable alternative path to modernity'[753] after several decades of opprobrium following the demise of authoritarian Japan and Germany sixty years ago. For Gat, the triumph of democracy over those states was more contingent than is usually assumed, and not necessarily linked to any intrinsic advantage of democracy itself. The success of the United States, and its global projection of democratic values, was as much the consequence of location (for example, a safe distance from the main theatres of war) and fortuitous timing (becoming militarily powerful at the right moment), as of intrinsic enlightenment values. There is therefore no reason that democratic values should necessarily follow economic development; China itself managed very well for several centuries under the late Ming and early Qing. So a powerful country as China has once again become could establish (has established?) a 'powerful authoritarian capitalist order that allies political elites, industrialists, and the military; that is nationalist in orientation; and that participates in the global economy on its own terms, as imperial Germany and imperial Japan did.'[754] The spectacular success of China, together with its huge population and domestic market, means that it could indeed accomplish this. And it is not inconceivable that such visible success could cause the country to be viewed as an alternative role to 'liberal democracy.'

For some, who have never dreamed of creating a liberal democracy, China appears as manna. This view was eloquently expressed in almost poetic terms by Robert Mugabe, when he explained that 'We have turned east where the sun rises, and given our back to the west, where the sun sets.'[755] But even for less corrupt and desperate countries in Africa, after decades of ineffective promises and aid, China indicates a model for feeding the people and building the necessary infrastucture for development as she has done at home. Such thoughts are made explicit in a speech such as that made by Ken Nnamani, President of the Nigerian Senate, in which he spoke of the 'paradox of development and democracy' in China and argued that the Chinese experience was an instructive lesson on the good that a focussed and patriotic leadership can do to realise prosperity and security. Many other African and Middle Eastern states would not find this unpalatable.[756]

Nor, indeed, would the middle-class Chinese, since many well-educated, and often Western-educated, Chinese agree with their political leaders that China is not ready for Western-style democracy. They fear something like the collapse of the Soviet Union with its negative consequences, and rarely fully trust the motivations of the United States in wishing to impose a democratic system on their country. According to a survey carried out by the Chinese newspaper *Global Times* (*Huan Qiu Shi Bao*), 79 per cent of urban Chinese (and thus the most educated) had negative views concerning American criticism of China's human rights abuses: half of the respondents thought that the United States is attempting to destroy stability in China, while nearly 20 per cent 'believe that America simply does not understand China's internal situation.'[757] Personal conversations bear this out.

Conversely, the Chinese do not really understand democracy.

Democracy is predicated on the importance of the individual: in simple terms, the citizen exchanges his personal vote for a series of individual 'rights'. In its modern sense, as understood by philosophers like Hobbes and Rousseau, it was based on the concept of 'natural rights', which in turn derived from self-interest. Hence the need for a social contract between the individual and the state and the vision of political freedom as a matter of individual liberty; fundamental values such as free speech, freedom of movement, health care and education are individual values. This is in complete contrast with Chinese thought, in which the individual is of importance only insofar as he belongs to a group or community – whether it be the family, the collective, or the Party. Confucian family values, and the centrality of a system of relationships to a Chinese individual's life, are well known. The *Record of Rites* provides the ten moral norms that still today inform Chinese relationships: 'The father is to be compassionate, the son filial, the elder brother kind and the younger brother respectful, the husband just and the wife obedient, the old person gracious and the young compliant, the ruler benevolent and the minister loyal. These ten are called the human norms.' This simple list is as good a basic guide to relationships in China today as we could imagine, for it sustains a patrilineal descent system in which the essential relationships are those between parents, especially fathers, and children, especially sons.[758] In an extended family, these values are the basis of trust, for a man who is not 'thoroughly imbedded in a network of kinship cannot be completely trusted because he cannot be dealt with in a normal way.'[759] In an earlier chapter, we saw how these fundamental values were able to transcend frontiers and nurture the business networks of the Overseas Chinese – whose most successful exponents are always families.

In his wise and profound study, *The Tyranny of History*, the sinologist W.J.F. Jenner shatters any doubt about the need for a deeper understanding of Chinese history and culture. He explains why democracy and political freedom have utterly different meanings for the Chinese, and how they effectively live in a 'feudal structure reminiscent of medieval Europe, in which vassals, the system bosses, hold their fiefs from a lord in return for duties and obligations and control their sub-vassals on a similar basis.'[760] In fact one of the most curious paradoxes about Chinese political theory is that while the Party publicly identifies itself with Marx, and President Hu Jintao exhorts his fellow leaders to study his works more deeply, it does not accept the Western-inspired Marxist ideal of the all-round development of the individual.[761] The new theory of today aims to create a harmonious society, not to produce outstanding indviduals.

This is all very theoretical. What does make sense, today, to the average Chinese, is that material improvement for the collective is tangible. Let us imagine the feelings of the millions of Chinese who lived through the purges, deprivations and sufferings of the Cultural Revolution – the majority of people one sees in any street everywhere. For them there is no question that life is much better, both for themselves and for younger members of their family, and there can be little doubt that they support the present government at least tacitly for maintaining the stability within which their family can prosper. At the same time, from their point of view individual freedoms are also hugely improved for people who until very few years ago needed permission from their work unit to travel to another city, or to obtain a divorce. Now there is almost total freedom of movement within China, and it becomes easier each year to travel abroad. There is also substantial freedom of speech in a private context, and intellectuals manage to live relatively well in a state of what one author has termed 'obedient autonomy'.[762] There are systems of involvement and grass-roots feedback at both central government and provincial levels through the 200 or so recognised political associations, such as the All-China Federation of Trade Unions, the Communist Youth League and the All-China Women's Federation. Things get done. Opinion polls have shown that as many as 67 per cent of the people believe that their living conditions have improved and 75 per cent that they will continue to do so in the future.[763]

Conversation with the underpaid textile factory girl or waitress will often reveal a different story from that of exploitation that we usually read. For she receives board, lodging and clothing from her employer and manages to send most of her meagre salary back to her family. A remittance that seems to us trivial might be enough to help a brother through university, or a parent through sickness. Those are her priorities. Immediate personal gratification is not necessarily the only measure of happiness, since there is also vicarious or filial happiness. Later, she will have time to find a boyfriend and think of her own life. She should not only be seen in the isolation of her work-bench or dormitory, but also as a part of the family and village system of her provenance. Similarly, from the parents' point of view, if their children are better off and are able to study at university, then they are content; if their son or daughter manages to buy a car, then they participate in the joy without resentment at not having had the same opportunity a generation ago. Indeed, in the eyes of many Chinese, Westerners are extremely selfish in assigning priority to personal gratification. For the purpose of our argument, there are two key points: first, that happiness need not necessarily be individual happiness; second, that he introduction of full democracy would not necessarily bring improvement in the eyes of people who have no wish for more personal expression than they already enjoy.

Peaceful democratisation in China in the short-term is therefore as likely as it was in Iraq, if we take advanced Western democracies as the model. For the moment, politics and opinions are still secondary to fulfilling basic needs and wants, and assuring through savings, investment and above all through education of the young that this new relative prosperity will not be truncated. According to a survey published in 2001, 70 per cent of parents expected their children to have a Master's degree and 45 per cent expected them to get a PhD,[764] ambitious requirements by any standard but an eloquent example of the value of education in Chinese eyes. Anything approaching those numbers, for parents who might themselves have missed a higher education in the turmoil of the Cultural Revolution and its aftermath, would represent a remarkable achievement. If some form of democracy emerges, it will do so when the circumstances are right. In other words, China is a country in which 'all men are in constant motion; and where society, transformed daily by its own operations, changes its opinions together with its wants.'[765] In that, it is no different to other countries in the past: these words were written of the United States in the middle of the nineteenth century by Alexis de Tocqueville, in his *Democracy in America*.

Given the same enthusiasm and raw energy as the United States possessed then, the exportation of such Chinese values as belief in the family, education and hard work might not be a bad thing.

Is Communism a Barrier to 'Going Out'?

The communism/capitalism conundrum continues to trouble Anglo-Saxon five-star-hotel bar-propping managers. Already fifty years ago, the American journalist Julian Schuman noted that: 'the presence of a healthy capitalism in this country avowedly being led by Communists towards the goal of socialism is a curious phenomenon.'[766] Capitalism was fostered and protected because China needed it then as it needs it today. But even in the early years of Mao's dominance, such pragmatism ruled. In the first Red State established under Stalin's protection in the town of Ruijin in south-east Jiangxi Province in 1931, the leadership exploited the largest deposit of tungsten in the world, which was to be found locally, to obtain salt, cotton, medicine and weapons from Cantonese warlords to the south who were, in theory, enemies from the 'White' faction of Chiang Kai-Shek.[767] A more recent American contributor to the debate asks the interesting question: 'How do you classify a country governed by a Communist regime but whose government share of GDP is less than half that of the US?'[768] China generates such paradoxes in profusion, creating the kind of contrast both professional photographers and tourists perennially enjoy between decrepit *hutong* and international architectural vision, between Mao's portrait on Tiananmen Gate and nearby Porsche and Rolls Royce dealerships.

Turning the question on its head, it can be cogently argued that some elements of the revolutionary and Maoist past have contributed positively to the recent record of economic development. Indeed, if we accept the definition of capitalism as 'the system in which humans seek to transform (or "conquer") nature in an eternally expansive way and to amass ever larger residues of this expansion',[769] then no man was a greater capitalist than Mao himself. One example of his contribution was the way in which commune and brigade entrepreneurship nurtured the dynamism of township and village enterprises,[770] a little-studied but fascinating example of this phenomenon. There are several cases of successful collective enterprises both at the village level and at the industrial level. An example of the former is the remarkable village of Huaxi in Jiangsu, known as 'China's richest village'. In Huaxi, fifty-eight companies are collectively owned by the village's 1,520 residents, so that while average annual income might still seem low to us at $15,000, each family is assigned a car and a 400 square metre villa, with completely free services including electricity, gas and medical insurance. The village collective was listed on the Shanghai Stock Exchange in 1995, and its revenues two years later amounted to about $3 billion. In the case of Huaxi, everything is controlled in military fashion by a dictatorial mayor, Wu Renbao, who governed for forty-eight years and was succeeded in 2003 by his son, Wu Xie'en, who was 'elected' with 100 per cent of the votes. Journalists are not officially allowed to interview the inhabitants, there is no bar, no karaoke club or internet café; instead, inhabitants attend a compulsory village meeting every weekend for their entertainment. To the Western individualist this probably sounds deeply unattractive, but there is a lengthy waiting list for potential residents. Indeed, the model is so well regarded and receives so many requests for visits that two years ago a plan was announced to teach 50,000 village leaders from all over the country how to replicate this success, all paid for by Huaxi.[771]

An excellent example at the industrial level is Haier, the white-goods manufacturer, which we have already discussed. A one-month initial training period for all employees is designed 'to give the new employees a sense of rule by discipline'. The sessions of public self-criticism required by workers after making mistakes, with huge footprints painted on the factory floor for them to stand in as they do so, are blatant hang-overs from the Cultural Revolution.[772] In fact, the Founder and CEO, Zhang Ruimin, lately much lauded by such capitalist stalwarts as *Forbes* and Harvard, was himself a teenage Red Guard, went in pilgrimage to Mao's birthplace, and rose to his original position as a manager by dint of becoming a model worker and a member of the Party.[773] Most importantly, at Haier his antiquated model actually works, and on my visits to the company there was a genuine satisfaction and sense of pride amongst employees.

A traditional focus on central planning for key national assets also works. In later 2006, these were defined by Li Rongrong, Chairman of the State Assets Supervision and Administration Commission, as armaments, power generation and distribution, oil and petrochemicals, telecommunications, coal, aviation and shipping industries, over which the state must, in his words have 'absolute control', since they are the vital arteries of the national economy and essential to national security.[774] This is the Party speaking. Yet such an approach is not dissimilar to that of an advanced democratic and capitalist nation like France.

It is also important to understand what Bruce J. Dickson has described as the 'residual impact' of success in 1949, that while communism was imposed on the people of most East European countries, 'the CCP came to power via an indigenous revolution that ousted a discredited and unpopular government.'[775] For that reason, to the surprise of many Westerners as they travel through China – especially off the beaten track, but even in the daily queue to visit his mausoleum in Beijing – Mao Zedong is still held in genuine esteem. The official verdict on his life from the Communist Party's website reflects this reality with a certain accuracy (disregarding, of course, the millions of deaths, which trouble a Western observer): 'It is true that Mao Zedong made gross mistakes in his later years, but when his life is judged as a whole, his indisputable contributions to the Chinese revolution far outweigh his mistakes, and his merits are primary and his errors secondary.'[776] The current Premier, Wen Jiabao, reflected this line of thought and the usual opinion of Chinese people today when he remarked in an article published in *People's Daily* that, in the past, 'we missed a major development opportunity because of some big policy mistakes, and particularly the disastrous ten-year-long "Cultural Revolution".[777] In any case, it was, to impose *a posteriori* a recent slogan, always communism with Chinese characteristics. The encompassing of professional and entrepreunerial figures, together with the loosening of control over everyday life, and the fact that the stability that all Chinese families desire more than anything after the turmoils of the '60s and '70s seems to them to be best guaranteed by the Party, led to a general acceptance of its power even by those who do not accept it on ideological grounds. Better the devil you know than the devil you don't know, as the proverb has it, especially when you can be left to your money-making activities without being disturbed. Every Chinese knows intuitively where the line is drawn, just as every southern Italian knows where to turn during the evening *passeggiata*.

The problem from the Party's point of view is that old habits die hard, and many of its leaders sound utterly out of touch with modern reality, at least in their public statements. A more or less random example might be pronouncements by Li Changchun, number eight in the Politburo and responsible for propaganda and ideology, made in 2006. At the end of a year-long research project on the application of Marxist theory to the economic and social development of China, marked by a conference with the title 'Marxism Theory Research and Construction Project', he remarked that 'results of the research should be able to enhance the appeal and influence of Marxism' and that 'people expect the project to provide theoretical guidance to the building of a well-off society in an all-round way.' So far, he argued, the project had been successful and would result in a relevant academic system and textbooks. It was a 'major measure to promote prosperity of philosophy and social sciences' and generally improve the situation in the country and the governance of the Party.[778]

This official mumbo-jumbo is of course a reference to the dogma mooted at the 16th Congress in 2002 that 'first we'll make everybody rich and then go back to communist ideals' (this is the idea behind *xiaokang*, or 'well-off' society, an expression that actually goes back to the Confucian *Book of Rites*, where it is mentioned as an alternative to *datong*, or 'great equality'). In the meantime, good economic management is the key.

One little-noted example of this is the management of the Beijing public bus system, in which 600 routes carry 4 million passengers daily with remarkable efficiency. Half of the transport budget for the Olympic Games (about $9 billion) was lavished on this system as part of a general strategy to 'consider public transportation as a part of social welfare and not to ignore social interests in the pursuit of economic gain', a statement with which it is difficult to argue. It is very much a utilitarian argument, planning a rotary park-and ride-style system to avoid congestion within the Third Ring Road, with bus fare prices recently reduced from three to one *yuan* to encourage usage. In a statement that speaks volumes for the 'communist' attitude to market forces, the deputy director of the Beijing Municipal

Committee of Communications, Li Jianguo, observed that 'History has proved that a market-oriented distribution of transportation capabilities will not ease traffic. So the government plans to develop the public transportation as a common wealth.'[779] The plan is to increase the utilisation rate of public transportation by 40 per cent within two years of the Games. Perhaps the English poet Alexander Pope said it best, in a brilliant couplet in his *Essay on Man*:

> For forms of government let fools contest;
> Whate'er is best administer'd is best.[780]

For no people is more pragmatic than the Chinese, our understanding of whom is undermined by the temporary aberrations of Mao's post-1959 errors.

The new mantra is neither Communism nor Capitalism, nor indeed any other 'ism', but performance. The Politburo formed in late 2007, and its confirmed president Hu Jintao, will be judged on its ability to fulfil China's many ambitions, address her many problems, and 'best administer' them.

Will the Base of the Stealth Empire itself Survive?

China's 'rise' generates conflicting views, which fluctuate from China as the future hegemon to China falling apart under social pressures too great to sustain. This was the subject of a closed-door discussion at Davos in 2007, which concluded that 'there is almost no chance that China will become the world's hegemonic superpower, or that the Chinese yuan will dislodge the US dollar as the key reserve currency in our life-times.'[781] That, of course, might depend on the age of the participants, but it is likely that China will come close, although a closed-door session at Davos came to the conclusion that China's rapidly ageing population and lack of 'new blood' will lead to a demographic implosion.

There is a long tradition of Cassandrian utterances about China's future. Here is one randomly chosen from many:

> Furthermore, China's senior political leadership is unstable. It is possible that the rising wealth produced by the economic transformation may encourage the continuation of recent progress. On the other hand, the ruling regime could crack, or even collapse, following the death of … …. Some fear that ethnic and political tensions in China will tear the country apart.

When was this written? Who is the 'present leader'? In fact, the missing name is Deng Xiao Ping, but it could just as easily have been Jiang Zemin. It is a statement written in 1995 based more on prejudice than on serious appraisal of the risks and an understanding of the average Chinese person and his or her expectations. Deng died a decade ago, and the 'rising wealth' continues to rise.

In point of fact, China is a remarkably stable country, having evolved into what one shrewd commentator has described as a 'decentralized predatory state'[782] with a constant and more or less accepted level of autocracy. It is still a Leninist Party-state, the foundations of whose phenomenal growth were actually laid in Maoist times at the height of authoritarianism. Comparisons with India over the past fifty years amply justify his insistence on basic healthcare, education, infrastructure (in particular the railways), much improved social conditions for women and improved living standards, in spite of the well-known collective political disasters.[783] No one was more Maoist than Deng Xiao Ping. But there is still much to be done.

China has one major advantage over Western nations: the ability to think and plan really long-term. Gordon Chang's bestselling book *The Coming Collapse of China* had a brief epilogue titled 'The State Begins to Disintegrate', referring to incidents in late 2000 and early 2001, and implied that the country would collapse soon after the accession of the new leadership and full implementation of WTO commitments.

In other words, at roughly the middle of the first decade of the twenty-first century. That date has now been surpassed without traumatic events. As if to emphasise the predilection for long-term planning, a twenty-volume work compiled by nearly 200 Chinese experts over the previous two years was published in 2007 under the title *An Outline of Sustainable Development in China*, in which strategic objectives for sustainable development in China by 2050 were outlined. It confidently predicts such things as an increase in the average length of the formal education process (from 8.2 years today to 14 years) and the contribution of scientific development to the national economy (75 per cent). It also predicts zero growth in the natural growth rate of the population by 2030; zero growth in the consumption rate of energy and resources by 2040; and zero growth in the degeneration rate of the environment by 2050. This is in accordance with the underlying notion of gradual change and development. It is no coincidence that Hu Jintao and Wen Jiabao are known in China as *tizhinei gaigezhe*, or 'within-the-system reformers',[784] whose by-word is caution.

The same work asserts that Shanghai will reach the level of 'moderately developed countries' in 2015, Beijing in 2018, and thirteen other major cities before 2050. Then, looking even further ahead, twenty-seven provinces, autonomous regions and municipalities will have reached their development goals by 2060, and the entire country by 2075. In fact, given the underlying conditions, the importance of such a large country and the vast population, this growth seems to be ineluctable. The Nobel laureate for economics, Robert Mundell, who often speaks in China, said in an interview in mid-2007 that the preeminence of the dollar would last another century and that 'it will be a long time before China's s standard of living will approach the U.S. It might be 100 years.'[785] But if we know that it is hard to make accurate predictions about the long-term future, we also know that it is important to set targets, and attempt to achieve them, and that Western politicians generally do not look beyond their own mandate. The very fact of being able to think of such long-term goals enhances the possibility of achieving them. For Professor Mundell (and most of the rest of us), 100 years lies in an literally unimaginable future because he knows as an individual that he will no longer be here, whereas the Chinese leadership sees it from the collective point of view of future generations of their Party and of their own families. The distant future is a reality to be planned for.

In a similar vein, many authors argue that inefficient State-Owned Enterprises (SOEs) and the large banks will eventually collapse into bankruptcy as the result of problems ranging from bad management to non-performing loans. But, as we have seen, China possesses sufficient financial resources to make such a scenario far-fetched. The issue for the government is to phase out or restructure the inefficient SOEs without increasing unemployment. Neither time nor funds is a problem. It believes that in the long-term present, subsidies will diminish and that the bad companies will either die a natural death in the evolved market economy or become profitable. There is no need to disrupt the SOE system today. The case of the enormously successful IPOs of state-owned banks, which outside observers only a couple of years ago predicted would collapse imminently, and the entry of important foreign banks as substantial shareholders, suggests government policy is right.

Two other major problems often cited as reasons for 'collapse' are the wealth gap and widespread corruption.

It is undeniable that on a statistical basis, the wealth gap is a terrible reality. Even the best spin-doctors cannot conjure an average monthly income of £50 into wealth, and there is no need to venture into the remote poor provinces and counties to see real poverty, since it exists within walking distance of most luxury shopping malls. The difference between urban and rural incomes is thought to be a multiple of anywhere between eight and ten. Yet, as in many other countries in the world, official statistics are only one part of the story. A survey carried out by the China Reform Foundation's National Economic Research Institute in 2005–6 calculated the total annual 'grey' or illegal income of urban residents in China to be 4.4 trillion yuan (about £284 billion). This means that urban residents are as much as 75 per cent better off than government statistics indicate, while even the poorest farmers have 53 per cent more.[786] Obviously, much of this comes from illegal activities such as drug dealing, illicit production of fake goods and a rampant sex trade. The latter alone, with somewhere between 10 and 20 million prostitutes around the country, has been calculated by one economist to generate revenues equal to around 6 per cent of GDP;[787] a fair proportion of this probably returns to the hometown as remittances just like those of the teenage seamstress. But much so-called grey income is also legal, such as speculation in property, since capital gains are untaxed. As in many European countries, teachers round out their salary with tax-free private lessons, while in China it is common for parents to assist their child by offering 'gifts' of cash to teachers in the traditional red envelopes used for weddings. The same treatment is reserved for doctors and surgeons, and anyone whose help is particularly appreciated.

There are many other tricks, such as the collective or temporary divorce racket (since marriage and divorce are both simple and quick). In 2006, for example, in a tiny village in Yibin County (Sichuan) eighty-six married couples from newlyweds to pensioners suddenly performed what the local press called a 'collective divorce' over a three-month period. But most remarried again soon afterwards, some within a matter of days. An even larger 'collective divorce' occurred in a suburb of Chongqing, involving 1,000 married couples. The reason for these 'outbursts' of divorce lay in the system of compensation payments for homes that were to be demolished for property development projects. If the couples occupying the building were married, then they would count as a single household, whereas as divorcees they would be counted as two households and receive twice as much money in compensation. This represented a perfectly legal, but morally 'grey', increase in their income.[788] Then there are the untaxed profits from the vibrant Stock Exchange in Shanghai, where some people managed 300 per cent gains in the period 2006–7, and the Chinese are as shrewd as anyone at making the best out of adverse circumstances.[789]

Bribery of officials is also commonplace, though often subtle and legally distanced. One example of my own experience is of government officials insisting that a large investment should be made through a consulting company whose chairman was a trusted friend of the officials concerned. In fact they, the officials, never asked for cash; it was the consultant who sought to justify his expectations by explaining in confidence (to someone he had known for three years and trusted to a certain extent) that he would have to reward them. There would be no traceable link to them, and some of the money would appear overseas for the payment of university fees. Large foreign companies, although they will always deny it, have in the past created slush funds for such payments. More brazenly, banks readily give loans to customers with official positions, who they describe as VIP clients.

According to an article in the Singapore-based Chinese-language newspaper *21st Century Business Herald*, there is a fairly normal scale of credit limits based on political power rather than guarantees or assets: thus low-level officials might be able to get 2–300,000 yuan (£13–19,000), a county level official 400,000 yuan (£26,000), and at the prefecture level around 800,000 yuan (£52,000).[790] The result of all these 'grey' activities is that in the survey quoted above the highest earning 10 per cent of urban households had a real per capita disposable income of 97,000 yuan (£6,270), compared to the official figure of 29,000 yuan (£1,800). It is still not much by Western standards, but much better.

The Chinese can wait for the wealth and freedom they are sure will come, since patience and hardship form part of their collective DNA, as does their natural, indeed obsessive, thrift. There is a deep-rooted, perhaps atavistic, attitude to parsimony in the Chinese, which enables them to survive (for those who know and love Italy, it is inevitable to make comparisons with the resilience and exuberant inventiveness of Neapolitans). There is a charming illustration of extreme thrift in Wu Ching-Tzu's novel *The Scholars*:

> Lying there at the point of death, Yen Ta-yu stretched out two fingers and refused to breathe his last; and when his nephews and servants made various wild guesses whether he meant two people, two events or two places, he simply shook his head.
>
> But now his wife had stepped forward to say: 'I'm the only one who understands you. You're worried because there are two wicks in the lamp – that's the waste of oil. If I take out one wick, it will be all right.'
>
> Suiting her actions to her words, she removed one wick. All eyes were fixed on Mr Yen, who nodded his head, let fall his hand, and breathed his last.[791]

Yen died happy, saving money for his family. He was not poor, since he left 200 taels (dollars) of silver to his brother. It is an attitude that is common in China, with hoteliers who save money by freezing guests, and small companies that conserve ancient computers and decrepit furniture even in a period of excellent revenue growth. Like Mr Yen, the average family simply wants more well-being than it has had in the past (in this, the often ridiculed *xiaokang* policy hits the nail on the head).

In a recent book, the long-time China-watcher James Mann writes of two possible scenarios for the short-term future that correspond to the hegemon-collapse pairing: what he terms the 'Soothing Scenario', the 'Upheaval Scenario'; then he proposes a 'Third Scenario' that seeks to build a middle way. In the first case, he means the comfortable option that most world leaders and journalists now appear to accept, that the past twenty-five years of growth will continue into the foreseeable future and bring China ever closer to Western mores and ways of thinking. This is the typical scenario of visitors who see the dynamic modern cities of Shanghai and Shenzhen, and some second-level cities such as Hangzhou and Xi'an, which are almost as impressive, and who deal with Western-educated Chinese managers or entrepreneurs – part of the new middle class that benefits from the current stability and would not wish to upset the apple-cart. He notes that China has defied gloomy predictions about its economy for decades, and suggests that his readers should get used to the idea that the country will not suddenly collapse in the next few years. Another attempt to draw up a 'balance sheet' concluded in similar fashion that while China faces many domestic challenges and possible economic slowdown, and a collapse cannot be ruled out, the 'strong likelihood is that China's leadership will undertake the further reforms necessary to meet its economic challenges'.[792] This, the authors argue in agreement with Mann, means that the United States, and by implication also other leading economic powers, should put its own house in order.

For Mann, the next hypothesis is the 'Upheaval Scenario', approximating to Gordon Chang's collapse. The wealth gap, restlessness among the rural poor and growing political awareness will lead to this upheaval, and could lead to a temporary or permanent break-up of the country. Yet Mann seems to accept that the inherent strength of China's political system, and its past ability to ride crises, makes this scenario unlikely. So he comforts himself (and us?) with a 'Third Scenario', which seems to be accepted by most Chinese of my acquaintance. This entails that China will muddle along more or less as it is with neither a shift towards democracy nor complete break-up of the country. The Communist Party might invent a new theory and even change its name, but it will still rule. There will be, as Mann says, 'no significant political opposition, no freedom of the press, no elections beyond the local level. There would be an active security apparatus to forestall organized political dissent. In other words, China, while growing stronger and richer, wouldn't change its political system in any fundamental way.'[793] It seems plausible enough as a scenario, though not as intriguing as the first scenario or as potentially exciting as the second.

So, if we accept something like Mann's conclusion and the weight of our own arguments, the answer to the question posed at the head of this section – 'will the base of the Stealth Empire itself survive?' – is, most certainly, yes.

Can the Chinese Environment Sustain the Empire?

The attainment of China's mission will place enormous strains on natural resources both within and outside the country. For this reason, the problems of the environment, especially water shortages, are often cited as one of the main possible causes of collapse.

Actually, up to now environmental history in China is consistent with that in most other countries in the world. No better, but no worse. It was, from around 650 to 1800, probably the 'most ecologically resilient and resourceful state on earth',[794] with ecological damage repaired over time by successive dynasties. There was of course deforestation, but that is a 'hallmark of civilisation' and occurred in most

European countries as well. The only aspect in which China may have exceeded some past great civilisations, such as those of Egypt and India, is in the degree of water manipulation, in particular the linking of the two main east–west river systems by means of a north–south canal. In many other ways, Chinese civilisation was conservationist *ante litteram*, the need for a balanced relationship between man and environment is explicit in landscape paintings and in the writings of both Confucian and Taoist philosophers. In one famous passage, Mencius wrote that:

> if you do not allow nets with too fine a mesh to be used in large ponds, then there will be more fish and turtles than [the people] can eat; if hatchets and axes are permitted in the forests on the hills only in the proper seasons, then there will be more timber than they can use.[795]

Mencius understood that forests needed to be cleared, and rivers widened and channelled, to make it possible for the Chinese to 'cultivate the ground and get food for themselves' and produce the five kinds of grain that were fundamental for their survival.[796] In fact, traditional Chinese agriculture was entirely based on recycling, and the avoidance of waste. Nothing was squandered: 'Human manure, for example, was fed to dogs and pigs, which are far more efficient digesters than humans and can use as food up to half of what we excrete. Weeds and straw were not composted directly but fed to pigs and cattle. Animal dung, as well as human waste in excess of the needs of the pigs, was the major fertiliser, along with all vegetable substances that were not choice animal food. Ashes, worn-out sandals, pulverised bricks and adobe, algal blossoms from pools, and above all the mud scooped from canal and stream bottoms were all critically important not only for supplying nutrients but also for maintaining the structure and texture of the soil.'[797] Recycling and conservationist logic were paramount, Ducks were used to remove weeds and insects from paddy fields, which could then be used to grow foods like watercress and lotus; cow's milk and cheese were not used because cattle needed it to feed their calves, which were vitally important for labour. There was even a logic to not eating cheese.

This traditional culture changed with industrialisation, and in particular with the Maoist variety of industrialisation between 1949 and 1976. Mao's slogan that 'Man Must Conquer Nature' encapsulated his attitude towards the environment, allowing forests to be destroyed to fuel the backyard furnaces of the Great Leap Forward, diverting underground rivers in cities to create bomb shelters, building dykes and damming rivers in the pursuit of his political dream. In 1945, he wrote an essay with the title 'The Foolish Old Man Who Removed the Mountains', in which he recounted a fable of the same title. This man lived in a south-facing house with the view and light blocked by two large peaks, and with the help of his sons began digging them up. Another old man who lived nearby laughed at their efforts, but the Foolish Old Man insisted that if they worked hard, even for several generations, the mountains could eventually be removed. 'High as they are,' he said, 'the mountains cannot grow any higher and with every bit we dig, they will be that much lower. Why can't we clear them away?'[798] The problem is that Mao seems to have begun with a pertinent fable, in which the two mountains represented imperialism and feudalism, and then attempted to apply the foolish old man's idea to Chinese reality by literally removing mountains. A piece of propaganda about the well-known and often cited examplar of Dazhai, a Shanxi village, which in 1964 became the national model for agriculture with the slogan 'In Agriculture, Learn from Dazhai', praises the inhabitants in these terms: 'Displaying the revolutionary spirit of the Foolish Old Man ... they have been struggling against nature for over ten years.'[799]

Yet Mao's attitude towards nature and its 'obstacles' was deeply embedded in Chinese culture, for in ancient and imperial China there were three traditional ways of interacting with nature. There was the Taoist tradition, which 'tended toward accommodation to nature's way', and a Buddhist one that taught reverence for all living beings. Then there was the Confucian tradition, which taught the mastery of nature by man, whose duty it was to harness its wealth and features to his own use.[800] But it must be said that the destructive forces of China's landscape, in particular that of the great rivers and the regular floods they caused, was an important force in encouraging man to tame his environment. To a certain extent, it was a land that needed taming, and in fact some of the earliest Chinese legends – such as that of the Emperor Yu taming the flood waters of the Huang He – express this need. But Mao went beyond the basic need to tame and exploit natural resources.

Oddly enough, the Chinese land-mass was relatively unexplored in geological terms until very recently. A seven year detailed geological survey providing accurate information was only completed in 2007. Until then, a vast area comprising the Tibetan Plateau, the southern of Xinjiang and the north of the Daxing'anling Mountains, nearly 25 per cent of China's territory, was described by the China Geological Survey as 'virgin regions'.[801] With only half this area now surveyed, it is thought that the plateau has gigantic reserves of copper, lead, zinc and iron ore. Given China's immense steel production and future needs, the presence of iron ore and zinc (used to make galvanized steel) could be extremely valuable. Viewed in these terms, the long-term future for natural resources changes rather dramatically, even though the harsh weather conditions in mines mostly over 4,000m in altitude means that exploiting these mineral deposits will not be easy.

There is also the negative aspect to the exploitation of natural resources, in terms of environmental damage and pollution, amply illustrated by authors such as Jared Diamond and Peter Navarro.[802] China is paying in environmental terms for the rapid industrialisation, urbanisation and population growth of the past half-century. In that period the population has doubled, in spite of the recent one-child policy, and the percentage of the population living in cities has grown from 13 per cent to 38 per cent. According to Diamond, the length of 'railroads, motor roads, and airline routes increased 2.5-, 10-, and 108-fold' in this period; in the past twenty-five years, the number of cars has increased 130-fold.[803] The effects are tangible to anyone visiting China: congested city roads, urban wastelands around the large cities, almost permanent smog, the effects on the air of a country in which most energy derives from coal, and hideous conurbations like Chongqing with a metropolitan area including around 30 million people. In mid-2007, the State Environmental Protection Agency (SEPA) announced that only 37.6 per cent of 585 cities surveyed had air quality 'indicating a clean and healthy environment'.

Add to these problems soil erosion, water pollution, fertility loss, salinisation, deforestation, desertification and the increase in man-made waste, and of course the natural disasters that such a huge and varied country suffers – such as dust storms, floods, droughts – and the picture is grim indeed. Diamond concludes that if China were to realise its aim of achieving First World living standards by mid-century, it would result in a doubling of 'the entire world's human resource use and environmental impact'.[804] This is the real problem, for while environmental pollution control policies have actually reduced pollution in some industrial sectors in the past decade, total energy consumption has increased with economic growth – as much as 70 per cent more between 2000 and 2005, with coal consumption increasing in the same period by 75 per cent.

Much the same message is conveyed in Elizabeth Economy's book *The River Runs Black*. She relates the disaster of the Huai River in 2001, when this vital river, which irrigates the land for 150 million people, turned into a torrent of sewage and dead fish, and the history of flooding, water scarcity and desertification that plagues China. Already in 2002, she argued, six of the ten most polluted cities in the world were in China, while over 75 per cent of the water in rivers flowing through urban areas is unsuitable for drinking or fishing[805] – indeed the places where older men can often be seen fishing within the large cities are often enough to make a weak stomach turn at the mere thought of eating what they might catch. A report three years later said that 'between 2001 and 2005, on average about 54 per cent of the seven main rivers in China contained water deemed unsafe for human consumption', and more specifically that the drinking water in 97 per cent of the 118 cities was polluted to some degrees.[806] One of the most striking facts is that while we might expect heavy pollution in the regions of greatest manufacturing output such as Guangdong and Jiangsu, in fact the areas with the worst air pollution are found in northern China (Qinghai, Ningxia, Beijing, Tianjin, Shaanxi, and Shanxi), as are the most heavily polluted rivers (the Liao, Hai, Huai, and Songhua).[807]

One summary of the water problem, based on various sources, lists frightening data that half of China's population has its water supplies contaminated by animal and human waste, and all coastal waters are polluted. Liver and stomach cancers deriving from water pollution are amongst the country's leading killers.[808] Driving from any randomly chosen city to another in southern Guangdong, the road will cross an infinite number of rivers, streams, canals, irrigation ditches and drains in which the nasty colours (brown, black, red and yellow, but never blue), foam, human waste, agricultural waste (China produces half of the world's pork), pesticides and fertilisers, create a disgusting soup. In Shanxi, entire villages and towns are as coal-black as the Nottinghamshire of D.H. Lawrence nearly 100 years ago.

The best-known project is the Three Gorges Dam, a 185m-high dam with five-tier locks set across the Chang Jiang (Yangtze). Entire books have been written about its consequences, for example the excellent account of villages and towns – not to mention devasting effects on the *feng shui* of the graves of ancestors – about to disappear beneath the waters in *Before the Deluge* by Deidre Chetham.[809] Their collective population of over a million has been displaced, with around half a million newly unemployed, and as many as 1,208 sites of key significance have been buried together with thirty-six plants unique to the area.[810] When I remember the changes made to the micro-climate of the valley in which I lived for many years in Italy as the consequences of a much smaller dam and new reservoir 50km away increased humidity and introduced winter fog where it had never been known, it is hard to imagine the magnitude of change that such a huge project will bring in the future. In fact, now that the dam itself has been completed, local government representatives have been emboldened by the drastic consequences on the towns and farmlands along the river to protest publicly. In an environment forum on the banks of the river at Wuhan, in September 2007, such protests resulted in the extraordinary (for China) admission that the dam has exerted a 'notably adverse' impact on the environment. A media report on the forum, under the headline 'China warns of environmental catastrophe from Three Gorges Dam', stated that the project 'has caused an array of ecological ills, including more frequent landslides and pollution, and if preventive measures are not taken, there could be an environmental "catastrophe".'[811] Naturally, this new report resonated throughout the world press, and provided hope that official recognition of the problems would lead to better management of the immediate environmental consequences such as landslides creating waves of 50m high, which crashed into the banks.

But the Three Gorges is only one of many dams. A few months previously, a WWF report with the title *Rivers at Risk* had identified twenty-one river basins in the world 'at severe risk of ecological degradation'. The worst case was the Chang Jiang, with forty-six dams. The report also observed that large numbers of dams in smaller basins can have 'greater cumulative impacts than the same number of dams spread through a larger basin'.[812] It is not only a matter of the Three Gorges.

When a World Bank working paper on the cost of pollution in China was published in the spring of 2007, rumour had it that the Chinese government has exerted pressure to cancel the conclusion that 750,000 people suffered premature death as a result of pollution-related disease each year. But even with that frightening statistic removed, there was enough for concern in the estimate that pollution could cost China as much as 5.8 per cent of its GDP.[813] A few months later, the OECD published an *Environmental Performance Review*, which forecast that by 2020 as many as 20 million people a year will suffer from respiratory diseases. In addition, there will be 'hundreds of thousands of premature deaths, and millions of cases of chronic bronchitis – with inevitable effects on the effectiveness of labour and health damage'. But this report went much further than the World Bank in suggesting that in the same year, 2020, the overall costs of environmental pollution and health costs could represent as much as 13 per cent of GDP. The report concluded that 'air quality in some Chinese cities remains among the worst in the world', 'China has very low water resources per capita (one quarter of the world average)', 'many water courses, lakes and coastal waters are severely polluted as a result of agricultural, industrial and domestic discharges', and that 'four hundred of the six hundred largest cities suffer from water shortages'.[814] But for the purposes of our argument here, the most powerful admonition comes from the conclusion that 'the target of quadrupling GDP between 2000 and 2020 requires commensurate strengthening of environmental management and finance, so that economic growth is environmentally sustainable.'[815] This, together with improving the people's health expectations, presents the most serious challenge to the declared ambition of creating a harmonious society rather than a steamrollering economic leviathan.

Later in 2007, the New York-based Blacksmith Institute published a list of the world's thirty most polluted places (the 'dirty thirty', as they call them).[816] There were six places in China on the list, some quite small places but including two provincial capitals Lanzhou and Urumqi, and one 'small' and unknown place, which nevertheless impacts on the lives of 3 million people. The four places in the lower part of the list include: *Huaxi* (a district of Donyang city, Zhejiang Province), with thirteen chemical estates in its Industrial Park; *Lanzhou* (Gansu), once named by the World Resources Institute as one of the most polluted cities in the world with both air and river problems and the country's highest pneumonia rates; *Urumqi* (Xinjiang), in the World Health Organization's top-ten most-polluted cities and Lanzhou's main rival in air pollution; and *Wanshan* (Guizhou), which bears the unhappy epithet of China's 'Mercury Capital', where 'concentrations in soil range from 24.3 to 348 mg/kg (16 to 232 times the maximum national standards for mercury contamination)'. The even more polluted, but unranked, top-ten places included two in China: *Linfen* (Shanxi) and *Tianyin* (Anhui). Linfen, in the north, which adds pollution from the automobile industry and other industrial emissions to Shanxi's severe problems with coal mines, was said by China's own State Environmental Protection Agency (SEPA) to have the worst air quality in the county, and it also suffers severe water shortages. In this case, the pollution affects a large population of around 3 million people, with widespread bronchitis, pneumonia, lung cancer and and epidemic of arsenicosis.[817] Tianying, in Central China, is a major lead-producing area, with a mixture of the country's worst problems such as lack of effective pollution controls, illegal operations, low technology and recycling plants, which have even higher pollution levels. According to Blacksmith, average lead concentrations in the area were between eight and a half and ten times higher than national health standards, while local crops and wheat were contaminated by lead dust at a level up to twenty-four times higher than national standards. Here, sadly, it is children who suffer most from lead poisoning, with problems such as 'lower IQs, short attention spans, learning disabilities, hyperactivity, impaired physical growth, hearing and visual problems, stomach aches, irritation of the colon, kidney malfunction, anaemia and brain damage.'[818]

In spite of the horror of these reports, especially for those who live in China, it should be recognised that most of them stress improvements in many areas of environmental protection in China in the past few years (both in Linfen and in Tianyin, for example, steps have been taken by local government and by SEPA to close contaminated mines). They also understand that the strain on urban resources placed by ever-increasing rural immigrants is an objective problem. It is also true that China still has much lower carbon emissions in *per capita* terms than Western nations. The IEA's Chief Economist said that from 2007 to 2015 China would 'install, as new, as much energy generating plant as currently exists today in all of the 25 countries of the expanded European Union – a total of 800 gigawatts.' As much as 90 per cent of this energy would derive from coal, which produces the highest amount of carbon dioxide – which will last for fifty to sixty years.'[819] Yet without this increase there would be no economic growth for China, which would also be a problem for the entire world. But as always, the statistics may be read in different ways. it is true that China produces almost half of the world's coal (44.8 per cent), which provides around 60 per cent of its total energy requirements – compared with 8.4 per cent globally.[820] But it is also true, according to the IEA's own statistics, that while over the period 1973–2004 the percentage of global carbon dioxide emissions produced by China has risen from 5.7 per cent to 17.9 per cent, that is still much less than the combined OECD total of 48.6 in which the United States is included.[821] It is not easy to clean up such a dirty act: one scientific study showed, for example, that while serious attempts were being made to improve the air for the Olympic Games, such as moving factories out of Beijing, in fact emission sources from far beyond the city, in industrial Shandong or on Tianjin, not to mention coal-burning Taiyuan, can 'exert significant influence on Beijing's air quality.'[822] In the end, it all depends on wind direction.

Yes, China is polluted, water is scarce and tap-water often undrinkable (if the household is fortunate enough to have it available). The air in major cities is among the worst in the world, and so on. But both government and citizens are increasingly aware of the problem, and international condemnations are more effective now than in the old, closed, Maoist China. But there is another question: is all this international criticism fair? Can we really expect China to become a manufacturing

centre for much of Western industry without necessarily creating the kind of pollution that we have been able to escape by exiling polluting industries to China? In
a certain sense, a city like London has become clean because dirty manufacturing
has been transferred to China.

The Chinese government itself is concerned, as it should be. The globalisation
of manufacturing has been followed by the globalisation of environmentalism
just like everywhere in the world. Robert P. Weller has noted that while in the
1970s there was very little interest in nature in either Taiwan or the People's
Republic, by the mid-1980s there were demonstrations against the building of new
factories in Taiwan and the creation of national parks;[823] the People's Republic is
undergoing a similar phase now, with a ministry-level National Environmental
Protection Agency since 1998, and frequent public activities such as tree-planting
days. At the inauguration of what was termed the 'Summer Davos' at Dalian in the
autumn of 2007, Wen Jiabao stressed environmental issues in his list of the main
problems facing China: 'They include excessively rapid economic growth, acute
structural tensions, the inefficient pattern of growth, depletion of resources and
environmental degradation, mounting pressure on price and entrenched structural
and institutional obstacles.'[824] In September, targets were set in a new five-year
plan to reduce energy consumption per unit of GDP by 20 per cent and reduce
'major pollutant discharges' by 10 per cent, with the focus on pollution control
and prevention.[825] One innovation that begins to have an impact on the ordinary
Chinese citizen is the rapid expansion in nature tourism and outdoor activities.
As the weather warms up after the long cold winter of northern China, the new
middle class enjoys nothing more than a family trip to 'scenic spots' on a sunny
spring day. And it wants them to be clean.

The Chinese people want more, not less, growth, and a better lifestyle; they
want to catch up. The level of industrial growth that is necessary for this, and the
more sophisticated housing they crave, means higher energy consumption. The
International Energy Agency has estimated that China will soon overtake the
United States in terms of carbon dioxide emissions, with an estimate of 6,020
million tonnes annually against 5,910 million tonnes from the US.

As far as the people themselves are concerned, in one sense the Chinese are
natural conservationists. The thrift mentioned above ensures that there is no waste.
Even the wealthy new middle class instinctively conserve their plastic bottles and
old newspapers, because every object has at least some intrinsic value and can
therefore be sold. China has what we might describe as a 'waste not, want not'
culture, which is not the consequence of the famines and material shortages of the
Mao era, as a Western reader might imagine, but was noted by many authors long
before Communism. The missionary Arthur Smith observed in 1895, for example,
how 'the tiniest scrap of foreign stuff is always welcome to a Chinese woman, who
will make it reappear in forms of utility if not of beauty, of which a whole parliament

of authoresses of "Domestic Economies" would never have dreamed.'[826] Still today, a woman will convert discarded cuffs and collars into clothing for babies, and waste merchants with their bicycle-drawn carts are a familiar sight in the streets of all major cities – one recent study has estimated there to be 120,000 rural migrants in Beijing alone who make a living by scavenging, with total annual profits of around $150 million.[827] Every neighbourhood has its own privately run collection and redistribution centre, often a piece of wasteland, where the loads of the bicycle carts are weighed, paid for, and transferred to lorries. In fact, China was promoting the recycling of household waste in propaganda posters as long ago as the 1960s, after Zhou Enlai had argued that the country should 'realize the transformation of unused materials into useful materials' and make the old and broken into the brand new.[828] There is much to be done, but the awareness is strong, so the outlook over the long-term is positive rather than negative.

Re-Naissance

An Italian art historian, Giovanni Previtali, once argued that around 1300 there was a *naissance* of Italian culture, with figures like Dante and Giotto, but that it was truncated in succeeding decades by war, famine and the Black Death. Art went into limbo. Then, in 1402, with the commission for the bronze doors of the Florentine Baptistery won by Lorenzo Ghiberti, there was a new start, which we know as the re-naissance. On this model, there was a *naissance* of modern China and an incipient stealth empire in the 1980s, which culminated with *River Elegy* and was truncated by the events of June 1989. The *re-naissance* begins in 2008, with a new Politburo assuming full powers and the Olympic Games taking place in August.

These apparently unrelated facts are brought together by the number 8, which is the most auspicious of all numbers for the Chinese since its pronunciation *ba*, is similar to that of *fa*, meaning 'prosperity' (it sounds odd as an explanation, but that is what the Chinese say). The octagon is considered an auspicious geometrical form, and is used in *feng shui* for protection. These beliefs may be seen in the desire to have as many '8's as possible in car number plates (which can be purchased) and phone numbers (especially in advertisements), and is also why the Olympic Games were programmed to begin at 8.00 p.m. on 8-8-2008 – on the north/south axis of Tiananmen and the Forbidden City, we will remember. A fine reminder of the persistence of ancient superstitions in a supposedly atheist and modern society. By that time, the new Politburo and State Council members will be settled in their new positions, and will draw inspiration from the Games for the remaining four years of their mandate.

Such a large country and population necessarily has a complex process of administration, honed over the centuries. In brief synthesis, it works as follows. The three essential and inter-locking organisations of power are the Communist Party of China, the Central People's Government, and the People's Liberation Army. In Figure 5 (Appendix 2), the Party is represented as enveloping the entire system, since most members of the other organisations are also Party members, and the Party reaches down into every subsidiary level of administration such as the provinces, cities and towns where each governor and mayor works beside – and slightly below – the Party Secretary. Senior managers of State-Owned Enterprises and even some private companies like Haier are also Party members.

Every five years, as in 2007, the Communist Party holds its National Congress, which in theory elects a Central Committee, which in turn appoints the twenty-two members of the Politburo and the smaller Standing Committee of the Politburo, which has nine members. The highest power in China resides in the Standing Committee of the Politburo, whose members share in varying measures the duties of running the State. The Chairman, currently President Hu Jintao, links the three organisations above in his person by being at the same time General Secretary of the Communist Party and Chairman of the Central Military Commission, which oversees the PLA. Hence the selection of new members of the Standing Committee, one of whom had recently died while others had reached retirement age, is the most significant act of the National Congress, which takes place each five years. For the president and premier who succeed Hu Jintao and Wen Jiabao in 2012 will be chosen from the other seven members of the Standing Committee nominated in 2007.

The premier presides over the State Council, which is equivalent to the 'government' of other countries. He chooses four vice-premiers, one of whom is likely to be groomed as future premier, each supervising one area of government activity. Beneath them are the ministries, government agencies and the entire mechanism of the state bureaucracy. The fifty or so members of the State Council meet once a month, while a smaller Standing Committee of eleven members including the premier and vice-premiers meets twice every week.

Two other members of the Standing Committee of the Politburo serve as Chairman of the National People's Congress and of the People's Political Consultative Conference, which complete the circle by referring upwards with proposals to the State Council and the Politburo. Exactly how this works in practice is unknown, due to the extreme secrecy of the Chinese governing process. No one writes personal memoirs, and there are usually no genuine leaks. It is a tightly organised and well-controlled system, and apparently effective.

Delegates of the National People's Congress (NPC), not to be confused with the quinquennial Communist Party National Congress, are selected by provincial congresses, and number around 3,000. Outside China, it is regarded as a rubber-stamp organisation, or even worse as an 'annual fortnight of wining, dining, snoozing and pressing the "yes" button' and 'pageant of legitimization'.[829] But it is also an important forum for the discussion of new ideas, problems and policies, and a pool of talent for future promotions. For members, especially those of the smaller Standing Committee, it is a forum for creating consensus and a potential springboard to greater power. The NPC meets every spring in Beijing, and makes formal proposals to the State Council, which are usually accepted as a consequence of pre-agreement.

The Chinese People's Political Consultative Conference (CPPCC) has a less direct role as an advisory organisation, although it too can make formal proposals both to the State Council and to the Standing Committee of the Politburo (to which its chairman belongs). The CPPCC also meets once a year in the spring, together with the NPC. Its members come from a much broader spectrum of society, and not all are members of the Communist Party. Indeed, members of the other eight official political parties are allowed to participate, along with prominent businessmen and representatives of the 200 or so political associations that are so important in Chinese life as an expression of lobbying powers. The most important of these are the All-China Federation of Trade Unions, the Communist Youth League, and the All-China Women's Federation. The organisations, and membership of the CPPCC, provide an alternative means of attracting attention and achieving political prominence.

The 17th National Congress of the Communist Party of China opened in Beijing on 15 October 2007, with the attendance of over 2,200 delegates at the Great Hall of the People on Tiananmen Square in Beijing. President Hu Jintao began the week with a two-and-a-half-hour speech, which summarised the successes of the past five years and outlined the aims of the next five. Then, after a week of closed-door sessions discussing this 'report', the delegates named a Central Committee of around 200 members, which in turn nominated the members of the new Politburo.[830]

The Congress perpetuated some of the ironies of identity mentioned above. For example, it was proudly announced that the international media presence had increased from 859 to 1,033 'overseas reporters' from forty-two 'countries and regions' since the previous Congress. Yet 342 of the journalists present, just over a third, were from Hong Kong, Macao and Taiwan. This of course reduces the genuine international presence, but sustains the paradoxical double myth that Taiwan is a fully-fledged province of China while Hong Kong and Macao remain outside.

From the beginning Hu Jintao stamped his authority on modern Chinese history by adding his own 'theory' to those of his predecessors as a formal adjunct to the Constitution. The original constitution was based on the twin pillars of Marxism-Leninism and Mao Zedong Thought. At the 14th Congress in 1992, the theory of building socialism with Chinese characteristics was added to these; then at the 15th Congress in 1997 Deng Xiaoping Theory was added; the last addition was that of Jiang Zemin's important thoughts (as they are always called) of

'Three Represents' at the 16th Congress in 2002. These are enshrined in the second paragraph of the Constitution, which reads: 'The Communist Party of China takes Marxism-Leninism, Mao Zedong Thought, Deng Xiaoping Theory and the important thought of Three Represents as its guide to action.'[831] Now President Hu has joined his 'scientific outlook on development' to the increasing list (which must be repeated in its entirety in newspaper articles about policy), though not to the same paragraph. After explaining each of the previous 'thoughts', the revised constitution adopted on 21 October 2007 states that the Central Committee has 'formulated the Scientific Outlook on Development, which puts people first and calls for comprehensive, balanced and sustainable development.'[832] This now becomes a guiding principle for the country, which 'keeps up with the times'. Thus Hu's thought achieves similar status to that of his predecessors and its inclusion in the Constitution gives him more than mere temporary power over the country.

Taiwan also figured high on the agenda. In the month leading up to the opening of the Congress a senior PLA officer with long experience of Taiwan affairs in the Nanjing military district, which faces the island and coordinates all military matters concerning it, received significant promotion. Army General Chen Bingde, who was previously Director-General of the General Armament, became Chief of the General Staff and now commands the entire PLA (see Figure 4, Appendix 2). General Chen represents the new high-tech PLA, having in his former post supervised the modernisation of military equipment and been responsible for the Chinese space programme; he has been a member of the Central Military Commission since 2005. There were also rumours that Liang Guanglie, who was the previous Chief of Staff and had served as Commander of the Nanjing district from 1999 to 2002 and as a member of the 13th, 14th and 15th CPC Central Committees, would become the new Minister of Defence.

In his opening address, when emphasising the common aspiration of the Chinese people to resolve problems with Taiwan, Hu Jintao proposed the establishment of a peace agreement with Taipei while calling for a formal end to the state of hostility that has existed across the Taiwan Straits since the Civil War ended in 1949. He asserted that: 'we are ready to conduct exchanges, dialogue, consultations and negotiations with any political party in Taiwan on any issue, as long as it recognizes that both sides of the Straits belong to one and the same China.' 'Let us', he said, in what he described as a solemn appeal, 'discuss a formal end to the state of hostility between the two sides, reach a peace agreement, construct a framework for peaceful development of cross-Straits relations, and thus usher in a new phase of peaceful development.'[833] This is an important novelty, since the Taiwan question has never previously been thus incorporated in what amounts to the doctrine of the Congress. Still on the subject of foreign policy, he insisted on the concept of peaceful development, and that China will follow 'a national defense policy that is defensive in nature, and it does not engage in arms race or pose a military threat to any other country.'[834] To this end also, the opening-up policy will be continued 'in accordance with internationally recognized economic and trade rules.'

Another significant emphasis was placed on the objective of quadrupling Chinese per capita GDP by the year 2020 (from 2000, when it was $800).[835] Hu also emphasised several of the business policies and strategies we have reviewed above, expanding the drive towards opening up the country, encouraging industry to focus on quality rather than quantity, further opening high-tech industry and manufacturing to foreign capital, and pushing more Chinese companies to invest abroad. To reduce his words to a single sentence, China's aim is to build a well-off society with balanced economic growth and social justice – with explicit recognition of the fact that this cannot be done without opening to the rest of the world: 'When the goal of building a moderately prosperous society in all respects is attained in China by 2020, China, a large developing socialist country with an ancient civilization, will have basically accomplished industrialization.'[836]

The Congress provided some insights into the Chinese concept of democracy, a word that many newspapers noted had been used no less than sixty times in Hu Jintao's inaugural address, and how far it is from the Western sense of the word. Several comments stressed the fact that 'intra-Party democracy' was an important feature of the Congress, with a selection process for the Central Committee including 'primary elections', which eliminates (rather than selects) around 8 per cent of the nominees. One expert argued that 'the increased margins between nominees and chosen candidates show that Chinese democracy has moved a big step forward,' and Hu himself stressed the need for 'democratic discussions within the Party' – a far cry from the Western notion of democracy.[837]

But the salient point of the Congress, and the only information that the Chinese themselves awaited with any interest, was the list of new names to be added to the Standing Committee of the Politburo – and which of the favourites would be excluded. The choice of other key figures is equally important: for example, to be selected as a Vice-Premier without entering the Politburo means a dead-end promotion since it means the next step is impossible; the same is true of an appointment to the State Council. This is effectively what happened to one of the up-and-coming names, Bo Xilai, whose ambitions are now truncated, while the rise of the second most powerful woman in China (and Hu protégé), Liu Yandong, has similarly come to a halt. Each will remain powerful, but since they will be respectively sixty-three and sixty-seven in 2012, it will be too late to move up a notch because it will be necessary to find fresh exponents of the fifth generation to rejuvenate the Politburo.

So who are the new members, and what influence might they have in the future?

The first announcement came on Sunday 21 October, when the list of 204 members of the 17th Central Committee of the Communist Party of China was elected and announced, together with 167 alternate members (one curious feature was that the first list was in order of the number of strokes composing their surnames, while the latter were listed in descending orders of votes received; 8 per cent of the total number of candidates failed to be chosen). This was the first confirmation of changes, since three members of the Standing Committee of the Politburo were not on the list and were therefore automatically excluded from the Standing Committee: Zeng Qinghong, Wu Guanzheng and Luo Gan, aged sixty-eight, sixty-nine and seventy-two respectively. Zeng Qinghong had also been China's Vice-President, and Hu Jintao's main counterbalance in the Standing Committee. Two other notable absentees were the vice-premiers Zeng Peiyan and Wu Yi, the latter having been recognised as the most powerful woman in China, and the Minister of Defence and Vice-Chairman of the Central Military Commission, Cao Gangchun. Most of these retirements were anticipated, and they left space for the final round of consultations and some very important roles to be filled. These 371 men and women will form the basis of Chinese power until 2012 and (in theory) on the next day approved the members of the Politburo and its Standing Committee.

The key names were announced in a rigidly formal press conference on Tuesday 23 October: in addition to the five remaining members of the Standing Committee (Hu Jintao, Wu Bangguo, Wen Jiabao, Jia Qinglin and Li Changchun), the newly appointed members were Li Keqiang, Xi Jinping, Zhou Yongkang and He Guoqiang. The first real interest lies in the potential rivalry between Li Keqiang and Xi Jinping, one of whom will probably become the next party chief and president in 2012. The immediate change was that Xi took charge of Party affairs as the head of the Secretariat, while Li became one of the four executive vice-prime ministers. This would strongly suggest that in 2012, in the minds of the puppeteers behind the scenes, Xi Jinping will succeed Hu Jintao as President of China and Li Keqiang will succeed Wen Jiabao, each with the requisite credentials and experience.

It is interesting to note, in spite of comments about humanities graduates above, that the preponderance of engineering graduates in the Politburo has been maintained. Given the likely importance of environmental and energy issues in the next five to ten years, it is worth observing that three of the new members have significant expertise and experience in directly related fields: Xi and He are both graduates in chemical engineering, while Zhou – although he is currently the Minister of Public Security – studied geophysical surveying and exploration at the Beijing Petroleum Institute and has spent most of his working life in the oil industry. Li Keqiang, on the contrary, holds a PhD in Economics. As usual in China, they are all technically highly competent in their professional fields and have vast experience in administration. These are the *sine qua non* for such promotion.

One further fact of importance concerns the out-going members of the Politburo, and how their departure may alter the balance within this tightly-knit group. One such member, Huang Ju, had been sick for some time and died before the Congress opened (although he had not been replaced). Huang was a Jiang Zemin protégé, ex-Mayor and Party Secretary of Shanghai, and even looked a bit like Jiang with his big glasses. As a proponent of Shanghai's success, he was in favour of continuing the development of the large cities, and thus a thorn in the side of Wen Jiabao who would 'have had an easier time implementing his reform programmes' if Jiang had chosen another of his protégés.[838] Of the others, Zeng Qinghong, another Jiang protégé and a notable 'princeling' is said to have resigned in favour of the 'princeling' Xi Jinping, son of a revolutionary and vice-premier, which effectively suggests both a Jiang permanence as counter-weight to Hu Jintao's cotery and a continuing shadow of the revolutionary elders cast forward over the leadership for the next ten years. But the imprint of Scientific Development guarantees Hu's continuing power and effective control over policy – in appointing successors and setting guidelines which cannot easily be changed – up to 2022.

The Harmonious Society

In the past half-century, China has seen 'Mao Zedong Thought', 'Deng Xiao Ping Theory' and Jiang Zemin's 'Three Represents' as the key doctrines of the Chinese Communist Party. Today, President Hu Jintao is contributing his doctrine of the 'Harmonious Society', which has resonated in his speeches for several years and is now enshrined in the charter of the Party by the 17th Congress as a cornerstone of the 'Theory of Scientific Development'.

In doing so, Hu is drawing deeply on Chinese history and culture. For, in the distant past, good government depended on harmonious relations between cosmic order and social peace, which one of the key meanings behind the Mandate of Heaven (not dissimilar in fact to the values expressed in Ambrogio Lorenzetti's fresco of 'Good Government' in the town hall of Siena). This harmony derived from three basic components: Truth, Benevolence, and Glory.[839] 'Truth' here refers to the moral truths represented in the divine person of the emperor, and in the scholars who devoted themselves to classical learning in order to reveal and refine these truths. 'Benevolence' means caring for the people, in the sense of providing stores of grain against drought, adequate supplies of water, orphanages, and public relief projects. 'Glory' means enhancing and spreading the glories of Chinese civilisation through the dissemination of language, through the tribute system, and by sporadic military conquest. Together, they constituted the legitimacy of the emperor and his rule.

These components find ready parallels in contemporary China, especially as they have been consciously renewed by Hu Jintao and his Politburo after virtual annihilation along with the 'four olds' in the time of late-Mao and the Cultural

Revolution. Moral truth is thought to derive from the Party and its political theories, which is one reason it remains so important in the eyes of Chinese leaders (though not for much of the population), and is sustained by the search for ever greater 'scientific' truths by institutions like the Chinese Academy of Social Sciences. In this case, the Academy fulfils a role similar to that of the venerable Hanlin Academy of imperial times, with the PhDs that the Chinese so venerate today substituting the old imperial examinations. Benevolence is also returning as a key value, in the form of thousands of NGOs and philanthropic institutions. This is the reason why at each official holiday the public is treated with television clips of Hu Jintao and Wen Jiabao visiting remote and poor villages to sit with rural families and listen to their problems. On the eve of the Spring Festival of 2007, for example, the President met farmers in a village near Dingxi in the western province of Gansu, while the Premier travelled to meet locals in Fushun in the north-eastern province of Liaoning. The glory is being provided by a programme of cultural exchange, a revival of classical art forms, and such official measures as the Confucius Institutes. But most of all it comes from the patronage and sponsorship of sport, in particular the Olympic Games. Thus we can see how the notion of a future harmonious society, in which many social evils will have been reduced if not eliminated, is a modern version of imperial legitimatisation of the Mandate of Heaven.

Let us therefore move to a conclusion on a note of optimism – both from China's point of view and from the Western point of view – with the vision of one of modern China's founding fathers, Sun Yat-Sen, in a long but pertinent paragraph written in 1927:

> If China gets only as far as Japan she will have the strength of ten Powers in her one state, and will then be able to recover her predominant national position. After China reaches that place, what then? A common phrase in ancient China was, 'Rescue the weak, lift up the fallen.' Because of this noble policy China prospered for thousands of years, and Annan, Burma, Korea and Siam, and other small states were able to maintain their independence. If we want China to rise to power, we must not only restore our national standing but we must also assume a great responsibility towards the world … Only if we 'Rescue the weak, lift up the fallen' will we be carrying out the divine obligation of our nation. We must aid the weaker and smaller peoples and oppose the Great Powers of the world. Then we will be truly 'governing the state and pacifying the world'.[840]

This is China's self-appointed mission. The main difference is that today the world is a more complex place, with China fully integrated into the global economic system but not yet into its political system. But need it be fully integrated to achieve its mission, as many Western observers argue? China is so vast, so complex, and its recent history so unlike that of any other country, that meaningful comparisons are impossible. This is why, in words spoken by Wen Jiabao that echo those of Sun, 'China's development is a long-term and daunting task. To achieve development, we need peace, we need friends and we need time.'[841]

Does such a mission even make sense today? Can the entire world be directed, monitored, supervised and reprimanded from the Oval Office or Zhongnanhai? We live in a world dominated, to use the buzz phrase of Davos 2007, with a 'shifting power equation' based on a fragmentation of traditional power. Power is shifting from the centre to the periphery, with traditional vertical command structures being replaced by horizontal networks and communities. Rapid air travel (for both passengers and cargo) and electronic communications have created a genuinely global neighbourhood often beyond the reach of governments. This is the space where the Chinese have thrived for centuries, their freedom from imperial control encapsulated in the phrase 'the mountains are high and the emperor is far away' and in the words of a popular country song quoted by Pearl Buck:

> When the sun rises I work;
> When the sun sets I rest.
> I dig the well to drink;
> I plow the field to eat.
> What has the Emperor to do with me?[842]

These sentiments are as apposite for the entrepreneurs of Wenzhou or Shenzhen today as they were for early twentieth century farmers. Because of this historical disassociation from the seat of political power no community is better suited to survive and prosper in the new multi-level and multi-polar world in which stealth power is the most apposite form of power.

The real fear is that China could, Icarus-like, extend itself too quickly. In this, perhaps the hawkish scholar Arthur Waldron is right when he suggests that the current Chinese leadership is overconfident, acting as if China were already 'the great power she aspires to be, rather than a still-poor and chaotic third world state.'[843] Such hasty extension could bring collapse or war. Yet it is also true that while in past empires such as that of Britain the idea of ruling distant overseas territories had what Edward Said has called 'a privileged status',[844] it enjoys no such status in China. If there is an empire, then it will certainly not be that kind of empire. The stealth approach will be less traumatic for other powers, but not will necessarily have less impact in the long term.

The institutions and governance structures that have traditionally dominated global power were based on the concept of nation states; but, as we have seen, China has never really been a nation state. Having been a disadvantage in the past 200 years in which nation-states controlled the world, and fought over it, a Stealth

Empire is today perhaps the best equipped of power systems to thrive in the global environment of shifting power equations, evading – perhaps unwittingly, it doesn't really matter – the predictions and fears of others and in a certain sense persisting in spite of itself. Defying gravity.

That is what China has always done, and what it will always do.

Appendices

Appendix 1: Maps of China

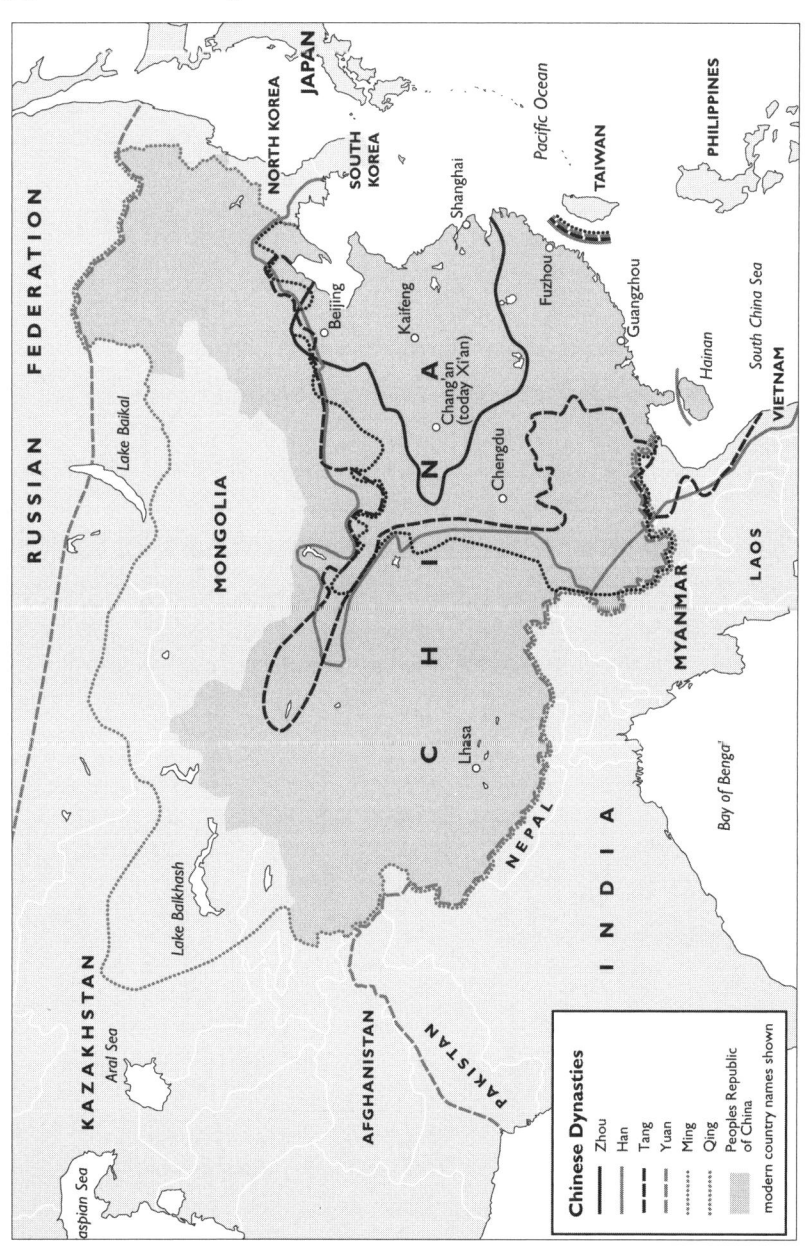

Map 1. Map of China showing Zhou, Han, Tang, Yuan, Ming, Qing and China today

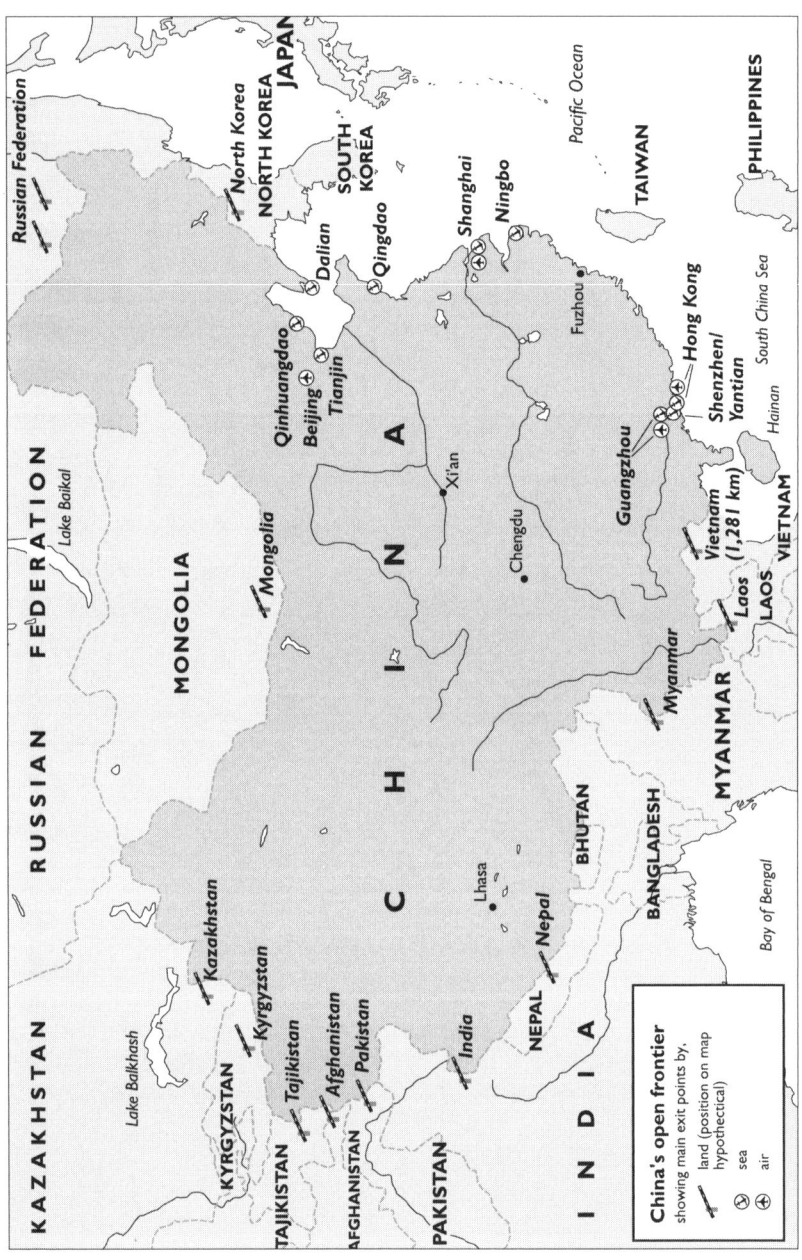

Map 2. China's opening frontier showing the main exit points: a) By land: HK, Vietnam, Burma, Russia, Kazakhstan, Pakistan, Korea, etc. b) By sea: HK, Shenzhen, Shanghai, Tianjin, Xiamen, Qingdao, etc. c) By air: international airports of HK, Beijing, Shanghai, Guangzhou, etc.

Map 3. The 'U-Shaped Line' (South China Sea, showing Taiwan/Pescadores/Ryukyu, etc.)

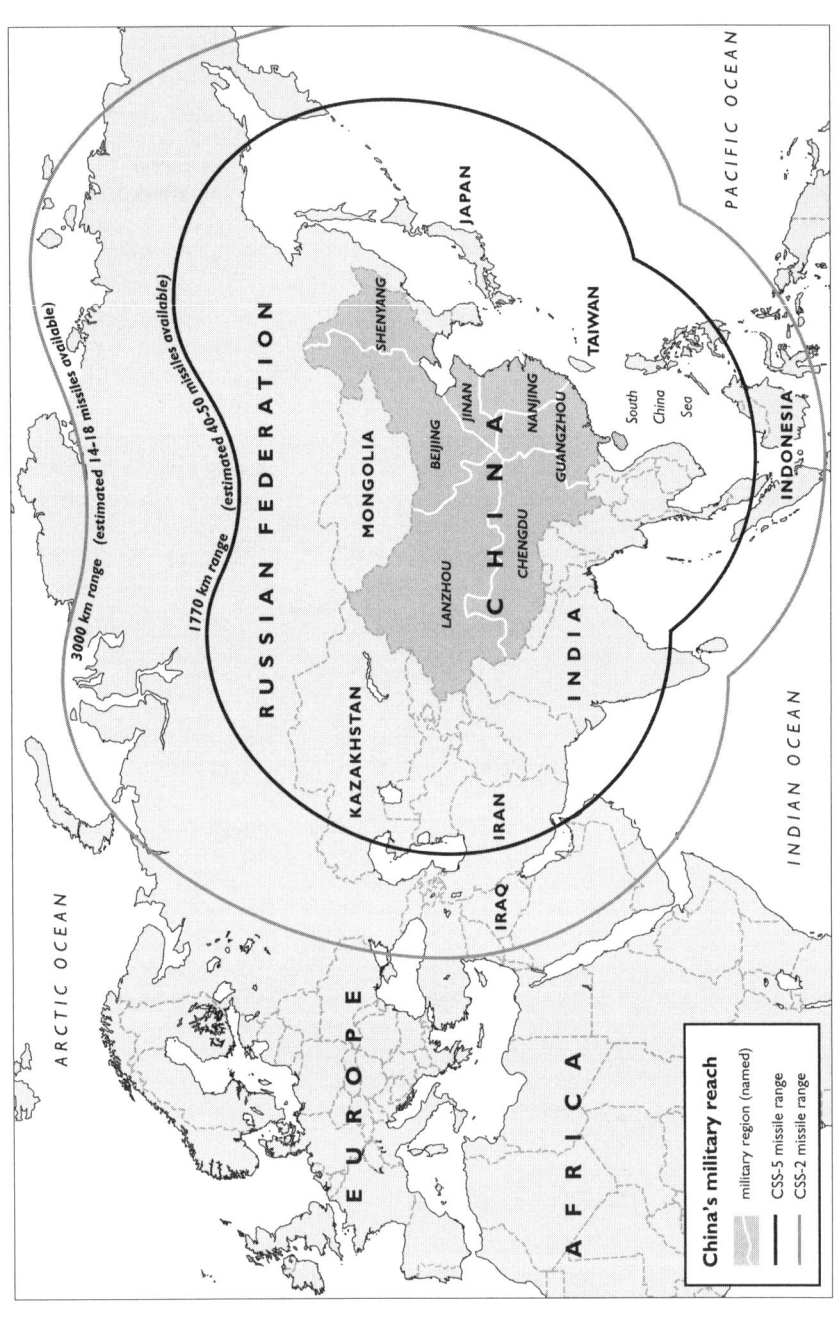

Map 4. China's military reach

Appendix 2: Figures

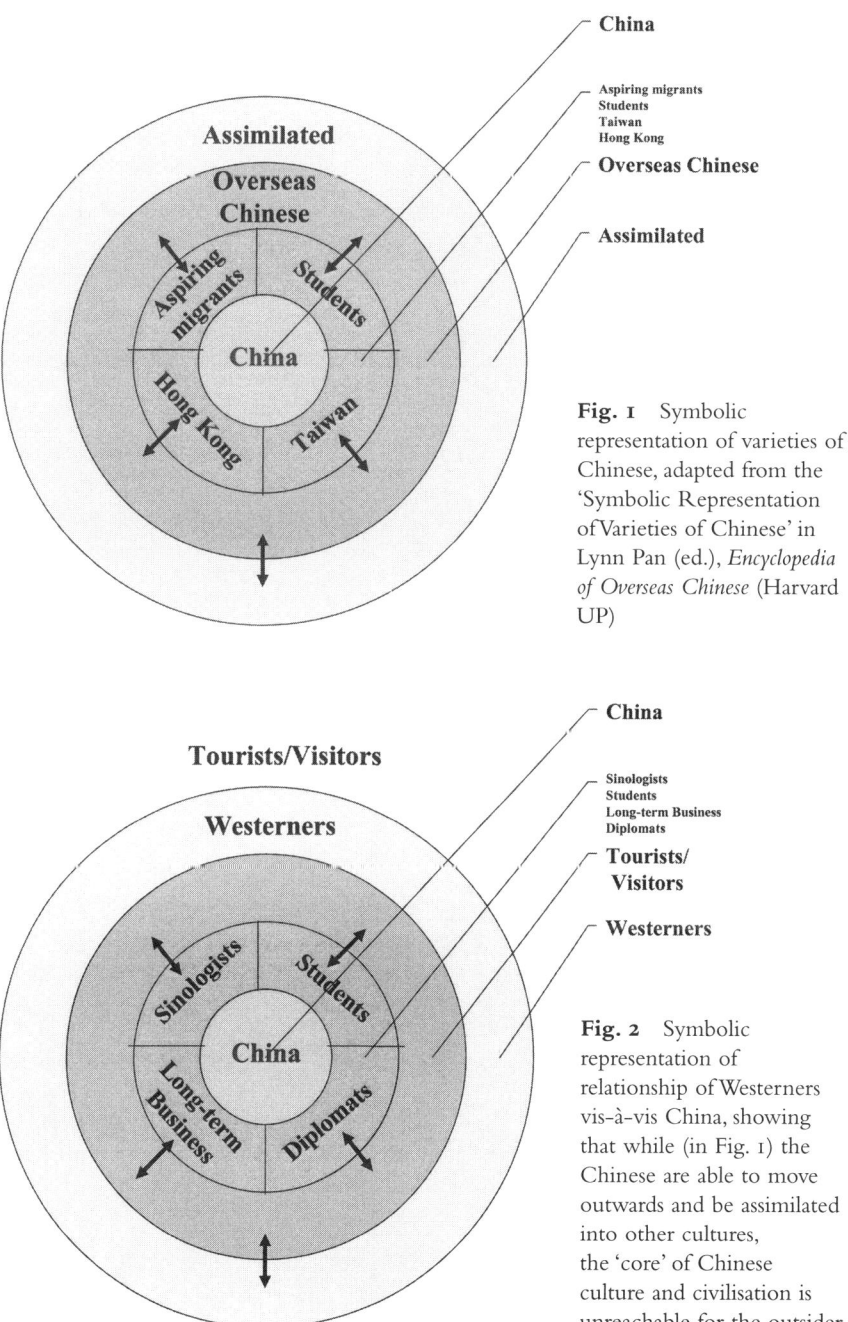

China

Aspiring migrants
Students
Taiwan
Hong Kong

Overseas Chinese

Assimilated

Fig. 1 Symbolic representation of varieties of Chinese, adapted from the 'Symbolic Representation of Varieties of Chinese' in Lynn Pan (ed.), *Encyclopedia of Overseas Chinese* (Harvard UP)

China

Sinologists
Students
Long-term Business
Diplomats

Tourists/ Visitors

Westerners

Fig. 2 Symbolic representation of relationship of Westerners vis-à-vis China, showing that while (in Fig. 1) the Chinese are able to move outwards and be assimilated into other cultures, the 'core' of Chinese culture and civilisation is unreachable for the outsider

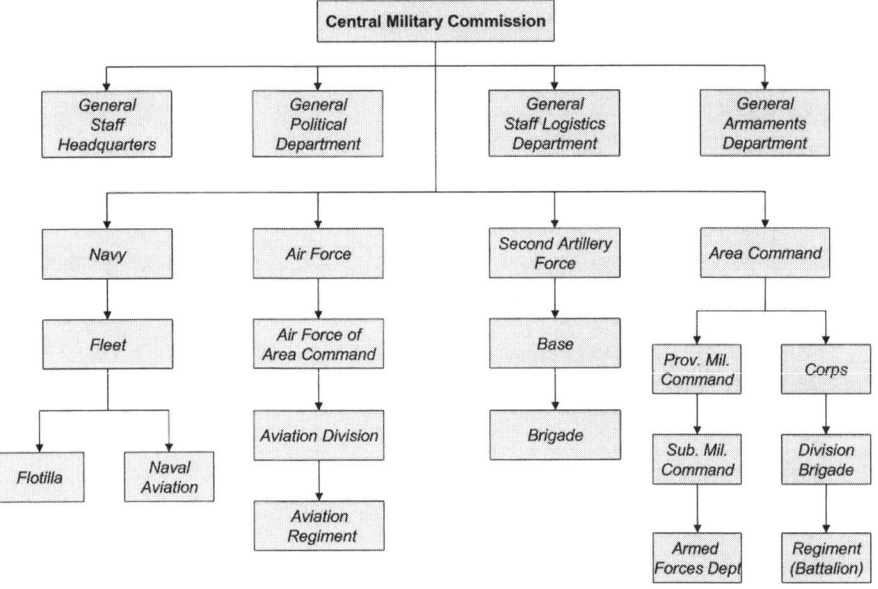

Fig. 3 PLA organisation chart (based on information in the *White Paper*, *China's National Defence in 2006*)

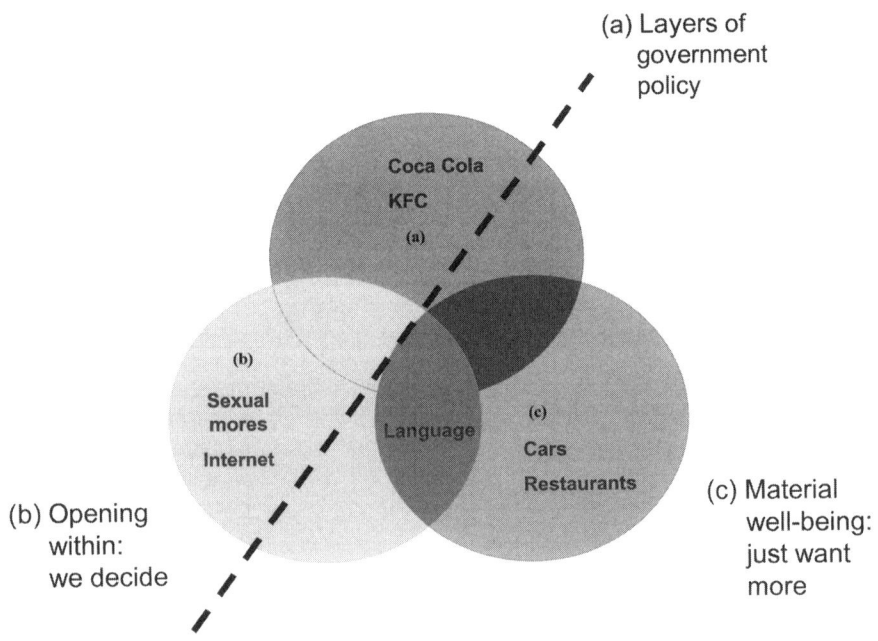

Fig. 4 China's opening to Western ideas and values

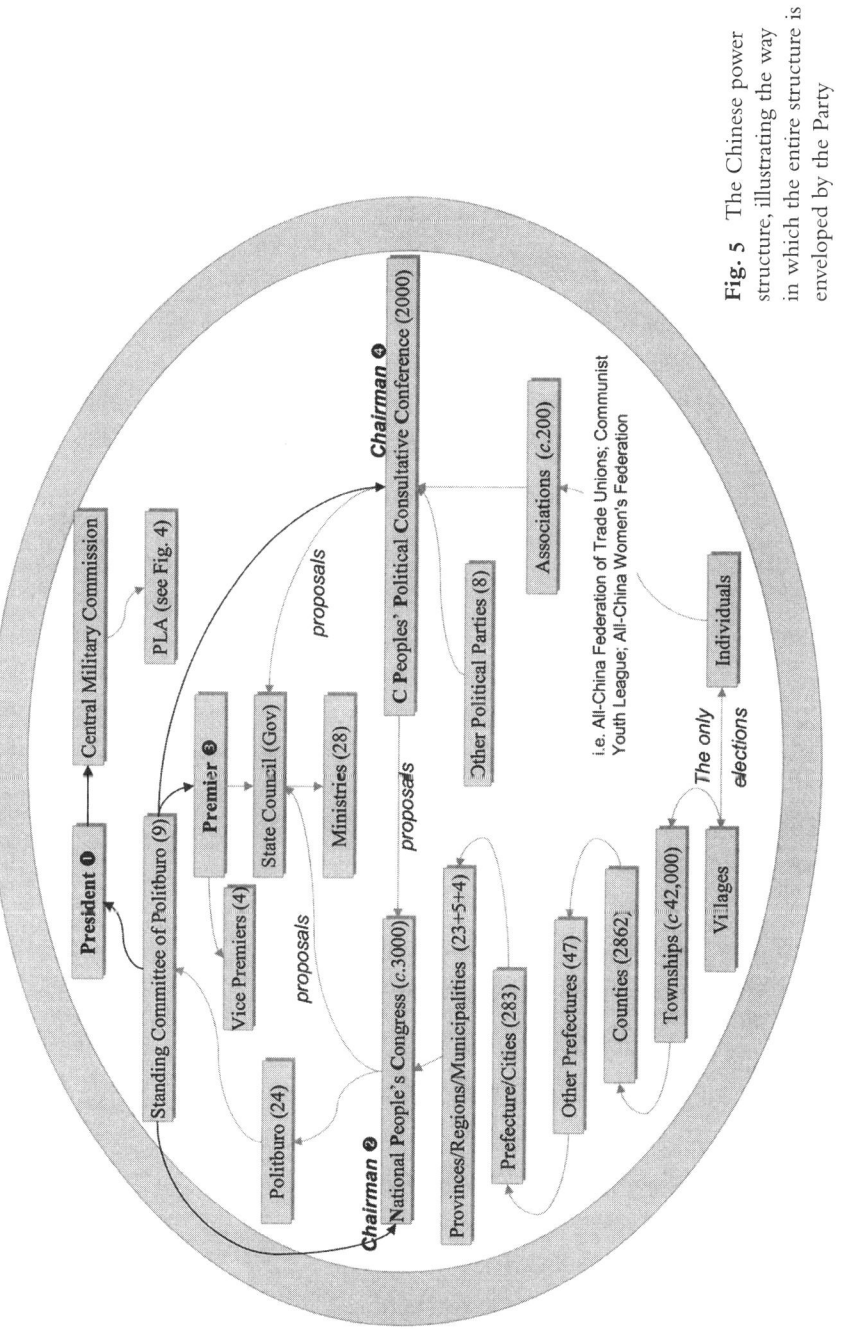

Fig. 5 The Chinese power structure, illustrating the way in which the entire structure is enveloped by the Party

Acknowledgements

Two people who have provided moral support and more throughout the writing of this book. The first is Ou Yang Xiao Hong, whose specialised knowledge as a financial journalist and enthusiasm for my project have been invaluable. The second is my Italian boon companion in Beijing, Francesco Sisci, whose profound knowledge of Chinese etymologies and thought has been invaluable.

I am also much indebted to Dr Ron Anton, SJ, the International Director of the Beijing Center for Chinese Studies, for his courtesy in allowing me full access to the services of its rapidly expanding library, to the librarian, Shan Yanrong, and also to the former Research Librarian Elisa Oreglia, who initially provided my reader's card. Librarians at the National Library of China in Beijing and at the Library of the London School of Oriental and African Studies were also courteous and unfailingly helpful during my visits. The Bibliography indicates which more recent books have been useful. Books that have been cited once or are not directly related to the topics in the Bibliography are given full reference in the Notes.

Finally, I would like to thank Christopher Feeney, formerly of Sutton Publishers, who first framed the question that enabled me to put my thoughts into their present shape, a variant of the basic what-if questions concerning Chinese isolationism: what if China had not turned inwards like its scholars' fingernails and permitted the European conquest of Far-Eastern trading outposts on its coast, and what if the voyages of the eunuch admiral Zheng He had spurred the Chinese themselves to overseas colonialism? Then there is the more disturbing question: what if they do it now?

Notes

1. Philip Stephens, *Financial Times*, 1 July 2005.
2. 'The Chinese Shadow', *New York Review of Books*, Volume 52, No. 18, 17 November 2005.
3. Jay Denby, *Letters of a Shanghai Griffin* (Shanghai: Shanghai Printing Company, 1910).
4. McGregor, *One Billion Customers: Lessons from the Front Lines of Doing Business in China*, p. 223.
5. The increasing length can be seen in published works as the decades pass, to take three random examples: 'thirty centuries' in André Malraux's *Human Condition* (London: Methuen, 1935), p. 120; 4,000 years in Jules Roy's *Journey Through China* (London: Faber and Faber, 1965, p. 30), to the title of a more recent China-based book like Lin Handa and Cao Yuzhang's Tales from *Five Thousand Years of Chinese History* (Shanghai: Shanghai Press & Publishing).

Introduction: Meanings of Empire

6. Lucien Pye, 'China: Erratic State, Frustrated Society,' p. 57.
7. Cranmer-Byng, 'The Chinese View of their Place in the World', p. 69.
8. Tu, Wei-ming, 'Cultural China: the periphery as the center', p. 153.
9. In Ming times, Russia stopped at the Ural Mountains, then it progressively added territory to the east: to Narym by 1598, to the Yenisey River by 1618, and on to the Sea of Okhotsk (including all of Siberia) by 1689. Advances further south, from the Caucasus to Kashgar, are recounted in the narrative of Anglo-Russian conflict by Peter Hopkirk, especially in the later chapters (Hopkirk, *The Great Game: On Secret Service in High Asia*, London: John Murray, 1990).
10. James A Millward, *Beyond the Pass: Economy, Ethnicity and Empire in Qing Central Asia, 1759–1864*, p. 15.
11. Cicero, *Cicerone Tusculanae*, Book V, 37; Cicero's *Tusculan Disputations*, Also Treatises on the Nature of the Gods and on the Commonwealth, Trs C.D. Yonge, (New York: Harper, 1877), p. 202.
12. Seneca, *L. Annaei Senecae Dialogorum Liber XII Ad Helviam Matrem de Consolatione*, Book VII, 7.
13. Herschel I. Grossman and Juan Mendoza, 'Annexation or Conquest: The Economics of Empire Building' (Cambridge, MA: National Bureau of Economic Research, Working Paper No.8109, February 2001).
14. Bayly, *The Birth of the Modern World 1780–1914*, p. 325.
15. Panjiazhuang is a remote village in the south of the province, closer to Jinan, the capital of Shandong Province, than to Beijing.
16. Arthur H. Smith, *Chinese Characteristics*, p. 330.
17. See virtually any of Hart's entries for a Sunday, when he evidently had time to write more and the Christian emphasis becomes strongest, in Richard Smith, John K. Fairbank and Katherine F. Brunner (eds), *Robert Hart and China's Early Modernization: His Journals, 1863–1866* (Cambridge, MA: Harvard University Press, 1991).
18. Vladimir Illyich Lenin, 'Imperialism, The Highest Stage of Capitalism', Petrograd, 1917.
19. Chang, *The Rise of the Chinese Empire*, p. 211.

20   Ibn Battuta, *Travels in Asia and Africa 1325–54*, p. 297.

21   Interestingly, translations of sections of this work were used to create the first Chinese history of the world, published as the *History of the Four Continents (Sizhou zhi)* under the editorship of Lin Zexu (founder of the first translation bureau in China).

22   Hugh Murray, *The Encyclopaedia of Geography, Comprising a Complete Description of the Earth*, Vol. II, p. 34.

23   In fact the use of China Proper continued well into the twentieth century, appearing for example in a 1942 Pocket Guide for American servicemen en route to China, where the country is divided into twenty-four provinces in China Proper plus three in Manchuria and Chinese Turkestan. *A Pocket Guide to China* (Washington D.C.: War and Navy Departments, 1942).

24   Watson, *The Frontiers of China*, pp. 26–8; in China this river is known as Heilongjiang and gives its name to the country's most north-easterly province.
      It is worth noting that Taiwan is not taken into consideration in the early 1950s.

25   Toynbee also wrote a less-known book on China called *A Journey to China, or Things Which Are Seen*, (London: Constable, 1931).

26   Gibbon, *Decline and Fall of the Roman Empire*, Vol. I, p. xxix.

27   *Ibid*, p. xxx.

28   Bai Shouyi, *An Outline History of China* (Beijing: Foreign Languages Press, 1982), pp. 361–2.

29   The phrase is used by Paul Kennedy in his *The Rise and Fall of the Great Powers*, where in three pages he describes China as an empire that began to 'fall' 600 years ago during the early Ming period and only began to rise again in the Deng Xiao Ping period after 1978 (Paul Kennedy, *The Rise and Fall of the Great Powers*, New York: Random House, 1987, p. 7).

30   Brzezinski and Mearsheimer, *Foreign Policy*, No. 146 (January–February 2005), 'Debate: Clash of the Titans', pp. 46–9, p. 46.

31   Ng and Wang, *Mirroring the Past: The Writing and Use of History in Imperial China*, pp. 253–4.

32   Hidehiro Okada, 'China as a Successor State to the Mongol Empire', in Amitai-Preiss and Morgan (eds), *The Mongol Empire and its Legacy*, pp. 261–2.

33   Millward, *Eurasian Crossroads: A History of Xinjiang*, p. 32.

34   Cohen, *Discovering History: American Historical Writing on the Recent Chinese Past*, p. 145.

35   Pan (ed.), *The Encyclopedia of Overseas Chinese*, p. 23.

36   Shih Chih-yu has argued that those who treat China 'as a piece of sovereign territory and claim knowledge of China cannot be exempted from Orientalism', that is, in Edward Said's terms, of constructing in their minds an entity that never existed and then going on to study it. The interesting thing, for Shih, akin to what we are doing here, would be to ask how 'celestial China has become territorial China.' *Navigating Sovereignty: World Politics Lost in China*, p. 27.

37   Ling, *The Lenovo Affair: The Growth of China's Computer Giant and Its Takeover of IBM-PC*, p. 90. And what, we might ask, was the translator doing in rendering the Chinese into English written as if for a Chinese reading the translation?

38   Xu, Guoqi, *China and The Great War: China's Pursuit of a New National Identity and Internationalization*, p. 58.

39   Morris, 'To Make the Four Hundred Million Move', p. 883.

40   Ernest Renan, 'What is a Nation'. A lecture delivered at the Sorbonne, 11 March 1882, in Geoff Eley and Ronald Grigor Suny (eds), *Becoming National: A Reader* (Oxford: OUP, 1996), pp. 41–55, p. 52.

41   Xu, Guoqi, *China and The Great War*, pp. 25–6.

42   Yuh Ying-shih, quoted in Michael Ng-Quinn, 'National Identity in Premodern China: Formation and Role Enactment', in Dittmer & Kim (eds), *China's Quest for National Identity*, p. 43.

43   Gallagher, *China in the Sixteenth Century: The Journals of Matthew Ricci*, p. 6.

44   Quoted in Liu, *The Clash of Empires: The Invention of China in Modern World Making,* p. 76.

45   Hummel, *Eminent Chinese of the Ch'ing Period (1644–1912)*, Vol. I, pp. 350–1.

46   In fact the use of a lunar calendar was never abolished, so that today the Chinese live with a dual calendar, and in the case of New Year a dual holiday since many companies give a two- or three-day holiday for the solar New Year as well as a week for the lunar New Year shortly afterwards. All traditional Chinese holidays and ceremonies run according to the lunar calendar, while some official holidays such as 1 May (and the subsequent three-day holiday) obviously follow the solar calendar.

47   Harrison, *China*, pp. 135–7.

48   Gerth, *China Made: Consumer Culture and the Creation of the Nation,* p. 92.

49   Jenner, *The Tyranny of History: The Roots of China's Crisis*, p. 6.

50   Ng and Wang, *Mirroring the Past*, p. 243.

51   Tu, Wei-ming, 'Cultural China', p. 146.

52   Translated in Frodsham (ed.), *First Chinese Embassy to the West: The Journals of Kuo Sung-t'ao, Liu Hsi-hung, and Chang Te-yi,* p. 110, p. 114.

53   Quoted in Teng & Fairbank, *China's Response to the West*, p. 153.

54   Wuchang and Hankow, on opposite banks of the Chang Jiang and linked by a bridge for the first time in 1957, were combined together with Hanyang in 1927 to form the present industrial city of Wuhan.

55   See his biography in Hummel, *Eminent Chinese*, Vol. I, pp. 27–31.

56   Teng & Fairbank, *China's Response to the West: a documentary survey 1839–1923*, p. 169.

57   Hummel, *Eminent Chinese*, p. 30.

58   Mao Zedong told the American journalist Edgar Snow in 1936 that when he was a sixteen-year-old schoolboy he had 'worshipped' Kang Youwei and Liang Qichao (*Red Star Over China*, pp. 134–5).

59   Gardner, *Chinese Traditional Historiography*, p. 70.

60   Quoted in Prasenjit, *Rescuing History from the Nation: Questioning Narratives of Modern China*, p. 35.

61   Quoted by Wang Hui, 'Modern Chinese Identity', in Yeh, *Becoming Chinese: Passages to Modernity and Beyond*, p. 241.

62   *Ibid.*, p. 36.

63   Gerth, *China Made,* pp. 8–11.

64   See the fascinating detailed case study in Chapter 8, 'Manufacturing Patriotic Producers' in Gerth, *China Made*, pp. 333–54; the quotation is from the note to Fig. 8.4 on p. 350.

65   Quoted in John Fitzgerald, 'The Invention of the Modern Chinese Self', in Mabel Lee (ed.) *Modernization of the Chinese Self,* p. 27.

66   *Ibid.*

67   *Ibid.*, p. 31.

68   Quoted from the translation of William A. Lyell, in Lu Xun, *Diary of a Madman and Other Stories* (Honolulu: University of Hawaii Press, 1990), pp. 29–30.

69   *Ibid.*, p. 41.

Chapter 1: Empire as Permanent Tribute

70   Xu Guoqi, *China and the Great War*, p. 22.

71   Quoted in Cécile and Michel Beurdeley, *Giuseppe Castiglione: A Jesuit Painter at the Court of the Chinese Emperors*, p. 31.

72   Sisci, *Another Country*, p. 32.

73   Gallagher, *China in the Sixteenth Century*, p. 43.

74   Giles, *Chinese Sketches*, 1875, No. II. It was this Giles, together with his predecessor as
      Professor of Chinese at Cambridge, Thomas Wade (1818–1895), who devised the Wade-
      Giles transliteration system. His son Lionel (1875–1958) was Keeper of Oriental Books and
      Manuscripts at the British Museum and a well-known translator of works from Chinese.

75   Article LI, reproduced in Lydia H. Liu, *The Clash of Empires: The Invention of China in
      Modern World Making*, p. 32.

76   Hebrew (*ha-Yam ha-Tikhon*); German (*das Mittelmeer*). Even the Roman *mare internum*
      carries similar connotations; see also the title of John Julius Norwich's book about the
      Mediterranean, *The Middle Sea* (London: Chatto, 2006).

77   Ch'ên Yüan, *Western and Central Asians in China Under the Mongols: Their transformation into
      Chinese*, p. 1.

78   See the account in Jeanette Mirsky, *The Great Chinese Travellers: An Anthology*, pp. 175–200.

79   Quoted in Wang Gungwu, 'Early Ming Relations with Southeast Asia: A Background
      Essay', in Fairbank (ed.), *The Chinese World Order*, p. 34.

80   Pan Guxi, 'The Yuan and Ming Dynasties', in Nancy S. Steinhardt (ed.), *Chinese
      Architecture*, pp. 222–5.

81   Abru, *A Persian Embassy, Being an Extract from Zubdatu't Tawarikh*, pp. 88–9.

82   Quoted by Staunton, in *An Authentic Account of an Embassy from the King of Great Britain
      to the Emperor of China*, Vol. I, p. 149; in a similar vein Simone de Beauvoir, who travelled
      through China with Sartre for two months in 1955, observed that there was 'no city
      more artificial than Peking' since it was sited 'arbitrarily' on an open plain and not on the
      banks of a river (*La longue marche, Essai sur la Chine*, Paris: Gallimard, 1957; cited from the
      Italian translation, *La lunga marcia*, Milano: Mondadori,, 2006, p. 33–4).

83   Naquin, *Peking*, 'Preface', pp. xxxiii–xxxiv, p. 255; she cites as an authority G.M.H.
      Playfair, *The Cities and Towns of China: A Geographical Dictionary*, (Taipei: Ch'eng-wen,
      1971, reprint of 1910 edition), pp. 432–3.

84   Paragraph based on Hae-Jong Chun, 'Sino-Korean Tributary Relations in the Ch'ing Period',
      in Fairbank (ed.), *Chinese World Order Order: Traditional China's Foreign Relations*, pp. 90–111.

85   Abru, *A Persian Embassy*, p. 65.

86   *Ibid.*, p. 112.

87   Gallagher, *China in the Sixteenth Century*, p. 9.

88   Laura Hostetler, *Qing Colonial Enterprise*, p. 42–3.

89   Slightly edited from John K. Fairbank, 'The Early Treaty System in the Chinese World
      Order', in Fairbank (ed.), *Chinese World Order*, p. 265.

90   *Troilus and Cressida*, Act I, Scene 3.

91   For recent examples in business books, see Tim Clissold, *Mr China*, pp. 166–7; James
      Kynge, *China Shakes the World*, p. 116; James McGregor, *One Billion Customers*, pp. 21–2. At
      second remove, things get worse to the point of silliness: in Friedman's *The World is Flat*,
      p. 411, an interviewee speaks of it in this way: '… think about the time when the emperor
      in China threw out the British ambassador.'

92   See the detailed account in Wills, *Embassies and Illusions*, pp. 25–37; Wills suggests that this
      ceremony was performed in the still-existing 'Pavilion for Practicing Ceremonies' in the
      Temple of Earth to the north of old Beijing.

93   See Teng and Fairbank, *China's Response to the West*, p. 20; also Hevia, *Cherishing Men from
      Afar: Qing Guest Ritual and the Macartney Embassy of 1793*, pp. 105–15.

94   John Bell, *Travels from St Petersburg in Russia to Diverse Parts of Asia*, Vol. II, p. 7.

95   Ellis, *Journal of the Proceedings of the Late Embassy to China*, Vol. I, p. 51.

96   Rowbotham, *Missionary and Mandarin: the Jesuits at the Court of China*, p. 273; Elman
      gives 131 scientific works between 1584 and 1790, out of a total of 437 translations or
      compilations, *On Their Own Terms: Science in China, 1550–1900*, p. 111.

97   Elman, *On Their Own Terms*, p. 63.

98   Gallagher, *China in the Sixteenth Century*, p. 477.

99   Elman, *A Cultural History of Modern Science in China*, p. 30.

100   Quoted in Hostetler, *Qing Colonial Enterprise*, p. 4.

101   His descendents were fascinated by Western technology, as this description of the imperial living-room in 1901 shows:

> There were clocks of every description from the finest French cloisonné to the most intricate cuckoo clocks from which a bird hopped forth to announce the hour, and each ticking its own time regardless of every other. Tables were placed in various parts of the room, on each of which were one, two or three clocks. Swiss watches of the most curious and unique designs hung about the walls.

> Isaac Taylor Headland, *Court Life in China: The Capital, its Officials, and People* (New York: Fleming H. Revell, 1909), p. 118.

102   Shen Fuwei, *Cultural Flow between China and Outside World*, pp. 261–6.

103   Spence, *Emperor of China: Self-Portrait of K'ang-Hsi*, p. 72.

104   Maddison, *Chinese Economic Performance in the Long Run*, p. 40.

105   Elman, *Cultural Examination of Civil Examinations in Late Imperial China*, p. 291.

106   Elman, *On Their Own Terms*, p. 207.

107   Jack A. Goldstone, 'Was the Early Qing 'Early Modern'?', in Struve (ed.), *The Qing Formation in World-historical Time*, pp. 259–61.

108   Paragraph 5 of the Treaty. An English translation of the Treaty, which was signed in Russian, Manchu and Latin versions, may be found in Joseph Sebes, *The Jesuits and the Sino-Russian Treaty of Nerchinsk (1689): The Diary of Thomas Pereira, SJ* (Rome: Institutum Historicum S.I., 1961), pp. 283–6.

109   Today known as K'achta, on the border between Russia and Mongolia, on the main road from Ulan Ud, south of Lake Baikal, to Ulan Bator; interestingly, when the telegraph line to Tianjin was cut during the Boxer Rebellion, communications were still possible via the other international telegraph line that passed through Kiakhta (see Nigel Oliphant, *A Diary of the Siege of the Legations in Peking During the Summer of 1900*, London: Longmans, Green, & Co, 1901, pp. 7–9).

110   S.C.M. Paine, *Imperial Rivals: China, Russia, and Their Disputed Frontier*, p. 30.

111   *Ibid.*, pp. 31–2.

112   See Newby, L.J., *The Empire and the Khanate: A Political History of Qing Relations with Khoqand c. 1760–1860*, (Leiden: Brill, 2005), pp. 133–4.

113   In the appendix to Cranmer Byng, J.L. (ed.), *A Journal of the Embassy to China; Lord Macartney's Observations Upon China*, pp. 252–4.

114   Rawski, *The Last Emperors: A Social History of the Qing Imperial Institutions*, pp. 200–1.

115   Joanna Waley-Cohen, 'Military Ritual and the Qing Empire', pp. 409–11; Evelyn Rawski, The Last Emperors, pp. 197–230.

116   Cranmer-Byng, *Journal*, p. 88.

117   Quoted in Ye Xiaoging, 'Ascendent Peace in the Four Seas', p. 99–100.

118   Quoted in Hevia, *Cherishing Men From Afar*, p. 143.

119   *Ibid.*, p. 170; the rites of hospitality are still maintained, and Kissinger noted how the Chinese had discovered President Nixon's favourite music and arranged for it to be played during formal banquets (quoted in Roberts, *China to Chinatown*, p. 117).

120   Cranmer-Byng, *Journal*, p. 70. Presumably the Madeira-like wine was Shaoxing wine, which is still offered warm in bowls on some occasions.

121   Mote, *Imperial China 900–1800*, p. 961.

122   Arnold, *Princely Gifts and Papal Treasures: The Franciscan Mission to China and its influence on the Art of the West*, p. 105.

123   *Journal*, Ed. Cranmer-Byng, p. 66.

124   *Ibid.*, p. 104.

125   Letter in Teng and Fairbank, *China's Response,* pp. 24–8.
126   Bland, J.O.P., *Houseboat Days in China* (London: Edward Arnold, 1909), p. 141.
127   Ellen Meiksins Wood, *Empire of Capital*, p. 28.
128   Hevia, *Cherishing Men From Afar*, p. 11.
129   'Spinoza entendió que todas las cosas quieren perseverar en su ser; la piedra eternamente quiere ser piedra y el tigre un tigre.' *Borges y Yo* (the 'eternamente', relevant to the Chinese Empire, disappears in the standard English translation).

Chapter 2: Chinese Emperors and Western-Style Conquest

130   Gibbon, *Decline and Fall,* Vol. I, p. 41.
131   Bai Shouyi, *Outline History*, p. 81.
132   Sima Qian, *Records of the Grand Historian: Qin Dynasty*, 1993, p. 38.
133   Giles' translation.
134   Quoted from Bodde, 'The State and Empire of Ch'in', p. 56.
135   Hevia, *Cherishing Men From Afar*, p.30.
136   One typical example may be found in a newspaper article discussing the 2008 British Museum exhibition:
         The First Emperor, Qin Shi Huangdi, was the founder of China: in the 11 short years of his rule between 221 and 210 BC, he united the separate states of China, standardised the written language, law, coinage, weights and measurements, and set up a centralised bureaucracy to administer his huge empire. Napoleon's rule of Europe approaches the First Emperor's extraordinary achievement, but while the French empire quickly fragmented, *the China united by Qin Shi Huangdi in 221 BC is the world's oldest political entity.* [My italics.]
         From *The Guardian*, 22 August 2007; http://arts.guardian.co.uk/art/heritage/story/0,,2153766,00.html.
137   Quoted from Steindhardt, *Chinese Imperial City Planning,* p. 53.
138   Sima Qian, *Records*, pp. 47–8
139   Quoted from Mair et al (eds), *Hawai'i Reader in Traditional Chinese Culture*, p. 157.
140   Bodde, 'The State and Empire of Ch'in', p. 61.
141   *Ibid.*, p. 56.
142   See the map in Steinhardt, *Chinese Imperial City Planning*, p. 21.
143   *Ibid.*, p. 263.
144   Quoted in Burman, *The World Before Columbus*, pp. 64–5.
145   Gibbon, *Decline and Fall,* Vol. 6, Chapter LXIV, Part II, and Footnote 28, p. 310.
146   Allsen, 'The rise of the Mongolian empire', p. 348.
147   J.D. Langlois, quoted in David Morgan, *The Mongols* (Oxford: Blackwell, 1986), p. 123.
148   Quoted from Arthur F. Wright, 'The Cosmology of the Chinese City', in Skinner, *The City in Late Imperial China,* p. 47.
149   Quoted from Nancy Steinhardt, *Chinese Imperial City Planning*, p. 33. This, as Steinhardt shows in her study, is a good rough description of any of the nine Chinese cities that have served as capital (Xi'an, Beijing, Luoyang, Nanjing, Kaifeng, Hangzhou, Datong, Chengdu and Ye – the last and least known being the Wei capital in Hebei in the third century BC) and many smaller imperial cities too. For of the 100 walled Eastern Zhou cities that were built, about twenty have been excavated and between them have only three different plans (*Ibid.*, p. 41).
150   Marco Polo, *The Travels of Marco Polo, The Complete Yule-Cordier Edition,* pp. 374–5 (Book II, Chapter XI).
151   Rossabi, 'The Reign of Khubilai Khan', p. 457. Later the Ming shifted the axis of the imperial city, centring it on the new Forbidden City and the area to its south, which later became Tiānānmén Square; thus the Drum Tower was no longer at the centre and one of

Qubilai's favourite places, the Miàoyīng Sì (Miaoying Temple), with its splendid white dagoba, lies off the main axis of the Ming city.

152 Mote, *Imperial China*, p. 450.
153 Franke, 'Could the Mongol Emperors read and write Chinese?', pp. 29–30.
154 Franke, 'Sino-Western Contacts under the Mongol Empire', p. 52.
155 Rossabi, 'The Reign of Khubilai Khan', p. 453.
156 Morgan, *The Mongols*, pp. 126–7.
157 Mote, *Imperial China*, p. 492.
158 Rossabi, 'The Reign of Khubilai Khan', p. 450.
159 Perdue, *China Marches West: The Qing Conquest of Central Eurasia,* p. 335.
160 *Ibid.*, p. 507; Waley-Cohen makes the same point in *The Culture of War in China: Empire and the Military under the Qing Dynasty,* pp. 90–1.
161 Quoted from John E. Herman, 'The Cant of Conquest: Tusi Offices and China's Political Incorporation of the Southwest Frontier', in Crossley, Pamela (ed.), *Empire at the Margins: Culture, Ethnicity, and Frontier in Early Modern China*, pp. 135–68, p. 160.
162 Joanna Waley-Cohen, 'Military Ritual and the Qing Empire', p. 405.
163 *Beijing, The Lonely Planet Guide,* 2002, p. 81.
164 Evelyn S. Rawski, *The Last Emperor*, 1998, p. 35.
165 Quoted in Ann Paludan's *Chronicle of the Chinese Emperors* (London: Thames and Hudson, 2003), p. 192.
166 Thomas Barfield, *The Perilous Frontier: Nomadic Empires and China, 221 BC to AD 175*, p. 267.
167 Waley-Cohen, *The Culture of War,* p. 73.
168 Waley-Cohen, 'Military Ritual and the Qing Empire', pp. 412–26, and *The Culture of War*, pp. 71–5.
169 S.C.M. Paine, *Imperial Rivals: China, Russia, and Their Disputed Frontier*, p. 4.
170 Hostetler, *Qing Colonial Enterprise*, p. 75.
171 Crossley, *A Translucent Mirror: History and Identity in Qing Imperial Ideology*, p. 221.
172 Gong Zizheng, *Xiyu zhi xingsheng yi,* in Wang Pei (ed.), *Gong Zizheng quan ji,* Beijing: Zhonghua Shuju, 1959, pp. 105–112.
173 Quoted in Millward, *Beyond the Pass*, p. 199.
174 Quoted in Teng and Fairbank, *China's Response,* p. 152.
175 Quoted in Watson, *The Frontiers of China*, p. 12.
176 Crossley, *Translucent Mirror*, p. 360.
177 Mao Tse tung, *Poems* (Beijing: Shangwu Publishing, 1976), pp. 46–8.

Chapter 3: The Persistence of Empire

178 See André Malraux's *Human Condition* (London: Methuen, 1935) p. 120; Jules Roy's *Journey Through China* (London: Faber and Faber, 1965, p. 30); and Lin Handa and Cao Yuzhang's *Tales from Five Thousand Years of Chinese History* (Shanghai: Shanghai Press & Publishing, 2004).
179 Lewis, *The Early Chinese Empires: Qin and Han*, p. 2.
180 Wilkinson, *Chinese History: A Manual*, p. 181.
181 Prasenjit, *Rescuing History from the Nation: Questioning Narratives of Modern China*, p. 41.
182 Quoted from Prasenjit, *Rescuing History*, p. 43.
183 Voltaire, *A Philosophical Dictionary, in The Works of Voltaire* (New York: E.R. DuMont, 1901), Vol. I, Part II, p. 158.
184 John Thomson, *Through China With a Camera* (London: Constable, 1898), p. 269.
185 Quoted from Richard Bodman's Introduction to Su and Wang, *Deathsong of the River*, p. 13.
186 Abru, *A Persian Embassy*, pp. 31–2.
187 Bell, *Travels from St Petersburg,* Vol. I, p. 331–2.

188 Here is a recent example from a gullible travel writer: 'Stretching about 4,000 miles – the distance from London to Chicago – from the Bay of Bohai on the Yellow Sea to Jiayguan in the Gobi desert, the wall stands about 23 feet high and dates back to the third century BC.' (Claire Wrathall, *The Independent*, 15 February 2007).

189 Cranmer-Byng, *Journal*, p. 57.

190 W.A.P. Martin, *The Awakening of China* (New York: Doubleday, Page and Company, 1907), p. 140.

191 Lattimore, *Inner Asian Frontiers of China*, p. 429.

192 Wheatley, *The Pivot of the Four Quarters: A preliminary enquiry into the origins and character of the ancient Chinese city*: the outer city wall was known as kuo, which 'acquired overtones associated with fortification and subsequently developed the secondary meaning of 'suburb', p.187.

193 From the Shih chi, translated by Burton Watson, *Records of the Grand Historian*, Vol. II, p. 160.

194 Waldron, *The Great Wall: From History to Myth*, p. 28.

195 *Ibid.*, p. 43.

196 Julia Lovell, *The Great Wall: China Against the World 1000 BC – AD 2000*, p. 229.

197 Martini, *Novus Atlas Sinensis*, p. 12.

198 Kircher, *China Monumentis qua Sacris quà Profanis*, p. 217.

199 Quoted in Waldron, *The Great Wall*, p. 206.

200 For example, in a speech in Nanjing in 1911, quoted in Harrison, *China*, p. 138.

201 *Ibid.*, p. 215.

202 Mao Tse-tung, *Poems*, p. 44.

203 Repeated in the travel article cited above: 'Most visitors from Beijing flock to places such as Shuiguan or Badaling, where you'll keep reading notices proclaiming, "He who does not reach the Great Wall is not a true man."' (Claire Wrathall, *The Independent*, 15 February 2007).

204 Tan, *Jianming Zhongguolishi*, Vol. 1., p. 59.

205 *China*, Lonely Planet, 2000, p. 228.

206 As if to stress the 'imperial' nature of British sea power, HMS *Cornwallis* was actually built in an Indian shipyard.

207 Spence, *The Search for Modern China*, p. 708.

208 http://www.hkex.com.hk/data/chidimen/CD_MC.htm.

209 Snow, *The Fall of Hong Kong*, p. 266.

210 *Ibid.*, p. 297.

211 In an interview with the British journalist Gordon Harmon, December 1946, quoted in Snow, *The Fall of Hong Kong: Britain, China and the Japanese Occupation*, p. 312.

212 *Ibid.*, pp. 345–7.

213 'Hu Recognises HK's desire for democracy', *South China Morning Post*, 10 April 2007.

214 Reported on the anniversary in *China Daily*, 1 August 2007.

215 This argument is developed in detail by Christopher R. Hughes in his *Chinese Nationalism in the Global Era*, pp. 14–19.

Chapter 4: Apparent Closure: the Ming Paradox

216 Bretschneider, *Medieval Researches from Eastern Asiatic Sources*, Vol. II, pp. 144–5.

217 *Ibid.*, p. 147.

218 Yen, *Coolies and Mandarins: China's Protection of Overseas Chinese During the Late Ching's Period (1851–1911)*, pp. 8–9.

219 Abru, *A Persian Embassy*, p. 56.

220 The most detailed account is in Susan Naquin's *Peking: Temples and City Life 1400–1900*, pp. 109–70.

221 Dreyer, *Zheng He: China and the Oceans in the Early Ming Dynasty 1404–1433*, p. 5.

222 Quoted in Wang Gungwu, 'Early Ming Relations with Southeast Asia: A Background Essay', p. 54.

223 Levathes, *When China Ruled the Seas: the treasure fleet of the Dragon Throne, 1405–1433*, p. 43; see also Donnelly, *The Chinese Junk and Other Native Craft*, pp. 15–16.

224 Ibn Battuta, *Travels*, p. 235.

225 Although these crews sound enormous, Marco Polo writes of crews of 300 men and of junks that can carry 5,000 to 6,000 baskets of pepper and have sixty cabins for merchants, *Travels*, op.cit., Vol. II, p. 250 (Book III, Chapter 1).

226 In Ma Huan, *Ying-yai Sheng-lan*, p. 56.

227 Pelliot, 'Les grands voyages maritimes chinois', pp. 273–74 .

228 Ma Huan, *Ying-yai Sheng-lan*, p. 19.

229 Abru, *A Persian Embassy*, p. 83.

230 *Ibid.*, pp. 84–5.

231 *Ibid.*, pp. 71–2.

232 Quoted in Needham, *Science and Civilisation in China*, IV, Part III, p. 488.

233 Quoted in Wang, 'Ming Foreign Relations', p. 311.

234 *Ibid.*, p. 92.

235 *Ibid.*, p. 85.

236 *Ibid.*, p. 129.

237 *Ibid.*, p. 97, p. 178.

238 *Ibid.*, p. 85.

239 *Ibid.*, p. 107.

240 *Ibid.*, p. 129.

241 *Ibid.*, p. 137.

242 *Ibid.*, p. 153.

243 *Ibid.*, p. 146.

244 Ma Huan, *Ying-Yai Sheng-Lan*, pp. 21–22; Levathes, *When China Ruled the Seas*, pp. 195–203.

245 Quoted in Levathes, *When China Ruled the Seas*, pp. 163–4; Taica lies on the south bank of the Chang Jiang, a few miles upstream from Shanghai, where presumably the ships in question were waiting to set sail.

246 Dreyer, *Zheng He*, p. 181.

247 Spence, *The Search for Modern China*, p. 7.

248 Lovell, *The Great Wall*, pp. 207–8.

249 Duyvendak, *China's Discovery of Africa*, p. 27.

250 Quoted in Needham, *Science and Civilisation in China*, IV, Part III, p. 525.

251 *Ibid.*, pp. 526 7.

252 Wang Gungwu, *China and the Overseas Chinese*, p. 127.

253 Gallagher, *China in the Sixteenth Century*, pp. 54–5.

254 Bell, *Travels from St Petersburg*, pp. 181–6.

255 The title *He Shang*, which literally means 'River' (*He*) 'Die ahead of one's time' (*Shang*), has been variously translated as 'River Elegy', 'River Dirge', 'The River Dies Young' and 'Deathsong of the River'. Although the last of these is the title of the English translation of the volume by the authors of the original film, 'River Elegy' seems to be used more often by other authors and is preferred here. The script, together with introductory material, commentary and criticism, was published soon afterwards, and may in found translated into English in Su, Xiaokang, and Wang, Luxiang, *Deathsong of the River: A Reader's Guide to the Chinese TV Series Heshang*, trans. W. Bodman and Pin P. Wan (Ithaca: Cornell University Press, 1991).

256 Su and Wang, *Deathsong*, p. 103.

257 *Ibid*, p. 130.

258 *Ibid*, pp. 130–1.

259 Quoted from Richard Bodman's introduction to *Deathsong of the River*, 'From History to Allegory to Art', p. 12.

260 Su and Wang, op.cit., p. 184; in fact some of these ideas appear in less dramatic form in Lyn Pan's book of that title: *China's Sorrow: Journeys Around the Yellow River* (London: Century, 1985).

261 Su and Wang, *Deathsong*, p. 190.

262 I remember, two years later, working in Rome with some Chinese telecommunications experts who had come from Shanghai. After two days of lectures about telecoms strategies and technical visits, they were given an afternoon free and asked whether they would like to visit St Peters or the Forum. But their only interest was to see the 'blue sea', so we took them to Anzio – where they spent an hour photographing the sea. The significance was lost on me at the time!

263 Su and Wang, *Deathsong*, pp. 211–3.

264 *Ibid.*, p. 214.

265 *Ibid.*, p. 216.

266 *Ibid.*, pp. 219–20.

267 Tu, Wei-ming, 'Cultural China', p. 152.

268 James Lull, *China Turned On: Television, Reform and Resistance,* p. 143.

269 Dittmer and Kim, 'Whither China's Quest for National Identity', in Dittmer & Kim (eds), *China's Quest for National Identity,* p. 268.

270 Speech at Harvard, 5 September 1943, on being awarded an honorary degree; available at http://www.winstonchurchill.org/i4a/pages/index.cfm?pageid=424the.

Chapter 5: The Invisible Chinese Empire

271 Bretschneider, *Medieval Researches,* Vol. II, pp. 316–23.

272 Attwater, *Adam Schall: A Jesuit at the Court of China 1592–1666,* pp. 98–100.

273 *Ibid.*, p. 98. A later example is that of the last emperor, Puyi, learning the use of a knife and fork and calling himself Henry as he imitated the habits of his tutor Reginald Johnston. He also liked to leave the palace and dine in Johnston's private home in a street demolished in 1950 and absorbed into Tiananmen Square (Raymond Lamont-Brown, *Tutor to the Dragon Emperor,* p. 80).

274 Michael Ng-Quinn, 'National Identity in Premodern China: Formation and Role Enactment', in Dittmer & Kim (eds), *China's Quest for National Identity,* p. 43.

275 Bodde, *Chinese Thought, Society and Science: The Intellectual and Social Background of Science and Technology in Pre-modern China,* p. 27.

276 As Professor John Wills pointed out in a letter to *The Economist*, this usage is in fact incorrect: 'The written language is Chinese; Mandarin and other names refer to its widespread standard pronunciation.' The Economist, 10 November 2006.

277 For a good succinct account of the transition from classical Chinese to Middle Chinese and then to Mandarin, see Wilkinson, *Chinese History,* pp. 18–28.

278 Harbsmeier, *Science and Civilisation,* Vol. 7, Part I, p. 29.

279 Blum and Jensen (eds), *China Off Center: Mapping the Margins of the Middle Kingdom,* p. 159.

280 For example, by Christoph Harbsmeier, in Needham, *Science and Civilisation,* Vol. 7, p. 29.

281 Derk Bodde, *Chinese Thought,* p. 19.

282 Joshua A. Fogel, 'Chinese Understanding of the Japanese Language from Ming to Qing', in Fogel (ed.), *Sagacious Monks and Bloodthirsty Warriors: Chinese Views of Japan in the Ming-Qing Period,* p. 63.

283 Jonathan Spence, *The Search for Modern China,* p. 118.

284 Wilkinson, *Chinese History,* pp. 194–5.

285 *Ibid.*

286 In Ronald Hyman, *Britain's Imperial Century 1815–1914* (London: Batsford, 1976), p. 37.

287 The European Diary of Hsieh Fucheng, *Envoy Extraordinary of Imperial China* (New York: St Martin's Press, 1993), p. 22.

288 Hobson, *The Eastern Origins of Western Civiliation,* p. 129.

289   Marco Polo, *Travels*, p. 423 (Book II, Chapter XXIV).

290   W. Montgomery Watt, *The Influence of Islam on Medieval Europe* (Edinburgh: Edinburgh University Press, 1972), p. 25.

291   For example, Robert Curzon and G.F Hudson, quoted in Hobson, *Eastern Origins*, pp. 185–6.

292   Needham, *Science and Civilisation*, Vol. 5, Part 7, p. 1.

293   *Ibid.*, p. 16.

294   Lach, *Asia in the Making of Europe*, Vol. II, Book Three, pp. 397–8.

295   Hobson, *Eastern Origins*, p. 131.

296   Bray, *Science and Civilisation*, Vol. 6, Part II, pp. 430–3.

297   See the section entitled 'Did China Contribute to Europe's Agricultural Revolution', in Bray, *Science and Civilisation*, Vol. 6, Part II, pp. 558–587.

298   Hobson, *Eastern Origins*, p. 204–5.

299   Bray, *Science and Civilisation*, Vol. 6, Part II, p. 571.

300   *Ibid.*, p. 174.

301   *Ibid.*, p. 377.

302   *Ibid.*, p. 585.

303   Quoted in Pomeranz, *The Great Divergence: China, Europe, and the Making of the Modern World Economy*, p. 45.

304   Hobson, *Eastern Origins*, pp. 213–4.

305   http://www.ironbridge.org.uk/our_attractions/the_iron_bridge_and_tollhouse/.

306   http://www.ironbridge.org.uk/our_attractions/coalbrookdale_museum_of_iron/.

307   Temple, *The Genius of China; 3,000 years of Science, Discovery, and Invention*, p. 68.

308   Hobson, *Eastern Origins*, p. 215.

309   Steinhardt, *Chinese Architecture*, pp. 125–7.

310   Wang Gungwu, *The Nanhai Trade: Early Chinese Trade in the South China Sea*, p. 26.

311   Needham, *Science and Civilisation*, Vol. IV, Part III, p. 488.

312   Shina Yoshinobu, 'Sung Foreign Trade: Its Scope and Organization', in Rossabi (ed.), *China Among Equals: The Middle Kingdom and Its Neighbors: 10th to 14th Centuries*, pp. 104–5

313   Ma Huan, *Ying-Yai Sheng-Lan*, pp. 98–9; the original translation has the older form of 'Kwang Tung'.

314   Ng, Chin-keong, *Trade and Society: The Amoy Network on the China Coast, 1683–1725*, p. 53.

315   Roderich Ptach, 'Ming Maritime Trade to Southeast Asia, 1368–1567: Visions of a System', in Ptach, *China, the Portuguese, and the Nanyang*, pp. 170–7.

316   John W. Wills, 'Relations with Maritime Europe', p. 334.

317   Atwell, 'Ming China and the Emerging World Economy, *c.* 1470–1650', p. 391.

318   *Ibid.*, n. 53.

319   *Ibid.*, p. 394.

320   *Ibid.*, p. 396.

321   Jonathan Hay, 'The Diachronics of Early Qing Visual and Material Culture', in Struve (ed.), *The Qing Formation*, p. 318.

322   Warrington Smith, *Mast and Sail*, Chapter XII.

323   Van Dyke, *The Canton Trade: Life and Enterprise on the China Coast, 1700–1845*, p. 31.

324   *Ibid.*, p. 127.

325   *Ibid.*, p. 133.

326   *Ibid.*, pp. 33–5.

327   John E. Wills, 'Contingent Connections: Fujian, the Empire, and the Early Modern World', in Struve, *The Qing Formation*, p. 186.

328   Cartier, *Globalizing South China*, p. 99.

329   Quoted in Robert K. Sakai, 'The Ryukyu (Liu-Ch'iu) Islands as a Fief of Satsuma', in Fairbank (ed.), *The Chinese World Order*, pp. 112–14.

330   Austin, *China's Ocean Frontier: International Law, Military Force and National Development,* pp. 98–99.

331   *Ibid.*, p. 137.

332   *Ibid.*, p. 131.

333   Weale, B.L. Putnam, *The Fight for the Republic in China* (London: Hurst & Blackett, 1918). This was the literary pseudonym of Bertram Lennox Simpson (1877–1930). He was the son of C.L. Simpson (1843–1909), who worked in the Chinese Maritime Customs Service for over forty years. Bertram Lennox followed his father into the Service, before turning to sensationalist journalism and novels.

334   Rowbotham, 'The Impact of Confucianism', p. 227.

335   Mungello, *Curious Land*, p. 260.

336   Quoted in Mungello, *Curious Land: Jesuit Accomodation and the Origins of Sinology,* p. 287.

337   Hobson, *Eastern Origins*, p. 195.

338   Theodore Michael Foss, 'The European Sojourn of Philippe Couplet and Michael Shen Fuzong', p. 129.

339   Quoted in *Ibid.*, p. 130.

340   Iris Chang, *The Chinese in America: a Narrative History*, p. 26.

341   Foss, *The European Sojourn*, p. 133.

342   Nicholas Standaert, *Handbook of Christianity in China,* Vol. I, p. 741.

343   A good reproduction may be seen at http://www.wga.hu/frames-e.html?/html/k/kneller/chinese.html.

344   Foss, *The European Sojourn*, p. 137; sadly, Michael died of an epidemic on the ship that was taking him back to China in 1691.

345   See the chapter 'Tea Comes to the West', in Macfarlane, *The Empire of Tea*, pp. 65–75.

346   Pepys, *Diary*, 25 September, 1660.

347   Pepys, *Diary*, 28 May 1665.

348   Roberts, in *China to Chinatown*, p. 171.

349   Iris Chang, *The Chinese in America*, p. 48.

350   *Ibid.*, p. 48; Roberts repeats this story in *China to Chinatown*, pp. 138–9; in Carl Crow's version from the 1930s, the Chinese restaurateur who improvised the dish translated it as 'beggar's hash' (*400 Million Customers*, p. 219).

351   Lynn Pan, *Sons of the Yellow Emperor*, pp. 333–4; Anderson, in his *The Food of China,* cites the autobiography of Li Shu-fan, *Hong Kong Surgeon* (1964) as stating that chop suey is a traditional dish from Toisan, south of Guangzhou, whence many immigrants left for the USA (p. 212).

352   Roberts, *China to Chinatown,* p. 136.

353   *Ibid.*, pp. 146–8.

354   *Ibid.*, pp. 156–7.

355   *Ibid.*, p. 174.

356   *Ibid.*, p. 181.

357   *Ibid.*, p. 193.

358   Quoted in *Ibid.*, p. 203.

359   The speech may be found at http://www.guardian.co.uk/racism/Story/0,2763,477023,00.html.

Chapter 6: The Overseas Chinese

360   The list may be seen at http://www.library.ohiou.edu/subjects/shao/databases_popdis.htm.

361   For example, Seagrave, *Lords of the Rim: The Invisible Empire of the Overseas Chinese*, p. 2; Yeung, *Globalization of Chinese Business Firms*, p. 7.

362   Weidenbaum and Hughes, *The Bamboo Network: How Expatriate Chinese Entrepreneurs Are Creating a New Economic Superpower in Asia*, p. 8.

363 Conference: 'I pronto moda cinesi: una risorsa da valorizzare', organised by Confartigianato Prato, Prato, 17 January 2005.

364 Quoted in William C. Hannas, *The Writing on the Wall*, p. 45.

365 Peter J. Kuhn and Carol McAusland, 'The International Migration of Knowledge Workers: When is a Brain Drain Beneficial?', Working Paper 12761, (Washington: National Bureau of Economic Research, December 2006).

366 Frank Dikötter, 'Race in China', in Nyíri and Breidenbach, *China Inside Out*, p. 203.

367 Lin Yutang, *My Country and My People* (Beijing: Foreign Language Teaching and Research Press, 1998), pp. 18–19; Thomas Barfield, *The Perilous Frontier*, p. 267.

368 Wills, 'Relations with Maritime Europeans', p. 357.

369 Iris Chang, *The Chinese in America*, p. 46.

370 Wang Gungwu, *The Chinese Overseas*, p. 47; earlier migrations, given the size of the country, were usually internal and in three types represented by the words *yimin*, 'moved people', *liumin*, 'dispersed people', and *nanmin*, 'refugees'.

371 Yen, *Coolies and Mandarins*, pp. 20–21.

372 Lin Yutang, *My Country*, p. 19.

373 Arthur H. Smith, *Chinese Characteristics*, p. 147.

374 Leong, *Migration and Ethnicity in Chinese History: Hakkas, Pengmin, and Their Neighbors*, p. 63.

375 Seagrave, *Lords of the Rim*, pp. 116–7; Lynn Pan, *Sons of the Yellow Emperor*, pp. 13–17.

376 Steven W. Mosher, *Broken Earth: The Rural Chinese* (London: Collier Macmillan, 1983), p. 36.

377 On 14 October 2006, the National Bureau of Statistics announced a list of the richest towns in China. No. 1 was in Jiangsu, but No. 2 was Humen, just across the Pearl River Delta from the Teochiu strongholds, about half-way between Macao and Guangzhou.

378 Waldinger, Roger, 'Immigrant Enterprise in the United States', in *Structure of Capital*, ed. Sharon Lukin and Paul DiMaggio (New York: CUP, 1990), p. 407.

379 E. Burton Holmes, *Travelogues: Down the Amur; Peking; The Forbidden City* (Chicago & New York: The Travelogue Bureau, 1914), pp. 134–5.

380 See Gordon Redding and Gilbert Y. Y. Wong, 'The Psychology of Chinese Organizational Behaviour', in Michael Harris Bond (ed.), *The Psychology of the Chinese People* (Oxford: OUP, 1986), p. 272.

381 Prasenjit, *Rescuing History*, p. 232.

382 Maria Chang, 'Greater China and the Chinese "Global Tribe"', p. 955.

383 Kao Cheng-shu, quoted in Yao, *Confucian Capitalism: Discourse, practice and the myth of Chinese enterprise*, p. 142.

384 'Suharto Inc', *Time*, 24 May 1999.

385 Quoted in Yao, *Confucian Capitalism*, p. 27.

386 Lever-Tracy, Ip and Tracy, *The Chinese Diaspora and Mainland China: An Emerging Economic Synergy*, p. 25.

387 From a Salim Group Brochure quoted in Marleen Dieleman and Wladimir Sachs, 'Economies of Scope and Economies of Connectedness: Illustrated by the Salim Group of Indonesia' (University of Leiden: Working Paper, July 2005), p. 10.

388 Lever-Tracy, Ip and Tracy, *The Chinese Diaspora*, p. 36.

389 http://www.cosco.com/en/global_offices/staff.jsp?catId=270; http://www.cosco-salim. com.cn.

390 Chatri Sophonpanich was No. 17 on Forbes Rich List for Thailand in 2006; http://www. forbes.com/business/global/2006/0724/045_2.html.

391 http://www.bangkokbank.com/Bangkok+Bank/About+Bangkok+Bank/History/default. htm.

392 http://www.bangkokbank.com/Bangkok+Bank/About+Bangkok+Bank/default.htm.

393 At the end of June 2006: Asia Financial Holdings Ltd, Interim Report 2006, p. 32.

394 'Overseas Chinese offer firm support', *China Daily*, 15 March 2005.

395   http://www.ln.edu.hk/lingnan_event/press_releases/press_releases_contents.shtml?060425.
       htm.

396   This biographical information is taken from Asia Financial Group's Annual Report 2006,
       available at: http://www.asia-financial.com/index.html.

397   Lever-Tracy, Ip and Tracy, *The Chinese Diaspora,* p. 104.

398   http://www.aca.co.id/.

399   Company Report for 2006, http://www.firstpacco.com/eng/ir/finreports.php; the interim
       report for the First Half of 2007 reported 20 per cent growth in profits, to $300 million
       (http://www.firstpacco.com/eng/ir/presentations.php).

400   *Ibid.*, p. 8

401   Marleen Dieleman and Wladimir Sachs, 'Economies of Scope and Economies of
       Connectedness: Illustrated by the Salim Group of Indonesia' (University of Leiden:
       Working Paper, July 2005), p. 8.

402   Company Report 2006, *Ibid.*

403   Pan (ed.), *The Encyclopedia of Chinese Overseas*, p. 113.

404   Yeung (ed.), *Globalization of Chinese Business Firms*, pp. 92–3.

405   Piruna Polsiri and Yupana Wiwattanakantang, *Business Groups in Thailand: Before and after
       the East Asian Financial Crisis* (Center for Economic Institutions, Hitotsubashi University,
       Working Paper No.13, 2004).

406   http://www.cpthailand.com/.

407   Quoted by Simon Long, 'The Overseas Chinese', *Prospect Magazine* (Issue 29), April 1998.

408   Lever-Tracy, *The Chinese Diaspora,* pp. 117–8.

409   http://www.forbes.com/lists/results.jhtml.

410   Wang Gungwu, *The Overseas Chinese*, p. 100.

411   Chang, *The Chinese in America*, p. 26.

412   *Ibid.*, p. 45.

413   The story is told by Robert Joe Stout, 'Chinese Immigrants on America's Western
       Frontier', at http://www.historynet.com/exploration/westward_expansion/3037936.
       html?featured=y&c=y.

414   Chang, *The Chinese in America*, p. 77.

415   Collis Huntingdon, quoted by Iris Chang, *The Chinese in America,* p. 57.

416   Mark Twain, *Roughing It* (Hartford (CT): American Publishing Company, 1871), p. 142.

417   Chang, *The Chinese in America,* p. 168.

418   *Ibid.*, p. 226.

419   *Ibid.*, p. 234.

420   http://www.house.gov/wu/bio.htm.

421   Pan (ed.), *Encyclopedia*, p. 304.

422   *Ibid.*, p. 306.

423   From Thomas Burke, 'The Chink and the Child', in *Limehouse Nights* (New York: Robert
       M. McBride & Company, 1917).

424   Obituary in *The Guardian,* Friday 17 December 2004; http://media.guardian.co.uk/site/
       story/0,14173,1375804,00.html.

425   http://www.ospp.com/index.jsp (only in Chinese).

426   Hsu, *Dreaming of Gold, Dreaming of Home*, p. 166; Chapter 6, pp. 156–75, is devoted to Chen Yixi.

427   *Ibid.*, p. 173.

428   Bureau of Archives of Taishan City; http://www.tsinfo.com.cn/en/xntls/1.htm ; see also
       Shen Shehong, *Being Chinese, Becoming Chinese American* (Chicago: University of Illinois
       Press, 2002, of which the relevant chapter, Chapter 4, is online at http://www.press.
       uillinois.edu/epub/books/chen/ch4.html).

429   *Wall Street Journal*, 12 October 2006.

430   Pan (ed.), *Encyclopedia*, p. 111.

431 Lever-Tracy, *The Chinese Diaspora*, p. 76, quoting the Fujian Statistical Yearbook.

432 *Ibid.*, p. 171.

433 John Whalley and Xian Xin, 'China's FDI and Non-FDI Economies and the Sustainability of Future High Chinese Growth' (Cambridge, MA: National Bureau of Economic Research, Working Paper 12249, May 2000), p. 3.

434 Quoted in Shen, 'Doing Chineseness': *Taiwanese Capital in China*, p. 9.

435 See, for example, the article in the local Milanese news in Corriere della Sera, 13 April 2007 (http://www.corriere.it/vivimilano/cronache/articoli/2007/04_Aprile/12/cinesi_sarpi_vigili.shtml).

436 In Teng and Fairbank, *China's Response to the West*, p. 269.

437 Bobbitt, *The Shield of Achilles: War, Peace and the Course of History*, p. 675.

438 Landes, *The Wealth and Poverty of Nations: Why Some Are So Rich and Some So Poor*, p. 477.

439 *Asia Times*, 10 December, 2002.

Chapter 7: Why Chinese Culture Stops at the Border

440 Joseph S. Nye, 'The Changing Nature of World Power', *Political Science Quarterly*, 105 (2), Summer 1990, pp. 177–92; pp. 181–2; see also 'Soft power', *Foreign Policy* 80, Fall 1990, pp. 153–171. A much earlier example of real 'soft power' in harness with 'hard power' was the introduction of Roman baths to barbarian Britain together with harsh military rule.

441 A joint prize was awarded for Physics in 1962 to Tsung-Dao Lee and Chien-Shiung Wu; Daniel Chee Tsui, who is Taiwanese-American, also won a prize for Physics, in 1998. All three did their graduate research in US universities, became Chinese Americans, and never returned to work in China. Many Chinese economists think that they should be given at least one Nobel Prize in recognition for the stunning economic achievements and growth of the past twenty-five years (See Gries, *China's New Nationalism: Pride, Politics, and Diplomacy*, p. 67).

442 Bodde, *Chinese Thought*, explains this in much greater detail, pp. 120–121; see also Wilkinson, *Chinese History*, pp. 185–6.

443 Gallagher, *China in the Sixteenth Century*, p. 27.

444 Biography and photographs may be found at http://news.tsinghua.edu.cn/new/news.php?id=511; the story is available in Chinese at many websites and blogs, for example http://www.chemilab.net/typo3/Classical-Prose-2.115.0.html. It may also be found in Tim Clissold's book *Mr China*, p. 162.

445 Bodde, *Chinese Thought*, p. 73.

446 See Sidney D. Gamble and John Stewart Burgess, *Peking, A Social Survey* (New York: George H. Doran, 1921), p. 55.

447 All quotes in this paragraph are from the translation by Victor H. Mair in Mair et al (eds), *Hawai'i Reader in Traditional Chinese Culture*, pp. 617–41.

448 Bodde, *Chinese Thought*, p. 85.

449 The 'hundred' (used in the sense of 'many') listed in verse all 438 surnames in use in the tenth century; as the child memorised these names the ritual chanting of the names echoed in his mind like a litany of society and emphasised the importance of family relationships. These still account for most surnames today.

450 Wang Shiqing, *Lu Xun: A Biography* (Beijing: Foreign Languages Press, 1984), pp. 15–6.

451 Elman, *Cultural Examination of Civil Examinations in Late Imperial China*, p. 737.

452 *Ibid.*, p. 293.

453 *Ibid.*, p. 76.

454 *Ibid.*, p. 164.

455 *Ibid.*, p. 141.

456   *Ibid.*, p. 291.

457   *Ibid.*, p. xxxix.

458   Fairbank, *The United States and China*, p. 43.

459   Bodde, *Chinese Thought*, p. 29.

460   Arthur F. Wright, quoted in Bodde, *Chinese Thought*, p. 30.

461   This phrase is from an article by a certain 'Mr Chi Li' quoted by Bertrand Russell in his book *The Problem of China* (London: George Allen & Unwin, 1922), p.37.

462   Hannas, *The Writing on the Wall*, p. 246.

463   Wang Wei, quoted in Sirén, *The Chinese on the Art of Painting*, p. 17.

464   Sirén, *Art of Painting*, p. 34–5.

465   Jullien, *In Praise of Blandness: Proceeding from Chinese Thought and Aesthetics*, p. 37.

466   Yao Tsui (*c.* 550), in Sirén, *Art of Painting*, p. 221.

467   Quoted in Rowbotham, *Missionary and Mandarin*, p. 275.

468   Kwo, *Chinese Brushwork in Calligraphy and Painting: Its History, Aesthetics, and Techniques*, p. 74.

469   Quoted from Susan Bush, 'The Essay on Painting by Wang Wei (415–453) in Context', in Cai, Zong-qi (ed.), *Chinese Aesthetics: The Ordering of Literature, the Arts, and the Universe in the Six Dynasties*, pp. 60–80, p. 70.

470   Naquin, *Peking*, p. 259.

471   Li Yü, in his *Summary of the History of Chinese Fine Arts* (Beijing, 1957); the second critic was Archbishop Lo Kuang of Tapei; both are quoted from Cécile and Michel Beurdeley, *Giuseppe Castiglione*, pp. 151–2.

472   Staunton, *An Authentic Account*, Vol. II, pp. 308–9; Michael Sullivan observes that 'the typical Chinese painting makes no use of scientific perspective, shading, or plastic three-dimensional modeling, and uses colour very sparingly or not at all.' He has examined all the major Chinese landscapes, for example, and found one single example of cast shadows (*Symbols of Eternity: The Art of Landscape Painting in China*, p. 8).

473   Quoted in Sullivan, *The Three Perfections: Chinese Painting, Poetry, and Calligraphy*, p. 46.

474   Quoted from Ronald Egan, 'Nature and Higher Ideals in Texts on Calligraphy, Music and Painting', in *Chinese Aesthetics*, op.cit., pp. 276–309, p. 278.

475   *Ibid.*

476   www.icbc-ltd.com.

477   Gallagher, *China in the Sixteenth Century*, p. 243.

478   One of the best short introductions to these techniques may be found in Steinhardt (ed.), *Chinese Architecture*, pp. 1–9.

479   Amiot, *De La Musique des Chinois*, p. 2.

480   Quoted in Standaert, *Handbook*, Vol. I, p. 856.

481   Gallagher, *China in the Sixteenth Century*, p. 336; see also p. 22.

482   Quoted by *An Authentic Account*, Vol. I, p. 262.

483   Levis, *Foundations of Chinese Musical Art*, p. 8.

484   *Ibid.*, p. 10.

485   *Ibid.*, p. 183.

486   *Ibid.*, p. 34.

487   The 'Canons of Shun', in *The Books of Documents*, quoted in Dewoskin, *Song for One or Two: Music and the Concept of Art in Early China*, p. 20.

488   In *The Book of Rites*, quoted in Levis, *Foundations*, p. 49.

489   *The Book of Rites* (Selections), Trans. Lao An, (Weifang: Shandong Friendship Press, 1999), p. 169; Chapters 37–39 of *The Book of Rites*, subtitled 'The Records of Music', discuss the role of music.

490   From *The Lingering Tones of Great Antiquity*, quoted by DeWoskin, *Song for One or Two*, p. 111.

491   Liang, *Music of the Billion: An Introduction to Chinese Musical Culture*, p. 209.

492   DeWoskin, *Song for One or Two*, p. 123.

493 Mentioned in Wu Zuguang, Huang Zuolin and Mei Shaowu, *Peking Opera and Mei Lanfang* (Beijing: New World Press, 1981, p. 65).

494 *Ibid.*, p. 198.

495 Bary, Wm. Theodore de, *The Trouble with Confucianism,* p. 45.

496 Quoted in John King Fairbank, *Chinabound: A Fifty-Year Memoir* (New York: Harper & Row, 1982), p. 89; Tsiang was Ambassador to the UN from 1947 to 1965.

497 Cao Xueqin, *A Dream of Red Mansions,* Trans. Yang Xianyi and Gladys Yang, (Beijing: Foreign Languages Press, 1994), 4 vols, Vol. I, pp. 5–6; this novel, originally published in 1791, enjoys the paradoxical double distinction of having been one of Mao Zedong's favourite books and having a dedicated theme park created during China's new boom.

Chapter 8: Finance, Brand and Sport: Fundamentals and Image

498 'China may be conducting a stealth attack on the Hong Kong stock exchange', *The Times*, 26 September 2007.

499 Goldstone, Jack A., 'The coming Chinese collapse', *Foreign Policy*, No. 99, 1995, pp. 35–52.

500 Julian Schuman, *Assignment China* (New York: Whitter Books, 1956), p. 237.

501 *Punch*, 10 February 1877.

502 *The Economist*, 26 October 2006; this example was given when reserves stood at $1 trillion.

503 Will Hutton, *The World We're In* (London: Abacus, 2003), p. 36.

504 'The United States and the Rise of China and India', published 11 October 2006, p. 34; available at http://www.thechicagocouncil.org/curr_pos.php.

505 Clay Chandler, 'Inside The New China Part communist, part capitalist – and full speed ahead', *Fortune*, 4 October 2004.

506 *World Economic Situation and Prospects 2007* (New York: United Nations, 2007), p. 4.

507 12-12-2005, 'China overtakes U.S. as world's leading exporter of information technology goods', OECD, http://www.oecd.org/document/60/0,2340,en_2649_201185_35834236_1_1_1_1,00.html.

508 Estimated by Sylvia Scwaag Serger in 'China: From Shop Floor to Knowledge Factory?' in *Internationalization of Corporate R&D. Leveraging the Changing Geography of Innovation*, ed. Magnus Karlsson (Stockholm: Institutet for Tillvaxtpolitiska Studier, 2006), p. 236.

509 http://www.wal-martchina.com/english/walmart/index.htm.

510 Navarro, *The Coming China Wars: Where They Will Be Fought and How They Can Be Won*, pp. 2–3.

511 Scwaag Serger, 'From Shop Floor to Knowledge Factory?', p. 236.

512 Eurostat, Euro-Indicators, 26 February 2007, http://epp.eurostat.ec.europa.eu/pls/portal/docs/PAGE/PGP_PRD_CAT_PREREL/PGE_CAT_PREREL_YEAR_2007/PGE_CAT_PREREL_YEAR_2007_MONTH_02/6-16022007-EN-AP.PDF.

513 Friedman, *The World is Flat: The Globalized World in the Twenty-First Century*, pp. 151–62.

514 The EICC, founded in 2005, has created 'standards to ensure that working conditions in the electronics industry supply chain are safe, that workers are treated with respect and dignity, and that manufacturing processes are environmentally responsible', is adhered to by all the major manufacturers with procurement in China, from Dell, IBM, HP and Lenovo to Philips, Sony, Intel and Cisco (see http://www.eicc.info/ for further information, and a Pdf copy of the Code). Compliance is required of all suppliers, including OEMs (Original Equipment Manufacturers) and ODMs (Original Design Manufacturers).

515 For example, in a speech on 1 April 2005, the Prime Minister Wen Jiabao said that 'science and technology are the decisive factors in the competition of comprehensive national strength.'

516 Fiona Gilmore and Serge Dumont, *Brand Warriors China: Creating Sustainable Brand Capital*, p. xvi–xvii.

517 This of course applies to brands. In terms of everyday products it is nearly impossible to escape products 'made in China', as Sarah Bongiorni proves amusingly in her book *A Year Without 'Made in China': One Family's True Life Adventure in the Global Economy* (New York: Wiley, 2007).

518 http://www.cqi.gov.cn.

519 See http://www.cohre.org/ and http://www.wsws.org/articles/2000/feb2000/olymp-f03. shtml respectively.

520 Beijing Organizing Committee (BOCOG), quoted in Close et al., *Beijing Olympiad: The Political Economy of a Sporting Mega-Event*, p. 15.

521 *Ibid.*, p. 20.

522 Quoted in Close et al., *Beijing Olympiad*, p. 95.

523 Bodde, *Chinese Thought*, pp. 295–6.

524 Headland Taylor, *Court Life*, p. 126

525 Crow, *400 Million Customers*, p. 240. Crow has recently been the subject of an entertaining biography: Paul French, *Carl Crow – A Tough Old China Hand: Life, Times, and Adventures of an American in Shanghai* (Hong Kong: Hong Kong University Press, 2006).

526 Yan Fu, *Yuan Qiang Xiudinggao*.

527 *Ibid.*, p. 15.

528 Liang Qichao, Xinmin Shuo Shi, pp. 108–9; translation in Morris, 'To Make the Four Hundred Million Move'.

529 Wu Wenzhong, *Zhongguo Tiyu Fazhan Shi*, p. 60.

530 L.C. Porter, quoted in Sidney D. Gamble and John Stewart Burgess, *Peking, A Social Survey* (New York: George H. Doran, 1921), p. 239.

531 Morris, 'To Make the Four Hundred Million Move', p. 889.

532 *Ibid.*, p. 892.

533 http://en.olympic.cn/games/summer/2004-03-27/121663.html; see also the account by Close et al., *Beijing Olympiad*, pp. 149–62.

534 On 16 November, as a result of this biased reporting, and probably jealousy about his success, Huang was obliged to resign his position as commentator for China Central Television (*China Daily*, 18 November 2006).

535 Larmer, *Operation Yao Ming: The Chinese Sports Empire, American Big Business. and the Making of an NBA Superstar*, p. 3–4.

536 In an interview from Colorado Springs, *Associated Press*, Saturday 5 August 2006.

Chapter 9: Nationalism, Militarism and Technology

537 Summarised from Q. Edward Wang, *Inventing China Through History: The May Fourth Approach to Historiography*, p. 174.

538 Quoted in Shih, *Navigating Sovereignty: World Politics Lost in China*, p. 38.

539 Su and Wang, *Deathsong*, p. 115.

540 Zhao Suisheng, *Chinese Foreign Policy: Pragmatism and Strategic Behaviour*, p. 66; *China's Pragmatic Nationalism*, p. 135.

541 Michael Hunt, in Dittmer and Kim (eds), *China's Quest for National Identity*, p. 63.

542 Steven W. Mosher, in *Hegemon: China's Plan to Dominate the World* (San Francisco: Encounter Books, 2000), p. 75.

543 See the section on the Senkaku incident in Gries, *China's New Nationalism: Pride, Politics, and Diplomacy*, pp. 121–5.

544 Gilley, *China's Democratic Future: How it Will Happen and Where it will Lead*, p. xiv.

545 Executive Summary, Annual Report to Congress: The Military Power of the People's Republic of China, Washington, Office of the Secretary of Defense, 2005 (no page number, but before p. i).

546 Executive Summary, Annual Report to Congress: The Military Power of the People's Republic of China, Washington, Office of the Secretary of Defense, 2007, p. 1.

547 Outlined in the White Paper, *China's National Defence in 2006*, Beijing: Information Office of the State Council of the People's Republic of China, 29 December 2006 (also available at http://english.people.com.cn/whitepaper/defense2006/defense2006.html).

548 Blasko, *The Chinese Army Today: Tradition and Transformation for the 21st Century*, p. 183. This book give the best updated and detailed account of the PLA's organisational structure, roles, units and manpower; a lot of basic information may be found at the PLA's website, http://english.chinamil.com.cn/.

549 See Ellis Joffe, 'The Chinese Army in Domestic Politics: Factors and phases', in Li Nan (ed.), *Chinese Civil-Military Relations: The Transformation of the People's Liberation Army*, pp. 8–24, in particular pp. 12–18.

550 For the American estimates see Figure 4, in Annual Report to Congress, op cit., p. 21. This Report argues (pp. 21–2) that the official budget does not include 'foreign weapons procurement (up to $3.0 billion annually from Russia alone), expenses for the paramilitary People's Armed Police, funding to support nuclear weapon stockpiles and the Second Artillery, subsidies to defense industries, some defense-related research and development, and local, provincial, or regional contributions to the armed forces.'

551 *People's Daily*, 5 March 2007; the 18 per cent increase in military expenditure was reported in most mainstream Western newspapers the next day.

552 Reported in *China Daily*, 2 August 2007.

553 Annual Report to Congress, 2006, Figure 4.

554 In a flurry of nationalistic pride both *China Daily* and *Xinhua* showed the new 'China-made' fighter in a series of photographs including a static runway display, training sessions and in-flight refuelling (31 December 2006).

555 *Xinhua*, 6 January 2007.

556 First announced by *Aviation Week & Space Technology*, 17 January 2007. Interestingly, Michael O'Hanlon, fellow of the Brookings Institution, warned a US House armed services subcommittee of the effects of a similar attack in June 2006, saying that 'I think most countries could pull off an anti-satellite strike on the first try.' (*New Scientist*, 23 June 2006).

557 http://www.ostp.gov/html/USper cent20Nationalper cent20Spaceper cent20Policy.pdf , p. 1.

558 *Ibid.*, p. 2; the Policy does however include a short paragraph on 'policies and practices aimed at debris minimization', which justifies complaints against China concerning the danger of orbital debris (p. 9).

559 The Harvard 'astronomer' was Jonathan McDowell, 'who tracks rocket launchings and space activity', *International Herald Tribune*, 19 January 2007; *The Times*, 19 January 2007. In fact, McDowell describes himself as an astrophysicist, maintains an online log of the positions of all satellites in the geosynchronous ring and produces a fortnightly newsletter (see http://www.planet4589.org/space/jsr/jsr.html for details), in which he provided more detailed technical information, that 'a kinetic-energy antisatellite weapon ... was launched on a suborbital medium range ballistic missile.' While a news search on 19 January revealed 392 articles on the event throughout the world, there was no mention in the three main Chinese domestic news websites or their printed newspapers (*People's Daily, China Daily, Xinhua*) in either the English or the Chinese versions. The first official recognition that the attack took place came from Foreign Ministry spokesman Liu Jianchao at a news conference on 24 January. Then, on 29 January, *Xinhua* announced that a new weather satellite, a Fengyun-3 (FY-3), would be launched in the

autumn 'to improve global weather monitoring capacity', but no reference was made to the satellite that had been destroyed.

560 Blasko, *The Chinese Army Today*, p. 20.

561 White Paper, *China's National Defence in 2006*.

562 Annual Report to Congress, 2006, p. 26.

563 Shambaugh, *Modernizing China's Military: Progress, Problems, and Prospects*, p. 159.

564 *Quadrennial Defense Review Report* (Washington: Department of Defense, 6 February 2006), p. 29. Such aims are not new: as long ago as 1964 the French author Jules Roy was told: 'So long as we are threatened by American imperialism, we will be obliged to prepare for our defense.' Roy, *Journey Through China*, p. 28.

565 White Paper, *China's National Defence in 2006*.

566 Lewis, *The Minimum Means of Reprisal China's Search for Security in the Nuclear Age*, pp. 25–7.

567 Howarth, *China's Rising Sea Power: The PLA Navy's Submarine Challenge*, p. 15.

568 *2006 Report to Congress of the U.S.-China Economic and Security Review Commission* (Washington: U.S. Government Printing Office, November 2006), p. 130.

569 *Quadrennial Defense Review Report*, op.cit., pp. 28–32.

570 Executive Summary, *Annual Report to Congress*, 2005.

571 *China's Peaceful Development Road*, State Council Information Office, 22 December 2005.

572 Scobell, *China's Use of Military Force: Beyond the Great Wall and the Long March*, p. 16.

573 Confucius, *The Analects,* Trans. Arthur Waley (New York: Macmillan, 1938), Chapter 13.

574 Sun Tzu, *The Art of War,* Trans. Lionel Giles (London: Luzac & Co, 1910), Chapter III, Paragraph 2.

575 Mott and Kim, *The Philosophy of Chinese Military Culture: Shih vs. Li*, p. 79.

576 See his reasons for this in the opening pages of Chapter V of the unfinished work entitled 'Problems of Strategy in China's Revolutionary War', in *Selected Military Writings,* pp. 103–6.

577 See Appendix 3 to Ka Po Ng's *Interpreting China's Military Power: Doctrine Makes Readiness,* pp. 159–64.

578 See Shih, *Navigating Sovereignty*, pp. 57–66.

579 *Ibid.* p. 58.

580 Mott and Kim, *Philosophy*, p. 18. Later in their book, they provide fascinating chapter-length discussions on the role of *shih* in the Chinese Civil War, the Korean War, the Sino-Indian War and the Sino-Vietnamese War.

581 Giles translation, XXII, 13.

582 See the fascinating chapter on 'How will the PLA fight', in Blasko, *The Chinese Army Today,* pp. 91–120, in which he shows how Mao's strategies were mostly consistent with Sun Tzu's thinking, and how the theories of both were incorporated into a more recent book used as a textbook for PLA officers (Wang Houqing and Zhang Xingye, eds, *On Military Campaigns*, Beijing: National Defense University Press, 2000); see also *Selected Military Writings of Mao Tse-Tung*.

583 Assistant Secretary of Defense Peter Rodman, in his testimony for the 2006 Report to Congress of the U.S.-China Economic and Security Review Commission, *2006 Report*, p. 130.

584 See, for example, the dramatically titled *Showdown: Why China Wants War With the United States*, by Ted Babbin and Edward Timperlake (Washington: Regnery Publishing, 2006), in which gung-ho chapters written in American military jargon are dedicated to each of these hypothetical scenarios.

585 In *The Progress and Present Position of Russia in the East: An Historical Summary* (London: John Murray, 1854, 4th Edition), pp. 100–101.

586 Needham, Joseph and Yates, Robin D.S., *Science and Civilisation in China,* Vol. V, Part 6, (Cambridge: CUP, 1994), p. 69.

587 In *Science and Civilisation,* Vol. 5, Part 7, p. 2.

588 Lewis and Xue, *Imagined Enemies: China Prepares for Uncertain Wars,* p. 25.

589 Isaacs, *Scratches on our Minds: American Views of China and India*, pp. 232–6.

590 Scobell, *China's Use of Military Force,* p. 193.

591 Gill, *Rising Star: China's New Security Diplomacy,* p. 66.

592 From 'Chapter I: The Security Situation', *White Paper on Defense,* December 2004, http://www.china.org.cn/e-white/20041227/index.htm.

593 *Ibid.,* Chapter II: National Defense Policy.

594 *Ibid.,* Chapter III: Revolution in Military Affairs with Chinese Characteristics.

595 Lewis and Xue, *Imagined Enemies,* p. 186.

596 *Ibid.,* p. 212. The above paragraph is based on their detailed analysis of Base 52 and Second Artillery strategy in Chapter 6 of their book, 'Redefining the Strategic Rocket Forces', pp. 173–213.

597 White Paper, *China's National Defence in 2006.*

598 Jean-Pierre Cabestan, 'The Taiwan Conundrum', in Chung (ed.), *Charting China's Future: Political, Social, and International Dimensions,* p. 173.

599 Ng, *Interpreting China's Military Power,* p. 124.

600 Lewis and Xue, *Imagined Enemies,* p. 276.

601 *Ibid.,* p. 261.

602 *Annual Report to Congress,* 2005, p. 4.

603 Lewis and Xue, *Imagined Enemies,* pp. 259–266; see also Scobell, *China's Use of Military Force*, Chapter 8: 'Show of Force: The 1995–6 Taiwan Strait Crisis', pp. 171–91, *passim.*

604 Quoted in Andrew J. Nathan and Robert S. Ross, *The Great Wall and the Empty Fortress: China's Search for Security* (New York: W.W. Norton, 1997), p. 206.

605 Quoted from Scobell, *China's Use of Military Force*, pp. 182–3.

606 *Ibid.,* III, 3

607 For example, Howarth, op.cit., pp. 140–2, and Lyle J. Goldstein and William S. Murray, 'The Submarine Force in China's Future Maritime Strategy', in Pollack, *Strategic Surprises,* op.cit., pp. 185–98, p. 191. See also the recent detailed scenario in an Appendix with the title 'Why China Could Not Seize Taiwan' in Bush and O'Hanlon's *A War Like No Other: The Truth about China's Challenge to America*, pp. 187–95.

608 Shambaugh, *Modernizing China's Military,* p. 243.

609 Victor N. Corpus, *America's Acupuncture Points*, a two-part article, *Asia Times Online*, 19–20 October 2006. Corpus is a retired Brigadier General and former Head of Intelligence of the Philippine Army, and holds a Master's degree in Public Administration from the Kennedy School of Government at Harvard.

610 *Annual Report to Congress,* 2005, p. 40.

611 See, for example, the article in the *Financial Times,* 3 September 2007, and many other newspapers and magazines.

612 *The Times,* 8 September 2007.

613 Navarro, *Coming China Wars,* p. 67.

614 Lewis and Xue, *Imagined Enemies,* p. 25.

615 You Ji, 'The PLA, the CCP and the formulation of Chinese defence and foreign policy', in Zhang and Austin (eds), *Power and Responsibility in Chinese Foreign Policy*, pp. 126–7.

616 *White Paper on Defense,* December 2004, p. 5; it should however be noted that the PLA officers' training manual cited above, *On Miltary Campaigns*, stresses that 'information warfare is a means, not a goal' and thus unlikely to be decisive factor (see Blasko, *The Chinese Army Today,* p. 106).

617 *Quadrennial Defense Review Report,* p. 29.

618 *White Paper on Defense,* December 2004, Chapter VII: Science, Technology and Industry for National Defense.

619 *Korea Times,* 6 April 2005, 'Technology Gap With China Narrowing Faster'.

620   The Chinese website has much more technical information, but the basics on the
       Forum are available in English at http://www.tdscdma-forum.org/en/index.asp .

621   The TD-SCDMA website has relevant information: www.tdscdma-forum.org.

622   Reported in *CNETAsia,* 28 October 2003.

623   *People's Daily*, 31 November 2006.

624   *China Daily,* 30 November 2006.

625   Information about products is available (in Chinese) at http://www.evd.cn/.

626   See www.on2.com/ and www.codingtechnologies.com

627   Estimate by Liu Gaozhuo, President of the China Aviation Industry Corporation, China
       Daily, 3 March 2004. CAIC already manufactures Embraer regional jets under license,
       and is developing its own 100-seat regional jet, the ARJ21, which will have its maiden
       flight as this book is published; CAIC has produced missiles and military aircraft for the
       PLA for many years. (http://www.avic1.com.cn/English/EnglishIndex.asp).

628   *People's Daily,* 22 March 2007.

629   See, for example, the speech by the founding father of the strategic missile programme,
       quoted in Feigenbaum, *China's Techno-Warriors: National Security and Strategic Competition
       From the Nuclear to the Information Age*, p. 1.

630   *Annual Report to Congress: Military Power of the People's Republic of China* (Washington:
       Office of the Secretary of Defense, 2006), p. 14.

631   Ng, *Interpreting China's Military Power,* pp. 90–1.

632   Much of the monitoring and collection of high-tech information is controversial,
       with many reports detailing how much is legally acquired and how much 'stolen'
       through espionage. See, for example, the three-volume congressional *Report of the
       Select Committee on US National Security and Military/Commercial Concerns with the
       People's Republic of China* (Washington: US Government Printing House, 1999).

633   Listed in Appendix 3 of Feigenbaum, *China's Techno-Warriors,* p. 248; the official website
       (with very little information in the English section) is available at http://www.863.org.
       cn/863_105/index.html.

634   Feigenbaum, *China's Techno-Warriors,* p. 184.

635   Quoted in *Aviation Week & Space Technology,* 19 October 2003.

636   *White Paper.* 'China's Space Activities in 2006', The State Council Information Office, 10
       October 2006, citing 'The Outline of the 11th Five-Year Program for National Economic
       and Social Development' and 'The National Guideline for Medium- and Long-term Plans
       for Science and Technology Development (2006–2020)'.

637   www.spacedaily.com/news   23 October 2000.

638   Segal, *Digital Dragon: High-Technology Enterprises in China,* p. 57.

639   Figures from the Ministry of Science and Technology, quoted in Sigurdson, p. 44.

640   'The National Guideline for Medium- and Long-term Plans for Science and
       Technology Development (2006–2020)', 9 February 2006.

641   Feigenbaum, *China's Techno-Warriors,* p. 196.

642   Sigurdson, *Technological Superpower China,* p. 12.

643   Ministry of Education; http://www.moe.edu.cn/english/planning_n.htm.

644   A healthy scepticism about Chinese educational statistics and their acceptance by the
       American media may be found in the amusing article by Gerald W. Bracey entitled 'Heard
       the One About the 600,000 Chinese Engineers?', *The Washington Post,* 21 May 2006.

645   'The Emerging Global Labor Market: Part II - The Supply of Offshore Talent in
       Services', McKinsey Global Institute, June 2005, p. 23.

646   *Ibid.,* p. 28.

647   Committee on Prospering in the Global Economy of the 21st Century, *Rising Above
       The Gathering Storm: Energizing and Employing America for a Brighter Economic Future*
       (Washington: The National Academies Press, 2006), p. 23.

648   *Ibid.*, p. 62.

649   Feigenbaum, *China's Techno-Warriors*, p. 199.

650   *Ibid.*, p. 223.

651   Sigurdson, *Technological Superpower China*, p. 178.

652   'China Gaining Ground in Global "Head and Brains" Race', *Batelle*, September 2006; available at http://www.battelle.org/news/06/09-29-06Globalper cent20R&D.stm.

Chapter 10: Stealth Foreign Policy

653   Tso-chuan (or Tso Chuen), in James Legge, *The Chinese Classics,* Vol. 5, p. 777.

654   Mark Mancall, 'The Ch'ing Tribute System: An Interpretative Essay', in Fairbank (ed.), *The Chinese World Order*, p. 72.

655   Quoted in the Introduction to Frodsham (ed.), *First Chinese Embassy*, p. xxvi.

656   See the account in Niu Jun's book *From Yan'an to the World: The Origin and Development of Chinese Communist Foreign Policy*, first published in 1992 and translated into English in 2005 (especially pp. 19–21), which opens with the sentence: 'One July day in 1936, a sharp-featured, blue-eyed foreigner, mounted on an old nag named Mongrel, rode into Baoan, the seat of the Chinese Communist Party.'

657   Snow, *Red Star Over China,* p. 99.

658   Quoted in Niu Jun, *From Yan'an to the World,* p. 38; see the partial version of this speech in 'Problems of War and Strategy', 6 November 1938, in *Selected Military Writings of Mao Tse-Tung*, pp. 269–285.

659   Shao, *Zhou Enlai and the Foundations of Chinese Foreign Policy,* p. 160.

660   Xu Guoqi, *China and The Great War,* p. 1.

661   Constantine C. Menges, *China: The Gathering Threat* (Nashville: Nelson Current, 2005), pp. 367–417.

662   Quoted in *Annual Report to Congress: Military Power of the People's Republic of China* (Washington: Office of the Secretary of Defense, 2006), p. 7. It derives from a history of similar formulae ideal for memorisation, such as Mao's sixteen-character formula for guerrilla warfare: 'The enemy advances, we retreat; the enemy camps, we harass; the enemy tires, we attack; the enemy retreats, we pursue.' In 'Problems of Strategy in China's Revolutionary War', in *Selected Military Writings*, op. cit., p. 111.

663   Larkin, *China and Africa 1949–70: The Foreign Policy of the People's Republic of China*, p. 13.

664   Francois Jullien, *A Treatise on Efficacy: Between Western and Chinese Thinking* (Honolulu: University of Hawaii Press, 2004), p. 20.

665   Mencius, Legge translation, 4a.14 and 7b4.

666   Published 22 December 2005, Ministry of Foreign Affairs.

667   'Eight Measures to Boost Overseas Chinese Teaching', Xinhua, 17 June 2005.

668   'The United States and the Rise of China and India', published 11 October 2006, p. 36; available at http://www.thechicagocouncil.org/curr_pos.php.

669   Fogel, 'Capitalism and Democracy in 2040', pp. 3–4.

670   Press Conference, 14 March 2006.

671   *The Hindu,* 20 June 2006.

672   *China Daily,* 6 July 2006.

673   Srivastava, Anupam, 'The Strategic Context of India's Economic Engagement with China', in *Indian Journal of Economics & Business, Special Issue: India & China,* 2006, pp. 1–19; available at http://www.icainstitute.org/publications.html.

674   http://www.transparency.org/policy_research/surveys_indices/cpi/2007.

675   William Boot, 'Burma's Bumper Energy Sale', *The Irrawaddy,* 30 September 2006.

676   The origins of this line are discussed in Austin, *China's Ocean Frontier: International Law, Military Force and National Development,* pp. 14–15, especially in Note 6 on p. 14, and in Li

Jinming and Li Dexia, 'The Dotted Line on the Chinese Map of the South China Sea: A Note', *Ocean Development & International Law*, No. 34, 2003, pp. 287–295.

677   https://www.cia.gov/cia/publications/factbook/geos/pf.html.

678   Austin, *China's Ocean Frontier,* p. 130.

679   https://www.cia.gov/cia/publications/factbook/geos/pg.html.

680   Austin, *China's Ocean Frontier*, p. 161.

681   25 March 2003; http://english.people.com.cn/200305/25/eng20030525_117192.shtml.

682   The oil reserves were announced in a report published that year by the UN Economic Commission for Asia and the Far East (ECAFE).

683   'The Basic View on the Sovreignty on the Senkaku Islands', Japanese Ministry of Foreign Affairs, http://www.mofa.go.jp/region/asia-paci/senkaku/senkaku.html.

684   Austin, *China's Ocean Frontier,* p. 176.

685   Pan, *Encyclopedia*, p. 64.

686   Larkin, *China and Africa*, p. 89; see the table of Chinese Diplomatic Relations with Africa, pp. 66–7.

687   *Ibid.*, p. 39 and p. 58.

688   *Ibid.*, p. 106. *The Economist*, with the headline 'Never Too Late to Scramble' (26 October 2006) was more cynical. In a sense, Tanzania went from one empire to another: Frances Wood recalls in her memoir of life in China in 1975–6 that a fellow student was 'outraged at the thought that a friendly African country with a nice new Chinese-built railway could be associated with the evil remnants of the British Empire.' (*Hand-Grenade Practice in Peking: My Part in the Cultural Revolution,* London: John Murray, 2000, p. 180).

689   Broadman, *Africa's Silk Road: China and India's New Economic Frontier,* p. 81.

690   *Ibid.*, p. 275.

691   *Xinhua*, 2 November 2006.

692   http://www.fmprc.gov.cn/zflt/eng/zxxx/t279811.htm.

693   *People's Daily,* 3 November 2006.

694   'Rioters Attack Chinese after Zambia Poll', *Daily Telegraph*, 3 October 2006.

695   John Rocha, 'A New Frontier in the Exploitation of Africa's Natural Resources: The Emergence of China', in Manji and Marks (eds), *African Perspectives on China in Africa,* pp. 15–34; pp. 24–5.

696   Quoted in the Introduction to Manji and Marks (eds), *African Perspectives on China in Africa,* p. 5.

697   Rocha, 'A New Fronier', p. 16.

698   Source: US-China Business Council (http://www.uschina.org/statistics/tradetable.html).

699   Quoted by Kenneth F. Scheve and Matthew J. Slaughter, 'A New Deal for Globalization', *Foreign Affairs*, July/August 2007. (http://www.foreignaffairs.org/20070701faessay86403/ kenneth-f-scheve-matthew-j-slaughter/a-new-deal-for-globalization.html).

700   *Ibid.*

701   President Nixon's phrase, recently repeated in the title of Margaret MacMillan's book, *Nixon and Mao: The Week That Changed the World* (New York: Random House, 2007).

702   By the Ministry of Foreign Affairs, http://www.fmprc.gov.cn/eng/ziliao/3602/3604/ t18056.htm.

Chapter 11: The Stealth Business Empire

703   Adam Smith, *The Wealth of Nations* (New York: Bantam Classic, 2003), pp. 855–6.

704   Jiang Zemin, in 'Accelerating Reform and Open Up', *Beijing Review*, 26 October 1992, pp. 9–32.

705   Shi Guangsheng, Minister of Foreign Trade and Economic Cooperation (MOFTEC), in his brief article 'China's Foreign Econmic Trade in the 21st Century' in Brahm (ed.), *China's Century: The Awakening of the Next Economic Powerhouse,* pp. 119–125, p. 122.

706 This is not a new denomination. Already in 1937 Carl Crow could write that 'the sundry goods shops, which sell odds and ends of foreign goods such as thermos bottles and aluminium ware are largely dominated by the Cantonese.' (*400 Million Customers*, p. 84).

707 http://www.newsgd.com/citiesandtowns/foshan/info/200309170062.htm.

708 Thomas Fuller, in the *International Herald Tribune,* 3 August 2006; see also Pietra Rivoli's *The Travels of a T-Shirt in the Global Economy* (New York: Wiley, 2006).

709 By the *International Herald Tribune,* 12 March 2007.

710 See, for example, Company Overview on the company's English-language website at http://www.huawei.com/about/info.do?cid=-1002.

711 Dan Margo, China Britain Business Council, in *Communications Week International,* 12/11/2001.

712 *The Globalisation of Chinese Companies,* Nomura Research Institute, 1 September 2003.

713 Data from the Ministry of Commerce in February 2007. The English language website may be found at http://english.mofcom.gov.cn/, but the Chinese version is more updated and complete.

714 http://www.haier.com.pk/abouthaier.asp.

715 Quoted in the *International Herald Tribune,* 18 April 2007 ('US Market important, but not like it once was, China Says').

716 'The fast and the furious: Are Chinese carmakers trying to do too much, too soon?' *The Economist,* 23 November 2006.

717 Gilmore and Dumont, *Brand Warriors China*, p. 92.

718 'TCl Multimedia's Global Agenda', *Business Week Online,* 22 August 2005.

719 *Financial Times,* 1 November 2006.

720 Reported in the article by Chris McGreal, 'Thanks China, now go home: buy-up of Zambia revives old colonial fears', in *The Guardian,* 5 February 2007.

721 Hundt, *In China's Shadow: The Crisis of American Entrepreneurship,* p. 43.

722 Ling, *The Lenovo Affair,* p. 13.

723 *Ibid.,* pp. 61–5.

724 *Ibid.,* p. 122.

725 *Ibid.,* p. 264.

726 *Ibid.,* p. 38, p. 49.

727 Quoted in *Ibid.,* p. 351.

728 Woetzel, *Capitalist China: Strategies for a Revolutionized Economy,* p. 42.

729 Yi and Ye, *The Haier Way: The Making of a Chinese Business Leader and a Global Brand,* p. 187.

730 Parts of the following section first appeared in Chinese in an article by the author published in the *Economic Observer,* one of China's two leading financial newspapers, on 2 February 2007.

731 Haier's Pakistan website celebrated the president's visit to the company during this visit with a page of photographs and country flags, with some curious linguistic errors in English. First, it unwittingly elevated Hu Jintao's status with its capitalisation: 'With Him ...' and then added that '... we are also *obliged* [my italics] to welcome President of Pakistan Mr. Pervaiz Musharaf and Prime Minister of Pakistan Mr. Shaukat Aziz'. (http://www.haier.com.pk/newsdetails.asp?newsid=22).

732 *The Indian Express,* 25 November 2006, http://www.indianexpress.com/story/17274.html.

733 *China Daily,* 5 February 2007.

734 *Lusaka Times,* 5 February 2007.

735 *China Daily,* 19 December 2006.

Chapter 12: The New Chinese Mindset and the Stealth Empire

736 Hsü, *The Rise of Modern China,* pp. 933–4; the last leading member of that generation, survivor of the Long March and ex-vice-premier Bo Yibo, father of the Bo Xilai mentioned in the next paragraph, died in January 2007 at the age of ninety-nine.

737 See the table in Cheng Li, 'Hu's New Deal and the New Provincial Chiefs', China Leadership Monitor, No.10, Spring 2004 (NB: The China Leadership Monitor is sponsored by the Hoover Institution on War, Revolution, and Peace at Stanford University; copies are available at http://www.hoover.org/publications/clm).

738 Cited from Bruce J. Dickson, 'Dilemmas of Party adaptation: The CCP's strategies for survival', in Gries and Rosen (eds), *State and Society in 21st-Century China: Crisis, Contention, and Legitimation*, pp. 141–158, p. 145. The lower figures for the previous generation are partly due to the closure of universities during the Cultural Revolution, which deprived many of the benefits of study.

739 Hundt, *In China's Shadow*, p. 111.

740 'The United States and the Rise of China and India', published 11 October 2006; available at http://www.thechicagocouncil.org/curr_pos.php.

741 *Ibid.*, p. 6.

742 *Ibid.*, p. 34.

743 'The United States and the Rise of China and India', op.cit., p. 35.

744 Quoted in the chapter by Yang Changzheng, 'Popular Culture among Chinese Youth', in Xi, Sun and Xiao, *Chinese Youth in Transition*, pp. 172–92, p. 177.

745 From a survey in *Parents' Reading Magazine*, quoted in *China Daily*, 18 March 2005.

746 The following discussion is based on Liu Junyan's chapter 'Chinese College Students', in Xi, Sun and Xiao, *Chinese Youth in Transition*, pp. 145–68.

747 *Ibid.*, p. 147.

748 In *Foreign Affairs*, 84:5, September/October 2005.

749 Hutton, *The Writing on the Wall*, p. x.

750 Fogel, 'Capitalism and Democracy in 2040', pp. 9–10.

751 Man, *The China Fantasy: How Our Leaders Explain Away Chinese Repression*, p. 10.

752 Huntington, Samuel P., *The Clash of Civilizations and the Remaking of World Order* (New York: Simon & Schuster, 1996), p. 218.

753 Gat, 'The Return of Authoritarian Great Powers', p. 60.

754 *Ibid.*, p. 66

755 In 2005. Quoted in John Blessing Karumbidza, 'Win-Win Economic Cooperation: Can China Save Zimbabwe's Economy?', in *African Perspectives on China in Africa*, op. cit., pp. 87–105; p. 87.

756 *Ibid.*, p. 41.

757 Gat, 'The Return of Authoritarian Great Powers', p. 60.

758 Jenner, *Tyranny of History*, op.cit., p. 104.

759 Quoted by Francis Fukuyama, in *Trust: The Social Virtues and the Creation of Prosperity* (London: Hamish Hamilton, 1995), p. 86.

760 Jenner, *Tyranny of History*, p. 54; on 'Democratic Confusions', see Chapter 9, *passim*.

761 Munro, *The Concept of Man in Contemporary China*, p. 187.

762 From the title of Erika E.S. Evasdottir's book *Obedient Autonomy: Chinese Intellectuals and the Achievement of Orderly Life* (Honolulu: University of Hawai'i Press, 2004).

763 Quoted by Fogel, in 'Capitalism and Democracy in 2040', p. 12.

764 Cited in Xi, Sun and Xiao (eds), *Chinese Youth in Transition*, 'Introduction', p. 4.

765 Alexis De Tocqueville, *Democracy in America*, Vol. II, Chapter XVIII.

766 Julian Schuman, *Assignment China* (New York: Whitter Books, 1956), p. 165.

767 Chang and Halliday, *Mao: The Unknown Story*, p. 109.

768 Shenkar, *Chinese Century: The Rising Chinese Economy and Its Impact on the Global Economy, the Balance of Power, and Your Job*, p. 21.

769 The phrase comes from Immanuel Wallerstein, seeking to amalgamate concepts by such varied authors as Landes, Carlyle, Marx, Keynes and Schumpeter in a single definition, in his chapter 'The West, capitalism, and the modern world-system', in Brook and Blue, *China and Historical Capitalism: Genealogies of Sinological Knowledge*, pp. 10–56, p. 15.

770 Perry, 'Studying Chinese Politics', p. 6.

771 See the fascinating articles in *China Daily*, 19 August 2003 and 16 January 2006, and in *The Guardian*, 10 May 2005.

772 See Yi and Ye, *The Haier Way*, pp. 49–51.

773 *Ibid.*, p. 163.

774 *China Daily,* 19 December 2006.

775 Bruce J. Dickson, 'Dilemmas of Party adaptation: The CCP's strategies for survival', in Gries and Rosen, *State and Society*, pp. 141–58, p. 144.

776 http://english.cpc.people.com.cn/66095/4468893.html.

777 An article by Wen in *People's Daily,* 27 March 2007.

778 Reported in *People's Daily*, 27 February 2006.

779 *China Daily*, 19 December 2006.

780 Alexander Pope, *Essay on Man,* Epistle IV.

781 Reported by Ambrose Evans-Pritchard, in 'Davos Diary', *Daily Telegraph Online,* 27 January 2007.

782 Pei, *China's Trapped Transition: The Limits of Developmental Autocracy,* p. 132.

783 *Ibid.*, p. 4.

784 Lam, *Chinese Politics in the Hu Jintao Era: New Leaders, New Challenges,* p. 34.

785 In an interview with Frederick Balfour, *Business Week, Asia Edition,* 7 May 2007.

786 Reported in *Asia Times Online* and other media, 11 July 2007; see also www.neri.org.cn (in Chinese).

787 Yang Fan, of the Chinese Academy of Social Sciences, in a comment reported in the *International Herald Tribune,* 14 December 2006. Given the paucity of information, the article 'A Close Look at China's "Sex Industry"', by Zhong Wei, in the Singapore newspaper *Lianhe Zaobao* on 2 October 2000, is still interesting (available at http://www.usembassy-china.org.cn/sandt/sex-industry.html).

788 Cited in *Asia Times Online,* 18 July 2007, based on a report in the Chinese language *Beijing Legal Daily,* at http://www.atimes.com/atimes/China/IG18Ad01.html.

789 Apart from personal knowledge and anecdotes, a detailed scholarly survey exists in the wonderfully titled *Managing Existence in Naples* by the Naples-born Oxford anthropologist Italo Pardo, who provides details on all the inhabitants' tricks for increasing income (Cambridge: CUP: 1996); this could easily be adapted to a Chinese city.

790 *21st Century World Herald,* 31 January 2007; www.21cbh.com.

791 *The Scholars*, p. 64 (the opening words of Chapter 6); I could imagine this scene in a play by Eduardo De Filippo, in one of his marvellously decadent Neapolitan bourgeois families.

792 Bergsten et al, *China: The Balance Sheet, What the World Needs to Know About the Emerging Superpower,* p. 39.

793 Mann, *The China Fantasy*, p. 11.

794 See J.R. McNeill, 'China's Environment in World Prespective', in Elvin, Mark and Liu, Ts'ui-jung (eds), *Sediments of Time: Environment and Society in Chinese History* (Cambridge: CUP, 1998), pp. 31–49, p. 35.

795 D.C. Lau, *Mencius* (Harmondsworth: Penguin, 1970), p. 51.

796 *Ibid.*, p. 61 (Legge, Ch. 19, para. 7), p. 131.

797 Anderson, *The Food of China*, p. 125.

798 'The Foolish Old Man Who Removed the Mountains', in *Selected Works of Mao Tse-tung* (Beijing: Foreign Languages Press), Vol. III, pp. 271–4, p. 272.

799 Quoted by Shapiro, in *Mao's War Against Nature: Politics and the Environment in Revolutionary China*, p. 103.

800 *Ibid.*, p. 7.

801 http://www.cgs.gov.cn/Ev/English.htm.

802 Diamond, *Collapse: How Societies Choose to Fail or Survive,* in particular Chapter 12; Navarro, *Coming China Wars, passim.*

803 Diamond, *Collapse*, p. 362.

804 *Ibid.*, p. 373.

805 Economy, *The River Runs Black: The Environmental Challenge to China's Future*, p. 18.

806 *Cost of Pollution in China: Economic Estimates of Physical Damage* (Washington (DC): World Bank: February 2007), p. 82.

807 *Ibid.*, p. xii.

808 Navarro, *Coming China Wars*, p. 144.

809 Deidre Chetham, *Before the Deluge: The Vanishing World of the Yangtze's Three Gorges* (London: PalgraveMacmillan, 2002).

810 *Ibid.*, pp. 188–9.

811 Report in *Xinhua*, 26 September 2007, taken up by most mainstream newspapers in the West. As always in China, there is the question: why now? Some reports suggested that it might be part of an attempt to discredit Jiang Zemin, who initiated the project, in view of the upcoming National Congress in mid-October.

812 *Rivers at Risk: Dams and the future of freshwater ecosystems,* WWF, March 2007, available at www.panda.org/dams.

813 World Bank, *Cost of Pollution in China.*

814 'Environmental Performance Review of China', (Paris: OECD, July 2007); quotes from 'Conclusions and Recommendations', *passim*, available at http://www.oecd.org/dataoecd/58/23/37657409.pdf.

815 *Ibid.*, p. 10.

816 See the report *The World's Most Polluted Places: The Top Ten (of the Dirty Thirty),* September 2007, available at http://www.blacksmithinstitute.org/.

817 *Ibid.*, p. 12.

818 *Ibid.*, p. 14.

819 *Reuters*, 24 April 2007.

820 *Key World Energy Statistics 2006* (Paris: International Energy Agency), p. 28.

821 *Ibid.*, p. 45.

822 David G. Streets et al., 'Air quality during the 2008 Beijing Olympic Games', *Atmospheric Environment,* 41 (2007), pp. 480–492, p. 490.

823 Weller, *Discovering Nature: Globalization and Environmental Culture in China and Taiwan,* pp. 1–3.

824 From the opening speech of the Inaugural Annual Meeting of the New Champions of the World Economic Forum's Summer Davos 2007 in Dalian, 6 September 2007.

825 *Xinhua*, 26 September 2007.

826 Arthur H. Smith, *Chinese Characteristics*, p. 22.

827 Joshua Goldstein, 'The Remains of the Everyday: One Hundred Years of Recycling in Beijing', in Madeleine Yue Dong and Joshua L. Goldstein (eds), *Everyday Modernity in China* (Seattle & London: University of Washington Press, 2006), pp. 260–302, pp. 261–2.

828 In a speech made in Guangdong in 1958, quoted in Goldstein, op.cit., p. 274.

829 *The Economist*, 8 March 2007; Bruce Gilley, *China's Democratic Future*, p. 28.

830 The speech was broadcast live on China Central Television's satellite and cable channel (CCTV9) with English subtitles. An English translation was posted on the *Xinhua* news agency's website on 16 October (Special Report on the Congress at http://www.chinaview.cn/17thcpc/), and the speech together with other key documents was published a few weeks later in book form as *Documents of the 17th National Congress of the Communist Party of China* (2007) (Beijing: Foreign Languages Press, 2007).

831 *Documents*, op.cit., p. 83.

832 *Ibid.*, p. 86. Hu explained this 'Outlook' in greater detail in his opening address (Documents, pp. 15–23), where unlike in the Constitution he also added it to a paragraph listing the achievements of Mao, Deng and Jiang in Section IX on the armed forces (Documents, p. 53).

833   *Ibid.*, p. 57.

834   *Ibid.*, p. 61.

835   *Ibid.*, p. 23.

836   *Ibid.*, p. 25.

837   *Xinhua*, 21 October 2007

838   Nathan and Gilley, *China's New Rulers: The Secret Files*, p. 127.

839   Vivienne Shue, in 'Legitimacy Crisis in China?', in Gries and Rosen (eds), *State and Society,* pp. 24–49, in particular pp. 30–34.

840   Quoted from Mead, Margaret and Métraux, Rhoda, *The Study of Culture at a Distance* (Chicago: University of Chicago Press, 1953), p. 472.

841   In a Press Conference on Monday 4 September 2006.

842   Quoted by Pearl Buck in her book *My Several Worlds* (1954), and cited by Peter Conn in his study *Pearl S. Buck: A Cultural Biography* (Cambridge: CUP, 1996), p. 54.

843   Arthur Waldron, 'The Pentagon's Latest China Report,' 24 May 2006, International Assessment and Strategy Center, http://www.strategycenter.net/research/pubID.110/pub_detail.asp.

844   Said, *Culture and Imperialism*, p. xxiii.

Bibliography

Abru, Hafiz, *A Persian Embassy to China, Being an Extract from Zubdatu't Tawarikh*, Trans. K.M. Maitra (Reprint of 1934 Lahore edition), (New York: Paragon Book Reprint Corp., 1970)

Adshead, S.A.M., *China in World History* (London: Macmillan, 2000)

Allsen, Thomas, 'The rise of the Mongolian empire and Mongolian rule in North China', in Herbert Franke and Denis Twitchett (eds), *The Cambridge History of China*, Vol. 6 (Cambridge: CUP, 1994), pp. 321–413

Amiot, Joseph Marie, *De La Musique des Chinois* (*Mémoires concernant les Chinois*, Vol. VI) (Paris: Imprimerie de Stoupe, 1779)

Amitai-Preiss, Reuvan and David O. Morgan (eds), *The Mongol Empire & Its Legacy* (Leiden: Brill, 2000)

Anderson, E.N., *The Food of China* (New Haven: Yale University Press, 1988)

Arnold, Lauren, *Princely Gifts and Papal Treasures: The Franciscan Mission to China and its influence on the Art of the West* (San Francisco: Desiderata Press, 1999)

Ash, Robert (ed.), *China's Integration in Asia: Economic Security and Strategic Issues*, (Richmond, Surrey: Curzon, 2002)

Assmann, Heinz-Dieter and Filseck, Karin Moser V., *China's New Role in the International Community: Challenges and Expectations for the 21st Century* (Transactions of the Interdisciplinary Roundtable held from June 19 to 23, 2004, at the Shanghai Institute for Advanced Studies), (Frankfurt am Main: Peter Lang, 2005)

Attwater, Rachel, *Adam Schall: A Jesuit at the Court of China 1592–1666* (Milwaukee: Bruce Publishing, 1963)

Atwell, William, 'Ming China and the Emerging World Economy, c1470–1650', in Denis Twitchett and Frederick W. Mote (eds), *The Cambridge History of China*, Vol. 8, Part 2 (Cambridge: CUP, 1998), pp. 376–416.

Austin, Greg, *China's Ocean Frontier: International Law, Military Force and National Development* (Canberra: Allen & Unwin, 1998)

Barfield, Thomas J., *The Perilous Frontier: Nomadic Empires and China, 221 BC to AD 1757* (Cambridge, MA: Blackwell, 1989)

Barmé, Geremie, 'TV Requiem for the Myths of the Middle Kingdom', *Far Eastern Economic Review*, 141.35 (1 September 1988), pp. 40–43

'To Screw Foreigners is Patriotic: China's Avant-garde Nationalists', *The China Journal*, No. 34, July 1995, pp. 209–34

Barnett, A. Doak, *China's Far West: Four Decades of Change* (Boulder, CO: Westview Press, 1993)

Bary, Wm. Theodore de, *The Trouble with Confucianism* (Cambridge, MA: Harvard University Press, 1991)

Bayly, C.A., *The Birth of the Modern World 1780–1914* (Oxford: Blackwell, 2004)

Becker, Jasper, *The Chinese* (New York: Free Press, 2001)

Bell, John, *Travels from St Petersburg in Russia to Diverse Parts of Asia* (Glasgow: Elibron Classics, 2005) 2 vols (facsimile of the 1763 edition)

Bergsten, Fred C and Gill, Bates Lardy, Nicholas R and Mitchell, Derek, *China: The Balance Sheet, What the World Needs to Know About the Emerging Superpower* (New York: Public Affairs, 2006)

Beurdeley, Cécile and Michel, *Giuseppe Castiglione: A Jesuit Painter at the Court of the Chinese Emperors* (Rutland, VT: Charles E. Tuttle, 1971)

Beurdeley, Michel, *Peintres Jésuites En Chine au XVIII Siècle* (Arcueil: Anthese, 1997)

Bland, J.O.P., *Houseboat Days in China* (London: Edward Arnold, 1909)

Blasko, Dennis J., *The Chinese Army Today: Tradition and Transformation for the 21st Century* (London: Routledge, 2006)

Blum, Susan D., and Jensen, Lionel M. (eds), *China Off Center: Mapping the Margins of the Middle Kingdom* (Honolulu: University of Hawaii Press, 2002)

Bobbitt, Philip, *The Shield of Achilles: War, Peace and the Course of History* (London: Allen Lane, 2002)

Bodde, Derk, 'The State and Empire of Ch'in', in Denis Twitchett and Michael Loewe (eds), *The Cambridge History of China*, Vol. 1 (Cambridge: CUP, 1986), pp. 20–102
    Chinese Thought, Society and Science: The Intellectual and Social Background of Science and Technology in Pre-modern China (Honolulu: University of Hawaii Press, 1991)

Bond, Michael Harris (ed.), *The Psychology of the Chinese People* (Oxford: OUP, 1986)

Boulger, Demetrius Charles, *The History of China* (London: W. Thacker, 1898), 2 vols

Brahm, Laurence J. (ed.), *China's Century: The Awakening of the Next Economic Powerhouse* (Singapore: John Wiley, 2001)

Bray, Francesca, *Science and Civilisation in China*, Vol. 6, Part II, *Agriculture* (Cambridge: CUP, 1984)

Bretschneider, E., *Medieval Researches from Eastern Asiatic Sources: Fragments Towards the Knowledge of the Geography and History of Central and Western Asia from the 13th to the 17th Century* (London: Trübner & Co., 1888), 2 vols

Broadman, Harry G., *Africa's Silk Road: China and India's New Economic Frontier* (Washington DC: The World Bank, 2007)

Brook, Timothy and Blue, Gregory (eds), *China and Historical Capitalism: Geneaologies of Sinological Knowledge* (Cambridge: CUP, 1999)

Brown, Kerry, *Struggling Giant: China in the 21st Century* (London: Anthem Press, 2007)

Brownell, Susan, *Training the Body for China: Sports in the Moral Order of the People's Republic* (Chicago: University of Chicago Press, 1995)

Brzezinski, Zbigniew and Mearsheimer, John J., 'Debate: Clash of the Titans', *Foreign Policy*, No. 146, January/February 2005, pp. 46–50

Burles, Mark and Shulsky, Abram N., *Patterns in China's Use of Force: Evidence from History and Doctrinal Writings* (Santa Monica, CA: Rand, 2000)

Burman, Edward, *The World Before Columbus 1100–1492* (London: WH Allen, 1989)

Burstein, Daniel and Keijzer, Arne de, *Big Dragon, China's Future: What It Means for Business, the Economy, and the Global Order* (New York: Simon & Schuster, 1998)

Bush, Richard C., and O'Hanlon, Michael E., *A War Like No Other: The Truth about China's Challenge to America* (Hoboken, NJ: John Wiley, 2007)

Cai, Zong-qi (ed.), *Chinese Aesthetics: The Ordering of Literature, the Arts, and the Universe in the Six Dynasties* (Honolulu: Univerirsity of Hawaii Press, 2004)

Cartier, Carolyn, *Globalizing South China* (Oxford: Blackwell, 2001)

Chan, Hok-Lam, 'The Chien-wen, Yung-lu, Hung-hsi, and Hsüan-te Reigns, 1399–1435', in Frederick W. Mote and Denis Twitchett (eds), *The Cambridge History of China*, Vol. 7, Part 1 (Cambridge: CUP, 1988), pp. 182–304

Chang, Chun-shu, *The Rise of the Chinese Empire, Vol One: Nation, State & Imperialism in Early China ca. 1600 B.C. – A.D. 8* (Ann Arbor: University of Michigan Press, 2007)

Chang, Gordon, *The Coming Collapse of China* (London: Century, 2001)

Chang, Iris, *The Chinese in America: a Narrative History* (London: Penguin, 2003)

Chang, Jung and Halliday, Jon, *Mao: The Unknown Story* (London: Jonathan Cape, 2005)

Chang, Maria Hsia, *Return of the Dragon: China's Wounded Nationalism* (Boulder, CO: Westview Press, 2001)

Chen, Chien-Hsun, Shih, Hui-Tzu and Chen, Jianxun, *Hightech Industries In China* (London: Edward Elgar, 2005)

Chen, Weixing & Zhong, Yang (eds), *Leadership in a Changing China* (New York: Palgrave Macmillan, 2005)

Cheng, François, *Souffle-esprit: textes théoriques chinois sur l'art pictural* (Paris: Seuil, 2006)

Cheng, Li, 'Anticipating Chinese leadership Changes at the 17th Party Congress', *China Brief*, Vol. 7, Issue 6 (21st March 2007), pp. 5–8

Cheng, Tun-jen, deLisle, Jacques, Brown, Deborah (eds), *China Under Hu Jintao: Opportunities, Dangers, and Dilemmas* (Singapore: World Scientific, 2006)

Ch'en, Yuan, *Western and Central Asians in China Under the Mongols: Their transformation into Chinese* (Los Angeles: Monumenta Serica at the University of California, 1966)

Cheong, Weng Eang, *The Hong Merchants of Canton: Chinese Merchants in Sino-Western Trade* (Richmond: Curzon Press, 1997)

Chung, Jae Ho (ed.), *Charting China's Future: Political, Social, and International Dimensions* (Lanham, MD: Rowman & Littlefield, 2006)

Clements, Jonathan, *Coxinga and the Fall of the Ming Dynasty* (Stroud: Sutton Publishing, 2005)
The First Emperor of China, (Stroud: Sutton Publishing, 2006)

Clissold, Tim, *Mr China* (London: Robinson, 2004)

Close, Paul, and Askew, David and Xu, Xin, *Beijing Olympiad: The Political Economy of a Sporting Mega-Event* (London: Routledge, 2007)

Cohen, Paul A., *Discovering History in China: American Historical Writing on the Recent Chinese Past* (New York: Columbia University Press, 1984)
China Unbound: Evolving Perspectives on the Chinese Past (London: RoutledgeCurzon, 2003)

Collotti Pischel, Enrica, La Cina, La politica estera di un paese sovrano (Milan: Franco Angeli, 2002)

Cologna, Daniele (ed.), La Cina sotto casa (Milan: Franco Angeli, 2002)

Cranmer-Byng, J.L. (ed.), *A Journal of the Embassy to China; Lord Macartney's Observations Upon China* (London: Longman, 1962)
'The Chinese View of Their Place in the World: An Historical Perspective', *China Quarterly*, No. 53 (Jan-March 1973), pp. 67–79

Creel, Herrlee Glessner, *Sinism: A Study of the Evolution of the Chinese World-View* (Chicago: Open Court, 1929)

Crespigny, Rafe de, 'Tradition and Chinese Foreign Policy', in Stuart Harris and Gary Klintworth (eds), *China as a Great Power* (New York: St Martin's Press, 1995), pp. 28–45

Crossley, Pamela Kyle, *A Translucent Mirror: History and Identity in Qing Imperial Ideology* (Berkeley: University of California Press, 1999)

Crossley, Pamela Kyle and Siu, Helen F. and Sutton, Donald S., *Empire at the Margins: Culture, Ethnicity, and Frontier in Early Modern China* (Berkeley: University of California Press, 2006)

Crow, Carl, *400 Million Customers: The Experiences – Some Happy, Some Sad of an American in China and What They Taught Him* (London: Hamilton, 1937)

Cushman, Jennifer Wayne, *Fields from the Sea: Chinese Junk Trade with Siam during the Late 18th and Early 19th Centuries* (New York: Cornell University (Southeast Asia Program), 1993)

Deng, Yong and Wang Fei-Ling (eds), *China Rising: Power and Motivation in Chinese Foreign Policy* (Lanham, MD: Rowman & Littlefield, 2005)

Des Forges, Roger and Fang, Qiang, 'Were Chinese Rulers above the Law? Toward a Theory of the Rule of Law in China from Early Times to 1949 CE', *Buffalo Legal Studies Research Paper Series*, Paper No. 2006–006

DeWoskin, Kenneth J., *Song for One or Two: Music and the Concept of Art in Early China* (Ann Arbour: Center for Chinese Studies, University of Michigan, 1982)

Diamond, Jared, *Guns, Germs, and Steel: The Fates of Human Societies* (New York: Norton, 1997)
Collapse: How Societies Choose to Fail or Survive (London: Penguin, 2006)

Di Cosmo, Nicola and Wyatt, Don. J. (eds), *Political Frontiers, Ethnic Boundaries, and Human Geographies in Chinese History* (London: RoutledgeCurzon, 2003)

Dittmer, Lowell and Kim, Samuel S. (eds), *China's Quest for National Identity* (Ithaca: Cornell University Press, 1993)

Dong, Jingxia, *Women, Sport and Society in Modern China* (London: Frank Cass, 2002)

Donnelly, Ivon A., *Chinese Junks and Other Native Craft* (Shanghai: Kelly & Walsh, 1924)

Dreyer, Edward L., *Zheng He: China and the Oceans in the Early Ming Dynasty 1404-1433* (New York: Pearson Longman, 2007)

Duyvendak, J.J.L., *China's Discovery of Africa*, London: Probsthain, 1949

East Asia: Seventh Report of Session 2005–6 (House of Commons Foreign Affairs Committee), (London: Stationery Office, 2006)

Eberhard, Wolfram, *A History of China* (Los Angeles: University of California Press, 1950)

Economy, Elizabeth C., *The River Runs Black: The Environmental Challenge to China's Future* (Ithaca: Cornell University Press, 2004)

Economy, Elizabeth and Oksenberg, Michel, *China Joins the World: Progress and Prospects* (New York: Council on Foreign Relations Press, 1999)

Ellis, Henry, *Journal of the Proceedings of the Late Embassy to China; Comprising a Correct Narrative of the Public Transactions of the Embassy, of the Voyage to and from China, and of The Journey from the Mouth of the Pei-ho to the Return to Canton* (London: John Murray, 1817), 2 vols.

Elman, Benjamin A., *Cultural Examination of Civil Examinations in Late Imperial China* (Berkeley: University of California Press, 2000)
On Their Own Terms: Science in China, 1550–1900 (Cambridge, MA: Harvard University Press, 2005)
A Cultural History of Modern Science in China (Cambridge, MA: Harvard University Press, 2006)

Elvin, Mark and Liu, Ts'ui-jung, *Sediments of Time: Environment and Society in Chinese History* (Cambridge: CUP, 1998)

Engardio, Pete, *Chindia: How China and India Are Revolutionizing Global Business* (New York: McGraw-Hill, 2007)

Enright, Michael J., Scott, Edith E. and Chang, Ka-mun, *Regional Powerhouse: The Greater Pearl River Delta and the Rise of China* (Singapore: John Wiley, 2005)

Fairbank, John King, *The United States and China* (Cambridge, MA: Harvard University Press, 1983)

Fairbank, John King, (ed.), *The Chinese World Order: Traditional China's Foreign Relations* (Cambridge, MA: Harvard University Press, 1970)

Feigenbaum, Evan A., *China's Techno-Warriors: National Security and Strategic Competition From the Nuclear to the Information Age* (Stanford: Stanford University Press, 2003)

Fernandez, Juan Antonio and Underwood, Laurie, *China CEO: Voices of Experience from 20 International Business Leaders* (Singapore: Wiley, 2006)

Fibicher, Bernhard and Frehner, Matthias, *Mahjong: Contemporary Chinese Art from the Sigg Collection* (Ostfildern-Ruit: Hatje Cantz, 2005)

Finkelstein, David M., and Kivlehan, Maryanne (eds), *China's Leadership in the 21st Century: the Rise of the Fourth Generation* (Armonke, NY: M.E. Sharpe, 2003)

Fishman, Ted C., *China Inc: The Relentless Rise of the Next Superpower* (London: Pocket Books, 2006)

Fogel, Joshua A. (ed.), *Sagacious Monks and Bloodthirsty Warriors: Chinese Views of Japan in the Ming-Qing Period* (Norwalk, CT: EastBridge, 2002)

Fogel, Robert W., 'Capitalism and Democracy in 2040: Forecasts and Speculations', *Working Paper 13184* (Cambridge, Mass.: National Bureau of Economic Research, June 2007)

Foss, Theodore Nicholas, 'The European Sojourn of Philippe Couplet and Michael Shen Fuzong, 1683–1692,' in Heyndrickx, Jerome (ed.), *Philippe Couplet, S.J. (1623–1693): The Man Who Brought China to Europe* (Nettetal: Steyler-Verlag, 1990), pp. 121–40

Franke, Herbert, 'Could the Mongol Emperors read and write Chinese?' *Asia Major*, Vol. 3, Part 1, 1953, pp. 28–41

'Sino-Western Contacts under the Mongol Empire', *Journal of the Hong Kong Branch of the Royal Asiatic Society*, Vol. 6 (1996), pp. 49–72

Friedman, Edward and Gilley, Bruce (eds), *Asia's Giants: Comparing China and India* (New York: Palgrave Macmillan, 2005)

Friedman, Thomas L., *The World is Flat: The Globalized World in the Twenty-First Century* (London: Penguin: 2006) Revised Edition

Frodsham, J.D. (trans.), *The First Chinese Embassy to the West: The Journals of Kuo Sung-t'ao, Liu Hsi-hung, and Chang Te-yi* (Oxford: Clarendon Press, 1974)

Gallagher, Kelly Sims, *China Shifts Gears: Automakers, Oil, Pollution, and Development*, (Cambridge, MA: MIT Press, 2006)

Gallagher, Louis J. (ed.), *China in the Sixteenth Century: The Journals of Matthew Ricci* (New York: Random House, 1953)

Ganea, Peter and Pattloch, Thomas, *Intellectual Property Law in China* (The Hague: Kluwer Law International, 2005)

Gang, Zhao, 'Reinventing China: Imperial Qing Ideology and the Rise of Modern Chinese National Identity in the Early Twentieth Century', *Modern China*, Vol. 32, No. 1, 3–30, 2006

Gardner, Charles S., *Chinese Traditional Historiography* (Cambridge, MA: Harvard University Press, 1983)

Garnaut, Ross and Song, Ligang (eds), *The China Boom and its Discontents* (Canberra: Asia Pacific Press, 2005)

Gat, Azar, 'The return of the Authoritarian Great Powers', in *Foreign Affairs*, Vol. 86, No. 4, July/August 2007, pp. 59–69

Gelber, Harry G., *The Dragon and the Foreign Devils: China and the World, 1100 B.C. to the Present* (New York: Walker & Company, 2007)

Gerth, Karl, *China Made: Consumer Culture and the Creation of the Nation* (Cambridge, MA: Harvard University Press, 2003)

Gertz, Bill, *The China Threat: How the People's Republic Targets America* (Washington: Regnery Publishing, 2000)

Gibbon, Edward, *The History of the Decline and Fall of the Roman Empire*, ed. J.B. Bury (New York: Fred de Fau & Company, 1906), 12 vols

Gifford, Rob, *China Road: A Journey into the Future of a Rising Power* (New York: Random House, 2007)

Gill, Bates, *Rising Star: China's New Security Diplomacy* (Washington: Brookings Institution Press, 2007)

Gill, Bates and Oresman, Matthew, *China's New Journey to the West: China's Emergence in Central Asia and Implications for U.S. Interests* (Washington: Center for International and Strategic Studies, 2003)

Gilley, Bruce, *China's Democratic Future: How it Will Happen and Where it will Lead* (New York: Columbia University Press, 2004)

'The 'End of Politics' in Beijing, *The China Journal*, 51, January 2004, pp. 115 35

Gilmore, Fiona and Dumont, Serge, *Brand Warriors China: Creating Sustainable Brand Capital* (London: Profile Books, 2003)

Gittings, John, *China Through the Sliding Door: reporting three decades of change* (London: Touchstone, 1999)

The Changing Face of China: From Mao to Market (Oxford: OUP, 2005)

Goldman, Merle and Elizabeth Perry, *Changing Meanings of Citizenship in Modern China*, 2002

Gong, Zizheng, *Xiyu zhi xingsheng yi* ('A Proposal to Establish the Western Regions as a Province', 1826

Goodrich, L, Carrington, and Fang, Chaoying (eds), *Dictionary of Ming Biography* (New York: Columbia University Press, 1976), 2 vols

Gries, Peter Hays, *China's New Nationalism: Pride, Politics, and Diplomacy* (Berkeley: University of California Press, 2004)

'China Eyes the Hegemon', *Orbis: A Journal of World Affairs*, Summer 2005, pp. 401–412

'China's "New Thinking" on Japan', *The China Quarterly*, Vol. 84, December 2005, pp. 831–50

'Forecasting US-China Relations, 2015', *Asian Security*, Vol. 2, No. 2, June 2006, pp. 1–23

Gries, Peter Hays and Rosen, Stanley, *State and Society in 21st-Century China: Crisis, Contention, and Legitimation* (London: Routledge, 2004)

Gu, Jiejang, *Zhongguo Jiangyu Yangeshi* (A History of the Evolution of China's Border Regions) (Changsa: Shangwu Yinshuguan, 1938)

Guthrie, Doug, *China and Globalization: The Social, Economic, and Political Transformation of Chinese Society* (New York: Routledge, 2006)

Hall, Richard, *Empires of the Monsoon* (London: Harper Collins, 1996)

Hannas, William C., *The Writing on the Wall: How Asian Orthography Curbs Creativity* (Philadelphia: University of Pennsylvania Press, 2003)

Hansen, Valerie, *The Open Empire: A History of China to 1600* (New York: Norton, 2000)

Harbsmeier, Christoph, *Science and Civilisation in China* (Needham, Joseph, ed.), Vol. 7, Part I: *Language and Logic* (Cambridge: CUP, 1998)

Harding, Harry, 'The Concept of "Greater China": Themes, Variations and Reservations', *China Quarterly*, No. 136, Special Issue: Greater China (Dec., 1993), pp. 660–686

Harrison, Henrietta, *China* (London, Arnold, 2001)

Harvey, Brian, *China's Space Program: From Conception to Manned Spaceflight* (Chichester: Praxis, 2004)

He, Zhaowu, Bu Junzhi, Tang Yuyuan and Sun Kaitai, *An Intellectual History of China* (Beijing: Foreign Languages Press, 1991)

Hershatter, Gail, Hong, Emily, Lipman, Jonathan N., Strauss, Randall, *Remapping China: Fissures in Historical Terrain* (Stanford: Stanford University Press, 1996)

Hevia, James L., *Cherishing Men from Afar: Qing Guest Ritual and the Macartney Embassy of 1793* (Durham & London: Duke University Press, 1995)

Heyndrickx, Jerome (ed,), *Philippe Couplet, S.J. (1623–1693): The Man Who Brought China to Europe* (Nettetal: Steyler-Verlag, 1990)

Hibbert, Christopher, *The Dragon Awakes, China and the West, 1793–1911* (London: Penguin, 1984)

Hobson, John M., *The Eastern Origins of Western Civilisation* (Cambridge: CUP, 2004)

Hostetler, Laura, *Qing Colonial Enterprise: Ethnography and Cartography in Early Modern China* (Chicago: University of Chicago Press, 2001)

Howarth, Peter, *China's Rising Sea Power: The PLA Navy's Submarine Challenge* (London: Routledge, 2006)

Hsü, Immanuel C.Y., *The Rise of Modern China* (Oxford: OUP, 2000)

Hsu, Madeline Yuan-yin, *Dreaming of Gold, Dreaming of Home: Transnationalism and Migration between the United States and South China, 1882–1943* (Stanford: Stanford University Press, 2000)

Hu, Shi, *China's own critics: A Selection of Essays by Hu Shih and Lin Yu-tang; with Commentaries by Wang Ching-wei* (Peiping: China United Press, 1931)

Hughes, Christopher R., *Chinese Nationalism in the Global Era* (London: Routledge, 2006)

Hummel, Arthur W., *Eminent Chinese of the Ch'ing Period (1644–1912)* (Washington: U.S. Government Printing Office, 1943–4), 2 vols

Hundt, Reed, *In China's Shadow: The Crisis of American Entrepreneurship* (New Haven: Yale University Press, 2006)

Hutton, Will, *The Writing on the Wall: China and the West in the 21st Century* (New York: Little, Brown, 2007)

Ibn Battuta, *Travels in Asia and Africa 1325–1354*, Translated and selected by H.A.R. Gibb (London: Routledge & Kegan Paul, 1929)

Iriye, Akira, *China and Japan in the Global Setting* (Cambridge, MA: Harvard University Press, 1992)

Isaacs, Harold R., *Scratches on our Minds: American Views of China and India* (Armonk, NY: M.E. Sharpe, 1980)

Jagchid, Sechin and Symons, Van Jay, *Peace, War, and Trade Along the Great Wall: Nomadic-Chinese Interaction through Two Millennia* (Bloomington: Indian University Press, 1989)

Jenner, W.J.F., *The Tyranny of History: The Roots of China's Crisis* (London: Allen Lane, 1992)

Jullien, François, *In Praise of Blandness: Proceeding from Chinese Thought and Aesthetics* (New York: Zone Books, 2004)

Jun, Niu, *From Yan'an to the World: The Origin and Development of Chinese Communist Foreign Policy* (Norwalk, CT: Eastbridge, 2005)

Karl, Rebecca E., *Staging the World. Chinese Nationalism at the Turn of the Twentieth Century* (Durham and London: Duke University Press, 2002)

Kircher, Athanasius, *China Monumenta qua Sacris quà Profanis* (Amsterdam: Joannem Janssonium à Waesberge & Elizeum Weyerstraet, 1667)

Kornberg, Judith F. and Faust, John R., *China in World Politics: Policies, Processes, Prospects* (Boulder, CO: Lynne Rienner, 2005)

Kuhn, Philip A., *Rebellion and its Enemies in Late Imperial China: Militarization and Social Structure 1796–1864* (Cambridge, MA: Harvard University Press, 1970)
   Origins of the Modern Chinese State (Stanford: Stanford University Press, 2002)

Kwo, Da-Wei, *Chinese Brushwork in Calligraphy and Painting: Its History, Aesthetics, and Techniques* (New York: Dover, 1981)

Kynge, James, *China Shakes the World: The Rise of a Hungry Nation* (London: Weidenfeld & Nicholson, 2006)

Lach, Donald F., *Asia in the Making of Europe. Vol. II: A Century of Wonder*, Book Three: *The Scholarly Disciplines* (Chicago: University of Chicago Press, 1977)

Lal, Rollie, *Understanding China and India: Security Implications for the United States and the World* (Westport, CT: Praeger Security International, 2006)

Lam, Willy Wo-Lap, *Chinese Politics in the Hu Jintao Era: New Leaders, New Challenges* (Armonk, NY: M.E. Sharpe, 2006)

Lamont-Brown, Raymond, *Tutor to the Dragon Emperor: The Life of Sir Reginald Fleming Johnston at the Court of the Last Emperor* (Stroud: Sutton, 1999)

Landes, David S., *The Wealth and Poverty of Nations: Why Some Are So Rich and Some So Poor* (London: Little Brown, 1998)

Lardy, Nicholas R., *Integrating China into the Global Economy* (Wasington D.C.: Brookings Instituion Press, 2002)

Larkin, Bruce D., *China and Africa 1949–70: The Foreign Policy of the People's Republic of China* (Berkeley: University of California Press, 1971)

Larmer, Brook, *Operation Yao Ming: The Chinese Sports Empire, American Big Business and the Making of an NBA Superstar* (New York: Gotham Books, 2005)

Lattimore, Owen, *Inner Asian Frontiers of China* (American Geographical Society, Research Series, No.21), (Irving-on-Hudson, NY: Capitol Publishing, 1951)
   Studies in Frontier History: Collected Papers 1928–1958 (London: OUP, 1962)

Lee, Mabel and Syrokomla-Stefanowska, A.D. (eds), *Modernization of the Chinese Past* (Broadway, NSW: Wild Peony, 1993)

Legge, James (trans.), *The Chinese Classics, Vol. 5, The Ch'un Ts'ew with the Tso Chuen* (London: Henry Frowde, 1872)

Lei Haizong, 'Duandai wenti yu Zhongguo lishi di fenqi' (The Problem of Periodization and the Division of Chinese History), *Shehui Kexue*, 2, No. 1 (October), 1936

Leong, Sow-Theng, *Migration and Ethnicity in Chinese History: Hakkas, Pengmin, and Their Neighbors* (Stanford: Stanford University Press, 1997)

Levathes, Louise, *When China ruled the seas: the treasure fleet of the Dragon Throne, 1405–1433* (New York: Simon & Schuster, 1994)

Lee, Yuan-Yuan and Shen, Sin-Yan, *Chinese Musical Instruments* (Chicago: Chinese Music Society of North America, 1999)

Levenson, Joseph R., *Liang Ch'i-Ch'ao and the Mind of Modern China* (Berkeley: University of California Press, 1967)

Lever-Tracy, Constance, Ip, David and Tracy, Noel, *The Chinese Diaspora and Mainland China: An Emerging Economic Synergy* (London: Macmillan, 1996)

Levis, John Hazedel, *Foundations of Chinese Musical Art* (New York: Paragon, 1963) Reprint of 1936 Peking edition

Lewis, Jeffrey G., *The Minimum Means of Reprisal China's Search for Security in the Nuclear Age* (Cambridge, MA: MIT Press, 2007)

Lewis, John Wilson, and Xue, Litai, *Imagined Enemies: China Prepares for Uncertain War* (Stanford: Stanford University Press, 2006)

Lewis, Mark Edward, *The Early Chinese Empires: Qin and Han* (Cambridge, MA: Harvard University Press, 2007)

Li, Jinming and Li, Dexia, 'The Dotted Line on the Chinese Map of the South China Sea: A Note', *Ocean Development & International Law*, No. 34, 2003, pp. 287–95

Li, Nan (ed.), *Chinese Civil-Military Relations: The Transformation of the People's Liberation Army* (London: Routledge, 2006)

Li, Yu-ning (ed.), *The First Emperor of China* (White Plains, NY: International Arts and Sciences Press, 1975)

Liang, Mingyue, *Music of the Billion: An Introduction to Chinese Musical Culture* (New York: Heinrichshofen, 1985)

Liang, Qichao, *Zhongguoshu xulun* (A Systematic Discussion of Chinese History),
   History of Chinese political thought: during the early Tsin period (London: K. Paul, Trench, Trubner, 1930)
   The great Chinese philosopher K'ang Yu-wei (San Francisco: Chinese World, 1953)

Lin Yutang, *My Country and My People* (Beijing: Foreign Language Teaching and Research Press, 1998)

Lindquist, Cecilia, *China: Empire of Living Symbols* (Reading, MA: Addison-Wesley, 1991)

Ling, Zhijun, *The Lenovo Affair: The Growth of China's Computer Giant and Its Takeover of IBM-PC* (John Wiley: Singapore, 2006)

Liu, Guoli, *Chinese Foreign Policy in Transition* (New York: Aldine de Gruyter, 2004)

Liu, Lydia H., *The Clash of Empires: The Invention of China in Modern World Making* (Cambridge, MA: Harvard University Press, 2004)

Lovell, Julia, *The Great Wall: China Against the World 1000 BC – AD 2000* (London: Atlantic Books, 2006)

Lull, James, *China Turned on: Television, Reform and Resistance* (London: Routledge, 1991)

Ma, Huan, *Ying-Yai Sheng-Lan: 'The Overall Survey of the Ocean Shores'*, Trans. J.V.G Mills (Bangkok: White Lotus Press, 1997)

Ma, Shu-Yun, 'The Role of Power Struggle and Economic Changes in the "Heshang Phenomenon" in China', *Modern Asian Studies*, Vol. 30, No. 1 (February 1996), pp. 29–50

Macfarlane, Alan and Macfarlane, Iris, *The Empire of Tea: The Remarkable History of the Plant That Took Over the World* (Woodstock & New York: The Overlook Press, 2004)

Maddison, Angus, *Chinese Economic Performance in the Long Run* (Paris: OECD Publishing, 1998)

   The World Economy: a Millennial Perspective (Paris: OECD Publishing, 2001)

Mair, Victor H., Steinhardt, Nancy S. and Goldin, Paul G. (eds), *Hawai'i Reader in Traditional Chinese Culture* (Honolulu: University of Hawaii Press, 2005)

Manji, Firoze and Marks, Stephen (eds), *African Perspectives on China in Africa* (Cape Town: Fahamu, 2007)

Mann, James, *The China Fantasy: How Our Leaders Explain Away Chinese Repression* (New York: Viking, 2007)

Mao, Tse-Tung, *Selected Military Writings of Mao Tse-Tung* (Peking: Foreign Languages Press, 1967)

Martini, Martino, *Novus Atlas Sinensis a Martino Martinio Soc. Iesv descriptis et Seren.mo Archiduci Leopoldo Gvilielmo Austriaco Dedicatus* (Amsterdam: Blaeu, 1665)

McGregor, James, *One Billion Customers: Lessons from the Front Lines of Doing Business in China* (New York: Free Press, 2005)

Menges, Constantine C., *China: The Gathering Threat* (Nashville: Nelson Current, 2005)

Mengin, Françoise (ed.), *Cyber China: Reshaping National Identities in the Age of Information* (New York: Palgrave Macmillan, 2004)

Menzies, Gavin, *1421: The Year China Discovered the World* (London: Bantam press, 2002)

Meyer, David R., Baker, Alan R., Dennis, Richard and Holdworth, Deryck, *Hong Kong as a Global Metropolis* (Cambridge Studies in Historical Geography), (Cambridge: CUP, 2000)

Millward, James A., *Beyond the Pass: Economy, Ethnicity and Empire in Qing Central Asia, 1759–1864* (Stanford: Stanford University Press, 1998)

   Eurasian Crossroads: A History of Xinjiang (New York: Columbia University Press, 2007)

Min, Anchee, Duo, Duo and Landsberger, Stefan R., *Chinese Propaganda Posters from the Collection of Michael Wolff* (Köln: Taschen, 2003)

Mirsky, Jeannette (ed.), *The Great Chinese Travellers: An Anthology* (Chicago and London: The University of Chicago Press, 1964)

Mitter, Rana, *Bitter Revolution: China's Struggle With the Modern World* (Oxford: OUP, 2004)

   Manchurian Myth: Nationalism, Resistance and Collaboration in Modern China (Berkeley: University of Caliornia Press, 2000)

Moore, Thomas G., *China in the World Market: Chinese Industry and International Sources of Reform in the Post-Mao Era* (Cambridge: CUP, 2002)

Morgan, David, *The Mongols* (Oxford: Blackwell, 1986)

Morris, Andrew, 'To Make the Four Hundred Million Move: The Late Qing Dynasty Origins of Modern Chinese Sport and Physical Culture', *Comparative Study of Society and History*, Vol. 42, Issue 04, October 2000, pp. 876–906

Mosher, Steven W., *Hegemon, China's Plan to Dominate Asia and the World* (San Francisco: Encounter Books, 2000)

Mote, F.W., *Imperial China 900–1800* (Cambridge, MA: Harvard University Press, 1999)

Mott, William H. and Kim Jae Chang, *The Philosophy of Chinese Military Culture: Shih vs. Li* (New York: Palgrave Macmillan, 2006)

Mulvenon, James C., et al, Chinese Responses to U.S. Military Transformation and Implications for the Department of Defense, Washington: National Defense Research Institute, 2006

Mungello, D.E., *Curious Land: Jesuit Accomodation and the Origins of Sinology* (Honolulu: University of Hawaii Press, 1985)

Munro, Donald J., *The Concept of Man in Contemporary China* (Ann Arbor: Center for Chinese Studies, University of Michigan, 2000)

Murray, Hugh, *The Encyclopedia of Geography, Comprising a Complete Description of the Earth* (Philadelphia: Lea and Blanchard, 1839), 3 vols

Naquin, Susan, *Peking: Temples and City Life 1400–1900* (Berkeley: University of California Press, 2000)

Nathan, Andrew and Gilley, Bruce, *China's New Rulers: The secret Files* (New York: New York Review Books, 2003)

Navarro, Peter, *The Coming China Wars: Where They Will Be Fought and How They Can Be Won* (Upper Saddle River, NJ: FT Press, 2007)

Needham, Joseph, Wang, Ling, and Lu, Gwei-Djen, *Science and Civilisation in China*, Vol. IV, Part III, *Civil Engineering and Nautics* (Cambridge: CUP, 1971)

Needham, Joseph, Ho, Ping-Yü, Lu, Gwei-Djen, and Wang, Ling, *Science and Civilisation in China*, Vol. 5, *Chemistry and Chemical Power*, Part 7: *Military Technology; The Gunpowder Epic* (Cambridge: CUP, 1986)

Ng, Chin-keong, *Trade and Society: The Amoy Network on the China Coast, 1683–1725* (Singapore: Singapore University Press, 1983)

Ng, Ka Po, *Interpreting China's Military Power: Doctrine Makes Readiness* (London: Frank Cass, 2005)

Ng, On-cho and Wang, Q. Edward, *Mirroring the Past: The Writing and Use of History in Imperial China* (Honolulu, University of Hawaii Press, 2005)

Nisbett, Richard E., *The Geography of Thought: How Asians and Westerners Think Differently* (New York: Free Press, 2003)

Nolan, Peter, *China and the Global Economy: National Champions, Industrial Policy and the Big Business Revolution* (Basingstoke: Palgrave, 2001)

Nyíri, Pál and Breidenbach, Joana, *China Inside Out: Contemporary Chinese Nationalism and Transnationalism* (Budapest: Central European University Press, 2005)

Odorico da Pordenone, *Viaggio del Beato Odorico da Pordenone*, ed. G. Pullé (Milan: Alpes, 1931)

Ong, Aihwa and Nonini, Donald M., *Ungrounded Empires: The Cultural Politics of Modern Chinese Transnationalism* (London: Routledge, 1997)

Paine, S.C.M., *Imperial Rivals: China, Russia, and Their Disputed Frontier* (Armonk, NY: M.E. Sharpe, 1996)

Pan, Lynn, *Sons of the Yellow Emperor: A History of the Chinese Diaspora* (New York: Kodansha International, 1994)

Pan, Lynn (ed.), *The Encyclopedia of Chinese Overseas* (Cambridge, MA: Harvard University Press, 1999)

Pan, Xiafeng, *The Stagecraft of Peking Opera: From its Origins to the Present Day* (Beijing: New World Press, 1995)

Panitchpakdi, Supachai and Clifford, Mark L., *China and the WTO: Changing China, Changing World Trade* (Singapore: John Wiley, 2002)

Paris, Matthew, *Chronica Majora: English History from the year 1235 to 1273*, Trans. J.A. Giles (London: Bohm, 1852), Vol. 1

Parker, Edward Harper, *Ancient China Simplified* (London: Chapman & Hall, 1908)

Peerenboom, Randall, *China Modernizes: threat to the west or model for the rest?* (Oxford: OUP, 2007)

Pei, Minxin, *China's Trapped Transition: The Limits of Developmental Autocracy* (Cambridge, MA: Harvard University Press, 2006)

Pelliot, Paul, 'Les grands voyages maritimes chinois au début du XVe siècle', *T'oung Pao*, 30 (1933), pp. 237–54

Perdue, Peter C., *China Marches West: The Qing Conquest of Central Eurasia* (Cambridge, Mass.: Belknap Press, 2005)

Perry, Elizabeth J., 'Studying Chinese Politics: Farewell to Revolution?', *The China Journal*, No. 57, January 2007, pp. 1–22

Peyrefitte, Alain, *L'Empire immobile ou le Choc des Mondes* (Paris: Arthèmes Fayard, 1989)

Pian del Carpini, Giovanni da, *Viaggio a' Tartari (Historia Mongolarum)*, ed. G. Pullé (Milan: Alpes, 1929)

Pollack, Jonathan D. (ed.), *Strategic Surprise? U.S. China Relations in the Early Twenty first Century* (Newport, RI: Naval War College Press, 2003)

Polo, Marco, *The Travels of Marco Polo, The Complete Yule-Cordier Edition* (New York: Dover, 1993), 2 vols

Pomeranz, Kenneth, *The Great Divergence: China, Europe, and the Making of the Modern World Economy* (Princeton: Princeton University Press, 2000)

Postiglione, Gerald A., Tang, James T. H., *Hong Kong's Reunion with China: The Global Dimensions* (New York: Armonk, NJ: M.E. Sharpe, 1997)

Prasenjit, Duara, *Rescuing History from the Nation: Questioning Narratives of Modern China* (Chicago: University of Chicago Press, 1997)

Prestowitz, Clyde, *Three Billion New Capitalists: The Great Shift of Wealth and Power to the East* (New York: Basic Books, 2005)

Ptak, Roderich, *China and the Asian Seas: Trade, Travel and Visions of the Other (1400–1750)* (Aldershot: Ashgate/Varorium, 1998)

China, The Portuguese, and The Nanyang: Oceans and Routes, Regions and Trade (c. 1000–1600) (Aldershot: Ashgate/Varorium, 2004)

Pye, Lucien, 'China: Erratic State, Frustrated Society,' *Foreign Affairs*, Vol. 69 (4), Fall 1990, pp. 56–74

Qian, Sima, *Records of the Grand Historian: Qin Dynasty*, Trans. Burton Watson (Hong Kong: Columbia University Press, 1993)

Ramo, Joshua Cooper, *Brand China* (London: The Foreign Policy Centre, 2007)

Rawski, Evelyn S., *The Last Emperors: A Social History of the Qing Imperial Institutions* (Berkeley: University of California Press, 1998)

Ready, Oliver G., *Life and Sport in China* (London: Chapman & Hall, 1904)

Reid, Antony (ed.), *Sojourners and Settlers: Histories of Southeast Asia and the Chinese* (Honolulu: University of Hawaii Press, 1996)

Richards, L., *Comprehensive Geography of the Chinese Empire and Dependencies*, Trans. M. Kennelly S.J. (Shanghai: T'usewei Press, 1908)

Roberts, J.A.G., *China to Chinatown: Chinese Food in the West* (London: Reaktion Books, 2002)
    The Complete History of China (Stroud: Sutton Publishing, 2003)

Roberts, Paul, *The End of Oil: the Decline of the Petroleum Economy and the Rise of a New Energy Order* (London: Bloomsbury, 2004)

Rossabi, Morris, *Khubilai Khan: His Life and Times*, (Berkeley: University of California Press, 1988)

'The reign of Khubilai Khan', in Herbert Franke and Denis Twitchett (Eds), *The Cambridge History of China*, Vol. 6, Cambridge: CUP, 1994, pp. 414–89

Rossabi, Morris (ed.), *China Among Equals: The Middle Kingdom and Its Neighbors: 10th to 14th Centuries* (Berkeley: University of California Press, 1983)

Rowbotham, Arthur H., *Missionary and Mandarin: the Jesuits at the Court of China* (Berkeley: University of California Press, 1942)

Said, Edward W., *Orientalism* (New York: Vintage, 1979)
    Culture and Imperialism (New York: Vintage, 1994)

Santangelo, Paolo, *Il sogno in Cina. L'immaginario collettivo attraverso la narrativa Ming e Qing* (Milan: Raffaello Cortina, 1998)

Scarpari, Maurizio, *La concezione della natura umana in Confucio e Mencio* (Venice: Cafoscarina, Venezia, 1991)

Schwartz, Benjamin, *In Search of Wealth and Power: Yen Fu and the West* (Cambridge, MA: Harvard University Press, 1964)

Scobell, Andrew, *China's Use of Military Force: Beyond the Great Wall and the Long March* (Cambridge: CUP, 2003)

Seagrave, Sterling, *Lords of the Rim: The Invisible Empire of the Overseas Chinese* (New York: G.P Putnam's Sons, 1995)

Segal, Adam, *Digital Dragon: High-Technology Enterprises in China* (Ithaca: Cornell University Press, 2003)

Shambaugh, David, *Modernizing China's Military: Progress, Problems, and Prospects* (Berkeley: University of California Press, 2002)

Shao, Kuo-Kang, *Zhou Enlai and the Foundations of Chinese Foreign Policy* (New York: St Martin's Press, 1996)

Shapiro, Judith, *Mao's War Against Nature: Politics and the Environment in Revolutionary China* (Cambridge: CUP, 2001)

Sheff, David, *China Dawn: The Story of a Technology and Business Revolution* (New York: HarperBusiness, 2002)

Shen, Fuwei, *Cultural Flow Between China and Outside World Throughout History* (Beijing: Foreign Languages Press, 1996)

Shen, Hsiu-hua, *'Doing Chineseness':Taiwanese Capital in China*, Asia research Institute Working Paper Series, No.46 (Singapore: National University of Singapore, 2005)

Shenkar, Oded, *Chinese Century: The Rising Chinese Economy and Its Impact on the Global Economy, the Balance of Power, and Your Job* (Upper Saddle River, NJ: Wharton School Publishing/Pearson Education, 2005)

Shi, Bo, *Between Heaven and Earth: A History of Chinese Writing* (Boston: Shambhala, 2003)

Shih, Chih-Yu, *Navigating Sovereignty:World Politics Lost in China* (New York: Palgrave Macmillan, 2003)

Shirk, Susan L., *China Fragile Superpower: How China's Internal Politics Could Derail Its Peaceful Rise* (Oxford: OUP, 2007)

Sigurdson, Jon, *Technological Superpower China* (Cheltenham: Edward Elgar, 2005)

Simon, Denis Fred and Goldman, Merle, *Science and Technology in Post-Mao China* (Cambridge, MA: Harvard University Press, 1989)

Sirén, Osvald, *The Chinese on the Art of Painting* (New York: Schocken Books, 1963)

Sisci, Francesco, *La differenza tra la Cina e il mondo. La rivoluzione degli anni ottanta* (Milan: Feltrinelli, 1994)

  Made in China: La vita quotidiana di un paese che cambia (Rome: Carocci Editore, 2003)

  Chi ha paura della Cina? (Milan: Ponte alle Grazie, 2006)

Skinner, G.William, *The City in Late Imperial China* (Stanford: Stanford University Press, 1977)

Smith, Arthur H., *Chinese Characteristics* (London: Kegan Paul, Trench, Trübner, 1895)

Snow, Philip, *The Fall of Hong Kong: Britain, China and the Japanese Occupation* (New Haven: Yale University Press, 2003)

Spence, Jonathan, *To Change China: Western Advisers in China* (New York: Penguin, 1980)

  Emperor of China. Self-Portrait of K'ang-Hsi (New York.Vintage, 1988)

  The Chan's Great Continent: China in Western Minds (New York: Norton, 1998)

  The Search for Modern China, 2nd Edition (New York: Norton, 1999)

Standaert, Nicolas, *Handbook of Christianity in China, Volume One: 635–1800* (Leiden: Brill, 2001)

Staunton, George, *An Authentic Account of an Embassy from the King of Great Britain to the Emperor of China* (London:W. Bulmer, 1797), 2 vols.

Steinhardt, Nancy Shatzman, *Chinese Imperial City Planning* (Honolulu: University of Hawaii Press, 1990)

Steinhardt, Nancy S. (ed.), *Chinese Architecture* (New Haven:Yale University Press, 2002)

Struve, Lynn A., *The Qing Formation in World-Historical Time* (Cambridge, MA: Harvard University Asia Centre, 2004)

Su, Xiaokang, and Wang, Luxiang, *Deathsong of the River: A Reader's Guide to the Chinese TV Series Heshang*, Trans.W. Bodman and Pin P.Wan (Ithaca: East Asia Program, Cornell University, 1991)

Sullivan, Michael, *The Three Perfections: Chinese Painting, Poetry, and Calligraphy* (New York: George Braziller, 1999)

  Symbols of Eternity: The Art of Landscape Painting in China (Stanford: Stanford University Press, 1979)

Sun,Yat-sen, *The International Development of China* (London: Hutchinson, 1922)

Sung,Ying-Hsing, *Chinese Technology in the Seventeenth Century: T'ien-Kung K'ai-Wu*, Trans. Sun, E-Tu Zen and Sun, Shiou-Chuan (Mineola, NY: Dover Publications, 1997)

Sutter, Robert G., *China's Rise in Asia: Promises and Perils* (Lanham, MD: Rowman & Littlefield, 2005)

Swaine, Michael and Tellis, Ashley J., *Interpreting China's Grand Strategy: Past, Present, and Future* (Santa Monica, CA: Rand, 2000)

Tan, Qixiang (Chief Editor), *Jianming Zhonguo lishi dituji* (Concise Historical Atlas of China) (Beijing: China Cartographic Publishing House, 1996)

Tang, Xiaofeng, *From Dynastic Geography to Historical Geography: A Change in Perspective towards the Geographical Past of China* (Beijing: Commercial Press International, 2000)

Temple, Robert, *Genius of China; 3,000 years of Science, Discovery, and Invention* (London: Prion, 1998)

Teng, Ssu-yü and Fairbank, John K., *China's Response to the West: a documentary survey 1839–1923* (Cambridge, MA: Harvard University Press, 1961)

Terrill, Ross, *The New Chinese Empire, and What it Means for the United States* (New York: Basic Books, 2003)

Thompson, Laurence G., *Ta T'ung Shu: The One-World Philosophy of K'ang Yu-wei* (London: George Allen & Unwin: 1958)

Tsai, Shih-Shan Henry, *Perpetual Happiness: the Ming Emperor Yongle* (Seattle: University of Washington Press, 2001)

Tsang, Steve, *Hong Kong: an appointment with China* (London: I.B. Tauris, 2004)
 A Modern History of Hong Kong (London: I.B. Tauris, 2004)

Tu, Wei-ming, 'Cultural China: the periphery as the center', *Daedalus*, Vol. 134, No. 4, Fall 2005, pp. 145–167

Tubilewicz Czeslaw (ed.), *Critical issues in Contemporary China*, (Abingdon: Routledge, 2006)

Van Dyke, Paul A., *The Canton Trade: Life and Enterprise on the China Coast, 1700–1845* (Hong Kong: Hong Kong University Press, 2005)

Wakeman, Frederic, *The Fall of Imperial China* (New York: Free Press, 1975)

Waldron, Arthur, *The Great Wall of China: From History to Myth* (Cambridge: CUP, 1990)

Waley-Cohen, Joanna, *Exile in Mid-Qing China: Banishment to Xinjiang, 1758–1820* (New Haven: Yale University Press, 1991)
 'Military Ritual and the Qing Empire', in Di Cosmo, Nicola (ed.), *Warfare in Inner Asian History (500–1800)* (Leiden: Brill, 2002), pp. 405–44
 The Culture of War in China: Empire and the Military under the Qing Dynasty (London: I.B. Tauris, 2006)

Wang, Edward Q., 'History, Space, and Ethnicity: The Chinese Worldview', *Journal of World History*, 10.2 (1999), pp. 285–305

Wang, Gungwu, *China and the Chinese Overseas*, Singapore: Times Academic Press, 1991
 'Ming foreign relations: Southeast Asia', in Denis Twitchett and Frederick W. Mote (eds), *The Cambridge History of China*, Vol. 8, Part 2 (Cambridge: CUP, 1998), pp. 301–332
 The Chinese Overseas: From Earthbound China to the Quest for Autonomy (Cambridge, MA: Harvard University Press, 2000)
 Don't Leave Home: Migration and the Chinese (Singapore: Eastern Universities Press, 2003)
 The Nanhai Trade: Early Chinese Trade in the South China Sea (Singapore: Eastern Universities Press, 2003)
 Ideas Won't Keep: The Struggle for China's Future (Singapore: Eastern Universities Press, 2003)

Wang, Q. Edward, *Inventing China Through History: The May Fourth Approach to Historiography* (Albany, NY: State University of New York Press, 2001)

Wang, T.Y. (ed.), *China After the Sixteenth Party Congress: Prospects and Challenges* (Toronto: de Sitter Publications, 2005)

Warrington Smyth, Herbert, *Mast and Sail in Europe and Asia* (London: John Murray, 1906)

Wasserstrom, Jeffrey N., 'Big Bad China and the Good Chinese', in Timothy B. Weston and Lionel M. Jensen (eds), *In China Beyond the Headlines* (Lanham, MD: Rowman & Littlefield, 2000), pp. 13–35

   China's Brave New World – And Other Tales for Global Times (Bloomington and Indianapolis: Indiana University press, 2007)

Watson, Francis, *The Frontiers of China* (New York: Frederick A. Praeger, 1966)

Weidenbaum, Murray L and Hughes, Samuel, *The Bamboo Network: How Expatriate Chinese Entrepreneurs Are Creating a New Economic Superpower in Asia* (New York: Free Press, 1996)

Weller, Robert P., *Discovering Nature: Globalization and Environmental Culture in China and Taiwan* (Cambridge: CUP, 2006)

Wheatley, Paul, *The Pivot of the Four Quarters: A preliminary enquiry into the origins and character of the ancient Chinese city* (Chicago: Aldine, 1971)

Wild, Leni and Mepham, David, *The New Sinosphere: China in Africa* (London: Institute for Public Policy Research, 2007)

Wilkinson, Endymion, *Chinese History: A Manual* (Cambridge, MA: Harvard University Press, 2000)

Williams, C.A.S., *Outlines of Chinese Symbolism and Art Motives* (New York: Dover, 1976)

Wills, John E., *Embassies and Illusion: Dutch and Portuguese Envoys to K'ang'hsi, 1666–1687* (Cambridge, MA: Council on East Asian Studies, 1984)

   'Relations with maritime Europeans, 1514–1662', in Denis Twitchett and Frederick W. Mote (eds), *The Cambridge History of China*, Vol. 8, Part 2 (Cambridge: CUP, 1998), pp. 333–75

Winters, L. Alan, and Yusuf, Shahid, *Dancing With Giants: China, India, and the Global Economy* (Singapore: World Bank and Institute of Policy Studies, 2007)

Wittfogel, Karl August, *Oriental Despotism: A Comparative Study of Total Power*, (New Haven: Yale University Press, 1957)

Woetzel, Jonathan R., *Capitalist China: Strategies for a Revolutionized Economy* (Singapore: John Wiley, 2003)

Wood, Ellen Meiksins, *Empire of Capital* (London: Verso, 2005)

Wright, Mary Clabaugh, *Last Stand of Chinese Conservatism: The T'ung-Chih Restoration, 1862–1874* (New York: Atheneum, 1957)

China in Revolution: The First Phase, 1900–1913 (New Haven: Yale University Press, 1968)

Wu, Zuguang, Huang Zuolin and Mei Shaowu, *Peking Opera and Mei Lanfang* (Beijing: New World Press, 1981)

Xi, Jieying, Sun, Yunxiao and Xiao, Jing Jian (eds), *Chinese Youth in Transition* (Aldershot: Ashgate, 2006)

Xu, Guoqi, *China and the Great War: China's Pursuit of a New National Identity and Internationalization* (Cambride, CUP, 2004)

Yamashita, Michael, *Zheng He: Tracing the Epic Voyages of China's Greatest Explorer* (Vercelli: White Star, 2006)

Yan, Fu, *Yuan Qiang Xiudinggao*, in Wang Shi, ed., Yan Fu Ji, Di Yi Ce (Beijing: Zhonghua Shuju, 1986)

Yao, Shujie and Xiaming Liu (eds), *Sustaining China's Economic Growth in the Twenty-First Century* (London: RoutledgeCurzon, 2003)

Yao, Souchou, *Confucian Capitalism: Discourse, practice and the myth of Chinese enterprise* (London: RoutledgeCurzon, 2002)

Yeh, Wen-hsin (ed.), *Becoming Chinese: Passages to Modernity and Beyond* (Berkeley: University of California Press, 2000)

Yen, Ching-Hwang, *Coolies and Mandarins: China's Protection of Overseas Chinese During the Late Ching's Period (1851–1911)* (Singapore: Singapore University Press, 1985)

Yeung, Henry Wai-chung and Olds, Kris (eds), *Globalization of Chinese Business Firms* (London: Macmillan, 2000)

Yi, Jeannie Jinsheng and Ye, Shawn Xian, *The Haier Way: The Making of a Chinese Business Leader and a Global Brand* (Dumont, NJ: Home & Sekey Books, 2003)

Zhang, Dainian, *Key Concepts in Chinese Philosophy* (New Haven: Yale University Press, 2002)

Zhang, Yongjin and Austin, Greg (eds), *Power and Responsibility in Chinese Foreign Policy* (Canberra: Asia Pacific Press, 2001)

Zhao, Suisheng (ed.), *Chinese Foreign Policy: Pragmatism and Strategic Behaviour* (Armonk, NY: M.E. Sharpe, 2004)

'China's Pragmatic Nationalism: Is It Manageable?' *The Washington Quarterly, Winter 2005–6*, 29:1 pp. 131–44

Zhao, Tingyang, 'Rethinking Empire from a Chinese Concept "All-under-Heaven" (Tian-xia)' *Social Identities*, Vol. 12, No. 1, January 2006, pp. 29–41

Zheng, Bijian, 'China's "Peaceful Rise" to Great-Power Status', in *Foreign Affairs*, September/October 2005, Vol. 84, No. 5, pp. 18–24

Zheng, Yongnian, *Discovering Chinese Nationalism in China: Modernization, Identity and International* Relations (Cambridge: CUP, 1999)

Zhongguolishi qi nianjiji (History of China for the 7th Year), (Beijing: People's Educational Publishing, History Course Material Development Centre, 2001), 2 vols

Zurndorfer, Harriet T., China Bibliography: A Research Guide to Reference Works about China Past and Present (Honolulu: University of Hawaii Press, 1999)

Index